Image-based Research

For Ian Lewis

Image-based Research

A Sourcebook for Qualitative Researchers

Edited by

Jon Prosser

Routledge
Taylor & Francis Group

LONDON AND NEW YORK

First published in 1998
Reprinted 2000
By Routledge,
2 Park Square, Milton Park, Abingdon, Oxon, OX14 4RN
270 Madison Ave, New York NY 10016

Transferred to Digital Printing 2006

Routledge is an imprint of the Taylor & Francis Group

A catalogue record for this book is available from the British Library

ISBN 0 7507 0706 2 cased
ISBN 0 7507 0649 x paper

Library of Congress Cataloging-in-Publication Data are available on request

Cover design by Caroline Archer

Typeset in 10/12 pt Times by
Graphicraft Typesetters Ltd., Hong Kong.

Every effort has been made to contact copyright holders for their permission to reprint material in this book. The publishers would be grateful to hear from any copyright holder who is not here acknowledged and will undertake to rectify any errors or omissions in future editions of this book.

Publisher's Note
The publisher has gone to great lengths to ensure the quality of this reprint but points out that some imperfections in the original may be apparent

Contents

Contents

Acknowledgments

I would like to thank all who have contributed to this book. A special thanks to those who have donated images. The author of Chapter 1, Marcus Banks, would like to acknowledge the following people, for giving permission to reproduce. Figure 1.1, Ruth Barnes courtesy of R.H. Barnes; Figure 1.3, National Film and Television Archive, © Cambridge University of Museum of Archaeology and Anthropology; Figure 1.4, Pitt Rivers Museum, University of Oxford; Figure 1.5, Chris Pinney, courtesy of Suhaag Studios, Nagda. The authors of Chapter 11 would like to thank Deakin University for permission to reproduce website pages. The authors of Chapter 15, Michael Schratz and Ulrike Steiner-Löffler, wish to thank Claudia Steindl and class 2A of Volksschule Stiftgasse, Vienna, for their commitment in sharing their experience in photo-evaluation with us, also Claudia Valsky for taking pictures of pupils' self-evaluation at work and for helping with the interviewing of the children. The author of Chapter 16, Terry Warburton, would like to acknowledge the kind permission of the cartoonist Les Gibbard (for Figure 16.2) and *Express Newspapers* (for Figure 16.1), who have allowed cartoons to be reproduced. The authors of Chapter 17 would like to acknowledge the kind permission of the Health Education Authority, London, to reproduce Figures 17.2, 17.3a, 17.4 and 17.8 and T. Nelson and Sons for permission to reproduce the text included in Figure 17.5. The author of Chapter 18, Elizabeth Chaplin, would like to acknowledge the kind permission to reproduce: John Constable's *The Cornfield* (National Gallery), 'Cornfield' wallpaper, (Colin and Anne Painter); and 'Cornfield' fire screen (also Colin and Anne Painter); and 'Most People Prefer the Original', Jordan's Oat Cereal advertisement, 1987 W. Jordan (Cereals) Ltd.

I would like to thank Anna Clarkson at Falmer Press for her guidance, patience and support. Finally, to my family, many thanks for allowing me those weekends 'playing' at editing this book when I should have been playing with you.

Introduction

Image making has spanned the evolution of humankind from ancient cave drawings to photographs of distant galaxies. Technological improvements are reflected in everyday visual communication, beginning with the use of natural dyes on limestone walls to illustrate a hunt to a single camera capable of making both still photographs and videos of family events. As an indicator of the urge humans feel to record their lives, last year Americans took over 20 billion photographs. We use images not only as representations of the objective world but also to communicate our deepest feelings.

Over the last three decades qualitative researchers have given serious thought to using images with words to enhance understanding of the human condition. They encompass a wide range of forms including films, photographs, drawings, cartoons, graffiti, maps, diagrams, signs and symbols. Taken cumulatively images are signifiers of a culture; taken individually they are artefacts that provide us with very particular information about our existence. Images provide researchers with a different order of data and, more importantly, an alternative to the way we have perceived data in the past.

This book is directed at a cross-section of qualitative researchers. Its intended audience are students, lecturers, methodologists, experienced and novice researchers from a wide range of disciplines and theoretical persuasions. The aim of the book is twofold: to encourage those already practising Image-based Research to reflect on their own work and to learn from the approaches used by others in different but related areas of Image-based Research; and secondly to encourage other qualitative researchers who have not used images in the past to consider the benefits they would bring.

One of the potential pitfalls of creating a book that appeals to a wide audience is that in creating a 'cookbook' of chapters which individually appeal to distinct groups of visual researchers the overall effect will be one of fragmentation. The contents of this book have been chosen to avoid this problem. Although specific chapters will inevitably appeal to particular groups of researchers, readers will find that many chapters contribute unique insights into problems that are common across Image-based Research. It is intended that workers from different disciplines, who focus on different topics and adopt different perspectives, will find the strategies and innovations that each brings to this book to be an enriching experience. It is intended that communal issues such as 'representation', 'trustworthiness', 'interpretation' and 'reflexivity' that are central to the qualitative research enterprise whatever the medium, are revisited and broaden our concept of Image-based Research.

The issues of 'representation', 'trustworthiness', 'interpretation', 'reflexivity', and others, are highly contested in visual and non-visual research. Image-based Research will appear more relevant to the wider research community *if* they are seen as shared problems to be resolved cumulatively rather than treated as battlegrounds of twenty-first century methodological theory. Implicit in this book is the belief that we should escape from the internal fighting within different approaches, recognize different starting points, and to seek out ways of building links between different approaches to Image-based Research. My hope is that in the future visual researchers will draw on several quite different approaches to conducting studies and yet provide an approach based on the commonality of thinking on how best to understand the visual world.

This sourcebook is the combined work of theoreticians and practitioners from diverse disciplines from different countries. They have stated their favoured positions clearly, avoiding reaching for the 'middle ground' of acceptability yet each has attempted to make their work accessible to a diverse audience.

The book is in three parts. Part 1 — A Theoretical Overview of Image-based Research — explores philosophical, theoretical and methodological issues. In addition it provides an overview of how anthropology, sociology and psychology have used and are using images. Part 2 — Images in the Research Process — is more practically orientated. It focuses on the various ways of thinking about conducting image-orientated qualitative research and particularly the role of images in the research process. Some chapters in this section are theoretically orientated whilst others use examples as an illustration of research design and methods in action. Part 3 — Image-based Research in Practice — tends towards a more pragmatic approach yet still retains a significant methodological input. The chapters offer, via a series of case studies, an insight into of how different researchers from different backgrounds and focusing on different issues have successfully applied images in a qualitative research context.

Knowing where to open a sourcebook can be difficult. Experienced image-based researchers have the option of working through the book from the initial theoretical chapters to more practical applications towards the end, or selecting particular chapters that meet their requirements. For less experienced visual researchers I suggest Chapter 7 would provide a helpful starting point because it considers much territory and would serve as a useful grounding in issues common to all forms of Image-based Research.

The first two chapters reflect the overall positions of visual anthropology and visual sociology respectively. In Chapter 1, Marcus Banks provides a synopsis of visual anthropology and describes how past and present theoretical and methodological thinking has, and is, shaping this major subdiscipline. He examines how visual anthropologists work with symbols, artefacts, non-verbal communication and rituals, that are significant manifestations of cultures. He goes on to identify the problems emanating from cross-cultural translation i.e., the culture of the image maker and those of the culture whose image is being 'taken'. In Chapter 2, Douglas Harper defines the complex parameters of visual sociology. He begins by discussing the origins and evolution of visual sociology before exploring its symbolic and empirical dimensions. What is distinctive about this chapter is its concern for locating visual sociology not only with its ethnographic and documentary past but also within contemporary thinking — semiotics, critical theory, cultural studies and postmodernism — which are influential in current methodology.

The following two chapters contain insights from two authors who possess a wealth of practical experience in addition to sound theoretical knowledge. In Chapter 3, Paul Henley covers 100 years of ethnographic filmmaking. He works through difficult terrain that is encompassed by a positivist approach to film as research on the one hand and an interpretative/hermeneutical approach on the other. Paul finally reflects on the possible future of ethnographic film following technological improvements and an increased capacity for many (rather than a few) to make, manipulate and receive film. Brian Winston, in Chapter 4, covers exactly the ground his title suggests — 'The Camera Never Lies':

The Partiality of Photographic Evidence. From its beginnings photography was claimed to be evidence of the external world. This was never the case. Brian explains how, following the development of digital systems that have made manipulation so much easier, the notion of photography as unequivocal evidence has been 'buried' and 'trustworthiness' thrust centre-stage.

The final three chapters in this section cover diverse but important topics. In Chapter 5, Órla Cronin presents a link between psychology and photographic theory. Using family snaps as a vehicle, she provides a critical review of the theoretical and therapeutic literature on the meaning and psychological significance of photographs. Many image-based researchers will recognize and relate to Órla's discussion of assumptions that underpin the use of photographs in research. We now shift perspective from psychology to sociology but the shift is not as traumatic as one would expect. In Chapter 6, Howard Becker explores the importance of external context or, more specifically, the context in which photographs are viewed, in shaping photographic meaning. Howie suggests that visual researchers will find legitimization not under a catchall heading to which a photograph is attached, such as 'documentary photography' or 'photojournalism', but through the response of viewers to the image. In the final chapter (Chapter 7) of this section Jon Prosser steps outside of traditional concerns of Image-based Research to ask *why* visual research plays a relatively minor role in qualitative research. The chapter briefly explores historical reasons for the limited status of images and methodological concerns of word-orientated researchers.

Part 2 opens with a very accessible chapter that considers the use of photographs within the sociological research process. In Chapter 8, Jon Prosser and Dona Schwartz consider research design, data collection and data analysis. Since theoretical and practical considerations are discussed within a conventional qualitative framework this chapter will be of interest to orthodox researchers who would like to use photography alongside traditional methods.

The following two chapters concentrate on two major issues — the use of photographs as a record in the field, and the context of making of photographs. In Chapter 9, Michael Ball reminds us of the importance of participation and observation in ethnographic fieldwork. He points out that we live in a time that is rich in cultural artefacts and cultural arrangements. Michael points out, using a case study of Himalayan fieldwork, of the insights to be gained by adopting a visual record approach alongside the more common textual form of representation. Clem Adelman, in Chapter 10, tackles the difficult topic of 'photocontext'. The thinking behind the construction of an image is a pivotal issue in Image-based Research. Here Clem examines the complex issue of the context of making a photograph and goes on to explore what he sees as more significant — the 'reflexive context of discovery' of the photograph.

Image-based Research is a contemporary form of structured investigation. In the final two chapters of Part 2 two quite different but vital areas of modern visually orientated research are described. In Chapter 11, Rob Walker and Ron Lewis provide a fascinating insight into the future possibilities provided by digitized images. They suggest that digitization will lead to new forms of research practice and shifts in methodological innovation, and support their arguments with illustrations from their 'Hathaway Project'. The final chapter takes us to what is a topical issue that but one that has been part of societies for a very long time — child abuse. Research into child abuse investigation is, technically and emotionally, extremely difficult work. Hollida Wakefield and Ralph Underwager, are very experienced researchers in this area and they draw on their wealth of knowledge. In

Chapter 12 they provide insights into the limitations of using anatomical dolls, books, puppets, drawings, projective cards, play dough, games, and toys during investigations. It is clear that many of these techniques, which are in use throughout the world, lack accepted standards of validity and reliability.

Part 3 opens with two studies of a similar nature in that they are both concerned with everyday photographs. In Chapter 13, Claudia Mitchell and Sandra Weber focus on school photographs both as phenomenon and method. Claudia and Sandra use old school photographs to elicit information from pupils and teachers illustrating how 'readers' are stimulated to 'narrativize' about the photographs before them. They pay attention to 'teacher culture' particularly teachers' professional identity and practice. Richard Chalfen investigates a broader spectrum of everyday images through his study family photography. Throughout Chapter 14, he provides the reader with informative and occasionally humorous insights into vernacular images using a descriptive model. Richard illustrates, via the 'construction, organization and consumption of family photographs' how everyday and taken-for-granted images aid our understanding of the human condition.

The next two chapters are the work of educational researchers who use their respective media for quite different ends. Like all institutions participants within schools are differentiated by their power status. This makes accessing the 'layers' of a school to obtain good quality data problematic. In Chapter 15, Michael Schratz and Ulrike Steiner-Löffler describe how they used photographs made by pupils to evaluate the climate of a school. They provide practical examples of how they gained insight into pupils' perspectives through 'making' a series of images with a particular focus in mind, and following discussion of the processed prints. To use images in this way to explore the 'inner world' of schooling is not only highly appropriate but also extremely effective. The chapter that follows is also about education but quite different in that it considers 'outsiders' viewpoint. Terry Warburton, in Chapter 16, draws on the work of cartoonists working for the national press, going about their black art of lampooning state education. Terry describes the use of a semiotic approach to the analysis of visual images. In this instance semiotics is used to explore cartoon representations of topical educational themes such as teacher culture, educational policy, and the activities of key decision makers.

The last two chapters of the book are situated at opposite ends of the visual research continuum. In Chapter 17, Noreen Wetton and Jennifer McWhirter demonstrate how an image-based approach can be used in a utilitarian way. They describe their 'draw and write' approach, which they use with children in order to improve curriculum development in health education. Noreen and Jenny have used this approach in various studies throughout Europe to great effect. They emphasize the importance of 'starting where the children are' and the importance of using children's own drawings and words to inform curriculum developers of children's perception of health and safety-related concepts. Chapter 18 also treats as problematic an image, in this case a painting, that is created by someone other than the researcher. Elizabeth Chaplin takes a contemporary look at the work of a well-known British artist (John Constable) and, by drawing on historical documents, constructs a case study which tells us a great deal about the artist and his associates and even more about the ebbs and flows of his growth in artistic status and reputation. Elizabeth, following on from the work of Howard Becker, provides a model for investigating what constitutes cultural negotiation of 'Fine Art' in other cultures.

Finally, I will end with a short story. I live in Dorset, the most English of English counties. Not far away in a quarry where limestone is excavated for rock gardens, fifty-two footprints made by a long necked, long tailed dinosaur were found. Palaeontologists could hardly contain their excitement at seeing the mother of all footprints, the largest being 112 cm (44 inches) across, laid down 140 million years ago. The expression on their faces served to remind me that visual evidence can very exciting for researchers who work with words and in the abstract. I hope this book provides readers not only with knowledge but also with the inspiration to pursue visual research for themselves. Image-based Research is not only useful but also illuminating, engaging, and stimulating.

Part 1

A Theoretical Overview of Image-based Research

Editor's note

The chapters in this section cover mostly historical, epistemological, theoretical and methodological overviews. They represent a cross-section of disciplines including anthropology, psychology and sociology and consequently a cross-section of perspectives on Image-based Research. However, they display a number of similarities in that each demonstrates an awareness of the limitations of visual research as well as its strengths. They also offer a framework for understanding how particular forms of Image-based Research are located in their respective disciplines.

Chapter 1

Visual Anthropology: Image, Object and Interpretation[1]

Marcus Banks

Abstract

Until recently, the subdiscipline known as visual anthropology was largely iden-tified with ethnographic film production. In recent years, however, visual anthro-pology has come to be seen as the study of visual forms and visual systems in their cultural context. While the subject matter encompasses a wide range of visual forms — film, photography, 'tribal' or 'primitive' art, television and cinema, computer media — all are united by their material presence in the physical world. This chapter outlines a variety of issues in the study of visual forms and argues for rigorous anthropological approaches in their analysis.

Anthropology and Visual Systems

In recent years there has been an apparent shift in anthropology away from the study of abstract systems (kinship, economic systems and so forth) and towards a consideration of human experience. This has resulted in a focus on the body, the emotions, and the senses. Human beings live in sensory worlds as well as cognitive ones, and while con-strained and bounded by the systems that anthropology previously made its focus, we not only think our way through these systems, we experience them. For anthropology, this has involved a shift away from formalist analytical positions — functionalism, structuralism and so forth — towards more phenomenological perspectives. Correspondingly, under the much misapplied banner of postmodernism, there has been an increased focus on ethno-graphy and representation, on the modes by which the lives of others are represented. At worst, this has been manifest in a depoliticization of anthropology, an extreme cultural relativism that concentrates on minutiae or revels in exoticism, and a deintellectualization of anthropology where all representations are considered equally valid, where analysis is subordinate to (writing) style, and where injustice, inequality and suffering are overlooked. At best, the new ethnographic approaches are historically grounded and politically aware, recognizing the frequent colonial or neo-colonial underpinnings of the relationship between anthropologist and anthropological subject, recognizing the agency of the anthropological subject and their right as well as their ability to enter into a discourse about the construc-tion of their lives (see Figure 1.1).

Until recently, visual anthropology was understood by many anthropologists to have a near-exclusive concern with the production and use of ethnographic film. In the first half of the century it was film's recording and documentary qualities that were chiefly (but not exclusively) valued by anthropologists. But while film could document concrete

Figure 1.1 Gabriel Reko Notan discusses his experience as a telegrapher for the Dutch East India government with anthropologist R.H. Barnes, in Witihama, Adonara, Indonesia

and small-scale areas of human activity that could subsequently be incorporated into formalist modes of analysis by anthropologists — the production and use of material culture, for example — it quickly became apparent that it could add little to our understanding of more abstract formal systems — in kinship analysis, for example. From the mid- to late-1960s onwards attention turned instead towards the pseudo-experiential representational quality of film, anticipating the appreciation of a phenomenological emphasis in written ethnography by a decade or two. Now film was to be valued for giving some insight into the experience of being a participant in another culture, permitting largely Euro-American audiences to see life through the eyes of non-European others.

While in some ways very different positions — film as science, film as experience — there is an underlying commonality between them. Both positions hold film to be a tool, something that allows 'us' to understand more about 'them'. More specifically, film was something 'we' did to 'them'. We can hypothesize that this is one of the reasons why ethnographic film came to dominate what became known as visual anthropology.[2] Ethnographic film produced using 16mm film cameras renders the anthropologist/filmmaker entirely active, the film subject almost entirely passive. Beyond altering their behaviour in front of the camera (or indeed, refusing to 'behave' at all) the film subjects have little or no control over the process. Partly for technical reasons they rarely if ever get to see the product before it is complete and they typically have no access to 16mm equipment to effect their own representations. Ethnographic still photography, probably more commonly produced than ethnographic film for much of the century, has been very much a poor second cousin to film in the traditional understanding of visual anthropology, perhaps because the active–passive relationship between anthropologist and subject is less secure: 'the natives' can have and have had more access to the means of production and consumption.

What was missed until recently was that film was one representational strategy among many. A particular division lies between written and filmed ethnography (see Crawford and Turton, 1992), but within the realm of the visual alone there are clearly differences between forms. For example, ethnographic monographs are frequently illustrated with photographs, very often illustrated with diagrams, plans, maps and tables, far less frequently illustrated with sketches and line drawings. Yet even this range of representations — some full members of what is traditionally understood to be the category of visual anthropology, some far less so — consists largely of visual forms produced by the anthropologist. Traditionally, the study of visual forms produced by the anthropological subject had been conducted under the label of the anthropology of art. Only very recently have anthropologists begun to appreciate that indigenous art, Euro-American film and photography, local TV broadcast output and so forth are all 'visual systems' — culturally embedded technologies and visual representational strategies that are amenable to anthropological analysis.[3] Visual anthropology is coming to be understood as the study of visible cultural forms, regardless of who produced them or why. In one sense this throws open the floodgates — visual anthropologists are those who create film, photography, maps, drawings, diagrams, and those who study film, photography, cinema, television, the plastic arts — and could threaten to swamp the (sub)discipline.

But there are constraints; firstly, the study of visible cultural forms is only visual *anthropology* if it is informed by the concerns and understandings of anthropology more generally. If anthropology, defined very crudely, is an exercise in cross-cultural translation and interpretation that seeks to understand other cultural thought and action in its own terms before going on to render these in terms accessible to a (largely) Euro-American audience, if anthropology seeks to mediate the gap between the 'big picture' (global capitalism, say) and local forms (small-town market trading, say), if anthropology takes long-term participant observation and local language proficiency as axiomatic prerequisites for ethnographic investigation, then visual studies must engage with this if they wish to be taken seriously as visual anthropology.[4] Not all image use in anthropology can or should be considered as visual anthropology simply because visual images are involved. It is perfectly possible for an anthropologist to take a set of photographs in the field, and to use some of these to illustrate her subsequent written monograph, without claiming to be a visual anthropologist. The photographs are 'merely' illustrations, showing the readers what her friends and neighbours looked like, or how they decorated their fishing canoes. The photographs are not subject to any particular analysis in the written text, nor does the author claim to have gained any particular insights as a result of taking or viewing the images. It is also possible for another anthropologist to come along later and subject the same images to analysis, either in relation to the first author's work or in relation to some other project, and to claim quite legitimately that the exercise constitutes a visual anthropological project.[5]

A second constraint returns us to a point I made in the opening paragraph. One of the reasons for the decline of formal or systems analysis in anthropology — particularly any kind of analysis that took a natural sciences model[6] — was the realization that formal analytical categories devised by the anthropologist (the economy, the kinship system) were not always that easy to observe in the field, being largely abstract. To be sure, earlier generations of anthropologists were confident both of the existence of abstract, systematized knowledge in the heads of their informants, and of their ability to extract that knowledge and present it systematically, even if the informants were unconscious of the systematic structuring. However, as these essentially Durkheimian approaches lost ground in the discipline, and as anthropologists concentrated more on what people actually did and actually thought about what they were doing, so doubts began to set in about how far any systematicity in abstract bodies of knowledge was the product of the anthropologists' own rationality and desire for order.[7] This does not, however, invalidate the current trend in anthropology towards seeing visual and visible forms as visual systems. The crucial difference between the visual system(s) that underlie Australian Aboriginal dot paintings and a particular Aboriginal kinship system is that the former is/are concrete, made manifest, where the other is not and cannot be except in a second-order account by an anthropologist. It is the materiality of the visual that allows us to group together a diverse range of human activities and representational strategies under the banner of visual anthropology and to treat them as visual systems. With some important exceptions, the things that visual anthropologists study have a concrete, temporally and spatially limited existence and hence a specificity that a 'kinship system' or an 'economic system' does not and cannot.[8]

In what follows, I shall unpack some of the ideas above, relating them more specifically to the history of visual anthropology, and some specific examples.

The Visual in Anthropology

The history of the visual in anthropology cannot be properly told or understood outside of an account of the history of anthropology itself, for it is intimately related to changes in what is understood to be the proper subject matter of anthropology, what methodology should be used to investigate that subject matter, and what theories and analyses should be brought to bear on the findings. Clearly this is not the place to rehearse the entire history of the discipline and the reader with less familiarity with anthropology's origins and subsequent development should turn to another account.[9] There have been one or two pieces by anthropologists, however, that have explicitly linked the parallel histories of anthropology and either photography (for example, Pinney, 1992c) or cinema (for example, Grimshaw, 1997).

Nonetheless, for much of anthropology's history the emphasis was on the study of indigenous visual systems (usually under the label of 'primitive art') and comments on the uses of film and photography by anthropologists were confined to methodological footnotes and the like until the last two decades or so. By and large, studies in the anthropology of art have mirrored wider theoretical concerns in the discipline as a whole, although, as Coote and Shelton note, the subdiscipline has 'hardly — if ever — taken the [theoretical] lead . . . [and] it is yet to significantly influence the mainstream' (1992, p. 3). Typically, from the early days of anthropology, we find works such as Haddon's *Evolution in Art* (1895) which attempts to trace the 'evolution' of stylistic devices by applying then-standard but now discredited social evolutionary theory developed in the second half of the nineteenth century (see Figure 1.2).

Yet despite the influence of 'Primitivism' on artists such as Picasso and the Cubists earlier generations of anthropologists resolutely confined themselves to the study of 'primitive art' in its own cultural setting and failed to set an agenda that would concern itself with 'art' as a broad category. This has not only led to an absence of anthropological studies of European 'fine art' and artists (and those elsewhere working within a European-influenced tradition) until recently, it has also led to an absence of anthropological studies of art in societies where anthropologists have long worked (such as China, Japan and India) but where the high culture of those societies, including their art forms, has been the preserve of other scholars.[10] Yet while these earlier studies insulated themselves from the traditions of art history and connoisseurship, they were nonetheless influenced (if

(a)

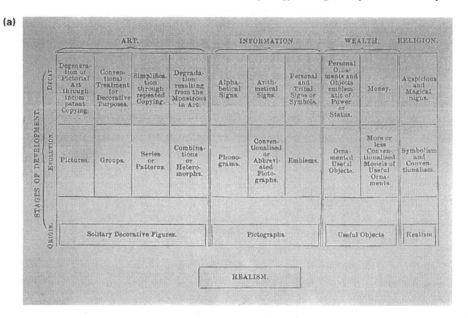

(b)

Figure 1.2   (a) Synoptic table of stylistic evolution and decay from Haddon's *Evolution in art* (1895: 8); (b) 'Skeuomorphs of Basketry' (Haddon 1895, Plate III) showing hypothetical origins of scroll designs (top) and examples of bronzework and pottery designs supposedly derived from these

unconsciously) by Euro-American categories of 'art' and the art object. It is only recently that the issue of aesthetics has been examined by anthropologists of art. Alfred Gell has urged the adoption of 'methodological philistinism', akin to the 'methodological atheism' adopted by sociologists of religion, in studies of art (1992). That is, anthropologists should abandon notions of aesthetics which are formed by the ethnocentric assumptions of the Euro-American 'art cult' (Gell, 1992, p. 42) and should consider art instead as a technical system. Conversely, Jeremy Coote cites philosopher Nick Zangwill who says 'one could do aesthetics without mentioning works of art! Sometimes I think it would be safer to do so.' (cited in Coote, 1992, p. 246). In other words, it is not only possible but perhaps also desirable to separate analytically the visual systems we term 'art' from the value systems (aesthetics) within which we normally understand 'art'.

In contrast, the anthropological approach to film and photography has been largely anti-aesthetic and focused upon the technological and methodological. While studies of non-western art were at least conducted within the framework of broader anthropological analysis, film — and to a lesser extent photography — has occupied a much more narrow and marginal place within the discipline. As an object of study, photography has received by far the more attention, with several studies devoted to a reading of historical photographs produced by others both as an insight into past (and present) ethnographic contexts (for example Geary, 1988; Ruby, 1995) and as an insight into the history of anthropology itself (for example Scherer, 1990; Edwards, 1992). There is also a literature on photography as an object of practice — that is, how can photographs be used in anthropological fieldwork and data collection? (See, for example, Collier and Collier, 1986.)

An anti-aestheticism is seen much more sharply at work in the anthropological writing on film, however. Here, there are almost no studies of non-ethnographic film, and very few of non-ethnographic film practice (though see Powdermaker, 1951 on the Hollywood film industry, and Dickey, 1993 and R. Thomas, 1985 on the Indian film industry). There are several studies, however, of ethnographic film practice. While some of these are insightful and relate the production of ethnographic film to the production of ethnographic knowledge more widely (for example, Loizos, 1993; MacDougall, 1978, 1992), others fall more into the 'how I made my movie' vein — or, as Loizos put it succinctly 'Look, Ma, I made a movie!' (Loizos, 1989, p. 25).

In general, visual anthropologists have been more concerned with the content of ethnographic film than with film as a medium. That is to say, there is little explicit anthropological consideration given to the properties of film as a medium of visual representation, beyond early endorsements of its powers as a medium of record (see, for example, most of the contributions to Hockings, 1995 — a re-issue of a volume that was first issued as a result of a conference held in the 1960s). Instead, there is a plethora of mostly short reviews of the content of particular ethnographic films (the journals *American Anthropologist* and *Visual Anthropology* both incorporate specific film review sections along with their book review sections), and some longer review pieces also exist. Many of these deal with a predefined corpus of film, whether the output of individual filmmakers, or the output of television.[11]

Issues

With a variety of initial positions established, and a brief assessment of some of the work that has been done on the visual in anthropology, it is now possible to address a number of issues that the study of the visual has raised.

Figure 1.3 Frame still of Torres Strait Islanders performing part of the Malu-Bomai ceremony for A.C. Haddon, 1898

First and foremost is the issue of veracity, of the visual as a medium of record. For earlier generations of anthropologists, operating within a more positivistic frame of analysis, the division between the visual forms of 'the informants' and their own visual forms — art vs. mechanical reproduction — seemed largely self-evident. Indigenous art was often non-representational (by the naturalistic conventions of post-Renaissance and pre-twentieth century European art) and needed to be interpreted, while photography and film apparently captured 'reality' unproblematically. There are however objections to such a simplistic dichotomy, some of which were noted at the time. For example, A.C. Haddon, a British anthropologist who shot the first ever fieldwork film footage in 1898 in the Torres Strait Islands (Australia), conducted his ethnography partially within a salvage or reconstruction paradigm — trying to gather data on the life of the Torres Strait Islanders as it was before European contact. In order to film a short section of a ritual dance, connected with an initiation cult that had already died out under missionary influence, he directed the Islanders to create cardboard replicas of the masks worn in the ceremony (see Figure 1.3). Thus the film is in one sense a record of what happened — men wore masks and danced — but in another sense is a fiction, an account of something that could not (or could no longer) be seen.[12]

Claims to veracity — or image as evidence — presume complete and authoritative control and intention lying with those who produce the image, and who have faith in their ability to record reality or their vision of reality convincingly. Yet the intention lying behind early (and later) uses of photography cannot be assumed to be unproblematic. Joanna Scherer has shown, for example, that studio portrait photographs of Sarah Winnemucca, a Northern Paiute (Colorado) woman, taken in the period 1879–84 cannot simply be read as representations of Native American women by (presumably) white, male, European photographers (Scherer, 1988). Indeed, Scherer demonstrates that Winnemucca seems to have exercised some control over her representations, by adopting certain poses, manner of dress, and so forth. But then as now the photographs — and the representations they embodied — formed part of a wider economy of photographic images, some of which were inserted into a still wider economy of discourse concerning the place of Indians in nineteenth century American society. Scherer assesses that Winnemucca seems to have mismeasured these economies, and that by conforming to a generalized 'Indian Princess' stereotype in her appearance and representations her photographs appear to have hindered her in her attempt to be taken seriously as a spokesperson for Indian rights. The formal studio portraits therefore reveal multiple levels of intentionality and meaning.

Figure 1.4   Photograph of Aranda boy, Central Australia, taken by Baldwin Spencer around 1901

Similarly, Howard Morphy has pointed out that while the early anthropologist of Australia, Baldwin Spencer, tended to work within the 'scientific' social evolutionary paradigm of late nineteenth and early twentieth century anthropology, his use of the camera can at times reveal a far more humanistic and subjective engagement with his supposed 'objects' of study (see Figure 1.4) (Morphy and Banks, 1997, p. 8).

A further issue of particular relevance to the anthropology of visual systems lies in the analytical separation of form and meaning. Although some earlier work in visual anthropology assumed the socio-cultural neutrality of photographic reproduction, at least in some circumstances, this idea now holds little currency.[13] A good example of cross-culturally variable linkages of form and meaning is provided by Chris Pinney's work on Indian photography (Pinney, 1992b). Pinney notes that certain formal or stylistic techniques, identified as montage and doubling, can be observed in a wide variety of visual media in India — popular bazaar prints, studio photographs and home video (see Figure 1.5). He also notes that these bear a superficial or formal similarity to uses of photomontage in Euro-American traditions of art photography, such as Dadaist uses.

Figure 1.5 'Doubled' portrait of a bride taken from a Central Indian wedding album, ca. 1983

However, Pinney warns that images from the two traditions should not be read in the same way. At least one of the intentions underlying photomontage doubling in the Euro-American tradition is to 'disrupt the unity of time and space . . . on which Western [narrative] realism depends' (Pinney, 1992b, p. 95); fracture and dissonance in the image subvert culturally specific notions of single-viewpoint perceptions of reality and attendant notions of narrative (how reality is represented and 'read'). By contrast, Pinney argues that Indian representational strategies rest, at least in part, on local notions of the person: divisible persons, in fact, whose inner core of personality cannot be directly perceived but is made visible through action. As actions (manifest through the body) are multiple, so multiple viewpoints of the body in photography are unproblematic. Montage and doubling in the Indian tradition are essentially conservative representational strategies, reinforcing rather than subverting a culturally specific view of reality.

Discussions such as these on how best to represent reality lie at the heart of the final issue to be discussed here — the fallacy of the so-called invisible camera. From the 1960s onwards ethnographic film production and documentary film production more generally sought to explore ways in which 'natural' and spontaneous human behaviour and interaction could best be observed by the motion picture camera. In some ways these endeavours, and the attendant debates, were direct descendants of the 'natural science' paradigm in pre-war anthropology and its (misplaced) enthusiasm for photographic media as neutral recording devices. However, with the paradigm shift to more interpretative anthropology, discussed above, styles of filmmaking were developed that sought to be sympathetic, even empathetic, with the rhythm of life as it is lived, and to be as reactive as possible to actual events in people's lives — the camera following, rather than dictating action.[14] Hence the observational cinema movement was born, appearing in recent years (albeit with some modifications) on British and other televisions as the 'fly-on-the-wall' documentary. At the heart of some, though not all, thinking in this area were attempts to get around some kind of Heisenberg observer-effect principle; if the film subjects could be persuaded to ignore or forget the presence of the camera, then their speech and actions thus recorded would be normal, unconscious, quotidian.

The classic view on this, and one closest to the old 'natural science of society' paradigm, was articulated by Margaret Mead who, apparently unconscious to the sociological embedding of technological development, predicted a brave new dawn for anthropology with 360 degree cameras 'preserv[ing] materials . . . long after the last isolated valley in the world is receiving images by satellite' and when 'large batches of material can be collected without the intervention of the filmmaker or ethnographer and without the continuous self-consciousness of those who are being observed' (to be achieved by self-loading, self-focusing cameras) (Mead, 1995, p. 9 — but first published in 1975).[15] The fallacy of course lies not in assuming that the camera can become invisible to those it films but in assuming that a socially, temporally and historical viewpoint can be overcome in what it sees. Even the classic 'invisible cameras' of modern industrial societies — high street bank security cameras, roadside traffic cameras, 'eye in the sky' surveillance cameras on helicopters — are socially located and 'see' from a particular, socially constructed viewpoint. The camera, whether strapped with a brace to the ethnographer's shoulder for permanent wearing (so that the subjects never know if they are being filmed or not), or positioned in a high corner of a building society ceiling, is a social actor and is inevitably involved in the social drama that unfolds before it. Its very presence confers importance and significance on the scene it reveals, to the viewer if not to the participants.

Material Visions

Finally, let us conclude by returning to the issue of the materiality of the visual form. A photograph, to take one example, is a material object with form as well as content. Once developed and printed it may be pasted by its owner into an album, shown to known and unknown others, sent to kin and friends, placed on display in a gallery, filed away in an archive, treasured by loved ones after the death of its owner, and so on. Once manifest in the world it begins a career and accumulates a series of linkages and social embeddings (cf. Appadurai, 1986). Part of its history is revealed by the object itself — traces of glue and paper on the reverse where it has been peeled from an album page, creases where it has been folded and tucked in a wallet, the name of the studio or photographer that created the image, and so forth. Another part of its history is revealed by its formal similarity or connection to other such objects — studio portraits, prison mugshots, family snapshots, anthropometric illustrations — and the social context within which such objects exist. 'History' here does not necessarily imply any particularly great time depth — a photograph taken by an anthropologist in the field and published within months to illustrate a journal article already has a history involving several persons and is embedded in a particular set of social, cultural and economic relations between those persons.

Take another example, this time of ethnographic film. In a review of several ethnographic films broadcast on British television in the 1970s, Peter Loizos notes that several anthropologists who reviewed individual films shortly after broadcast were rather critical of them, demanding in particular more information (Loizos, 1980). Loizos notes that these reviewers, who were often specialists in the ethnography of the societies portrayed, seemed to be reviewing the films as though they were reviewing an academic monograph. In effect, they were making a material category error; by focusing on the content of the films, they failed to appreciate the form and the historical trajectory of the object (a television programme created for, and broadcast to, a non-specialist mass audience) and thereby failed to read it correctly.

While the materiality of the visual object is important, so too are the technologies for the production, dissemination and viewing of the object. Anthropologists are well aware that there are no socially neutral technologies — all are embedded in complex historical, social and ideological frameworks (hence the fallacy of the 'invisible camera' mentioned above). For example, the film historian Jean-Louis Baudry, has pointed out that there is nothing 'natural' about the dimensions of a cinematic image, its framing or its composition, all of which derive from a western Renaissance aesthetic (Baudry, 1985, p. 534 — first published 1970), and the same is obviously true for all other visual media.

What all this points to is that visual anthropology is a subdiscipline of great complexity, a complexity that is generated not by spurious theorizing on the part of its practitioners, but by the very complexity of human social relations. Visual anthropology is not merely making and watching ethnographic movies, nor a pedagogic strategy, nor a tool to be employed in certain fieldwork contexts. Rather, it is an exploration by the visual, through the visual, of human sociality, a field of social action which is enacted in planes of time and space through objects and bodies, landscapes and emotions, as well as thought.

Notes

1 My thinking in this article has been strongly influenced by a number of colleagues, but most specifically by Howard Morphy and Elizabeth Edwards, to both of whom I am very grateful. Most of the ideas were developed while I was working on an ESRC-funded project to compile an online catalogue of early ethnographic film (award number R000235891), during the course of which I developed a much stronger appreciation of the use of visual media in anthropological research, but also of the materiality of visual media and their social location.

2 There are other reasons too for ethnographic film's dominance, especially in recent years. See Banks, 1988, 1990.

3 Recent collections of essays in visual anthropology that embody this approach include Banks and Morphy, 1997; Devereaux and Hillman, 1995; Taylor, 1994. Compare these with Hockings,

1995, the second edition of a work that appeared first in 1975; both editions are dominated by articles on ethnographic film — largely emphasizing the documentary, recording aspect — and almost no articles consider the possibility that visual anthropology might concern itself with visual forms produced by anyone other than the anthropologist.

4   My right to speak for sociology is far less grounded than my self-claimed but challengable right to speak for anthropology; nonetheless, I would assume that with appropriate changes to the definition this statement would hold true for visual sociology.

5   Indeed, Evans-Pritchard's photographs of the Nuer of the southern Sudan, published in his various ethnographies, have been subject to just such re-analysis, and although neither Farnell (1994, p. 929) nor Hutnyk (1990) to my knowledge claim to be visual anthropologists I find both, but particularly Farnell, to offer some highly relevant comments.

6   A classic starting point for this kind of approach is Radcliffe-Brown's book *A natural science of society* (1957)

7   The classic case for anthropologists — whether they agree with it or not — is Rodney Needham's claim that 'there is no such thing as kinship' (Needham, 1971, p. 5). I should perhaps stress that Durkheim is nonetheless alive and well in some branches of anthropology, and that the exploration of systematic bodies of knowledge is still highly relevant in some areas — ethnobotanical classification, for example.

8   The exceptions all broadly group together under the heading of performances — be they of dance, ritual, music, theatre, etc. — which often have an important visual aspect, as well of course as their other sensory and emotional aspects. Also somewhat transiently concrete are visual forms that are very quickly effaced — body decoration, for example. However, while the idea of such forms is clearly abstract, the performances themselves nonetheless exhibit temporal and spatial specificity. The relationship between the idea of ritual and the specificity of its performances has been explored in part by Humphrey and Laidlaw (1994), and although they do not make it explicit, there is a visual anthropological subtext to their analysis.

9   A wide variety of texts exist which aim to present an overview or history of anthropology, though few of them make specific mention of the visual. For a general account of the specific-ally British approach Kuper (1996) is probably the most straightforward, while Langham (1981) is a more detailed account of the early period. Two recent encyclopedias probably offer the most wide-ranging overviews — Ingold (1994) and Barnard and Spencer (1996). Other works which specifically address the place of the visual in anthropology will be mentioned elsewhere in the main text of this chapter.

10 Recent writing in the anthropology of art has moved in two related directions — a study of the place of non-western art in the contemporary art markets and galleries of Europe and America, leading to an anthropological evaluation of 'western' aesthetics, and a study of the place of non-western art in the ethnographic museums of the nineteenth century, contributing to the anthropological evaluation of 'the primitive' in European society. For the former, see recent work by Dussart (1997), Morphy (1995), and N. Thomas (1997), while MacClancy (1988) provides an insightful account of London auction house practice. For the latter, see Stocking (1985). Anthropological approaches to the 'high' art of India, China and Japan are thin on the ground, though significant insights are to be found in a recent series of essays on Indian Jain art (Pal, 1994), while Chris Pinney has done more than most to address the popular arts of India in an anthropological framework (for example, 1992a, 1992b).

11 Peter Loizos considers a number of filmmakers in his 1993 book, while Mick Eaton (1979) concentrates on Jean Rouch as does Paul Stoller (1992). A variety of articles have con-cerned themselves with corpuses of television ethnographic film, particularly concentrating on Granada Television's (UK) 'Disappearing World' series — see Banks (1994), Ginsburg (1988), Henley (1985), and Loizos (1980).

12 I am very grateful to Paul Henley for making me see this point (in the 1996 Paul Spencer Lecture at the University of Kent). See also Balikci (1995) on reconstruction in ethnographic film.

13   There are several examples of this assumption, but two well-known ones are the position adopted by Margaret Mead and the actual work conducted by Sol Worth and John Adair. Mead's position (1995, p. 9, but first published in 1975) regarding the static surveillance camera is discussed below. Worth and Adair (1972) attempted to translate the Sapir-Whorf hypothesis concerning the cognitive determinism of language to the realm of the visual by training cinematographically illiterate Navaho to use 16mm film cameras, under the initial impression — later modified — that the cameras would, as it were, see in Navaho. See also the discussion of Jean-Louis Baudry (1985) on the historically cultural bias of the cinematic image, below.

14   In some formulations of the history of documentary and ethnographic cinema, a certain technological determinism can be detected, arguing that the development of lightweight film cameras (and later, video cameras) and crystal synchronization between film camera and sound recorder, obviating the need for a cumbersome cable linking camera operator and sound recordist, brought about the development of observational cinema. Such arguments of course rest on the assumption that technological development is essentially asocial, that technology is developed independently of social need or social construction, something for which sociologists of science have failed to find evidence (e.g., Latour, 1996).

15   The irony is that while the empiricist positivism of Mead's position, not to say its hints of laboratory behaviourism, is wildly out of fashion today, most fieldworking anthropologists would welcome several hours of relatively unmediated footage of this kind if it came from a period before that for which adequate written ethnography and other texts exist. It is for this reason that I began the HADDON Project in Oxford to compile an online computerized catalogue of archival film footage of ethnographic interest. HADDON can be reached at the following URL: http://www.rsl.ox.ac.uk/isca/haddon/HADD_home.html

References

APPADURAI, A. (1986) (ed.) *The Social Life of Things: Commodities in Cultural Perspective*, Cambridge: Cambridge University Press.

BALIKCI, A. (1995 [1975]) 'Reconstructing cultures on film', in HOCKINGS, P. (ed.) *Principles of Visual Anthropology*, Berlin and New York: Mouton de Gruyter.

BANKS, M. (1988) 'The non-transparency of ethnographic film (Editorial)', *Anthropology Today*, **4**, 5, pp. 2–3.

BANKS, M. (1990) 'Experience and reality in ethnographic film', *Visual Sociology Review*, **5**, 2, pp. 30–3.

BANKS, M. (1994) 'Television and anthropology: An unhappy marriage?', *Visual Anthropology*, **7**, 1, pp. 21–45.

BANKS, M. and MORPHY, H. (1997) (eds) *Rethinking Visual Anthropology*, London and New Haven: Yale University Press.

BARNARD, A. and SPENCER, J. (1996) (eds) *Encyclopedic Dictionary of Social and Cultural Anthropology*, London: Routledge.

BAUDRY, J.-L. (1985 [1970]) 'Ideological effects of the basic cinematographic apparatus', in NICHOLS, B. (ed.) *Movies and Methods Volume II*, Berkeley and Los Angeles: University of California Press.

COLLIER, J. JN and COLLIER, H. (1986) *Visual Anthropology: Photography As a Research Method*, Albuquerque: University of New Mexico Press.

COOTE, J. (1992) '"Marvels of everyday vision": The anthropology of aesthetics and the cattle-keeping Nilotes', in COOTE, J. and SHELTON, A. (eds) *Anthropology, Art and Aesthetics*, Oxford: Clarendon Press.

COOTE, J. and SHELTON, A. (1992) 'Introduction', in COOTE, J. and SHELTON, A. (eds) *Anthropology, Art and Aesthetics*, Oxford: Clarendon Press.

CRAWFORD, P. and TURTON, D. (1992) (eds) *Film As Ethnography*, Manchester: Manchester University Press in association with the Granada Centre for Visual Anthropology.

DEVEREAUX, L. and HILLMAN, R. (1995) (eds) *Fields of Vision: Essays in Film Studies, Visual Anthropology and Photography*, Berkeley: University of California Press.

DICKEY, S. (1993) *Cinema and the Urban Poor in South India*, Cambridge: Cambridge University Press.

DUSSART, F. (1997) 'A body painting in translation', in BANKS, M. and MORPHY, H. (eds) *Rethinking Visual Anthropology*, London and New Haven: Yale University Press.

EATON, M. (1979) (ed.) *Anthropology–Reality–Cinema: The Films of Jean Rouch*, London: British Film Institute.

EDWARDS, E. (1992) (ed.) *Anthropology and Photography 1860–1920*, New Haven: Yale University Press in association with The Royal Anthropological Institute, London.

FARNELL, B.M. (1994) 'Ethno-graphics and the moving body', *Man*, **29**, 4, pp. 929–74.

GEARY, C. (1988) *Images from Bamum: German Colonial Photography at the Court of King Njoya, Cameroon, West Africa, 1902–15*, Washington: Smithsonian Institution Press.

GELL, A. (1992) 'The technology of enchantment and the enchantment of technology', in COOTE, J. and SHELTON, A. (eds) *Anthropology, Art and Aesthetics*, Oxford: Clarendon Press.

GINSBURG, F. (1988) 'Ethnographies on the airwaves: The presentation of anthropology on American, British and Japanese television', in HOCKINGS, P. and OMORI, Y. (eds) *Senri Ethnological Studies No. 24: Cinematographic Theory and New Dimensions in Ethnographic Film*, Osaka: National Museum of Ethnology.

GRIMSHAW, A. (1997) 'The eye in the door: Anthropology, film and the exploration of interior space', in BANKS, M. and MORPHY, H. (eds) *Rethinking Visual Anthropology*, London and New Haven: Yale University Press.

HADDON, A.C. (1895) *Evolution in Art: As Illustrated by the Life-histories of Designs*, London: Walter Scott.

HENLEY, P. (1985) 'British ethnographic film: Recent developments', *Anthropology Today*, **1**, 1, pp. 5–17.

HOCKINGS, P. (1995) (ed.) *Principles of Visual Anthropology* (2nd ed.), The Hague: Mouton.

HUMPHREY, C. and LAIDLAW, J. (1994) *The Archetypal Actions of Ritual: A Theory of Ritual Illustrated by the Jain Rite of Worship*, Oxford: Clarendon Press.

HUTNYK, J. (1990) 'Comparative anthropology and Evans-Pritchard's Nuer photography', *Critique of Anthropology*, **10**, 1.

INGOLD, T. (1994) (ed.) *Companion Encyclopedia of Anthropology*, London: Routledge.

KUPER, A. (1996 [1973]) *Anthropology and Anthropologists: The Modern British School* (3rd revised edition), London: Routledge and Kegan Paul.

LANGHAM, I. (1981) *The Building of British Social Anthropology: W.H.R. Rivers and His Cambridge Disciples in the Development of Kinship Studies*, Dordrecht: D. Reidel.

LATOUR, B. (1996) *Aramis, or the Love of Technology*, Cambridge, Mass.: Harvard University Press.

LOIZOS, P. (1980) 'Granada television's disappearing world series: An appraisal', *American Anthropologist*, **82**, pp. 573–94.

LOIZOS, P. (1989) 'Film and fidelity', *Anthropology Today*, **5**, 3, pp. 25–6.

LOIZOS, P. (1993) *Innovation in Ethnographic Film: From Innocence to Self-consciousness, 1955–85*, Manchester: Manchester University Press.

MacCLANCY, J. (1988) 'A natural curiosity: The British market in primitive art', *Res*, **15**, pp. 163–76.

MacDOUGALL, D. (1978) 'Ethnographic film: Failure and promise', *Annual Review of Anthropology*, **7**, pp. 405–25.

MacDOUGALL, D. (1992) 'Complicities of style', in CRAWFORD, P. and TURTON, D. (eds) *Film As Ethnography*, Manchester: Manchester University Press in association with the Granada Centre for Visual Anthropology.

MEAD, M. (1995 [1975]) 'Visual anthropology in a discipline of words', in HOCKINGS, P. (ed.) *Principles of Visual Anthropology*, Berlin and New York: Mouton de Gruyter.

MORPHY, H. (1995) 'Aboriginal art in a global context', in MILLER, D. (ed.) *Worlds Apart: Modernity through the Prism of the Local*, London: Routledge.

MORPHY, H. and BANKS, M. (1997) 'Introduction: rethinking visual anthropology', in BANKS, M. and MORPHY, H. (eds) *Rethinking Visual Anthropology*, London and New Haven: Yale University Press.

NEEDHAM, R. (1971) 'Remarks on the analysis of kinship and marriage', in NEEDHAM, R. (ed.) *Rethinking Kinship and Marriage*, London: Tavistock.

PAL, P. (1994) (ed.) *The Peaceful Liberators: Jain Art from India*, Los Angeles/New York: Los Angeles County Museum of Art/Thames and Hudson Inc.

PINNEY, C. (1992a) 'The iconology of Hindu oleographs: Linear and mythic narrative in popular Indian art', *Anthropology and Aesthetics*, **22**, pp. 33–61.

PINNEY, C. (1992b) 'Montage, doubling and the mouth of god', in CRAWFORD, P.I. and SIMONSEN, J.K. (eds) *Ethnographic Film Aesthetics and Narrative Traditions: Proceedings from NAFA 2*, Aarhus: Intervention Press.

PINNEY, C. (1992c) 'The parallel histories of anthropology and photography', in EDWARDS, E. (ed.) *Anthropology and Photography, 1869–1920*, New Haven and London: Yale University Press in association with The Royal Anthropological Institute, London.

POWDERMAKER, H. (1951) *Hollywood, the Dream Factory: An Anthropologist Looks at the Moviemakers*, Secker and Warburg.

RADCLIFFE-BROWN, A.R. (1957) *A Natural Science of Society*, Glencoe, Ill: Free Press.

RUBY, J. (1995) *Secure the Shadow: Death and Photography in America*, Cambridge, Mass.: MIT Press.

SCHERER, J. (1988) 'The public faces of Sarah Winnemucca', *Cultural Anthropology*, **3**, 2, pp. 178–204.

SCHERER, J. (1990) (ed.) *Picturing Cultures: Historical Photographs in Anthropological Inquiry* (a special edition of *Visual Anthropology*, **3**, pp. 2–3), Harwood Academic Publishers.

STOCKING, G. (1985) (ed.) *Objects and Others: Essays on Museums and Material Culture*, Madison: University of Wisconsin Press.

STOLLER, P. (1992) *The Cinematic Griot: The Ethnography of Jean Rouch*, Chicago: University of Chicago Press.

TAYLOR, L. (1994) (ed.) *Vizualizing Theory: Selected Essays from V.A.R. 1990–4*, New York: Routledge.

THOMAS, N. (1997) 'Collectivity and nationality in the anthropology of art', in BANKS, M. and MORPHY, H. (eds) *Rethinking Visual Anthropology*, London and New Haven: Yale University Press.

THOMAS, R. (1985) 'Indian cinema — pleasures and popularity', *Screen*, **26**, 3–4, pp. 116–32.

WORTH, S. and ADAIR, J. (1972) *Through Navajo Eyes: An Exploration in Film Communication and Anthropology*, Bloomington: Indiana University Press.

Chapter 2

An Argument for Visual Sociology

Douglas Harper

Abstract

This paper extends arguments I have developed over several years concerning the relationship between visual sociology and several forms of 'visual discourse'. I suggest that visual sociology is a useful framework for integrating traditions which first began with visual ethnography in anthropology and with documentary photography. In the meantime, new ways of thinking about ethnography, semiotics, documentary expression and science itself, often referred to as 'postmodern', both challenge and enlarge the potential scope of visual sociology.

This paper extends a case I previously made for visual sociology as an aspect of qualitative methodology (Harper, 1993). In this and other essays I described visual sociology as a two-headed beast; separating the empirical from the symbolic.[1] My argument included the simple suggestion that sociologists record the visual aspects of reality as part of relatively conventional research activities. Though commonplace in the natural sciences, and even in anthropology, this simple idea still seems revolutionary in sociology.

I contrasted the empirical visual sociologists with those who dwell in the universe of the symbolic. I had in mind analysis, typically based on semiotics, of visual texts. Subject matter includes landscape ('made', or found) (Pugh, 1990; Mitchell, 1994) and all human-made texts, including those made by photographers, filmmakers or cartoonists.[2] The discussions between empiricists and symbolists have produced a lively energy among visual sociologists, as captured in listserv exchanges during the winter of 1996 (Faccioli, 1996, pp. 50–9). Since semiotics scholars have studied secondary meanings of constructed sign systems such as photography and film, the arguments have turned in on themselves; semiotically minded visual sociologists easily absorb the visual texts of their empiricist colleagues! Thus a lot of us have noted that continuing the separation between these orientations is certainly counterproductive (Grady, 1996) and probably largely arbitrary. Added to this conundrum is the question of the relevance of cultural studies for visual sociology. It is the spirit of merging perspectives, noting overlaps and challenges posed by bringing ideas together, that I offer the following.

I begin by seeing visual sociology in the context to visual ethnography, documentary photography and semiotics. Postmodern thinking continues to influence all of these orientations, and, as I will note, these postmodern criticisms lead to interesting possibilities for a newly integrative visual sociology. Critical theory has its own history, which includes the production of visual, critical texts. These too, have been drawn upon by contemporary artists/social critics, which may be a natural part of the emerging subfield. Thus visual sociology has one foot in old traditions, and the other in the experimental thinking currently found in most of the social sciences and humanities. Visual sociology must trace its roots to this shifting ground, holding on to what is valuable while adopting elements of the new.

Visual Ethnography and the Realist Tale

Anthropology emerged at the end of nineteenth century and was first closely related to biology, at that time primarily a science of classification. Photography provided visual information used to categorize human races and these data supported theories of social evolution, the main preoccupation of early anthropology. Photography's role in this early history is well told by Elizabeth Edwards (1992), who notes that photography was first thought of 'as a simple . . . truth-revealing mechanism' (1992, p. 4). Photography, however, declined in importance in anthropology, both because of emerging emphasis on social organization (thought to be less visual), and because photography itself had begun to lose its general cultural influence. By 1920 Edwards suggests that:

> photography had become just another ancillary tool in the fieldworker's arsenal. Photographs became . . . marginal to the process of explanation rather than becoming part of a centrally conceived resource . . . a technique perceived as recording surface rather than depth, which was the business of the anthropologist. (Ibid.)

From this rather unpromising situation, Gregory Bateson and Margaret Mead largely reinvigorated the use of the visual methods in anthropology. While their book, *Balinese Character* (Bateson and Mead, 1942) showed the potential of visual ethnography in the study of culture, it did not inspire a revolution in visual ethnographic methods. The importance of *Balinese Character* however, remains (see also Elizabeth Chaplin's artful discussion, 1994, pp. 107–218). Bateson and Mead had each studied and written about Balinese culture for nearly a decade when they turned to photographic methods:

> . . . we were separately engaged in efforts to translate aspects of culture never successfully recorded by the scientist, although often caught by the artist, into some form of communication sufficiently clear and sufficiently unequivocal to satisfy the requirements of scientific inquiry . . . [our several monographs on the Bali] all attempted to communicate those intangible aspects of culture which had been vaguely referred as its ethos. As no precise scientific vocabulary was available, the ordinary English words were used, with all their weight of culturally limited connotations, in an attempt to describe the way in which the emotional life of these various South Sea people was organised in culturally standardised forms . . . (Bateson and Mead, 1942, p. xi)

Finding words inadequate by themselves, they added photographs to their analysis:

> . . . we are attempting a new method of stating the intangible relationships among different types of culturally standardised behaviour by placing side by side mutually relevant photographs . . . By the use of photographs, the wholeness of each piece of behaviour can be preserved, while the special cross-referencing desired

can be obtained by placing the series of photographs on the same page. (op. cit., p. xii)

The authors worked as a team; Bateson photographing as Mead directed. They made more than 25,000 photographs over a two-year field experience from which they selected 759 photographs for *Balinese Character*. The photographs were sorted into categories which had emerged from their study, including: 'spatial orientation and levels', 'learning', 'integration and disintegration of the body', 'orifices of the body', 'autocosmic play', 'parents and children', 'siblings', 'stages of child development' and 'rites of passage'. The categories included cultural topics specific to the Balinese and subjects which could be applied to any ethnographic study. Several themes addressed social organization, which anthropology had previously found unsuitable for visual study.

Their book offered a new model for integrating images and text. For example, in the chapter on 'Rites of Passage', photographic plates (pages with between six and ten photographs each) visualize subtopics such as tooth filing, marriage, funerals, exhumation and other rituals. The photographs are in numbered sequences and face pages of detailed explanation, image by image. The analysis moves from the level of concept to detailed study of specific events, elements or moments.

The significance of the Bateson and Mead project is that the photographs were regarded as a part of the process of observation. Bateson writes:

In general we found that any attempt to select for special details was fatal, and that the best results were obtained when the photography was most rapid and almost random. (op. cit., p. 50)

Mead and Bateson catalogued and sorted images to present several perspectives on a single subject, or in sequences which showed how a social event evolved through time. Single images were used to construct longer visual statements. Organizing the images this way presented problems a filmmaker routinely confronts when assembling a soundtrack for a film. The anthropologists limited themselves to an arbitrarily determined amount of space — just as flowing images on a film limit how much can be said on a film. The gain for Bateson and Mead has been that the images remain adjacent to their informing texts.

There have been no visual ethnographies which equal *Balinese Character*. Several visual monographs have applied some of Bateson and Mead's methods and styles of presentation. These include Danforth and Tsiaras' (1982) study of death rituals of rural Greece, which follows the format of *Balinese Character* but concentrates on a single ritual; Cancian's (1974) visual ethnography of Mexican peasant culture which studies deviance and social disorganization, and Gardner and Heider's (1968) visual ethnography of the largely ritualistic war of Dani of New Guinea. These and a small number of other visual ethnographies are at the more experimental end of what John van Maanen (1988) called the 'realist tale' of ethnography.

The conventions of the 'realist tale' — taken-for-granted in traditional ethnography — obscure problems inherent in the anthropologist's attempts to gain scientific legitimacy. These conventions, according to Van Maanen, define the author as scientific expert. Scientific discourse depends on technical language, which naturally excludes personal reporting or emotional reflections. In the realist tale, the anthropologist observes objectively and interprets according to anthropological theory. The points of view of the subjects are offered in quotes separated from the rest of the text, maintaining the control of the voice of the author (Van Maanen, 1988, pp. 46–9).

Photography, thought of as a 'reflection' rather than an 'interpretation' of what was photographed, has a natural place in these reports. George and Louise Spindler, writing in the Foreword to John Collier's classic text on visual anthropology, commented:

> Usually an anthropologist takes a photograph to illustrate a finding that he has already decided is significant . . . He [sic] waits until whatever it is happens, then points his camera at it. His camera then is incidental to his research activity and comes into use late in the fieldwork period. He uses the camera not as a research technique, but as a highly selective confirmation that certain things are so, or as a very selective sample of 'reality'. (Collier, 1967, p. x)

The Spindlers later comment that Collier has argued for a more inductive photographic ethnography (particularly in the use of photographs to elicit interviews, which I will discuss later), but the Table of Contents of Collier's text shows photography in the service of the traditional ethnography. Collier argues that visual ethnography is an efficient way to survey and map material culture or social interaction, contributing to techniques such as sociometric analysis.

The use of still photography by anthropologists in ethnography has not developed much beyond the experiments cited here. In nine years of the publication of the journal of *Visual Anthropology*, the handful of visual ethnographic studies include Norman's portrayal of a primary health care system in underserved communities in Florida (1995), Frese's (1992) study of American yard decoration as gendered space, and Schwartz's visual ethnography of a rural Legion Post (1989). Several studies used historical photographs to understand earlier cultural forms, such as Dohm's study of architecture and privacy in Pueblo housing (1992); and others have studied the changing historical depiction of cultural groups (Cheung, 1996). In Lucien Taylor's collection of four years of the publications of the *Visual Anthropology Review* (1994), there is nothing resembling visual ethnography as the 'realist tale'.

As a result, the subdiscipline of visual anthropology has become mostly a discipline of film and video, with texts written in service of the films and videos. These are typically studies of the meaning of images as mediation between the anthropologist and the subject, and queries into the nature of visual representation.[3] Other texts, such as Connor, Asch and Asch (1986) accompany and explain films. The Connor, Asch and Asch monograph provides background on their four films on a Balinese healer, Jero Tapakan; it is 'an integrated set of materials that different people could use in a variety of ways . . .' (1986, p. 2).

Thus, the 'realist tale' has become a discredited form in visual ethnography, at least within publications sponsored by the discipline of anthropology. It is seldom seen and yet often criticized. Taylor's editorship of the *Visual Anthropology Review*, the publication of the American Anthropological Association's Society for Visual Anthropology, represented this trend. The journal has evolved to a slightly anthropological version of otherwise familiar essays in cultural criticism. Despite the sense that anthropology has turned its back on visual ethnography, it is a tradition which continues to offer a model for contemporary visual sociologists bent on the visualization of social life in field work research.

Visual Sociology and the Realist Tale

Visual sociology came into existence during the 1960s. Only a few sociologists interested in the visual have been aware of, or involved with the parallel movement in anthropology. Rather, the first visual sociologists tended to be inspired by documentary photographers working on many of the issues which sociologists felt were missing from the sociological agenda of the times. These included the photographic studies of drugs and drug culture (Clark, 1971); black ghetto life (Davidson, 1970); small-town southern poverty and racism (Adelman, 1972); the southern Civil Rights movement (Hansberry, 1964), institutionalization (Lyon, 1971; Jackson, 1977); social class (Owens, 1973; Estrin, 1979); the unionization of migrant farm workers (Fusco and Horowitz, 1970); the counter-cultural life (Simon and Mungo, 1972); the anti-war movement (Kerry, 1971), the freespeech movement (Copeland, 1969) and the social irresponsibility of corporate capitalism (Smith and Smith, 1975). Aspiring visual sociologists drew inspiration from the liberal humanist tradition of documentary photography which dated to Jacob Riis's (1971 [1890]) examination of the poverty of the urban immigrant, the Farm Security Administration photographic documentation of poverty during the 1930s (Stryker and Wood, 1973; Agee and Evans, 1941), and, more indirectly, Robert Frank's photographic portrait (1969 [1959]) of an alienated, materialistic American culture in the 1950s. These books were primarily photographs, sometimes with lengthy texts (for example in Smith and Smith, 1975) which generally provided background and personal commentary. The documentary photographers were not sociologists, and while their books lacked sociological frames or theories, the documentarians did have a great deal to offer sociologists seeking a more direct and critical sociology. Sociologists looking for a visual method recognized that the documentary photographers often had deep involvement with their subjects, and thus an insider's knowledge, much as would a sociological field worker. Adelman's study of southern poverty and racism, for example, emerged from his experiences as a VISTA worker; Eugene and Aileen Smith, while writing *Minamata*, lived for several years in the Japanese village poisoned by corporate mercury dumping. Some of these studies were 'culturally autobiographical' and showed the importance of insider knowledge; Estrin (1979) photographed her upper class family and friends and Owens (1973) photographed his own suburban community. Others, like Robert Frank, a Swiss photographer, simply travelled around America making photographs, but his images (1969) resonated with widely held sociological ideas such as alienation or anomie. In the documentary movement there was very little, if any discussion of the issues of representation, ideology, or how the relationships with subjects influenced these photographic studies. As mentioned, these studies were characterized by the sense that the photographer should expose social problems in order to educate the public in order to change society. This idea, we shall see later, has lost of a great deal of its currency.

Howard S. Becker's lead article in Volume 1, Number 1 (1974) of *Studies in the Anthropology of Visual Communication*, the first journal in either sociology or anthropology devoted to the study of visual communication, defined visual sociology within accepted conventions of sociology. Becker noted that photography and sociology had about the same birth date, and that they had both been concerned with, among other things, the exploration of society. Early issues of the *American Journal of Sociology* routinely used photographs (Stasz, 1979); Lewis Hine's early twentieth-century photographic surveys of social problems were supported by the Russell Sage Foundation. From the beginning of photography, however, there was a split between those who saw photography as description ('documentary' photography) and those who saw it as art. As sociology has become more like science, Becker points out, photography has become more like art. Thus sociology and photography had ceased, by the time of the writing of the article, to have much to do with each other; his article was intended to begin dialogue between the two. Sociologists should study photography, Becker suggests, because photographers have studied many of the same things which sociologists routinely study, including communities, social problems, work, social class, the 'ambience of urban life', and more abstract themes such as the social types or modal personalities.

An important theme raised by Becker concerns the role of theory in photographic representation. While photographs are potentially packed with information, photographers:

> tend to restrict themselves to a few reiterated simple statements. Rhetorically important as a strategy of proof, the repetition leads to work that is intellectually and analytically thin. (Becker, 1974, p. 11)

To make the photographs 'intellectually denser', Becker suggests the photographer must become conscious of the theory that guides one's photography. That theory may be 'lay theory' — taken-for-granted assumptions about how the world is organized — or it may be 'deep, differentiated and sophisticated knowledge of the people and activities they investigate . . . for photographic projects concerned with exploring society it means learning to understand society better' (1974, p. 11). Recall that Bateson and Mead both spent several years in the field, and had completed ethnographic studies before they then turned to the subject with their cameras. The theories they explored with photographs were grounded in anthropological knowledge.

Becker reminded us that photographs, often thought of as 'truth', are more precisely reflections of the photographer's point of view, biases, and knowledge, or lack of knowledge. Thus the integration of photography and sociology must begin with the understanding of just how much unsociological photography we are accustomed to seeing. Sociological photography may be guided by sociological concepts which develop as one's theories are revised.

Becker addresses how issues of validity, reliability and sampling are treated by the visual sociologist. In simple terms, these are the questions: 'has the ethnographer reported accurately what she or he has seen? Is the event reported on repeated enough times so that the single event can be understood to stand for a regularly repeating class of events? Do the events reported characterize the behavior of the group?'

We recognize that the photographic image is 'true' in the sense (physical or electronic manipulation aside) that it holds a visual trace of a reality the camera was pointed at. But more fundamentally, all images, despite their relationship to the world, are socially and technically constructed. Their credibility should be based on common-sense reasoning and evidence, rather than debates about the essential quality of the photograph. In other words, we adopt a pragmatic response to this question: the more we know about how the photograph came into existence the more we can judge its validity. Thus to the question of whether the photograph represents the only truth of a particular setting, the answer lies in 'distinguishing between the statement that X is true about something and the statement that X is all that is true about something' (Becker, 1986, p. 252). The problem of validity and reliability is related to access; whether the photographer has been able to observe and photograph a full range of activities that explore the particular question he or she is interested in. The camera makes access more difficult; in some circumstances it makes it impossible. Because photographing is much more active than observing, it certainly influences how the fieldworker is received in the field.

Because the camera portrays people clearly, ethical issues, important to all field-workers, is especially important to visual ethnographers. Steven Gold, a sociologist who has photographed a variety of field settings, suggests that for the visual ethnographer:

> Sensitivity is rooted in a covenantal rather than contractual relationship between researcher and host. Unlike a contract that simply specifies rights and duties, a covenant requires the researcher to consider his or her relationship with subjects on a much wider level, accepting the obligations that develop between involved, interdependent persons . . . For visual sociology, the concepts of sensitivity and convenantal ethics are clearly related. A researcher cannot engage in the reciprocal relationship required by the covenant without making efforts to understand his or her hosts' beliefs, values, and views of the world. Similarly, the covenantal ethnic reminds the researcher to consider his other subjects' needs when researching and publishing. (Gold, 1989, pp. 104–5)

This important point can be summarized by the recognition that while the ethical considerations of each project vary, ethical concerns are particularly important since the camera intrudes and reveals more than other method. Sociologists must keep the cultural perspectives of subjects at the forefront of their consciousness.

Thus visual sociology draws on traditions of ethnographers us in cameras to record what were thought to be 'exotic' cultures, and of concerned people photographing society for some of the same reasons sociologists study it, as well as from field work practices in sociology. It has been said by many that the camera is a telling symbol of modernism; a machine which advances the purposes of an empirical science, of which sociology has traditionally been a part; a science whose existence itself was due to the liberal agenda of social reform. But the assumptions which underlie sociology, documentary photography and ethnography have shifted since Becker wrote what was a clarion call for sociologists to take up cameras. The larger mandate of science itself is questioned; as is sociology's status as a science; liberalism, for many has lost its potency; photographs are seen as problematical and tentative statements rather than reflections of truth. Thus while visual sociology must recognize its roots in the traditions of ethnography and documentary, it must acknowledge and integrate the insights of the new critical comment in these areas as well.

I shall now introduce the critical takes on ethnography and photography, and evaluate their usefulness for visual sociology.

Methodological Critique: New Ethnography

The idea of ethnography as 'partial truth' rather than 'complete document' lies at the basis of the new ethnography. The book or film (or other mode of communication) which represents culture is partial, or incomplete, because culture itself is not precisely boundaried and continually evolves. For example, Dorinne Kondo, an American of Japanese descent who wrote an ethnography of a Japanese workplace through an analysis of her own complex partially cross-cultural experience, writes:

Culture . . . is no reified thing or system, but a meaningful way of being in the world, inseparable from the 'deepest' aspects of one's 'self' — the trope of depth and interior space itself a product of our own cultural conventions. These cultural meanings are themselves multiple and contradictory, and through they cannot be understood without reference to historical, political and economic discourses, the experience of culture cannot be reduced to these nor related them in any simple, isomorphic way. (Kondo, 1990, pp. 300–1)

Kondo constructs cultural description through her own negotiation of a liminal status and thus teaches us as much by looking inward as through her interaction with other members of the culture she visits.

Ethnographic knowledge traditionally derives from the interaction between the 'subject' and the 'researcher'. The postmodern critique questions the normal assumptions surrounding this interaction. Steven Tyler, for example, suggests an ethnographic model consisting of '. . . a co-operatively evolved text consisting of fragments of discourse intended to evoke in the minds of both reader and writer an emergent fantasy of a possible world of common-sense reality . . .' (Marcus and Fischer, 1987, p. 125). Paul Stoller's account of his apprenticeship among sorcerers in western Niger (Stoller and Olkes, 1987) emerged from cultural collaboration at the level of personal transformation. Stoller became a spiritual being in a culture which was previously unknown to him. Stoller's account is narrative and conversational, and engages the subject through the question of his personal transformation. Other experiments are written in a way which intends to bring the reader to the cultural world, rather than to report on it from a distance. For example, to communicate the cyclical nature of the tramp experience (Harper, 1982), I wrote a narrative of five weeks on the road in the company of tramp workers. The book describes work and migration, elements of a repeating pattern in a migrant lifestyle, much as the experience itself unfolded. The centre of the book is the relationship between the writer and the tramp; a variation of a typical social bond: momentary but culturally organized.

Finally, the new ethnography challenges the very idea of analysis: 'Post-modern ethnography . . . does not move toward abstraction, away from life, but back to experience. It aims not to foster the growth of knowledge but to restructure experience; not to understand objective reality, for that is already established by common sense, nor to explain how we understand, for that is impossible, but to reassimilate, to reintegrate the self in society and to restructure the conduct of everyday life' (Marcus and Fisher, p. 135). For example, David Sudnow's (1978) study of the 'organisation of improvised conduct' attempts to communicate 'what the hand feels or thinks' as one plays keyboard jazz or types one's ideas. The language violates taken-for-granted assumptions about action and motive, and the description ventures into areas which had not been described before. Whether the inquiry is 'successful' by the standards of traditional ethnography (speaking of 'demonstrable truth') is beside the point. We know a truth about the accomplishment of jazz through Sudnow's research, but this knowledge is more an empathetic understanding than a basis for prediction.

From the vantage point of the new critique, then, ethnography is most usefully thought of as a created tale which describes reality more successfully if it does not attempt to fulfill the impossible and undesirable (for ethnography) standards of science. Ethnography should draw upon narrative; emphasizing the point of view, voice, and experience of author.

There are relatively few examples of this 'new ethnography', applied to visual methods, and published within the canon of visual anthropology. From my vantage point, there is a flood of critique, yet few attempts to bring the critiques to life. Seremetakis' visual/textual montage of her Greek grandmother (1994) provides a suggestive example.

The Critique, Part Two: Postmodernism and Documentary

The postmodern critique of documentary photography begins with the idea that the meaning of the photograph is constructed by the maker and the viewer, both of whom carry their social positions and interests to the photographic act.[4] We are often reminded that the powerful, the established, the male, the colonizer typically portray the less powerful, established, female and colonized. Even exceptions such as Hubbard's (1991) collection of photographs by homeless children, or Ewald's (1985) portraits and stories by Appalachian youth, projects which give voice to marginalized groups, emerge from a corporate publishing world which reflects the priorities of the market and is largely controlled by Anglo males.

The postmodern critique reminds us that the meaning of the photograph changes in different viewing contexts. The history of photography shifts from a history of the images of 'great photographers' to a history of the uses of photographs, and whole photographic traditions. Excellent contemporary examples are case studies in the above cited (Edwards, 1992) history of anthropological photography. The case studies studied in the Edwards volume are not interesting because they tell us the size, shape and material culture of long-disappeared Third World people, but because they tell us how the colonial portrayed, and thus categorized the colonized.

These insights confront the idea that photographs carry documentary 'truthfulness' in the manner taken for granted in early anthropological or documentary photography. They also challenge the oft-stated notion that documentary photographs show 'the human condition' — something we all supposedly recognize, but cannot define.

A second common theme in this perspective is the assertion that even if documentary was once a part of liberal humanism, liberal humanism is now a failed program, based on naive assumptions that have not stood the test of new theory. In Martha Rosler's words:

> In the liberal documentary, poverty and oppression are almost invariably equated with misfortunes caused by natural disasters: causality is vague, blame is not assigned, fate cannot be overcome . . . Like photos of children in pleas for donations to international charity organisations, liberal documentary implores us to look in the face of deprivation and to weep (and maybe to send money . . .) (Rosler, 1989, p. 307)

Documentary photography advances the false causes of a liberal system because it does not see the ideological aspects of its own patterns of representation. Documentary typically focuses on the specific and thus hides or mutes the critiques of the system; social problems are portrayed as personal stories and social ugliness is made beautiful or provocative. All of these characteristics of documentary photography, so say the postmodern critic, obscure the very social realities the documentarian wishes to portray. These critical themes may be uncomfortable for many, they cannot be ignored.

The Critique, Part Three: Cultural Studies and Visual Texts

Many argue that visual sociology must transcend its methodological orientation to embrace the theoretical, as situated at the level of the whole society. The natural intersection is critical theory, currently known as cultural studies. Certainly the critical theory perspective, represented in several decades of twentieth-century scholarship through the work of major figures as Lukacs, Benjamin, Adorno and Marcuse,[5] developed the idea that art reflects the social organization — specifically, the class structure — which produces it. Gramsci contributed the important idea that revolutionary socialists, to overturn capitalism, had to 'do more than seize power — they had to built a counter-culture of their own' (Chaplin, 1994, p. 29). This counter culture would consist of 'initiatives' against the hegemony of capitalist ideas, naturally advanced and developed in all aspects of the institutional life of the society (the 'superstructure', in Marxian terminology). Chaplin suggests that it is Benjamin's 'idea of the true revolutionary author [as] one who instructs in criticism, placing an improved critical apparatus at our disposal' (40).

Theorists, however, have mostly written about the role of art in creating critical consciousness, rather inspiring by the critical sensibility by making visual texts. Contemporary sociologically minded artists (such as Victor Burgin, who I will discuss below), however, are producing work within the mandate of creating an 'improved critical apparatus'.

Typically, these artists have relied on one or another form of juxtaposition. For example, in the 1920s photographers such as El Lissitzky and Alexander Rodchenko used photomontage to inspire an understanding of the socialist revolution in the Soviet Union. The Russian filmmaker Dziga Vertov employed montage in his films 'Man with a Movie Camera', and 'Three Songs to Lenin', to jolt viewers into the revolutionary moment. In these cases, art as critical sensibility inspired support for an emerging socialist revolution. Artist/critics also relied on visual juxtaposition. John Heartfield, in the best know example, used photomontage to ridicule German Nazism (Ades, 1976). Of course, once the Russian revolution became totalitarian, state-supported art became socialist realism: visual texts to inspire loyalty rather than critical reflection. Heartfield, and other similar artists did not survive long in Nazi Germany. The art of state fascism reflected ideologies of the time.

The idea of documentary images as a part of a critical text is surprisingly rare. Baudrillard's 1986 essay on American culture contains several full page photos. Some of these are banal and predictable: an image of Ronald Reagan in a foolish pose. But other images, particularly by the photographer Chris Richardson, develop Baudrillard's critical slant. They are not captioned but juxtaposed to chapter titles on the facing pages. These establish an ironic dialogue between text and image; at times overstated, often suggestive. Is this sociology? Most would see this project as cultural commentary; the images sometimes develop or elaborate ideas, but they do so on the basis of agreement, rather than research.

Building a Visual Sociology

How has visual sociology emerged from these unlikely roots? How is it most usefully to evolve?

Douglas Harper

Salvaging assumptions from traditional sociology?

While the postmodern critique has meant that visual sociology cannot treat business as usual, there are many elements in traditional ways of doing things, many outlined in Becker's first outline of visual sociology, which remain useful (see also Prosser, 1996). Most important may be the realization that to accomplish in-depth understanding one must complete 'immersive' field research driven by theoretical questions. We must remember that when we enter the field we initially see and photograph through our own cultural lenses. We must learn to see through the lenses of the cultural Other — in the ways field workers always have gained cultural knowledge. The irony for visual sociology is that one can take an extraordinary number of photographs in a very short time (National Geographic photographers, for example, routinely expose a hundred rolls of film — 3,600 separate images per day) and creating so much information tricks one into thinking one has created knowledge. Thus the first step to a vital visual ethnography is the same level of commitment which is necessary for all field research. Diane Hagaman's (1996) study of religious institutional practices is provocatively titled 'How I learned not to be a photojournalist' precisely because it was her experience that to develop a complex theory of her subject required involvement that could not emerge in the typical photojournalist's role. Recent documentary projects, including Olive Pierce's visual ethnography of a Maine fishing village (1996), Helen Stummer's portrait of life in the inner city of Newark, New Jersey (1994), James Barker's study of subsistence among Alaskan Eskimos (1993), and John Miller's (1992) visual ethnography of deer hunting continue to remind us that documentary based on in-depth involvement still inspires a 'realist tale' visual ethnography.

The role of theory cannot be overstressed. Our photographic work be guided by ideas which, directly or indirectly, derive from sociology. Theory guides teaching visual sociology as well as doing it. When we assign visual sociology students the task of photographing sociological ideas they are confronted with the need to put some form to their sociological thinking. It is often disarmingly difficult to answer the question, as the group gazes at the students' photos: 'What sociological idea are you exploring with these photographs?' 'How might have you better explored these ideas?' The discussions typically lead from a very simple idea to several levels of complexity. Of course, this is not to say that all sociological ideas can be photographed, an issue which leads to other useful dialogues.

There are several recent models for this form of visual sociology. Jon Rieger masterfully demonstrated how social change may be visualized through the re-photography process (1996); Steven Gold studied the relationship between setting and urban interaction (1995); Margolis analyzed ideology in the portrayal of Colorado Coal Camps, and Van Mierlo studied the comparative gestures of prayer (1994). Within this perspective photography is as an information-gathering process; the information must subsequently be organized and presented from a sociological perspective. If we do not make this second step we may create visual information which will unconsciously reflect our personal taken-for-granted assumptions — the very thing that sociologists should suspend as they enter and try to understand the worlds of others.

Visual sociology should, I think, begin with traditional assumptions and practices of sociological field work and sociological analysis. The photograph can be thought of as 'data'; in fact the unique character of photographic images force us to rethink many of our assumptions about how we move from observation to analysis in all forms of sociological research. But note that I suggested that image making and analysis begins with these and other traditional assumptions and practices. It does not end there!

Lessons from the Critique?

Sociology embraces the assumptions of the scientific report — the use of third person; the pretence of 'objectivity'; the language of analysis-qualified, dispassionate, precise and arid. The new ethnography embraces diametric oppositions to these forms: the first person, the understanding that all presentation is subjective, the language of narrative-vibrant, suggestive, engaged and passionate. Photographs can, of course, serve either function. As suggested above, photography in traditional ethnography was often used to simply gather information. Our understanding of the constructed nature of photography, however, leads us to see photography as a natural part of a new ethnography.

Tales can easily become visual; we are accustomed to the idea of images-through-time in film. Images can be organized in sequences which explore sociological ideas; these visual narratives might explore cycles in a cultural life (Harper, 1987b) — the migration, work and drinking sprees of migrant workers, or the peasant pilgrimages of Europe (Bot, 1985). Emmet (1989) uses a photo narrative to describe nearly ten years in the lives of a family of migrant farmworkers. These experiments in visual narrative scratch the surface of a potential method in a new ethnography.

The new ethnography asks for a redefinition of the relationship between the researcher and the subject. The ideal suggests collaboration rather than a one-way flow of information from subject to researcher. The technique of photo-elicitation promises a particularly apt alternative; a model for collaboration in research. Photo elicitation, first described by Collier (1967), is a very simple variation on the theme of open-ended interviewing. The open-ended interview is an exchange initiated and guided by the researcher in which the subject hopefully provides in-depth responses to complex questions. The open-ended interview rests on the assumption that the researcher will ask questions that are culturally meaningful to the subject. As most people who have done this kind of research know, that is more easily described than accomplished. In the photo-elicitation interview, interview/discussion is stimulated and guided by images. Typically these are photographs that the researcher has made of the subject's world (Harper, 1987a; Gold, 1991). A shocking thing happens in this interview format; the photographer, who knows his or her photograph as its maker (often having slaved over its creation in the darkroom) suddenly confronts the realization that she or he knows little or nothing about the cultural information contained in the image. As the individual pictured (or the individual from the pictured world) interprets the image, a dialogue is created in which the typical research roles are reversed. The researcher becomes a listener and one who encourages the dialogue to continue. The individual who describes the images must be convinced that their taken for-granted understanding of the images is not shared by the researcher, often a startling realization for the subject as well!

This method has yet to catch on as a recognized sociological method, yet its potential is nearly endless. The photo interview may use photographs people have in their home collections, as many of my students have done. The photos may come from an historical archive, and may be used to recreate 'ethnographic memory', which I am doing in a study of labour exchange among dairy farmers in the 1940s. Or, the method may stretch the collaborative bond, so that the subjects direct the photography before interpreting them in interviews, a method used by five Dutch students in a study of a Dutch neigh-bourhood (Van der Does, *et al.*, 1992). The photo-elicitation interview may redefine the relationships between subject and sociologist, and the interview material may be presented in any of a number of creative ways. These sensibilities from the new ethnography open the door for a creative and engaged visual ethnography. Given the expressive potential of photography and the intellectual ferment surrounding experiments in ethnography, the marriage of visual methods and ethnography seems natural.

Taken at its extreme, however, the postmodern critique of documentary is perhaps the greatest challenge to visual sociology. This critique calls for the end of photography, linking the photographic gaze to politically reactionary voyeurism. As noted above, this critique has characterized traditional documentary as linked to the prevailing power centres, thus reinforcing existing social arrangements even when it attempts to criticize. Part of this is due to the fact that photography typically focuses on discernible individuals or events; the power arrangements of the society are visually abstract; perhaps invisible. A response is to create photographic/textual statements which are critiques of documentary-de-masking how prevailing forms of documentary communicate (Rosler, 1989). These acts of decon-struction are defined as Marxist because they suggest how social groups gain and maintain control through cultural manipulation, and informed by a Freudian critique which asserts that our own act of seeing in the traditional documentary is fuelled by voyeuristic pleasure (Clough, 1992). Visual sociology must confront this critique. Some will, of course, take it seriously enough to never photograph in the field again. Others will continue to form creative solutions which address at least some of the critique.

Visual Sociologist as Cultural Critique?

There remains the question of the visual sociologist as a cultural critic, picking up on themes and working methods created by the artist/critics of the 1920s and 1930s. It has become common for contemporary artists to 'appropriate' images from the culture, usually from mass media, and juxtapose these images (or parts of images) to other scraps from the culture; words, phrases from mass culture or other sources. A small number of visual sociologists have been inspired by these examples. Leo Frankenberger, for example, (1991) assembled photomontages from documentary photographs of a neighbourhood to be demolished and images of the neighbourhood residents. The photomontages take us inside the exteriors of the soon-to-be-destroyed buildings to empathize with the personal losses the destruction represents. These projects work through metaphor; they are suggest-ive, empathetic and descriptive.

Some of the statements which emerge from these practices lead us to see class and gender relations and oppression in new and provocative ways. Victor Burgin (1986) juxtaposes texts and photographic images to jolt viewers into deconstructing ads from mass media, billboards or the built environment. His texts have two elements: he borrows fonts and layout from the ad he mimics, but the message may be taken from an eco-nomics or sociology text; usually a statement about the distribution of wealth or other social inequities. The act of expressing sociological insights in the dress of the message it mimics, and playing the text onto the image often produces awareness of secondary meanings. It is an example of the 'critical apparatus' called for by critical theorists for most of the century. It also poses the question of what constitutes data in visual sociology, and whether one uses the method to 'instruct' the society to the insights one has arrived at, or whether images are part of the process of discovery of those insights.

While I have cast the definition of visual sociology into one sea after another, I do believe that there are some genuine dead ends for visual sociology. One is in an emerging form of documentary expression, published as art, which claims to investigate sociological themes. For example, Nan Goldin's 'visual diary' (1986) claims to reveal codes of sexual behavior in their natural settings. We find self portraits and portraits of her friends, typically facing the camera in a cold, cool stare, or seemingly engaged in sex or parodies thereof. The photographs tell us that Goldin's friends and lovers have sex in tawdry settings; they occasionally beat each other up; they seem to look at the preceding generation as mannequins. They may have supplied ethnographic data but it is not on the subject promised.

Where, then, is the contribution of the postmodern criticism of the documentary to an emerging visual sociology? First, postmodernism leads us away from study of the 'great artists of the documentary' to the study of the history of the uses of photography. Here visual sociology becomes a form of critical history, well demonstrated in Edwards, cited above.

Secondly, the new criticism allows us to confront the problem of ideology; the manner in which unequal relationships are hidden or ignored in the practice of photography. Traditionally this meant that photography has been implicated as part of the power and domination which lie behind the relationship of the colonized or the native (the subject of the ethnography) and the colonizing culture, that of the ethnographer, but it includes issues of gender and class. Noteworthy examples are Solomon-Godeau's (1991) several studies of gendered photography, including her deconstruction and reconsideration of erotic photography; her development of Jean Clair's characterization of 'the gaze as erection of the eye' in order to '. . . better understand   in order to effectively combat — the complex network of relations that meshes power, patriarchy, and representation' (1991, p. 237), and her several essays which begin to define a feminist photographic aesthetic and practice.

The new ethnography must understand power relationships outside of the small social units they study, and they need to see their own work in the context of larger frames of power. To these ends, the visual sociologist working in the area of social criticism has much to gain from the sensibilities of those working in what has come to be known as the postmodern left.

Finally, the critical perspective sometimes shows how critical consciousness can live within the sociological urge to know another world. Jacob Holdt's decades-long voyage through the American underclass (Holdt, 1985), for example, takes on the practice of making social problems beautiful or artful-Holdt used a cheap pocket camera and drugstore developing and did not frame images with an artist's eye. The images seem to be ripped out of experience, They are captioned by a lengthy text which tells where the photographer went; who he met, and what he thought along the way. Nick Waplington (1991) takes us to the mundane events of British working-class weekends; his photographs document the energetic, chaotic, person-filled 'backstages' of life — people laying around, bodies askew on rough and serviceable furniture; kids playing a hundred games of their own invention; families drinking beer and pinching each other; men fixing old cars on the streets in front of their flats; women shopping, laden with their kids. The emphasis on the mundane, for Waplington, vitalizes a documentary practice which has tended to emphasize the spectacular. The result is visual ethnography of daily life which explores concepts of front stage/back stage familiar to all students of social interaction. Jo Spence's 'political, personal and photographic' autobiography (1988) shows that narrative self reflection combines powerfully with images pulled from one's past or made in the process of self study. Quinney places images made as fine art in the context of personal and philosophical reflection: '. . . a visual sociology not of direct formulation, not for the testing of hypotheses, nor for the collection of data, but a practice in the living of a life.' (1995, p. 61). These, and other experiments at the interpretative extreme of documentation use images as metaphor and allegory rather than literal data. Without rejecting sociology they extend the borders.

I take a practical attitude toward the future of visual sociology. Rather than build boundaries and engage in intellectual battles, I hope that visual sociology will draw on several quite different traditions and practices to organize an approach based on the commonality of the visual world. Images allow us to make statements which cannot be made by words, and the world we see is saturated with sociological meaning. Thus it does not seem peculiar to suggest that images enlarge our consciousness and the possibilities for our sociology. Oddly, we remain revolutionaries in an enormously conservative discipline. But while our colleagues continue to resist such an attractive, useful, interesting and engaging proposition, visual sociologists have continued to do research, publish in our own journal of *Visual Sociology*, hold international conferences, and continually redefine ourselves and our research in the process — as we are all Dziga Vertov's, constantly spinning.

Notes

1 See Harper, 1987b. Elizabeth Chaplin (1994) suggests different fault lines, separating the 'critical' from the 'empirical'. Her analysis integrates cultural theory and empirical sociology quite successfully. Chaplin's impressive argument has had a great impact on my thinking as reflected in my discussion of critical theory, which is largely inspired by her work.
2 For example, see Barthes,1970, for the semiotic study of photography; Nichols, 1991 for an analysis of ethnographic and documentary film; Goldman, 1992 for a study printed advertisements. These are only the tip of the iceberg.
3 See David McDougall, 1994; Lansing, 1989; and Lydall, Bishop, and Tomaselli's contribution to Boonzajer and Harper, 1993.
4 This perspective, however, is rooted in a Marxist frame. For example, John Tagg states: 'The photograph is not a magical "emanation" but a material product of a material apparatus set to work in specific contexts, by specific forces, for more or less defined purposes' (1988, 3).
5   This brief reference points only to a sampling of the major texts, which would profitably include Adorno, 1984; Benjamin, 1973; Lukacs, 1971; and Marcuse, 1964.

References

ADELMAN, B. (1972) *Down Home*, New York: McGraw-Hill.
ADES, D. (1976) *Photomontage*, New York: Pantheon.
ADORNO, T. (1984) *Aesthetic Theory*, London and New York: Routledge and Keegan Paul.
AGEE, J. and EVANS, W. (1941) *Let Us Now Praise Famous Men*, Cambridge, Massachusetts: Riverside Press.
BARKER, J.H. (1993) *Always Getting Ready*, Yup'ik Eskimo Subsistence in Southwest Alaska (Upterrlainarluta), Seattle: University of Washington Press.
BARTHES, R. (1970) *Camera Lucida*, New York: Hill and Wang.

BATESON, G. and MEAD, M. (1942) *Balinese Character: A Photographic Analysis*, New York: New York Academy of Sciences.

BAUDRILLARD, J. (1986) *America*, London: Verso.

BECKER, H.S. (1974) 'Photography and sociology', *Studies in the Anthropology of Visual Communication*, **1**, 1, pp. 3–26.

BECKER, H.S. (1986) *Doing Things Together*, Evanston: Northwestern University Press.

BENJAMIN, W. (1973) 'The work of art in the age of mechanical reproduction', *Illuminations*, London: Fontana, pp. 219–53.

BERGER, J. and MOHR, J. (1982) *Another Way of Telling*, New York: Pantheon.

BOLTON, R. (ed.) (1988) *The Contest of Meaning: Critical Histories of Photography*, Cambridge: MIT Press.

BOONZAJER FLAES, R. and HARPER, D. (eds) (1993) *Eyes across the Water, volume II*, Amsteram: Het Spinhuis Press.

BOT, M. (1985) *Misere: The Great Pilgrimages of Penance in Europe*, Rotterdam, Holland: Marrie Bot.

BURGIN, V. (1986) *Between*, London: Basil Blackwell.

CANCIAN, F. (1974) *Another Place*, San Francisco: Scrimshaw Press.

CHAPLIN, E. (1994) *Sociology and Visual Representation*, London: Routledge.

CHEUNG, S.C.H. (1996) 'Change of Ainu images in Japan: A reflexive study of pre-war and post-war photo-images of Ainu', *Visual Anthropology*, **9**, 1, pp. 1–24.

CLARK, L. (1971) *Tulsa*, New York: Lunstrum Press.

CLIFFORD, J. and MARCUS, G. (eds) (1986) *Writing Cultures*, Berkeley: University of California Press.

CLOUGH, P.T. (1992) *The End(s) of Ethnography: From Realism to Social Criticism*, Newbury Park: Sage Publishers.

COLLIER, J.Jr. (1967) *Visual Anthropology: Photography As a Research Method*, New York: Holt, Rinehart and Winston.

CONNOR, L., ASCH, P. and ASCH, T. (1986) *Jero Tapakan: Balinese Healer. An Ethnographic Film Monograph*, Cambridge: Cambridge University Press.

COPELAND, A. (ed.) (1969) *People's Park*, New York: Ballantine Books.

DANFORTH, L. and TSIARAS, A. (1982) *Death Rituals of Rural Greece*, Princeton: Princeton University Press.

DAVIDSON, B. (1970) *E100 Street*, Cambridge: Harvard University Press.

DOHM, K.M. (1992) 'Architecture and privacy in Pueblo housing', *VisualAnthropology*, **5**, 1, pp. 1–15.

EDWARDS, E. (ed.) (1992) *Anthropology and Photography 1860–1920*, New Haven: Yale University Press.

EMMET, H.L. (1989) *Fruit Tramps*, Albuquerque: New Mexico University Press.

ESTRIN, M.L. (1979) *To the Manor Born*, Boston: Little Brown.

EWALD, W. (1985) *Portraits and Dreams*, New York: Writers and Readers.

FACCIOLI, P. (1996) *L'Immagine Sociologigica: Relazioni Famigliari e Ricerca Visuale*, Milan: Franco Angeli.

FRANK, R. (1969) (1959) *The Americans*, New York: Aperture.

FRANKENBERGER, L. (1991) 'Going out of business in Highland Park', *Visual Sociology Review*, **6**, 1, pp. 24–32.

FRESE, P.R. (1992) 'Artifacts of gendered space: American yard decoration', *Visual Anthropology*, **5**, 1, pp. 17–42.

FUSCO, P. and HOROWITZ, G.D. (1970) *La Causa*, New York: Collier.

GARDNER, R. and HEIDER, K. (1968) *Gardens of War: Life and Death in the New Guinea Stone Age*, New York: Random House.

GOLD, S.J. (1989) 'Ethical issues in visual field work', in BLANK, G., McCARTHY, J. and BRENT, E. *New Technology in Sociology: Practical Applications in Research and Work*, New Brunswick: Transaction Publishers.

GOLD, S. (1991) 'Ethnic boundaries and ethnic entrepreneurship: A photo-elicitation study', *Visual Sociology*, **6**, 2, pp. 9–23.

GOLD, S. (1995) 'New York/LA: A visual comparison of public life in two cities', *Visual Sociology*, **10**, 1–2, pp. 85–105.

GOLDIN, N. (1986) *The Ballad of Sexual Dependency*, New York: Aperture.

GOLDMAN, R. (1992) *Reading Ads Socially*, London: Routledge.

GRADY, J. (1996) 'The scope of visual sociology', *Visual Sociology*, **11**, 2, pp. 10–24.

HAGAMAN, D. (1996) *How I Learned Not to Be a Photojournalist*, Lexington: University of Kentucky Press.

HANSBERRY, L. (1964) *The Movement*, New York: Simon and Schuster.

HARPER, D. (1982) *Good Company*, Chicago: University of Chicago Press.

HARPER, D. (1987a) *Working Knowledge: Skill and Community in a Small Shop*, Chicago: University of Chicago Press.

HARPER, D. (1987b) 'The visual ethnographic narrative', *Visual Anthropology*, **1**, 1, pp. 1–19.

HARPER, D. (1993) 'On the authority of the image: Visual sociology at the crossroads', in DENZIN, N. and LINCONN, Y. *Handbook of Qualitative Sociology*, Beverly Hills: Sage, pp. 403–12.

HOLDT, J. (1985) *American Pictures*, Copenhagen: American Pictures Foundation.

HUBBARD, J. (1991) *Shooting Back: A Photographic View of Life by Homeless Children*, San Francisco: Chronicle Books.

JACKSON, B. (1977) *Killing Time*, Ithaca: Cornell University Press.

KERRY, J. (1971) *The New Soldier*, New York: Macmillan.

KONDO, D. (1990) *Carfting Selves*, Chicago: University of Chicago Press.

LANCING, J.S. (1989) 'The decolonization of ethnographic film', in BOONZAJER, F.R. (ed.) *Eyes Across the Water*, Amsterdam: Het Spinhuis Press.

LUKACS, G. (1971) *History and Class Consciousness*, Studies in Marxist Dialectics, London: Merlin Press.

LYON, D. (1971) *Conversations with the Dead*, New York: Holt, Rinehart and Winston.

MACDOUGALL, D. (1994) 'Whose story is it?', in TAYLOR, L. (ed.) *Visualizing Theory: Selected Essays from V.A.R. 1990–4*, London: Routledge, pp. 27–37.

MARCUS, G. and FISCHER, M. (1987) *Anthropology as Cultural Critique*, Chicago: University of Chicago Press.

MARCUSE, H. (1964) *One Dimensional Man*, New York: Beacon Press.

MARGOLIS, E. (1994) 'Images of struggle', *Visual Sociology*, **9**, 1, pp. 4–26.

MILLER, J. (1992) *Deer Camp: Last Light in the Northeast Kingdom*, Boston: MIT Press.

MITCHELL, W.J.T. (ed.) (1994) *Landscape and Power*, Chicago: University of Chicago Press.

NICHOLS, B. (1991) *Representing Reality*, Bloomington: Indiana University Press.

NORMAN, W.R.JR. (1995) 'The San Joachim clinic', *Visual Anthropology*, **7**, 3, pp. 209–31.

OWENS, B. (1973) *Suburbia*, San Francisco: Straight Arrow Books.

PIERCE, O. (1996) *Up River*, Hanover: The University Press of New England.

PROSSER, J. (1996) 'What constitutes an image-based qualitative methodology?', *Visual Sociology*, **11**, 2, pp. 25–34.

PUGH, S. (ed.) (1990) *Reading Landscape*, County, City, Capital. Manchester: Manchester University Press.

QUINNEY, R. (1995) 'A sense sublime: Visual sociology as a fine art', *Visual Sociology*, **19**, 1–2, pp. 61–84.

RIEGER, J. (1996) 'Photographing social change', *Visual Sociology*, **11**, 1, pp. 5–49.

RIIS, J.A. (1971) (1890) *How the Other Half Lives*, New York: Dover.

ROSLER, M. (1989) 'In, around and afterthoughts (on documentary photography)', in BOLTON, R. *The Contest of Meaning: Critical Histories of Photography*, Cambridge: MIT Press.

SCHWARTZ, D. (1989) 'Legion post 189: Continuity and change in a rural community', *Visual Anthropology*, **2**, 2, pp. 103–33.

SEREMETAKIS, C.N. (1994) 'The memory of the senses: Historical perception, commensal exchange, and modernity', in TAYLOR, L. (ed.) (1994) *Visualizing Theory: Selected Essays from V.A.R. 1990–4*. London: Routledge, pp. 214–29.

SIMON, P. and MUNGO, R. (1972) *Moving on Standing Still*, New York: Grossman.

SMITH, W.E. and SMITH, A. (1975) *Minamata*, New York: Holt, Rinehart and Winston.

SOLOMON-GODEAU, A. (1991) *Photography at the Dock: Essays on Photographic History, Institutions and Practices*, Minneapolis: University of Minnesota Press.

SPENCE, J. (1988) *Putting Myself in the Picture: A Political, Personal and Photographic Autobiography*, Seattle: The Real Comet Press.

STOLLER, P. and OLKES, C. (1987) *In Sorcery's Shadow*, Chicago: University of Chicago Press.

STASZ, C. (1979) 'The early history of visual sociology', in WAGNER, J. (ed.) *Images of Information: Still Photography in the Social Sciences*, Beverly Hills: Sage.

STRYKER, R. and WOOD, N. (1973) *In This Proud Land*, Greenwich: New York Graphic Society.

STUMMER, H.M. (1994) *No Easy Walk: Newark, 1980–93*, Philadelphia: Temple University Press.

SUDNOW, D. (1978) *Ways of the Hand: The Organization of Improvised Conduct*, Cambridge: Harvard University Press.

TAGG, J. (1988) *The Burden of Representation: Essays on Photographies and Histories*, Basingstoke: Macmillan.

TAYLOR, L. (ed.) (1994) *Visualizing Theory: Selected Essays from V.A.R. 1990–4*, London: Routledge.

VAN DER DOES, S.E., GOOSKENS, I., LIEFTING, M. and VAN MIERLO, M. (1992) 'Reading images: A study of a Dutch neighborhood', *Visual Sociology*, 7, 1, pp. 4–68.

VAN MAANEN, J. (1988) *Tales of the Field*, Chicago: University of Chicago Press.

VAN MIERLO, M. (1994) 'Touching the invisible', *Visual Sociology*, 9, 1, pp. 43–51.

WAPLINGTON, N. (1991) *Living Room*, New York: Aperture.

Chapter 3

Film-making and Ethnographic Research

Paul Henley[1]

Abstract

Until the 1950s, most ethnographers considered film to be no more than a means of objective documentation. Film-making in ethnographic research thus remained separate from documentary-making generally, often conventionally defined as 'the creative treatment of actuality'. The subsequent synthesis of documentation and documentary approaches has been associated with much stylistic and technical innovation, as well as with increased quantity of production. But only recently have changes in the dominant paradigms of anthropology, coupled with further technical development, finally opened the door for genuine rapprochement between text- and film-based ethnography.

Claiming the Real: The Status of Ethnographic Film

Ever since they first became widely available almost a century ago, moving image cameras have had fervent advocates amongst ethnographers. However, since those early days, ideas about the precise role that moving image film should have in ethnographic research have varied considerably, partly as a result of technical developments, but more importantly, as a result of changing theoretical paradigms in social and cultural anthropology generally. Yet throughout the history of ethnographic film, certain issues have been the focus of recurrent debate. Of these, one of the most fundamental is the status of the 'claim upon the real' that is implicit in an ethnographic film document (cf. Winston, 1995).[2]

Central to this issue is the ontological ambiguity neatly described by Marcus Banks (1995) in his comment that 'while film, video and photography do stand in an indexical relationship to that which they represent they are still representations of reality, not a direct encoding of it'. Or, to put it a somewhat less elegant way, although such representations may be based on the chemical or magnetic registration of the objective physical features of the things represented, their realization is influenced by both subjective and cultural factors. Indeed, in the view of some authors, even the objectivity of the physical image itself is in doubt: after all, a film image is not a literal reproduction but rather a two dimensional object purporting to represent a three-dimensional reality, which — if all the travellers' tales of native peoples' first reactions are to be believed — it takes a little time to learn how to read. It has also been argued that conventional camera and lens construction reproduce the world according to a set of perspectival conventions based on a single and unified point of view. This is not a universal nor objective perspective, it is claimed, but rather the product of a particular cultural tradition which originated in Europe around the time of the Renaissance (Comolli, 1985, p. 43, Morris, 1994, pp. 15, 27).

There are obviously also some more prosaic considerations about the circumstances in which filming generally takes place which clearly impose limits on the objectivity of cinematographic images. Any ethnographic film production requires the maker to take a series of decisions about when, where and how long to film, where to place the camera(s), how to frame the shot, how to determine its duration. All these decisions, and many more pertaining to the selection of material at the editing stage are all inevitably subject to cultural bias or to idiosyncratically personal factors of gender, age, relationship to the subject, political interest, aesthetic taste and so on.

The reaction of some ethnographic film-makers to these contingencies of production has been to formulate procedures designed to minimize the corruption of film as a reliably objective record. Typically, this will involve the elaboration of rules to maximize the effacement of the physical presence of the film-maker during production (so that life will go on 'as if the camera were not there') whilst minimizing the film-maker's authorial signature in the rushes (no 'dramatic camerawork'). So too is a concern with typicality, which is to be established by randomizing strategies and/ or by appropriate detailing of the circumstances of production in an accompanying text. For those who advocate this approach, the camera should be comparable to the instruments of the natural sciences — the camera as telescope, the camera as microscope — neutral, impersonal, dispassionate, distant (Sorensen and Jablonko, 1995; Fuchs, 1988).

But for others, all such strategies to ensure the objectivity of the cinematographic image are bound to fail. Even if it were possible, through some sufficiently ingenious or laborious means to produce film sequences that might be considered somehow to be an objective physical record of a cultural event, there would still remain the question of the meaning of that event, in the first instance to the protagonists, but also to the film-maker. This meaning, they would argue, can only be determined by means of an active engagement on the part of the film maker with the protagonists of the film and this is bound to involve some measure of subjectivity. For ethnographic film-makers of this persuasion, the camera acts as a catalyst, provoking events, situations and relationships that are revealing precisely because of their atypicality. Some have even claimed that the camera can act as the medium of a trance-like state whereby the film-maker becomes fully engaged in the lives of the film's protagonists and thereby achieves an understanding that is inaccessible to those who insist on remaining neutral and distant (Rouch, 1995, pp. 89–90). The implicit theory of knowledge underlying this approach is that true social reality is not to be found in the superficial observable details of everyday life but rather in the underlying relationships, sentiments and attitudes which sustain them. These, it is claimed, come to be exposed only in extraordinary circumstances. The very process of making of a film can serve to generate such revelatory 'epiphanies' (Denzin, 1989, pp. 15–18). If these underlying significances do not arise in the actual act of shooting, they may well do so during the process of editing where the juxtaposition of sequences gives new meanings to each.

In effect, these two very different approaches are nothing more than the manifestation within the specialist domain of ethnographic film of the long-standing tussle within the social sciences between the positivist approach, associated with the aspiration to develop a natural science of society based on controlled observations by a dispassionate observer, and the various hermeneutical/interpretative approaches in which society is conceived as a text or language whose meaning must be explicated by an analyst who has achieved sufficient 'communicative competence' in the relevant cultural norms and practices. In anthropology, since the end of the last century at least, it has been accepted that this competence can only be achieved through direct personal engagement with the protagonists of the study in the course of fieldwork (Giddens, 1976; Hastrup and Hervik, 1994). Despite their differences, the two approaches, the positivist and the interpretative, have not, in actual practice, been mutually exclusive, at least not in anthropology. In recent years though, the positivist approach has been in decline whilst the interpretative approaches have become more influential (Marcus and Fisher, 1986).

This shift of emphasis can also be traced in recent developments in ethnographic film. One of its most significant indicators are changing attitudes towards narrative conventions. For those adopting a positivist approach, the production of a film should be aimed exclusively at documentation, i.e., the collection of visual data in the most objective possible manner. The material recorded may be subsequently re-arranged in the course of being presented as evidence in support of a verbal argument. This will typically tend to be of an entirely external nature (i.e., not offered by the protagonists themselves) and to be presented in the form of a voice-over soundtrack. But any such re-arrangement should be strictly controlled, openly declared and directly subject to the requirements of the verbal argument.

In contrast, ethnographic film-makers sympathetic to the interpretative approach have been inclined to structure their films around a story-line that emerges from within the action itself since in this way they have been able to communicate the meaning of the events filmed to the protagonists. Further, they have often been prepared to edit these story-lines according to narrative conventions already well established within documentary cinema generally (Nichols, 1983; de Bromhead, 1996). Such manipulation of the cinematographic record would be anathema to those who think of the camera as an objective recording medium. But ethnographic film-makers drawing on documentary conventions argue that they are not distorting the material so much as using the medium to its best effect to evoke their understanding of the situations portrayed. In this sense, they claim, they are no different from the authors of ethnographic monographs who, it is increasingly recognized, routinely call upon their writerly skills and the conventions of textual presentation to communicate their understandings (Hammersley and Atkinson, 1995, pp. 239–62).

Documentation versus the Documentary

The moving image camera was initially conceived simply as a means to retain a supposedly objective image of the world for subsequent detailed analysis. For most of the century in which moving image cameras have been used in ethnographic research, the field has been dominated by those who have sought to use them in this way. This was certainly the aim of pioneers such as Regnault in France, Haddon in Britain and Boas in North America (de Brigard, 1995; Long and Laughren, 1993; Morris, 1994, pp. 55–66). It was also the primary objective of Margaret Mead and Gregory Bateson (former students of Boas and Haddon respectively), whose 16mm filming and 35mm photography in Bali in 1936–9 represent by far the most significant ethnographic research use of visual media in the first half of this century (Mead and Bateson, 1942, pp. 49–54). None of the three earlier pioneers ever edited their materials into films structured by any sort of narrative. Although Mead did eventually edit the Balinese material into a coherent film form, this was only some fifteen years later and even then, it was used in a highly didactic manner to provide visual evidence in support of a voice-over analysis.)

The early use of film by ethnographic researchers thus remained completely separate not just from all the major developments in documentary film which took place before, during and immediately after the Second World War (Barnouw, 1983), but even from the more specialized genre of 'ethnographic documentary' which is conventionally deemed to have originated with the work of Robert Flaherty amongst the Inuit in the 1920s.[3] Indeed, it was not until the 1950s that film-makers with some sort of association with academic life began to make films that combined an academic concern for ethnographic documentation with the narrative devices of documentary cinema generally.)

This division between those interested in documentation and those interested in documentary has been overlain and to some extent cross-cut by another that is possibly more significant, not just in relation to film-making but within ethnographic practice generally. This is the difference between those whose aim is to represent the world as it is and those whose concern has been 'salvage ethnography', i.e., the recording of 'traditional' ways of life on the verge of extinction through contact with a wider social universe. The latter have sometimes resorted to full-scale reconstruction or re-enactment of a way of life before outside influences made themselves felt.[4] But frequently this testamentary attitude affects ethnographic film-making in ways that are more difficult to detect: thus, for example, at both production and editorial stages, material evidences of contact are eliminated whilst the views of traditionalists (usually older protagonists) are favoured over the views of those who welcome change. The very themes chosen as the subject-matter of the film, the particular communities, the narrative devices — all can silently conspire to emphasize some idealized notion of the 'traditional' past at the expense of the realities of the present. In recent years however, there has been increasing suspicion of anything that smacks of 'salvage ethnography', be it in films, texts or museum collections. There has also been a growing corresponding commitment to representing the ways in which once largely autonomous communities are developing hybrid cultural forms as a means of dealing with integration into a world economic and social system (Clifford, 1986; Morris, 1994).

The films of both Haddon and Boas were motivated by acute salvage ethnography concerns and were based on the re-enactment of abandoned ceremonial events performed at the request of the film-makers. In the case of Mead and Bateson on the other hand, the film-makers aimed rather to minimize the effects of the presence of the camera through the use of a right-angle viewfinder and other techniques. The only events which they staged specifically for the camera were certain theatrical performances which had to be performed in daylight since they did not have the lighting equipment to film them at night (Mead and Bateson, 1942, p. 49; de Brigard, 1995, p. 27). But in Mead's work generally, there is a strong salvage ethnography concern, as is clear from her celebrated introduction to the landmark volume *Principles of Visual Anthropology* (1995, pp. 9–10).

Perhaps the most elaborate ethnographic reconstruction is *The Netsilik Eskimo*, a series of nine films about the Inuit of the northwestern shores of Hudson's Bay. Shot in 1962 under the anthropological direction of Asen Balikci, a one-time student of Mead's, these films mostly deal with migratory subsistence practices as they would have been forty years earlier, before the arrival of rifles led to a major change in hunting strategies and before the establishment of a Catholic mission led to a change in settlement patterns. Yet although Balikci specifically eschewed 'the classic documentary format with its linear narrative structure, evolving story-line and closed statement at the end' (Balikci, 1989,

p. 6), the shooting and editing of the film nevertheless conforms to certain documentary codes. This is particularly noticeable in some of the later films, which were shot by the distinguished documentary cameraman Robert Young. Also, the films are constructed around the person of Itimanguerk, a fifty-year old man whom, 'in the Flaherty tradition', Balikci selected as his 'principal actor', relating most community activities to him and his small family (Balikci, 1995, p. 187). Thus although the films were originally conceived as neutral documents, they took on many of the attributes of the documentary form in the actual process of realization.

The more intentional synthesis of documentation and documentary in ethnographic film-making took place more or less simultaneously in various parts of the world in the 1950s. Perhaps the first to engage in it in a systematic way was the French film-maker Jean Rouch. Since the 1940s, he has made over a hundred ethnographic films, mostly based on his own research in West Africa. However, in contrast to most previous ethnographic film-makers, he has not been afraid to use documentary editorial devices and even, on occasion, to make films which he has described as 'ethnographic fictions'. These were developed in conjunction with the protagonists and played with the boundaries not only between fact and fiction and between observer and observed, but also with the equally ambiguous boundary between tradition and modernity (Stoller, 1992).

Particularly influential for Rouch were Flaherty and Dziga Vertov, the Polish film-maker who worked in the Soviet Union in the interwar period. It was Vertov who first elaborated the idea of *kinopravda,* later to be rendered into French as *cinéma vérité*. The connotation of this phrase is notoriously slippery and it is often now used to refer to so-called 'fly-on-the-wall' documentary styles in which the interference by the film-makers is minimal. The implication here is that by minimizing the mediation by the film-makers such an approach produces a film that is a faithful reproduction of reality. But in its original acception, *kinopravda* had an entirely different meaning: it referred not to the truth of everyday reality but rather to the particular truth of the cinema, which is quite different and, by implication, more profound. In contrast to observations from one fixed position, as is normally characteristic of the natural human eye, Vertov believed that the camera should be constantly moving, entering where it pleases, 'catching life unawares'.

Rouch has described Flaherty and Vertov as 'the inspired precursors' of ethnographic film-making: 'it is to these two filmmakers that we owe all of what we are trying to do today' (Rouch, 1995, pp. 81–4). However the exact nature of Rouch's own debt to these two film-makers, whose works are also very different one from another, cannot be easily tied down to any particular stylistic characteristics. There is a particularly large gulf between Rouch's films, which, even though they may involve some fictionalization, are realist in a very literal sense and the surrealist montages of Vertov's best-known film, *Man with a Movie Camera.* The debt seems to lie rather at the level of general approach and attitude: with Flaherty, Rouch shares a commitment to active participation with the protagonists in the creation of his films, even to the point of jointly collaborating in the fictionalization of their lives; with Vertov, he shares a belief in the camera as a means of insight beyond the surface features of everyday observable reality. To these characteristics, he has added an additional dimension, namely the use of improvization and fantasy as a means of exploring people's lives, a method that resonates with his interest in trance and possession in West Africa (Loizos, 1993, pp. 45–9).

Not long after Rouch began to introduce documentary conventions into ethnographic documentation, similar syntheses were taking place in the work of film-makers based in

North America and Australia. Particularly prominent amongst the latter were Ian Dunlop and Roger Sandall, both of whom were involved initially in documentation projects funded by government agencies. These were aimed at recording Aboriginal customs before they disappeared and often entailed re-enactment. But later they began to produce films that were genuinely documentary and which were concerned with showing how Aboriginal peoples have continued to develop their cultural identities in the context of modern Australia. Sandall's film *Camels and the Pitjantjara* (1969) is a particularly good example of this. However, even in this later work, there is often a strong documentation element. This is especially true of the work of Dunlop, whose films are often extremely long as a result. They include *Towards Baruya Manhood* (1972), about male initiation in Highland New Guinea and *Djungguwan at Gurka'wuy* (1990), concerning an Aboriginal secondary burial ceremony. At 395 and 233 minutes respectively, they must be amongst the longest ethnographic documentaries ever made.

The Netsilik films were partly inspired by a series of earlier films about the San 'Bushmen'. These were shot by John Marshall, who first went to southern Africa in 1951 whilst still a teenager, accompanying his parents on an ethnographic expedition in which it was his role to make a film record. Neither Marshall nor his parents had been trained as anthropologists, but his parents were friendly with Margaret Mead and, inspired by her, they emphasized to him the importance of producing 'a record, not a movie'. This he duly did over the following years, producing more than 250 hours of footage shot in a observational style but with a vividness and intimacy that derived from his extended cohabitation with the protagonists. The early films were shot in black-and-white and without synchronous sound, but by the end of the 1950s, he was shooting 'in synch' and in colour (Loizos, 1993, pp. 21–2).

In contrast to the Netsilik films, the Marshall San films involved no self-conscious reconstruction. But the work of Edwin Wilmsen, an anthropologist specializing on the Khoisan-speaking peoples (of whom the San are one) suggests that if Marshall's films are considered as objective documentation of the world as it is, they are similarly unreliable. The San and other 'Bushmen' groups have often been represented within the anthropological literature as a 'window to the Pleistocene', i.e., as surviving representatives of the hunter-gathering stage of human social evolution. But according to Wilmsen, the way of life of the San is not some remnant from prehistory, but rather a function of their present marginal state on the edge of the Kalahari desert which has come about as a result of the invasion of their former lands, first by Bantu-speaking peoples from the north and latterly by Europeans. To the extent that the early Marshall films do nothing to reveal this broader social and economic context, they help to further the illusion of primordiality in the anthropological literature (Wilmsen, 1989, in press).

There is also a certain similarity between the Netsilik and San films in that although the film-maker may have set out with a genuine intention to generate film documents rather than documentaries, the actual realization gave rise to an end product that conformed to many of the features of the documentary genre. Perhaps the most extreme example of this is Marshall's best known film, *The Hunters* (1958). As a narrative, there is little to differentiate this film from the classics of the Flaherty *oeuvre* in that it concerns an epic struggle of man against nature (in this case a giraffe hunt by men confronting starvation and armed only with puny bows and arrows), realist fictionalization (four giraffe hunts are collapsed into one, the presence of the crew with their four-wheel drive vehicle and plentiful supplies of food and water is not acknowledged) and allegorical characterization of the principal protagonists. This manipulation of the material has attracted criticism from both anthropologists and film-makers, but it was nevertheless one of the most widely distributed ethnographic films for at least twenty years after its release (Heider, 1976, pp. 31–2; Weinberger, 1994, p. 8).[6]

In editing this early material, Marshall collaborated with two other film-makers who have also had an important influence on ethnographic film-making. One was Robert Gardner, who would go on to make a series of influential documentaries, of which perhaps the best known are one of the earliest, *Dead Birds* (1963), concerning traditional warfare in western Highland New Guinea (now Irian Jaya) and one of the latest, *Forest of Bliss* (1985), a portrait of the funeral industry in Benares. An important theme linking these two films, and one running through many of his other films, is the contemplation of mortality. In these films, the ethnographic interest in documentation for its own sake has been completely displaced in favour of metaphorical, poetic interpretations that seek to link the particularities of the cultural phenomena represented to the generalities of the human condition (Loizos, 1993, pp. 139–68).

The other collaborator was Timothy Asch, with whom Marshall developed the so-called 'event-sequence' or 'reportage' technique. They reasoned that through extended fieldwork, anthropologists should learn what was significant to their hosts about particular events and this would provide them with the necessary guidelines as to how they should be shot. By this means, one could ensure that the representation of the event would not only begin and end at the right time, but would also include all the significant stages. Ideally, it should also contain all the contextualizing material regarded as significant by the participants. If this could not be included in the actual film itself, it could be laid off on to an accompanying text. These sequences could act as complete films in themselves or be built up into a series to create a longer film. The latter might require some manipulation of the material, but if so, the sequence should be preserved archivally in its original form (Asch, Marshall and Spier, 1973; Marshall and de Brigard, 1995).

In order to put his ideas about sequence filming into practice, Asch later collaborated with Napoleon Chagnon on the production of a series of forty films of varying lengths on the Yąnomamö of Venezuelan Amazonia (Chagnon, 1974, pp. 260–6). These films also featured certain technical innovations, such as the use of synchronous sound recording in the field and the use of subtitles at the editing stage. Perhaps the two best known are *The Feast* (1970), a collective ceremony at which two previously hostile groups cement a political alliance and *The Ax Fight* (1975), which presents a single event from three different perspectives: the rushes with an immediate reaction interpretation from Chagnon in voice-over, a chronologically edited version governed by an analytical argument couched in terms of kinship structure complete with genealogical diagrams, and finally, a version cut in such as way as to maximize the seamlessness of the editing.

In one sense, the event-sequence approach can be interpreted as an attempt to circumvent the dichotomy between positivist and hermeneutical approaches in the social sciences. On the one hand, the documentation was to be rigorous and objective: the camera could be to the anthropologist 'what the telescope is to the astronomer or what the microscope is to the biologist' (Asch, Marshall and Spier, 1973). But it was to be rigorous within the culturally relative terms defined by the protagonists, thereby providing a meaningful account of those events at the same time. But as Loizos has pointed out, there are several sorts of problems surrounding this approach which are related to the implicit assumption that there is such a thing as a typical event which has an established meaning that all protagonists would agree with. Moreover, even if the significance of certain basic technical processes may be relatively unproblematic, the meaning of more complex social events, both to the participants and to the anthropologist is bound to be contested to a far greater degree (Loizos, 1993, pp. 19–20).] *continued*

In his subsequent work, Asch became more sceptical about the objectivity of film documentation. Also, although he continued to stress the importance of fieldwork and anthropological expertise in his later work on a Balinese healer with his wife Patsy Asch and anthropologist Linda Connor, he also laid great emphasis on the importance of indigenous exegesis and collaboration in the making of ethnographic films. [In addition to their *More* research value, he also became particularly concerned about the value of ethnographic *concerns* films as teaching media and about the readings that students and other western viewers *problems* might make of them (Connor, Asch and Asch 1986; Loizos, 1993, pp. 39–42; Asch and Asch, 1995; Martinez, 1995).] *what becomes the pap purpose of the work*

[As Loizos has observed, although there is now widespread scepticism in academic anthropology about the capacity of the moving image camera to produce ethnographic documentation that is objective in any significant sense, it is unlikely that scholars will ever regret that these documents have been made. Just as an historian considering textual documents would do, one should think of these film documents as providing evidence rather than facts and still less, the truth. One should always ask what interests governed their making, how complete they are, how reliable other documents produced by the same source have been (Loizos, 1993, p. 20). Anthropological photographs have long been subject to this form of critical assessment and it is to be hoped that given the promise offered by new technology of making film archives more accessible the practical obstacles to a similar treatment of anthropological film documents will be removed.[7]

excellent Summary of who are should think of documentary work the way it is

great Summary and critique

[Film and Anthropological Theory]

development of ethnography into ethnographic documentary)

As the 1960s progressed, technological developments allowed for the production of much more sophisticated ethnographic documentaries: synchronous sound and subtitling gave the protagonists a voice which they had never had before whilst the development of lightweight equipment and fast colour film stocks allowed film-makers to operate in remote locations with the minimum of disruption to those whose lives they were filming. To use the moving image camera simply for documentation seemed increasingly unimaginative in the light of the new opportunities that these technological developments offered. Indeed the last twenty-five years have been a period both of great stylistic and of technical innovation in ethnographic film-making as well as of greatly increased production, sustained in part by the patronage of television (Loizos, 1993; Henley, 1985; Ginsburg, 1995; Ichioka, 1995).

how technology changed the approach but has not importance.

However the theoretical place of film in anthropology has remained problematic. Most of the innovations in 'ethnographic' film came from those who were marginal to the academic mainstream in anthropology or who came from completely outside it. Whilst rejecting the positivist perception of film as a means of objective documentation, they did not frame their own views in terms that struck an immediate chord with the then dominant theoretical paradigms in anthropology either. Typical of these new ideas were *look up* the trio of articles by Jean Rouch, Colin Young and David MacDougall which appeared together in the original edition of *Principles of Visual Anthropology*. In striking contrast to the general documentation ethos of the collection, these authors argue that far from

Paul Henley

being used simply as a passive means of recording visual data, the camera should be an active, catalyzing element within the triangle of relationships between film-maker, protagonists and audience, and should be used as such to generate meaningful events and interpretations. Each speaks from a slightly different position within the cluster of approaches associated with the tradition of *cinéma vérité*: whilst Rouch emphasizes the role of the film-maker in provoking the action of a film, Young underlines rather the importance of allowing viewers enough latitude to construct their own meanings whilst MacDougall advocates the importance of involving the protagonists in the construction of the meaning of the film. But the differences between them are more a question of emphasis than of kind and they are unanimous in their rejection of the idea that film can be objective in any simple sense. Yet rather than attempt to limit the subjectivity involved, they see this as one of the strengths of the film-making process (Rouch, 1975; MacDougall, 1975; Young, 1975, see also MacDougall, 1978).

Those from within the academy who were also seeking at this time to theorize a role for documentary film in anthropology were rather more cautious. Early attempts to do so are represented by the writings of Ruby (1975), Heider (1976) and somewhat later but still in the same vein, by those of Rollwagen (1988). Although there were differences of emphasis in their writings also, all shared a common concern to develop a film-making model that conformed to the canons governing the presentation of evidence in written texts. Accordingly, in varying degrees, they each argued that to be anthropologically legitimate, a film must be based on extended fieldwork and on familiarity with the distinctively anthropological approach to the study of cultural and social life, that the theoretical presuppositions and methodological procedures on which any particular film is based should be made explicit, and that the action represented in the film should be contextualized within broader social and economic frames of reference. If these conditions could not be achieved within the film itself, then they must instead be met in an accompanying text.

The problem with these prescriptions was that they were very difficult to fulfil given the nature of film as a communicative medium. The crux of the matter was a fundamental mismatch between the theoretical ambitions of anthropology generally at that time and the kind of knowledge that an ethnographic film can deliver. For until the 1980s, all the dominant theoretical paradigms were based on general principles of abstraction and generalization. In contrast, film, by its nature is resolutely concrete and particular. It is most effective at representing the performative aspects of culture defined in the broadest sense — political events, religious rituals, aesthetic endeavours of the most diverse kinds, the symbolic aspects of everyday life. It is also particularly good at giving some idea of what these experiences mean to those who participate in them. This it does by showing the emotional or psychological impact that these experiences have or by providing the protagonists with the opportunity to give their own interpretations of them. But within a generalizing theoretical paradigm, such performative or emotional aspects of social and cultural life would be regarded merely as epiphenomena of underlying principles or structures whilst the interpretations given by the protagonists themselves should not be taken at face value but rather treated as part of the data to be explained.

But whenever any attempt is made to provide such explanatory theoretical frameworks within a film, usually in voice-over, the result is usually at best a very pedestrian film in which the images are swamped with words. At worst, it can have the effect of belittling the beliefs and behaviours of the protagonists. Even if the commentary does not sound pretentious at the time that it is scripted, it is very likely to do so in the future, for nothing dates as quickly in a documentary as its commentary. In any case, all this is usually to no avail anyway since the soundtrack of a film rarely provides enough time to draw out all the sociological significances of the events portrayed.

However, as a consequence of recent changes in the intellectual climate of anthropology generally, it has become easier to theorize a role for ethnographic film-making that plays to its strengths. The most important aspect of this change has been the emergence of interpretative approaches as the dominant orthodoxy of anthropology at the expense of the positivist tradition. As described by Marcus and Fisher (1986, p. 26), this has entailed a shift of emphasis 'from behaviour and social structure, undergirded by the goal of "a natural science of society", to meaning, symbols, and language, and to a renewed recognition . . . that social life must fundamentally be conceived as the negotiation of meanings'. In this paradigm, social life is not considered the mere expression of underlying structures, but rather as a processual matter, which depends on a day-to-day basis on social performances of many different kinds. Ethnographic description thus becomes a process of describing and elucidating these performances rather than demonstrating their function or role in an abstract system. At the same time, there is now widespread disenchantment with grand generalizing theories and an emphasis instead on the description of particular ethnographic cases.

These changes favour the use of film within anthropology in a number of different ways. The emphasis on the negotiation of meanings at the expense of the identification of underlying structures plays to the particular strengths of film as a medium of ethnographic description and analysis. There are already many ethnographic films, often constructed around critical ritual or political events, that demonstrate the value of film as mode of ethnographic description of this kind: two that spring immediately to mind here are *The Wedding Camels* (1976), David and Judith MacDougall's film on the negotiations surrounding a Turkana marriage and Kim McKenzie and Les Hiatt's film of Aboriginal secondary burial, *Waiting for Harry* (1980). Both demonstrate how the meanings of major ritual events are matters of constant negotiation that are minutely tied up with local political issues. At the same time, both films provide insights into the broader society of which these events are merely a part.

Similarly, the shift in emphasis from the elaboration of general schemas to the understanding of particular ethnographic cases also narrows the gap between what is regarded as good practice in the writing of anthropological texts and the making of ethnographic films. In films, general theoretical contexts and comparative examples inevitably have to be introduced as 'outsider' commentary with all the aesthetic disadvantages referred to above, usually resulting in films that satisfy no-one. But when greater emphasis is laid on the individual ethnographic case, contextualization can emerge from within the film, often in the form of comments made by the protagonists themselves. Over time, such comments will retain their cultural integrity and be less vulnerable to fluctuations in theoretical fashion.

The difference between anthropological text-making and film-making has also been narrowed by the increasing awareness of the realist genre conventions that influence the writing of ethnographic monographs. All documentary film-makers are keenly aware of the paradox entailed by the need to manipulate one's rushes at the editing stage so that they no longer provide a literal account of reality whilst at the same time maintaining the illusion of realism. However as a result of the analyses of Geertz (1988), Marcus and Cushman (1982) and others, it is now more broadly recognized that

ethnographic texts are influenced by realist genre conventions that in many ways are very similar.

However these recent changes in the general climate of anthropology has not been limited to purely epistemological matters. It has also had institutional and political corollaries. Just as in literature-based anthropology, there has been a call for 'dispersing' the authority of the text by integrating native voices into 'polyphonous' or 'dialogical' accounts (Clifford and Marcus, 1986), so too in ethnographic film there has been an interest in collaborative film-making projects with those who had previously been restricted to the role of protagonists of ethnographic film-making: peoples of the Third and Fourth Worlds, the poor and dispossessed (MacDougall, 1994).

In fact, in ethnographic film-making there is a long tradition of involving the protagonists themselves, going back at least as far as the 1960s when anthropologists at the University of Philadelphia gave 16mm cameras to Navajo Indians and to inner city teenagers, as well as to their own students and sought to relate both the form and the content of the films produced to the social or cultural circumstances of the makers (Worth and Adair, 1972; Chalfen, 1992). However these original experiments were motivated exclusively by academic research interests, whereas more recent collaborative ventures between ethnographers and indigenous film-makers have tended to have a more political character, involving demands for the reparation of past injustices and claims to a series of rights including, most importantly, rights over traditional lands. Even so, these films have continued to be of interest for academic researchers over a broad range of issues (Michaels, 1986; Turner, 1991; Ginsburg, 1994).

Yet for some authors, such projects of collaboration with indigenous subjects, be it with the latter as active participants in the development of the film or even as film-makers themselves, are politically suspect. For them, these projects represent attempts to overcome the so-called 'representational crisis' by pretending that indigenous peoples have thereby been 'given a voice' whereas in fact they are merely being brought in as supporting bit-players in the perpetuation of self-interested western constructions of the world (Faris, 1992; Moore, 1994). Indeed, in the view of the most radical of such critics, the whole tradition of ethnographic research, be it in films or texts, merely contributes to the general regimentation and control of peoples of the Third and Fourth Worlds. The realist genre conventions that characterize ethnographic narratives are said to be, at best, paradigmatic examples of the Gramscian hegemonic discourse, namely a culturally specific construct that disguises itself as natural, universal, historically inevitable (Morris, 1994, pp. 22–38). At worst, they are also a specialized form of pornography, sharing with films and literature more conventionally classified as such the combination of a voyeuristic interest in the intimate details of other people's lives with the maintenance of distance and, in a desperate search for a lost Eden, the fetishistic cathexis of the Other. For these radical critics, the ethnographic enterprise is beyond redemption except as a form of autoethnography by those Others who live in various marginal or liminal conditions within the West, or who have traditionally been the mere objects of study of anthropology (Chen and Trinh, 1994; Nichols, 1994).

Those who have defended anthropology against such criticisms have argued that they are often based on empty formal parallelisms and/or outmoded and simplistic descriptions of ethnographic practice and above all, on an over-simplification and indeed an overestimation of the relationship between anthropology as an academic discipline and the loci of genuine power in western society (Turner, 1992; Loizos, 1993, pp. 206–7; Moore, 1994, see also Ruby, 1991). To the extent that such criticisms are also derived from the premises of psychoanalytically based film theory, they also present difficulties on account of what one author has referred to as the 'phallocentric and culturally relative lineage' of these ideas (Morris, 1994, pp. 53–5, 77).

Film as Ethnography: The Promise of the Future

After a century of ethnographic film-making, the general intellectual conditions of anthropology would appear finally to favour the incorporation of the moving image camera as an important tool of social research. These favourable intellectual conditions are further reinforced by the most recent technological developments. Video cameras are becoming increasingly easier and cheaper to use whilst new digital systems have brought broadcast standard technical quality within the budgetary reach even of university departments. Once gathered, visual images are now much easier and cheaper to manipulate, be it in non-linear edit suites, in the context of CD-Rom devices or simply for the purposes of projection, which has also improved greatly in recent years.

There remain some difficult practical problems still to be resolved. The acquisition of film-making skills continues to be both essential and time consuming. The actual technical knowledge now required to make films may be a great deal less than it used to be but directorial and editorial skills remain as important as they ever were. The demand for opportunities to acquire these skills is presently much greater than the supply. Another major problem is that there is currently no satisfactory archival medium for video. According to some technical experts, deterioration can begin to set in after a single year, and will certainly affect all tapes within ten years. It seems very unlikely that any tape recorded today will be playable fifty years from now, if only because the playback technology will have changed so much. But here too digital technology may prove more satisfactory than the analogue video systems that they are beginning to replace.

With the exception of these two problems, both of which seem superable in the near future, there is now no major practical obstacle to the use of moving image cameras in ethnographic research. Present circumstances allow one to contemplate a variety of uses. Provided that one remains aware of the inevitable selectivity involved in any film-making act, there is no reason why one should not still use the moving image camera for the purpose for which it was originally devised, namely, as a simple recording device. There are a wide range of possible contexts for such a use, though the anthropology of performance, particularly music and dance, is one that is particularly obvious (see Baily, 1989).

However it is in its potential role as one of the means whereby general ethnographic accounts may generated in the course of primary fieldwork-based research that film-making offers the greatest promise for the future. Fieldwork remains at the core of the academic discipline of anthropology and film-making will only become of significance if it becomes one of the range of skills with which an anthropologist is equipped prior to going to the field. In the past, most authors have tended to assume that film-making gives rise only to a 'second order account', i.e., one that merely reproduces results or understandings that have been achieved by other means (e.g., Ball and Smith, 1992, p. 4). But whilst this has often been the case in practice, film-making can also play an important role in the actual generation of ethnographic understanding.

One of the first aspects to be considered here is the question of the most appropriate filmic approach. This will greatly depend on a variety circumstances, including the subject matter, the relationship of the film-maker to the protagonists, the time and other

Paul Henley

resources available. But in many instances, for the purposes of a general ethnographic account, the approach advocated by the practitioners of *cinéma vérité* broadly defined has much to recommend it. As Banks (1992) has pointed out, there are many 'startling' similarities between the canons of practice of the various *vérité* documentary approaches and 'the features which distinguish anthropological research and writing from any other form of human observation'. Perhaps the most important of these is the common assumption that the product generated (notes in one case, rushes in the other) along with the insights that they embody, arise out of an in-depth personal knowledge of the protagonists. Both anthropologists and *vérité* film-makers vary in the relative importance they give to participation on the one hand and observation on the other. But whatever the exact mix, there is a common belief that understanding should be achieved through a gradual process of discovery, that is, through sharing the lives of the protagonists over an extended period.

However a *vérité*-based strategy need not be used exclusively. In just the same way that a general ethnographer may combine informal participant observation with formal interview procedures, so too an ethnographic film-maker may combine *vérité* shooting with highly constructed 'talking head' interviews. So that this interview material may be subsequently cut so as to eliminate redundancies and irrelevancies, and/or used in combination with archival or synchronous *vérité* material, it is advisable to employ a particular range of techniques. The most important of these concern the placing of the interviewee and interviewer, the placing of the camera and the movement of the lens as well as the framing and ordering of the questions (Rabiger, 1987, pp. 57–68).

An aspect of ethnographic film-making referred to by many practitioners is the catalytic effect that it has on the participant–observer process. Even in the video era, there is a limit on how much one can actually film. This serves to concentrate the film-maker's mind whilst still in the field as to what is really important to him/her about the host community. Nor is it only one's own mind that the presence of the camera concentrates. It can also concentrate the minds of the protagonists as to what it is about their lives that they specifically want to present to the film-maker. The camera can also serve to give an anthropologist a *raison d'être* that is understandable to his/her hosts. Someone making a film is obviously working: a person making occasional marks in a notebook may be more suspect. Furthermore, by screening the rushes, the film-making anthropologist is able to give his/her hosts another chance to understand if not actually to sympathize with what he/she is doing. This is not a new technique: Flaherty used it with his Inuit hosts over seventy years ago. But a Manchester doctoral student, Carlos Flores is currently taking it a step further in his ethnographic study of a Q'echi Mayan village. As a Ladino Guatemalan working in a community that has suffered terrible repression from counter-insurgency military activity in recent years, Flores felt that it was very important that his work be as transparent as possible. He is therefore working with a local community video team financed by the Catholic Church, making films about local customs. The community film-makers learn about him whilst he learns about them as they collaborate in these joint projects.

Nor is the screening of rushes merely potentially good for establishing closer relationships with one's hosts. It can also generate all manner of new insights as the protagonists' comments bring to light facts or connections that previously they had not thought worthy of comment. By objectifying the traditions in which they may have unthinkingly participated before, the viewing of film rushes can even lead protagonists to make connections that are new even to them. Some film-makers have made a point of encouraging

54

protagonists to join them in the edit suite and to continue this process of commenting on the material as the various cuts of the film are completed (Morphy, 1994). But even without the presence of a protagonist, the editing of a film can also be part of the process of enlightenment. In a manner analogous to the sifting through of field notes, the logging and organization of rushes can yield new insights simply through intensive engagement with the material. Later, the requirement to produce a film with a coherent narrative can lead one to juxtapose shots or sequences that generate new meanings for each. Even features of the final 'dressing' of the film, such as the exact formulation of commentary points or the translation of subtitles can all draw one's attention to certain important issues that have previously been neglected.

The knowledge thereby generated need not necessarily be integrated into the film itself. It can be incorporated instead into an accompanying text or indeed into some other text on the same subject which is not specifically dependent on the film. The point to stress here is that one should not think of a film simply as an end-product but rather as means to a general ethnographic account which will probably include written texts as well. Indeed it seems very unlikely that films will ever entirely replace texts in the anthropological enterprise. Film-making is merely an alternative means of representing certain aspects of social reality, which in certain contexts may be more effective than writing a text but which in others, is certainly less effective. One should therefore be looking for ways of using films in a complementary fashion with texts so as to enrich the anthropological research process as a whole.

Here CD-Rom technology and 'hypermedia' software appear to offer a practical vehicle for exploring the range of possible relationships between texts and images in the post-production of ethnographic accounts. But as Seaman and Williams (1992) have warned, the up-front resource costs of producing such CDs, particularly the investment of time, are likely to be very high. Moreover, in order to take full advantage of the technical possibilities, not only the authors (which includes film-makers in this context) but also the users of CD-Roms will have to learn new skills. From the author's point of view, perhaps the most critical of these relates to the fact that the user can move with ease backwards, forwards and across large bodies of information in a range of different media. Instead of maintaining a single train of thought, as in a linear textual medium, 'the ethnographer will have to establish a structure that allows multiple points of access while still maintaining a consistent point of view' (Seaman and Williams, 1992, p. 310).

This raises some very important questions about the place of authorship and narrative in hypermedia ethnographic accounts. As we saw above, the recent history of ethnographic film-making has involved a move away from an approach based simply on supposedly objective documentation strategies to one that presupposes the eventual production of a documentary which will inevitably have involved some degree of subjectivity in its making, both in the relationships established between film-maker and protagonists during production as well as in the later editorial structuring of the material. But the ideology associated with the new CD-Rom technology generally runs against the grain of this history. For there is a tendency for CD-Roms to be presented as authorless aggregates of objective information which the user can wander over at will, constructing his or her own narrative threads. In this sense, these CDs are more akin to an encyclopaedia than they are to an authored ethnographic text. In fact, in this ideology there is an uncanny echo of the naive enthusiasm of those who first advocated the use of the moving image camera as an objective documentation device a century ago. If the technology presently being developed is to be used to build on the most recent trends in the use of film in ethnographic research, it is vitally necessary for the role of authorship and narrative in these CD productions to be more clearly established.

Notes

1   This chapter was written at a time when I held a Leverhulme Research Fellowship and I am very grateful to the Trust for its support.

2   In this article, unless otherwise specified, I shall refer generically both to the medium of moving image representation and to the final edited artefact as 'film', though in many particular instances the medium actually used may have been magnetic videotape rather than celluloid. Although the differences between the two media can have significant consequences both in terms of style as well as in relation to production strategies, a discussion of these lies beyond the scope of this chapter.

3   Flaherty's film *Nanook of the North*, concerning an Inuit family living around Hudson's Bay and shot in 1921, is regarded by many as the original 'ethnographic' documentary, though it is predated by some seven years by Edward C. Curtis' *In the Land of the Headhunters*. Less well known than Flaherty's work, the latter is set amongst the Kwakiutl and Curtis was advised by George Hunt, the part-English, part-Tlingit assistant who also acted as Franz Boas' principal ethnographic rapporteur (Holm and Quimby, 1980).

4   Loizos has suggested that one should distinguish between 're-enactment' when the protagonists are asked to perform a task which they themselves have previously customarily performed, even if they now no longer do so and 'reconstruction', when protagonists are asked to recreate an activity in which their ancestors may have engaged but which is something which they themselves have never done (1993, p. 30).

5   In Haddon's case, the sense of a need for salvage ethnography appears to have been particularly strong (Edwards, in press). The men's dances shown in the opening sequences of his 4-minute Torres Straits film originally formed part of a male initiation ceremony closely connected with head-hunting practices abandoned some twenty-five years before when the islanders converted to Christianity. The masks worn by the dancers, originally featuring the jaw bones of captured enemy heads, had to be refashioned from cardboard supplied by Haddon himself (Haddon, 1901, pp. 47–9). Similarly, in his 1930 film of the Kwakiutl, Boas filmed traditional dances and potlatch oratory in front of an artificial backdrop set up in the front yard of a non-Indian house (Jacknis, 1996, p. 199, see also Ruby, 1983).

6   Much later, after a number of years working with the Leacock-Pennebaker direct cinema documentary group, Marshall was to make *N!ai: The Story of a !Kung Woman* (1980). This provided a much less romantically allegorical portrait of San life and foregrounded the contacts that they have with the outside world and their consequences: alcoholism, prostitution and military conscription (Wilmsen, in press).

7   See the chapter in this volume by Marcus Banks, in which he discusses both the critical assessment of anthropological photographs as objects that are the product of a particular social history, and HADDON, the online computerized catalogue of archival ethnographic film documents which he himself has created.

References

Asch, T. and Asch, P. (1995) 'Film in ethnographic research', in Hockings, P. (ed.) *Principles of Visual Anthropology*, 2nd ed., Berlin and New York: Mouton de Gruyter, pp. 335–60.

Asch, T., Marshall, J. and Spier, P. (1973) 'Ethnographic film: Structure and function', *Annual Review of Anthropology*, **2**, pp. 179–87.

BAILY, J. (1989) 'Film-making as musical ethnography', *The World of Music*, **21**, 3, pp. 220–3.

BALIKCI, A. (1989) 'Anthropology, film and the Arctic peoples: The first Forman lecture', *Anthropology Today*, **5**, 2, pp. 4–10.

BALIKCI, A. (1995) 'Reconstructing cultures on film', in HOCKINGS, P. (ed.) *Principles of Visual Anthropology*, 2nd ed., Berlin and New York: Mouton de Gruyter, pp. 181–91.

BALL, M. and SMITH, G.W.H. (1992) *Analyzing Visual Data*, Qualitative Research Methods, vol. 24, Newbury Park, London, New Delhi: Sage.

BANKS, M. (1992) 'Which films are the ethnographic films?', in CRAWFORD, P. and TURTON, D. (eds) *Film as Ethnography*, University of Manchester Press, pp. 116–29.

BANKS, M. (1995) 'Visual research methods', *Social Research Update*, **11**.

BARNOUW, E. (1983) *Documentary: A History of the Non-fiction Film*, Revised edition: Oxford University Press.

CHAGNON, N. (1974) *Studying the Yąnomamö*, Holt, Rinehart & Winston.

CHALFEN, R. (1992) 'Picturing culture through indigenous imagery: A telling story', in CRAWFORD, P. and TURTON, D. (eds) *Film as Ethnography*: Manchester University Press, pp. 222–41.

CHEN, N. and TRINH, T.M. (1994) 'Speaking nearby', in TAYLOR, L. (ed.) *Visualizing Theory: Selected Essays from Visual Anthropology Review 1990–4*, New York and London: Routledge, Originally published in 1992 in *Visual Anthropology Review*, **8**, 1, pp. 433–51.

CLIFFORD, J. (1986) 'On ethnographic allegory', in CLIFFORD, J. and MARCUS, G.E. (eds) *Writing Culture: The Poetics and Politics of Ethnography*, Berkely, Los Angeles and London: University of California Press, pp. 98–121.

CLIFFORD, J. and MARCUS, G.E. (1986) (eds) *Writing Culture: The Poetics and Politics of Ethnography*, Berkely, Los Angeles and London: University of California Press.

COMOLLI, J-L. (1985) 'Technique and ideology: Camera, perspective and depth of field', in NICHOLS, B. (ed.) *Movies and Methods* vol. 2, Originally published in 1977 in *Film Reader* 2, pp. 40–57.

CONNOR, L., ASCH, P. and ASCH, T. (1986) *Jero Takapan, Balinese Healer: An Ethnographic Film Monograph*: Cambridge University Press.

DE BRIGARD, E. (1995) 'The history of ethnographic film', in HOCKINGS, P. (ed.) *Principles of Visual Anthropology*, 2nd ed., Berlin and New York: Mouton de Gruyter, pp. 13–43.

DE BROMHEAD, A. (1996) *Looking Two Ways: Documentary's Relationship with Cinema and Reality*, Højbjerg: Intervention Press.

DENZIN, N.K. (1989) *Interpretive Interactionism: Applied Social Research Methods*, vol. 16, Newbury Park, London, New Delhi: Sage.

EDWARDS, E. (in press) 'Torres Straits expedition of 1898: Making histories', *Journal of Pacific Studies*.

FARIS, J.C. (1992) 'Anthropological transparency: Film, representation and politics', in CRAWFORD, P.I. and TURTON, D. (eds) *Film as Ethnography*, Manchester: Manchester University Press, pp. 171–82.

FUCHS, P. (1988) 'Ethnographic film in Germany: An introduction', *Visual Anthropology*, **1**, 3, pp. 217–23.

GEERTZ, C. (1988) *Works and Lives: The Anthropologist as Author*: Stanford University Press.

GIDDENS, A. (1976) *New Rules of Sociological Method: A Positive Critique of Interpretative Sociologies*, London: Hutchison.

GINSBURG, F. (1994) 'Culture/media: A (mild) polemic', *Anthropology Today*, **10**, 2, pp. 5–15.

GINSBURG, F. (1995) 'Ethnographies on the airwaves: The presentation of anthropology on American, British, Belgian and Japanese television', in HOCKINGS, P. (ed.) *Principles of Visual Anthropology*, 2nd ed., Berlin and New York: Mouton de Gruyter, pp. 363–98.

HADDON, A.C. (1901) *Headhunters: Black, White and Brown*, London: Methuen.

HAMMERLSEY, M. and ATKINSON, P. (1995) *Ethnography: Principles in practice*, 2nd ed., London and New York: Routledge.

HASTRUP, K. and HERVIK, P. (1994) (eds) *Social Experience and Anthropological Knowledge*, London and New York: Routledge.

HEIDER, K. (1976) *Ethnographic Film*, Austin and London: University of Texas Press.

HENLEY, P. (1985) 'British ethnographic film: Recent developments', *Anthropology Today*, **1**, 1, pp. 5–17.

HOLM, W. and QUIMBY, G.I. (1980) *Edward S. Curtis in the Land of the War Canoes: A Pioneer Cinematographer in the Pacific Northwest*, Thomas Burke Memorial Washington State Museum Monograph no.22, Seattle and London: University of Washington Press.

ICHIOKA, Y. (1995) 'Ethnographic filmmaking for Japanese television', in HOCKINGS, P. (ed.) *Principles of Visual Anthropology*, 2nd ed., Berlin and New York: Mouton de Gruyter, pp. 441–56.

JACKNIS, I. (1996) 'The ethnographic object and the object of ethnology in the early career of Franz Boas', in STOCKING, G.W. (ed.) *Volksgeist as Method and Ethic: Essays on Boasian Ethnography and the German Anthropological Tradition*, Wisconsin: University of Wisconsin Press, pp. 185–214.

LOIZOS, P. (1993) *Innovation in Ethnographic Film: From Innocence to Self-consciousness 1955–85*, Manchester: Manchester University Press.

LONG, C. and LAUGHREN, P. (1993) 'Australia's first films: Facts and fables. Part Six: Surprising survivals from colonial Queensland', *Cinema Papers*, **96**, pp. 32–6.

MACDOUGALL, D. (1975) 'Beyond observational cinema', in HOCKINGS, P. (ed.) *Principles of Visual Anthropology*, 2nd ed., Berlin and New York: Mouton de Gruyter, pp. 13–43.

MACDOUGALL, D. (1978) 'Ethnographic film: Failure and promise', *Annual Review of Anthropology*, **7**, pp. 405–25.

MACDOUGALL, D. (1994) 'Whose story is it?', in TAYLOR, L. (ed.) *Visualizing Theory: Selected Essays from Visual Anthropology Review 1990–4*, New York and London: Routledge, pp. 27–36. Originally published in 1991 in *Visual Anthropology Review*, **7**, 2.

MARCUS, G.E. and CUSHMAN, D. (1982) 'Ethnographies as texts', *Annual Review of Anthropology*, **11**, pp. 25–69.

MARCUS, G.E. and FISCHER, M.M.J. (1986) *Anthropology as Cultural Critique: An Experimental Moment in the Human Sciences*, Chicago and London: University of Chicago Press.

MARSHALL, J. and DE BRIGARD, E. (1995) 'Idea and event in urban film', in HOCKINGS, P. (ed.) *Principles of Visual Anthropology*, 2nd ed., Berlin and New York: Mouton de Gruyter, pp. 133–45.

MARTINEZ, W. (1995) 'The challenges of a pioneer: Tim Asch, otherness, and film reception', *Visual Anthropology Review*, **11**, 1, pp. 53–82.

MEAD, M. (1995) 'Visual anthropology in a discipline of words', in HOCKINGS, P. (ed.) *Principles of Visual Anthropology*, 2nd ed., Berlin and New York: Mouton de Gruyter, pp. 3–10.

MEAD, M. and BATESON, G. (1942) *Balinese Character: A Photographic Analysis*, Special Publications of the New York Academy of Sciences, vol. 2, New York.

MICHAELS, E. (1986) *The Aboriginal Invention of Television in Central Australia, 1982–6*, Canberra: Australian Institute of Aboriginal Studies.

MOORE, H. (1994) 'Trinh T. Minh-ha observed: Anthropology and others', in TAYLOR, L. (ed.) *Visualizing Theory: Selected Essays from Visual Anthropology Review 1990–4*, New York and London: Routledge, pp. 115–25. Originally published in 1990 in *Visual Anthropology Review*, **6**, 2.

MOORE, R. (1994) 'Marketing alterity', in TAYLOR, L. (ed.) *Visualizing Theory: Selected Essays from Visual Anthropology Review 1990–4*, New York and London: Routledge, pp. 126–39. Originally published in 1992 in *Visual Anthropology Review*, **8**, 2.

MORPHY, H. (1994) 'The interpretation of ritual: Reflections from film on anthropological practice', *Man*, **29**, pp. 117–46.

MORRIS, R.C. (1994) *New Worlds from Fragments: Film, Ethnography, and the Representation of Northwest Coast Cultures*, Boulder and Oxford: Westview Press.

NICHOLS, B. (1983) 'The voice of documentary', *Film Quarterly*, **36**, 3, pp. 17–30. Reproduced in NICHOLS, B. (ed.) *Movies and Methods* vol. 2, Berkeley, Los Angeles, London: University of California Press, pp. 258–73.

NICHOLS, B. (1994) 'The ethnographer's tale', in TAYLOR, L. (ed.) *Visualizing Theory: Selected Essays from Visual Anthropology Review 1990–4*, New York and London: Routledge, pp. 60–83. Originally published in 1991 in *Visual Anthropology Review*, **7**, 2.

RABIGER, M. (1987) *Directing the Documentary*, Boston and London: Focal Press.

ROLLWAGEN, J. (1988) 'The role of anthropological theory in "ethnographic" filmmaking', in ROLLWAGEN, J. (ed.) *Anthropological Filmmaking: Anthropological Perspectives on the Production of Film and Video for General Public Audiences*: Harwood Academic Press, pp. 287–309.

ROUCH, J. (1975) 'The camera and man', in HOCKINGS, P. (ed.) *Principles of Visual Anthropology*, 2nd ed., Berlin and New York: Mouton de Gruyter, pp. 79–98.

RUBY, J. (1975) 'Is an ethnographic film a filmic ethnography?', *Studies in the Anthropology of Visual Communication*, **2**, 2, pp. 104–11.

RUBY, J. (1980) 'Exposing yourself: Reflexivity, anthropology and film', *Semiotica*, **30**, 1/2, pp. 153–79.

RUBY, J. (1983) 'An early attempt at studying human behavior with a camera: Franz Boas and the Kwakiutl 1930', in BOGAART, N.C.R. and KETELAR, H.W.E.R. (eds) *Methodology in Anthropological Film-making*, Göttingen: Herodot.

RUBY, J. (1991) 'Speaking for, speaking about, speaking with, or speaking alongside — An anthropological and documentary dilemma', *Visual Anthropology Review*, **7**, 2, pp. 50–63.

SEAMAN, G. and WILLIAMS, H. (1992) 'Hypermedia in ethnography', in CRAWFORD, P. and TURTON, D. (eds) *Film as Ethnography*, Manchester: Manchester University Press, pp. 300–11.

SORENSEN, E.R. and JABLONKO, A. (1995) 'Research filming of naturally occurring phenomena: Basic strategies', in HOCKINGS, P. (ed.) *Principles of Visual Anthropology*, 2nd ed., Berlin and New York: Mouton de Gruyter, pp. 147–59.

STOLLER, P. (1992) *The Cinematic Griot: The Ethnography of Jean Rouch*: University of Chicago Press.

TURNER, T. (1991) 'The social dynamics of video media in an indigenous society: The cultural meaning and the personal politics of video making in Kayapo communities', *Visual Anthropology Review*, **7**, 2, pp. 68–76.

TURNER, T. (1992) 'Defiant images: The Kayapo appropriation of video', *Anthropology Today*, **8**, 6, pp. 5–16.

WEINBERGER, E. (1994) 'The camera people', in TAYLOR, L. (ed.) *Visualizing Theory: Selected Essays from Visual Anthropology Review 1990–4*, New York and London: Routledge, pp. 3–26. Originally published in 1992 in *Transition* 55.

WILMSEN, E.N. (1989) *Land Filled with Flies: A Political Economy of the Kalahari*: Chicago University Press.

WILMSEN, E.N. (in press) 'Knowledge as a source of progress: The Marshall family testament to the Bushmen', *Trikster*.

WINSTON, B. (1995) *Claiming the Real: The Documentary Film Revisited*, London: British Film Institute.

WORTH, S. and ADAIR, J. (1972) *Through Navajo Eyes: An Exploration in Film Communication and Anthropology*, Bloomington: Indiana University Press.

YOUNG, C. (1975) 'Observational cinema', in HOCKINGS, P. (ed.) *Principles of Visual Anthropology*, 2nd ed., Berlin and New York: Mouton de Gruyter, pp. 99–113.

Chapter 4

'The Camera Never Lies': The Partiality of Photographic Evidence

Brian Winston

Abstract

We do not hesitate to say that the reagents discovered by M. Daguerre will accelerate the progress of one of the sciences, which most honours the human spirit. With its aid the physicist will be able henceforth to proceed to the determination of absolute intensities; he will compare the various lights by their relative effect. (Eder, 1972, p. 238)

(From a speech made by François Arago
in the French Chamber of Deputies, 3 July 1839)

It is certain that through M. Daguerre's invention physics is today in possession of a reagent extraordinarily sensitive to the influence of light, a new instrument which will be to the study of the intensity of light and of luminous phenomena what the microscope is to the study of minute objects. (Eder, op. cit., p. 242)

(From a speech made by the chemist Joseph Louis Gay-Lussac
in the French House of Peers, 30 July 1839)

From its beginnings photography has made a claim on science which has allowed it to be considered as evidence. Yet from the beginning this claim has been, in some sense, too strong, the opportunities for manipulation too great, to allow the photographic image to stand, of itself, as evidence of the external world. As the archive of great photographs is combed for traces of inauthenticity and as the possibilities of digital image manipulation sunder any connection between the camera and the things it photographs, the illusion of evidence is ending.

155 years after Arago and Gay-Lussac successfully argued that the French nation should acquire the Daguerre patents for the world, Andrew Bennett, the Labour member for Denton and Reddish, rose in the House of Commons to request 'that leave be given to bring in a bill to require news media to prepare a code of practice to cover the principles by which pictures may be edited, altered and changed using computer techniques . . .' (Hansard, 1994, p. 951). Bennett's request does not, however, signal how much more sophisticated we are today than we were at the time of photography's birth. On the contrary, the worry which brought him to his feet in the Commons speaks most powerfully to the persistence of the vision of Arago and Gay-Lussac. Bennett claims, with good reason, that : 'Most people are aware of the old adage "the camera never lies".

It seems to me that many people still believe it. . . . Most people believe pictures, particularly those accompanied by a well-respected voice on the television.'

Of course, in photography's founding moment, it was understood that photographs had artistic potential; but that was not the line taken by Arago and Gay-Lussac to persuade the government of the day to cough up a handsome annuity for Daguerre. Instead they positioned photography as science and located its social importance in its ability to produce evidence of all kinds of phenomena. This included evidence of the natural world (as with the suggestion that meteorological records could now include photographs of weather conditions), as well as man-made artefacts (as with the example that hieroglyphs could be more easily and accurately reproduced photographically than by any other means). In all this, the photographic process was almost hidden, its complexity a mere matter of necessary, mechanistic manoeuvres rather than an opportunity for human intervention and manipulation.

The result was that even the most acute of nineteenth-century minds accepted uncritically the photograph as evidence. Charles Peirce, for example, felt photographs operated as a sort of death mask whereby the photographic plate was 'physically forced to correspond point by point to nature'. Thus photographs were a 'sign' of nature made 'by physical connection' (Peirce, 1965, pp. 143, 159). The French law also initially assumed no significant human intervention was involved in making a photograph. No question of intellectual property, nor therefore of copyright, could arise (Edelman, 1979, pp. 44ff).[1] It is scarcely any wonder that when, in the 1870s, Dr Barnardo's famous 'before and after' photographs, showing the supposedly beneficent effects of his homes on an urchin, were revealed as having been taken on the same day an outraged cleric was moved to sue for public fraud. Or that, in the 1880s, the Parisian policeman Alphonse Bertillon created a system of criminal identification based on measurements and photographic 'mug shots' (Sekula, 1986, p. 18).

Yet, from the outset, a certain cognitive dissonance also comes into play, conceding the limitations of photography's evidentiary power. Even as Bennett suggested people believed the old 'adage', he also acknowledged that this was 'in spite of the fact that many of them are aware that over the ages pictures have been faked'. It is possible that these two contradictory ideas about photography arise because faking, deliberate manipulation, is beyond our common experience. For most people, from the age of the Box Brownie to the era of the instant Polaroid and the camcorder, a photographic image is good evidence of the reality it captures. That is indeed how we looked on our day trip to the beach, when we were married, at our sixth birthday party. Bennett understands, as we all do, that this record might be partial: 'Perhaps there sits on the mantelpiece a photograph of Uncle Albert with a broad grin on his face, yet we know that, except for that one picture, he almost never grinned in his whole life'; but it is, nevertheless, a recognizable image of Uncle Albert. It is not 'faked'. We clicked the shutter on our automated camera; the chemist passed the film through the automated processor and out came Albert's image. The evidence is partial not because the photograph was tampered with at any stage but rather because, unusually, Albert was actually grinning when the shutter clicked. Most of us would simply not know how to alter the photographic record even if we so desired.

The manipulations that produced trick images, such as the composite of the Cottingley Fairies or joke postcards of farmers posing by huge animals and vegetables, were hidden (as it were) behind the everyday veracities of Box Brownie. Obviously manipulated photographs become a species of exception which prove the evidentiary rule. Yet even with these images very often, as with Arthur Conan Doyle's naive belief in the Cottingley pictures, the scientific heritage swamped any awareness of the potential for manipulation which might have existed. On balance then, for more than a century, we have assumed, with a justice based on our own experience of the technology, that although manipulation is possible the chances are that the camera is not lying to us. It is only comparatively recently that the balance of probabilities has started to shift, and then only as far as public, published photographic images are concerned. Increasingly, we are subjecting these to a searching examination for authenticity and are finding more and more great photographs to be less than they seem.

The contemporary point is that confidence in the evidential strength of the photograph was misplaced. While it was true that the apparatus recorded what was before it, there were no guarantees that such material had not been tampered with by the photographer. Lighting alone could do this and is a significant source of meaning in many images but even harder to detect is the physical manipulation of objects before the lens. For example, within forty-eight hours of the end of the Battle of Gettysburg, Andrew Gardner and his team were on the field making images of the aftermath. One photograph, entitled *Home of a Rebel Sharpshooter*, shows a confederate corpse sprawled in a trench. Another image, again of a dead soldier, is called *A Sharpshooter's Last Sleep*. This body is not so obviously a member of the Confederate Army. In fact, its quite hard to tell which side he was on but Gardner's published caption suggests he was a Union man. Both corpses are in a similar attitude lying in the lower third of the frame but the terrain is different. The 'Rebel' is in a trench while the other lies on more open ground. The 'Rebel's' rifle is propped between his legs against the rocky side of the trench whereas in the other image the rifle lies at the man's head. Experts have identified the spots as being about forty yards apart. Others have identified the corpse as being identical in both shots. The only explanation is that Gardner was lugging a body around with him, re-costuming it as he went and even, some suggest, turning the head despite rigor mortis (Fulton, 1988, pp. 23–8).

The perfect composition of the image of four marines raising the Stars and Stripes on Mt. Suribachi, Iwo Jima seventy-nine years after Gettysburg caused the editors of *Life* pause. The photographer, Joe Rosenthal, always claimed it was authentic picture but it is generally agreed that the flag is a replacement for the one initially raised. The issue is: who arranged for the replacement? The suggestion is that the larger flag was prepared for hoisting at Rosenthal's instigation and the implication is that this vitiates the authenticity of the image — despite the fact that the photograph, without question, shows four 'real' marines (three of whom were to die in the battle then raging) with a 'real' flag on the actual island of Iwo Jima. These doubts did not prevent the photographer winning a Pulitzer prize in 1945 or the photograph from being used for a war bond poster, appearing on a 3c stamp and becoming the basis of a statue placed outside the Arlington national Cemetery in Washington. Manipulated or not, the image has been described as a record of 'the soul of a nation' (Fulton, 1988, pp. 160–1).

In 1950, *Life* published a rather different 'soul of a nation' image. The magazine commissioned Robert Doisneau to photograph the romantic French, specifically engaging in such activities as kissing on the street. *The Kiss* is the perfect image of young Parisians in love. A debonair man, tieless, tousled hair, scarf casually tucked into his jacket, has his arm round a lithe young woman. She leans back into the embrace as he kisses her oblivious of the people around. One of these, a gaunt-faced 'Frenchman' with beret, coat, tie and pullover, appears to be staring past the couple in studied disapproval. In fact,

Doisneau treated the assignment as a photo-love-story shot and cast an actor, Jacques Carteaud and his girlfriend, Françoise Bornet, as the couple. The stereotypical Frenchman in the beret behind them has been identified as the late Jack Costello, a Dublin auctioneer, on a motorbike pilgrimage to Rome, a bit lost in Paris looking for his travelling companion (Lennon, 1993).

These examples, chosen almost at random, deal only with the question of manipulation taking place before the camera. Beyond this, what necessarily remained outside of the frame could have profound, and clearly unknowable, effects on what was within it. Let us take one example from documentary film. In a famous sequence in his 1934 classic *Man of Aran*, Robert Flaherty, the 'father' of Anglo-American documentary, has his Aran family laboriously transforming a rocky field into soil using seaweed. It is an eloquent testimony to the hardiness of the islanders and their indomitable spirit in the face of grinding poverty. In his 1976 film about Flaherty on Aran, *Man of Aran: How the Myth was Made,* American documentarist George Stoney pans from the seaweed field across the headland to reveal perfectly good land nearby. Stoney tells us in commentary that when the original film was shot these fields belonged to absentee owners, a complication with which Flaherty simply did not wish to deal.

Beyond manipulations before the lens of lighting and objects and framing selectivities, there are the inevitable further selectivities of lenses, angles, shutter speed and aperture. Each of these carries semantic force — some obvious, others less so. Extreme wide angles clearly distorted reality but the confusions of depth caused by long focus telescopic lens, which can force unreal juxtapositions, are less easy to detect. Likewise, extreme low or high angles, with their clear culturally determined connotations of power or subservience, could be seen but less extreme angles more subtly conveying the same meaning are often not consciously noted. And all this is before we get into the darkroom.

There has been no public scandal about the lead photograph of a famous W. Eugene Smith *Life* photo-essay on Albert Schweitzer but, again, it can be questioned. Smith had complained about the quality of the photo labs prints *Life* photographers usually put up with. He had demonstrated his prints were superior and the editors therefore allowed him the privilege of avoiding the labs. We can note that he routinely adjusted his images at this stage, always in line with accepted professional practice (Willumson, 1992, pp. 248–50). Manipulations included correcting underexposure in portions of the negative and bleaching to achieve high contrast prints that would reproduce well on the press. This did not offend against *Life*'s policy at this time, the 1950s, although further manipulations other than cropping were not permitted.

Toilers, captioned 'Schweitzer and a carpenter watch hospital building', shows the doctor, in white shirt and pith helmet, standing before an unfinished structure. Behind him, on the structure, sits a African. Both are looking out of the frame towards something that seems to be causing them concern. They both looked worried. Silhouetted against Schweitzer's shirt is the handle of a saw and a gesturing hand (Anon, 1954, p. 161). This is actually a composite, a real superimposition. The arm and saw-handle are from another shot. The editors of *Life*, who had forbidden such practices, never knew. The deception (if it can be so called) was discovered, thirty and more years on, by Glenn Willumson going through Eugene Smith's negatives while writing his biography (Willumson, 1992, pp. 211–13).

Perhaps more significantly, Willumson also notes (pp. 193–203) that, as with the smiling image of Uncle Albert, these eleven magazine pages failed to capture Smith's ambivalent attitude to Schweitzer, a tetchy and authoritarian man, who was being turned by events from a symbol of Christian charity into the very model of the paternalistic colonial. The essay celebrates the symbol, ignoring the politics of decolonization.

Despite all this, it would be as foolish now to doubt every image in the archive as it was, previously, naive to believe them. For instance, it has also been suggested that Robert Capa staged his *Death In Spain* (aka *Death of Loyalist Soldier*), the famous photograph of a Spanish loyalist militiaman at the moment of death as he runs down a slope his rifle flung wide in his right hand. The lack of uniform and the curiously ornate leather cartridge belt have been questioned. And how come, if this is the moment of death, the rifle is still being gripped? However, it was finally established in 1996 that this is indeed the last moment of loyalist militiaman and member of the anarchist trade union's youth movement, Frederico Borell Garcia from Alcoy at the battle of Cerro Muriano in defence of Cordova seven weeks into the war, on 5 September 1936 (*Observer*, 1996).

My point in that many of these arguments and scandals turn on quite fine questions of intervention rather than deliberate fraud and are only raised because our expectations of photography's evidentiary capacity is still, as it was at the outset, far too high. This is why, as Sekula persuasively argues, Bertillon needed the aggregate power of an archive to provide evidence of the criminal. To make a positive ID measurements and other photographs were essential, exactly because 'of an acute recognition of the 'inadequacies' and limitations of ordinary visual empiricism' (Sekula, 1986, p. 18; emphasis in original). In other words, photography offers at best partial evidence despite the richness of the data is presents.

The promise of Arago and Gay-Lussac has turned out to be false. Photography does not provide unambiguous, instantly compelling data of the sort they initially envisaged — however hard it tries. For example, no social science has made greater efforts to use the photographic image than has anthropology. And few anthropological films have tried more strenuously to produce an evidentiary record than *The Ax Fight* (1975), made among the Yanomamö of Venezuela by anthropologist Napoleon Chagnon and leading ethnographic film maker Timothy Asch. The film consists of various presentations of twelve shots taken hurriedly by Asch as a fight broke out on the afternoon of 28 February 1971 in the large Yanomamö village of Mishimishiböwieö-Teri. All this we learn from titles or voice-overs in the film; that is to say (obviously), we do not learn where we are and the date and time from the photographic record itself.

First we are told in an intertitle: 'That the fight began when a woman was beaten in the garden.' A voice-over idents the footage and says: 'Two women are fighting with each over. . . . Bring your camera over here. It's going to start.' Then we see what a superimposed titles says is: 'the unedited record of this seemingly chaotic and confusing fight just as the field workers witnessed it on their second day in the village.' The twelve shots appear for the first time, the film makers adding only subtitles to two of them to translate what a screaming women is saying. It is clear from these, though, that despite what we first heard, the fight is not among the women but between some men. There follows a sound sequence with no pictures in which the anthropologists are heard discussing various possible explanations of the causes of the fight. The next sequence, which begins with an intertitle: 'First impressions can be misleading. . . .', re-uses the footage but this time with slow-motion and super-imposed arrows to explain how the fight developed, who the main protagonists were and how they were related. This information is then formally expanded in the next sequence which represents, in diagrammatic form, the familial and lineage relationships involved. Finally the shots are re-edited, leaving out some material extraneous to the fight.

This exhaustive presentation, however, is not compelling evidence of what actually occurred. In fact, as many questions are raised as are answered. First, to be charitable, this was not Asch's finest moment as a cameraperson. The main protagonist's critical blow to his major opponent with the blunt side of the axe is obscured at the edge of the frame. His felling of this opponent's brother is not seen at all. The voice-over — Chagnon — tells us that there are repeated blows but we only see one blow connect. Chagnon tells us that a woman is screaming at the other lineage but she seems to me to be yelling just as much at her own family. Chagnon tells us that a man is knocked unconscious but we only see him sitting on the ground seemingly wide-awake. More generally, Chagnon says the people are enraged but most just seem to be bystanders. The subtitled screaming woman at the end is said to be provoking the other side but I do not know, from the image, they can even hear her.

In short, we are relying on Chagnon far, far more than would seem to be the case at first sight. Moreover, it is his interpretation which tells us how to read the incident. It is his diagram which confidently explains the implications of the fight. He explains what is at stake. He knows that, prior to this fight, 'the women have scores of their own to settle'. He determines the real reason for the fight. Above all he reads the incident as a very good example of how the Yanomamö — whom he sees, as one of his books calls them, as *A Fierce People* — usually behave.

But, given that Asch's images offer no evidence of any of this, why should I take his word? There could be other explanations which his Yanomamö informants have not given him. Different groups — the women, say, as opposed to the men — might explain the incident differently. Lévi-Strauss has pointed out how common it is for anthropologists to be given different accounts of social structures by different informants exactly because social organization is 'too complex to be formalised by means of a single model' (Lévi-Straus, 1968, p. 134). Anyway, are these Yanomamö so very fierce? Rage and anger are not so great as to cause the men to use the sharp sides of the axes. Order is restored by an unarmed man wielding nothing more than his personal authority and some feathers on his arms — or so we are told.

Let me say that I am not, of course, suggesting for a moment that Chagnon is wrong, much less that he is deliberately misrepresenting the situation for some reason. Rather, my point is simply that all the apparatus of this film — the repeated footage, the arrows, the diagrams, the way in which the film-making process is revealed rather than remaining hidden as it usually does — is insufficient to compel support for Chagnon's version of events. While the footage does not in anyway contradict him, nevertheless the photographic record is too ambiguous for his to be the only available reading. As Bill Nichols, considering this same film, has written:

> We can see with our own eyes and ears what the camera and tape recorder has provided for us. It is already more than a chronicle or assembly of data, much more. It has the same mix of transparent obviousness (often absent from data) and impenetrability (often abundant in data) that forms of lived encounter also possess. (Nichols, 1996, p. 8)

Nevertheless, the screen does not 'yield facts as they are normally regarded or encountered, in service to subsequent interpretation' (Nichols, 1996, p. 9). Thus, although '(w)ith film, rigorous description attains a qualitatively distinct level . . . the filmed record of actual events is not quite as firm a guarantee of what really happened as we may at first thought' (Nichols, 1996, p. 8).

The problem with *The Ax Fight* is not Chagnon's commentary but the fact that he is relying on the scientific heritage of the camera to make a strong claim — a very strong claim — that he is presenting evidence of the real world. However, the claim is built on the sands of inference rather than the rock of objectivity. To make any sense of the images, Chagnon takes what Uberto Eco might call 'an inferential walk' and comes up with a monological account of the data.[2] The ability of the material as evidence to sustain such an account is never questioned. We, like strangers gazing at the photo of Uncle Albert and thinking him a friendly soul, are told that these are fierce tribal people and that this footage is authentic evidence of that ferocity.

However, as we have seen with the examples I have given, the authenticity of the photographic image is complex. It is a real Civil War corpse, but that is not where it fell nor how it was dressed. It is a real Stars and Stripes but it comes to be in the frame because of the photographer rather than because of the military. It is a real kiss in a real street but the lovers are actors — actors who happen to be lovers in what I suppose we must call 'real life' but would not have been in that place at that time had the photographer not asked them to be. It is a real tribal fight but its causes are not clear, its course is confused and its outcome is obscure. There is, in fact, within any one photographic image a 'continuum of authenticity' — if you will — a complex range of relationships with the real world depending in different ways and different degrees on the plastic materials and action within the frame as well as the manipulations and interventions of the photographer. Understanding these relationships depends as much on the contextual inferential walks taken by the deconstructing viewer as on anything within the frame. As a result, photographic images in general can only be considered as evidence of the real world in limited and complex ways — more limited and more complex than we commonly allow.

So, we are now too sophisticated to believe a photographic image is like a window on the world, a window unmarked by the photographer's finger-prints. But to acknowledge the presence of the photographer is not necessarily to deny totally that you can still see something of the world. You can. I would describe this as making a weak claim for the photograph as evidence, adopting (as it were) 'a mild realist position'.

To take such a position, however, is to move a long way from the traditional view we have of photographic technologies. Such a move has considerable implications for how our audiovisual culture works. If we stop making strong claims for photos as evidence, in effect we transfer the onus of the claim on the real from the image to the viewer. That is to say, we stop pretending authenticity — truth, even — can be found within the frame. Instead we rely on our inferential walks to test for authenticity and truth. We would be moving the legitimacy of the realist image from *representation* — the screen or the print — where nothing can be guaranteed to *reception* — by the audience or the viewer — where nothing need be guaranteed.

Robert Fairthorne, a radical film critic, wrote in 1933 that ' "actuality" is not a fundamental property' of the photographic image. He said it was like fast- or slow-motion. To understand *them* you needed to have prior knowledge of speed in the real world (Fairthorne, 1980, p. 171).

More generally then, to understand what is authentic in the image, a general understanding of the real world — which, of course, we all have — is needed.[3] The illusion that the photograph provides simple, compelling evidence about the real world is ending. But it is only the illusion that photographs are somehow *automatic* — scientific — reflections of the world which should be abandoned. In its place must come the idea that the photograph can provide evidence of the real world but in a way more akin to the evidence provided by painting or writing. We must finally acknowledge the photographer as a subjective presence even while the science of his or her camera allows us to continue to test, in a qualitative way, for authenticity.

I believe that such a change, which would obviously need decades to be accomplished, now becomes a necessity. Somewhat paradoxically, this is exactly because the computer technology which brought Andrew Bennett MP to his feet now makes it extremely easy to manipulate photographs more extensively than ever before. Digitization allows for a degree of alteration not previously possible while also rendering such manipulations undetectable. There need be no negatives any longer to provide the historian or biographer with evidence of fabrication. Photographs, even in newspapers, need have no necessary correspondence to reality. *The Sun* published a photograph of a monk and his girl friend. The man had been caught walking down the street dressed in shirt and trousers. The paper used computer technology, a Scitex, to give him a habit and when challenged said: 'We have superimposed the monk's habit to make it clear to the readers that the story is about a monk.' If our commonsense, everyday understanding of the camera's ability to capture images of the world is to be maintained in this environment, then a weak realist position which throws the onus of evaluating the images' authenticity onto the viewer might just be sustainable. It is clear that the traditional Arago/Gay-Lussac 'scientific-evidence' claim, always dubious, now cannot be maintained at all. Andrew Bennett's attempt to legislate in Parliament for the strong realist position is quixotic.

Notes

1   Edelman notes that the rapid growth of a dageurreotyping industry forced the French to re-consider which they eventually did by allowing photographs to be an art as well as a science. In the materialist Common Law tradition, there was no copyright difficulty because there was no concept of intellectual property. The copyright of the photograph belonged to the person furnishing the photographic plate.
2   Eco develops this concept specifically in connection with narrative but it would apply here just as well: 'An inferential walk has much to do with a rhetorical entymeme. As such, it starts from a probable premise picked up in the repertory of common opinion, or *endoxa*, as Aristotle said. The endoxa represent the store of intertextual information . . .' (Eco, 1984, pp. 215–6).
3   This assumes that there is a real world — something upon which philosophers seem to find it quite difficult to agree. For the purposes of this argument, I am simply taking Dr Johnson's line on the idealist thought of Bishop Berkeley. Johnson rejected the Berkeleian notion that the material world depended on the perceiving mind by giving a stone a hefty kick, saying: 'I refute him, thus'.

References

Anon (1954) 'A man of mercy', *Life*, XXXVII/20, 5 November.
Eco, U. (1984) *The Role of the Reader: Explorations in the Semiotics of Texts*, Bloomington: Indiana University Press.

EDELMAN, B. (1974) *Ownership of the Image: Elements for a Marxist Theory of Law*, KINGDOM, E. (trans) London: Routledge and Kegan Paul.

EDER, J.M. (1972) *History of Photography*, New York, Dover.

FAIRTHORNE, R. (1980) 'The principles of the film', in MACPHERSOU, D. (ed.) *Traditions of Independence*, London: BFI.

FULTON, M. (1988) *Eyes of Time: Photojournalism in America*, New York: New York Graphical Society.

HANSARD (1994) 30 March.

LENNON, P. (1993) 'It started with a kiss', *Guardian*, 2, 6 January.

LÉVI-STRAUSS, C. (1968) *Structural Anthropology*, JACOBSON, C. and GRUNFEST SCHOEF, B. (eds), London: Allen Lane, The Penguin Press.

NICHOLS, B. (1996) 'What really happened: The ax fight reconsidered', *Media International Australia*, **82**, November.

PEIRCE, C. (1965) *Collected Papers: Vol. II*, Cambridge, Mass.: The Belnap Press at the Harvard Press.

SEKULA, A. (1986) 'The body and the archive', *October*, **39**, Winter.

THE OBSERVER (1966) 1 September.

WILLUMSON, G. (1992) *W. Eugene Smith and the Photographic Essay*, Cambridge, Mass.: Cambridge University Press.

Chapter 5

Psychology and Photographic Theory

Órla Cronin

Abstract

The purpose of this chapter is to provide a critical review of the theoretical and therapeutic literature on the meaning and psychological significance of family photographs. A series of assumptions underpinning the use of photographs in research and clinical contexts is evaluated. These assumptions are:

1 that there are two types of photograph: those which contain information and those which provoke an emotional reaction;
2 that the essence of a photograph, which differentiates it from other forms of representation, is its relationship to time;
3 that the use of photographs tends to be grounded within either a 'realist' or a 'symbolist' folk myth;
4 that the meaning of a photograph arises in a narrative context;
5 that family photographs can either 'tell' us something about family dynamics, or can convey an impression of family unity and cohesiveness; and
6 that family photographs are used to create personal histories.

The arguments surrounding these assumptions, and empirical data which illuminate them, are discussed, and a set of recommendations which emphasize the socially constructed nature of photographic meaning are presented.

Introduction

Since the camera's invention, it has passed through many different phases of use; it was, and still is, a tool of the artistic and cultural elite; it had and still has many practical uses in art and science. But perhaps the single most important development in photography from the point of view of the 'ordinary person' was the democratization of camera ownership. The movement of photography from the realms of science, technology and art to that of a practice indulged in as a hobby, or a habit, by the 'snapper' is perhaps most succinctly summed up by Kodak's advertising jingle, coined in the 1930s: 'you press the button, we'll do the rest'.

This accessibility of photography was never more evident than in the 1990s. According to the 1992–3 Wolfman Report (a large scale market research survey carried out periodically on behalf of the photographic industry), 17.2 billion photographs were taken in the US in 1993, in comparison with the 8.9 billion photos taken in the US in 1977, and

3.9 billion in 1967. While, according to the same source, the market for photographic goods aimed at the skilled amateur/professional is declining, amateur 'instant' photography is still a growth area. In the UK, the 'Kodacolor Gold' Survey (1990) reported that 80 per cent of households owned cameras.

Smaller scale social science surveys on camera ownership and photography have reported prevalence information as an adjunct to more psychological and sociological findings. For instance, Bourdieu (1965) claimed on the basis of photographic industry reports that in 1965 there were 8,135,000 cameras in working order in France, at least one camera in half of all households, and 845,000 cameras sold each year. It would appear, therefore, that notwithstanding the advent of the video camera, still photographs are extremely common in Western homes.

Despite this prevalence, with some exceptions (e.g., Chalfen, 1987), the meaning and functions of family photography are remarkably under theorized, and even more under-researched in the social sciences, particularly in psychology. This is perhaps a reflection of the more general neglect of psychological aspects of material culture (Dittmar, 1992).

However, if one turns to the discipline of visual communication, a field spanning visual anthropology, visual sociology and cultural studies, in which one would expect theories regarding the nature and functions of photographs to be well developed, a similar lacuna exists. Burgin (1982) claims that there is no one photographic theory to date, but rather a multiplicity of micro theories. The proliferation of these micro theories makes life difficult for a social scientist seeking a 'foot in the door', as the assertions embodied in them are rarely supported with empirical evidence.

However, our relative ignorance of the meaning and functions of photographs in everyday life has not stymied their use as a research and therapeutic tool in social science. 'Phototherapy' is the generic name given to the use of photographs as an adjunct to psychotherapy. As Weiser (1985) points out, the term 'phototherapy' does not refer to a homogeneous set of practices or procedures. However, there are a number of common elements in the ways photographs are used and the therapeutic goals they support. There are also a number of implicit assumptions about the nature of photographs and their functions in everyday life which link the various approaches to phototherapy. It can be argued, though, that given the prevalence of 'vernacular' photography, the assumptions regarding the nature of photography, its appropriate uses, and its functions in everyday life need to be examined and made explicit before photography is adopted as a 'neutral' research or therapeutic tool.

The purpose of this chapter, therefore, is to provide a critical review of the assumptions prevalent in the theoretical and therapeutic literature on the meaning and psychological significance of family photographs. The purpose of this is twofold: first of all, it is helpful to see photographic research and theorizing, and therapeutic uses of photography as being an extension of 'lay' uses of photographs. Considering the origins of our assumptions enables us to be reflexive in our work and helps to break down the often artificial distinction between academics and the 'lay person'. Secondly, it enables us to challenge taken for granted myths regarding the nature of photography, which is a necessary stage for the formulation and investigation of valid research questions.

The following review of the existing literature on clinical and psychological uses of photographs is based on a variety of sources reflecting a range of disciplinary approaches. For ease of discussion, the literature is presented in the form of a series of identified assumptions underpinning the uses of photograph in therapeutic settings. Each assumption is described and discussed in relation to theories of photography. Where possible, empirical evidence which enables us to evaluate the assumption is presented, and suggestions regarding possible directions and methodology for future research are included.

There Are Two Types of Photographs: Those which Contain Information and Those which Provoke an Emotional Reaction

The therapeutic uses of photographs which seem to be premised upon the existence of either information or an emotional stimulus are the use of photographs to obtain information about the client's background (Meloche, 1973; Sedgwick, 1979), and the use of photographs as a 'projective' technique (Gosciewski, 1975; Weiser, 1984; Wolf, 1976).

The 'information' which has been obtained from photographs by therapists ranges from the inferring of socio-economic status and home environment of the client, based on, for example, the appearance of the neighbourhood, the physical state of repair of the home and the depiction of domestic possessions. Other factual information might include family topography, i.e., networks of relatives and generational links.

The employment of photographs to stimulate the release of strong emotions is premised on the existence of a 'punctum' or trigger for emotions in photographs. Phototherapists working within a psychoanalytic model, for instance, argue that defence mechanisms which may prevent the open expression of feelings can be challenged using photographs.

Barthes (1980), a cultural theorist who attempted to define the 'essence' of photography, claimed that photographs could be divided into those which contained a 'studium' (informational and aesthetic value) and those which contained a 'punctum' (a shock, thrill or emotion elicited by the photograph). Barthes claims that the informational and aesthetic value of a photograph is available to anyone, i.e., a photograph is interpretable in a similar way by any two individuals who have access to the same cultural codes. The punctum, however, is specific to the individual. Barthes describes it as 'a subtle beyond' (p. 59); he sees the source of the shock or thrill of the photograph as located in the viewer. The punctum could be described as a small detail in a photograph which triggers a succession of personal memories and unconscious associations, many of which are indescribable by the individual. Lesy (1980) expresses similar sentiments when he stated that '[photos are] like frozen dreams, whose manifest content (what is actually visible in the photograph) may be understood at a glance, but whose latent content (the meaning of a photograph) is enmeshed in unconscious associations' (p. xiv).

Both Barthes and Lesy appear to take for granted the accessibility of the manifest content. However, Barnes and Sternberg's (1989) study of people's ability to decode non-verbal cues in photographs found that they were not universally able to do so accurately. This study does seem to challenge the ease with which Barthes and Lesy claim we acquire information from photographs.

Barthes' notion of the punctum, on the other hand, underpins much of the use which is made of photographs in therapy. Photographs are 'dreams, slips of the tongue', according to Akeret (1973). However, what is missing in Barthes' treatise, and in the use of photographs to stimulate affect in therapy, is any acknowledgment of the link between individual phenomenology and culture. Implicit in the notion of the 'punctum' is the assumption that 'culture' somehow exists 'out there' and that it does not impinge on individual affect. However, this conceptualization of the punctum as pure, unadulterated feeling does not sit well with any notion of reality as being constructed, or memory and emotion being to some extent collective (e.g., Halbwachs, 1950; Edwards and Middleton, 1988) or with a conception of archetypes (Jung, 1968), which can be defined as the images and constellations of feeling which crystallize universal human experiences and which have been claimed to universally permeate human memory. Therefore, to divide the message of a photograph into a 'studium' and 'punctum' is to create an artificial dichotomy between the 'public' or overt message of a photograph, and the private, personal interpretation. This practice risks polarizing research into two topics: phenomenology, and photography, thereby neglecting the processes involved in the interpretation of photographs.

The Essence of a Photograph which Differentiates it from Other Forms of Representation, Is Its Relationship to Time

The awareness of the passage of time, and the reifying of time into discrete units, is inherent in some uses of photographs in therapy. The client's demeanour, depicted in photographs taken during the course of therapy, is said to reveal changes in emotional state; photographs are therefore treated as a 'slice of time', and are used as a dependent variable or index of therapeutic progress (Akeret, 1973; Graham, 1967). These practices assume a relationship between photographs and time which is echoed in 'lay' uses of photography.

Colson (1979) claims that 'people take up photography at times of rapid change in their lives when the photograph is most clearly expressive of the wish to hold time still, to have greater opportunity to consolidate the ordinarily fleeting experience of the moment' (p. 273). If one accepts that photographs can be used as a tool to manipulate our subjective experience of time, Colson suggests, then 'the rapid and often bewildering changes in life style and technology which characterise our culture and the reduced stability of the family unit' (p. 274) make the current popularity of photography more understandable. Colson is a psychoanalyst, and his thesis was based on five sources of information: the psychoanalytic literature, his own familiarity with photography and photographers, biographical works about photographers, and interviews and articles appearing in popular magazines and photographic portfolios. He also conducted clinical work with several patients who had a major interest in photography, including six psychiatric hospital patients, and conducted interviews with four mental health professionals who practised photography as a hobby.

Time is one of the 'punctums' identified by Barthes. He claimed that, unlike a painting, which may or may not be a figment of fantasy, when we see a photograph we cannot deny that its referent once *existed*. A photograph is therefore an emanation of a *past* reality. Bazin (1967), who theorized photographs from the standpoint of cultural studies, also emphasizes the relationship of photographs to time, but extends the argument to suggest that photographs, like statues and other icons, exist in order to create an ideal world which has its own trajectory through time. Similarly, Walker and Kimball-Moulton (1989), sociologists who examined albums created by amateur photographers in order to investigate the psychological and social functions of photo albums (and their value to scholars as documents of social life), claim that photography has always been about time. They state that 'the act of photography anticipates the future by ripping the appearance of a moment out of its time, creating a tangible image for the future of what will be the past. The things photographed have their own dynamic (which means an unseen but implied past and future)' (p. 157).

Other sociologists have highlighted the relationship between photographs and time. For example, Boerdam and Martinius (1980) reiterate Bourdieu's (1965) statement that photographs are a protection against time. More precisely, they argue, on the basis of twelve interviews with couples about photography, that photography has the function of helping one to overcome the sorrow of the passing of time, either by providing a magical substitute for what time has destroyed, or by making up for the failures of memory, acting as a mooring for the evocation of associated memories; in short, by providing a sense of the conquest of time as a destructive power.

With the exception of Barthes, all the theorists who emphasize the relationship of photography to time allow for a social dimension to time. They acknowledge that conceptions of time are socially and historically relative. There have also been attempts to evaluate some of these claims empirically. For example, Kotkin (1978) suggested on the basis of 'hundreds' (sic) of photographs, that we conceive of our lives as a series of eras and stages and our albums reflect and reify the way we think of those units of time. However, it is difficult to evaluate such 'evidence' as the above researchers provide; few direct quotations from respondents or other illustrations of the data underpinning their claims are provided, and therefore the relationship between the identified themes and the qualitative data on which they were based is impossible to elucidate. In effect, any description of the interpretative process which would enable us to evaluate, or even trace the origins of the authors' conclusions, is lacking in the reports of their research.

With regard to the plausibility of its relationship to time being a valuable attribute of a photograph: the value of the structuring of time to the individual has been documented by psychologists. For example, when Fryer and Payne (1984) studied a sample of people identified as coping with unemployment in a creative and positive way, they found that one of the distinguishing characteristics of this group was the ability to generate their own personal structuring of time. It is therefore clear that a sense of time contributes to an individual's phenomenology, and thus, that photographs may contribute to our subjective experience of time.

Time did emerge as a significant aspect of photographs in an interview study with lay photographers (Cronin, 1996). The relationship of photographs to time was primarily governed by the manifest content, according to the participants in this study, who felt that photographs could be used to document change, and who claimed that they took many photographs of rites of passage. This was borne out by an archival study (Cronin, 1996), in which I found that rites of passage, which serve to mark the passage of time in the family, were well represented in the photographic collection. I also found that peaks in photo-taking activity occurred during times in the family life cycle when families were undergoing rapid change. However, developmental milestones were not particularly well represented in the collections, and therefore it could be argued that the time which is at issue in the photographic collection is 'family' time, i.e., the whole family's trajectory through time, rather than the development of any one individual. This yields a caveat for any research conducted with pre-existing family photographs: the 'slices of time' which they embody may not necessarily represent the way in which any one member of the family would carve up their own life, and therefore, they must be interpreted with caution if they are being used to provide such material as life lines

Lay Perceptions of the Nature of Photographs Can Be Described as Being Grounded in Either a 'Realist Folk Myth' or a 'Symbolist Folk Myth'

The last assumption invoked the issue of instrumentality and photography, i.e., what do people *use* photographs for? This brings us to the issue of what the 'lay person' (i.e., someone who is neither a professional theorist nor a professional photographer) thinks about photographs, what significance is attributed to them, and what he or she does with them.

The use of photographs by some phototherapists appears to be based on an assumption of realism: it has been suggested that 'photographs may be used to stimulate memories of the past' (Weiser, 1984), to 'check on the accuracy of recollections of family events or characteristics' (Meloche, 1973), and 'to track continuities between past and present' (Anderson and Malloy, 1976). None of these uses take into account the functions of photographs in the *present* for the client. A more dangerous, though less common manifestation of a realist myth in clinical settings, is the use of photographs as a diagnostic technique. Therapists infer a variety of emotional, dysfunctional or pathological states from individual photographs and collections belonging to clients. For example, the client is said to reveal their depression through facial expression (Diamond, 1856; Graham, 1967), or their poor capacity for personal relationships through the choice of inanimate subject matter for their photographs (Ziller and Smith, 1977).

This use of photographs as mirrors of reality illustrates the 'binary folklore' which Sekula (1975), discussing the nature of the photograph, claimed exists around photography. He claimed that photographic communication occurs within a 'symbolist folk myth' or a 'realist folk myth'.

The 'symbolist folk myth' entails photographs being treated as a 'blank canvas', i.e., a photograph by itself doesn't mean anything until it is interpreted, and the meaning of a photograph will not necessarily be apparent from the manifest content. This echoes the sentiments of Silber (1973), who stated that 'the snapshot is in many ways a symbolic form of communication, relatively independent of the literal identification of the events portrayed' (p. 10).

The 'realist folk myth', on the other hand, treats the photograph as a copy of 'reality'. O'Connell (cited by Leon, 1981) suggested that 'the image by its flatness and precision persuades us to accept the moment it portrays as the essential one.' Sontag (1977) attributes the 'realist' position to the population in general. She states that 'photographed images do not seem to be statements about the world so much as pieces of it, miniatures of reality that anyone can make or acquire'. She goes on to discuss the evidential power of photos, claiming that 'the picture may distort; but there is always a presumption that something exists, or did exist, which is like what's in the picture. A photograph seems to have a more innocent, and therefore more accurate, relation to visible reality than do other mimetic objects' (p. 5). Schwartz (1992) sums up this view nicely:

> Both history and popular lore have encouraged us to view photographs as direct, unmediated transcriptions of the real world, rather than seeing them as coded symbolic artifacts whose form and content transmit identifiable points of view. (Schwarz, 1992, p. 95)

If the assumption that photographs can be interpreted from either a realist or a symbolist standpoint is valid, one would expect that 'lay', as opposed to 'theoretical' conceptions of the nature of photographs would fall into one or other of these 'myths'.

There is some empirical support for the existence of the 'realist' myth. O'Connor, Beilin and Kose (1981), in their empirical investigation of children's belief in photographic fidelity, found that six-year-old children treat photographs as reflecting reality with greater fidelity than drawings. Vial (1988) claimed, on the basis of interviews with twelve participants, that the realist myth was distinguishable in the discourse of lay photographers. She stated that people treat the photograph as proof that something occurred, and that its power derives from the fact that it transcends the boundaries of time and space and the fact that its referent is instantly recognizable. Because of this, she says, the viewer runs the risk of taking the representation for the referent, i.e., treating the photograph as 'true'. This is likely to be no less true of the researcher or therapist working with photographs than it is of the 'lay' observer.

The general tenor of the discussion of realist myths seems to be that 'lay' people do not have the privileged access to semiotic theory which academics do, and therefore are somewhat naive in their dealings with photographs. This may indeed be the case, but it could be argued that the theorists just described have fallen into what Wetherell and Potter (1988) term an 'old-fashioned' view of language, whereby there is an assumption of a direct mapping of a person's internal mental event onto the language they use. Accounts are taken to be simple, unintrusive, neutral reflectors of real processes located elsewhere. However, Wetherell and Potter point out that in sociology, philosophy, and literary theory, as well as in social psychology, there has been a shift towards examining the 'action oriented' nature of discourse. This recent emphasis on 'what talk *does*' renders the mere identification of symbolist and realist myths regarding photography somewhat trivial unless we carry the issue further and ask the empirical questions 'To what uses are these myths put?' 'What does treating a photograph as a direct reflection of reality *achieve*?' 'What does treating a photograph as a symbolic representation *achieve*?' We need not ask 'what is it about this photograph that 'causes' an emotional reaction in the observer', but rather 'once a photograph is identified as being significant for an individual, what is it used for?'

An interview study of the meaning of family photographs (Cronin, 1996) challenged the dichotomy between realism and symbolism to some degree. Qualitative analysis of interviews conducted with thirty adults indicated that though the two myths were discernible, no individual was exclusively located within either of them; rather, individuals moved freely between them. A distinction between a theoretical meaning and a practical meaning emerged, i.e., when talking about photographs in the abstract, my participants tended towards the symbolist myth; whereas they switched to the realist myth when talking about specific photographs (e.g., 'this photograph shows . . .'). Therefore, Sontag's (1977) suggestion, that the realist myth is somehow attributable to a naive realism on the part of lay photographers, does not capture the complexity of the interaction. Rather, there is a favouring of stories occurring, i.e., the owner of the photograph seems to be saying implicitly 'given the manifest content of the photograph, here's my story; someone else may have a different story'. There doesn't seem to be a presumption of truth, i.e., that one story is better or truer than the other. This interpretation of the invoking of realist and symbolist myths has important implications for research on photographs; it enables what Beloff (1993) called the 'rhetorical battle' regarding the meaning of a photograph to occur in the interactional context in which photographs are viewed. This leads us to the next assumption:

The Meaning of Photographs Arises in a Narrative Context

The tendency of photographs to be embedded in a narrative context is exploited by phototherapists who assume that photographs provide a non-threatening topic of discussion, and who, therefore, use them to 'break the ice' in the initial stages of therapy (Gerace, 1989; Gosciewski, 1975; Weiser, 1984). A somewhat more sophisticated use of the narrative stimulated by albums or individual photographs is the use of photographs to trigger discussion about the client's family life (Entin, 1983; Fryrear, 1980).

The notion of photographs gaining their meaning in a narrative context not only raises questions regarding the use of photographs as springboards for narrative, but also regarding their use as memory aids, particularly if one construes remembering as primarily a social activity (Ruby, 1982). Spence and Holland (1991) pose the question of whether there might be a 'collective narrative' which surrounds family photos and, if so, whether it differs from individual narratives.

Walker and Kimball Moulton (1989) concentrated on exploring the structure of the narratives accompanying the presentation of family albums, and the role of these narratives in creating the meaning of the family album. They argue that the accompaniment of a family photographic collection by a verbal narrative is one of the four key features of family photographs, the other three being that the family photographic collection is essentially a private collection, is available only to small audiences, and assumes a possessor who will preside over its display.

They further claim that every photograph album is constructed on the basis of some implicit narrative, although as Lesy (1980) suggests, the narrative may take several different approaches. Some narratives are addressed to the reality that lies behind the images, so that the photographs and the narrative are related as illustration is to text. Some focus more explicitly on the photograph itself, i.e., they directly address the photographic image rather than the reality which underlies the image. Walker and Kimball Moulton (1989) claim that their 'narrators' recognize the problematic relationship between photograph and reality, that there is an incomplete correspondence between a photographic image and the reality it records, and that an active camera changes the reality it is engaged in. (This is in contrast to the stark dichotomy of realism and symbolism discussed above.)

Musello (1980) claimed that his sample of middle-class 'Euro-American' families approached photographs as 'mechanical recordings of real events', not as symbolic articulations, stating that 'meanings and interpretations are most often based on a belief in the photograph's value as a document of natural events and on recognition of its iconic referents'. However, he goes on to state that

> The use of the 'home mode' [domestic photography] seems heavily reliant on verbal accompaniment for the transmission of personal significances. Photographs presented to others are typically embedded in a verbal context delineating what should be attended to and what significances are located in the image, and providing contextual data necessary for understanding them. (Musello, 1980, p. 39)

With regard to the social aspects of remembering, Edwards and Middleton (1988) point out that relationships are both a determinant of remembering, providing a criterion of significance (defining what is worth remembering and how memories are linked together to tell the story of people's lives) and providing also a forum for the process itself (a context within which communicative remembering is done). In the other direction, remembering is a determinant of relationships. Relationships can be defined, negotiated, redefined consolidated, disputed, through conversations about the past.

Edwards and Middleton place particular emphasis on the use of photographs in joint remembering. They state that learning how to remember the past through conversations about family photographs involves learning how to 'take meaning' from such pictures in a sense similar to Heath's (1982) notion of taking meaning from written texts. That is to say, using family photographs as *aides mémoires* entails the family seeing photographs as depictions of events from a shared family history. It is the clues available in photographs which enable them to serve the family as reminders of the context of events. Those events themselves are then recreated and conventionalized in conversation about the photographs. These reconstructive aspects of memory are well documented in the psychological literature on memory (e.g., Bartlett, 1932; Loftus and Loftus, 1980).

Placing emphasis on the narrative context of photographs has several important implications for any research into the meaning of photographs. Firstly, it implies that any such investigation needs to pay as much attention to the contexts in which photographs are used as it does to their manifest content. Secondly, it reinforces the message (which is implicit in the discussion of the other assumptions) that the function of photographs is primarily the creation and maintenance of meaning, and to this end a hermeneutic approach, which concentrates on the meaning woven around a photograph, is desirable.

Inferences Regarding Family Dynamics Can Be Drawn from the Manifest Content of Photographs vs Family Photographs May Draw on Ancient Themes of Unity and Cohesiveness

These two assumptions are in direct opposition to each other. On the one hand, therapists have used photographs to explore family systems. Family dynamics, power relations and affectional bonds are sometimes inferred by phototherapists from photographs. Proximity and distance between family members, degree of physical contact, pairings of family members, inclusion and exclusion and location within the group are all used as indices of structure and process within the client family (Akeret, 1973; Entin, for example, 1980). This usage is exemplified in Hirsch's (1981) claim that the layout of formal portraits often appears to describe a plane: we see triangles with bases and apexes, configurations with points and angles which make us ask who in the family is at the top, who is subordinate, who is out of line, who has power, who submits and who defies.

On the other hand, we have Hirsch's suggestion that family photographs are selective and culturally patterned: she claimed that 'family photography . . . masks statistics of adultery, divorce, mental breakdown, and juvenile delinquency (p. 32): therefore [photographs] sustain the myth and the notion of family as institution; therefore they have a social utility'. Sontag (1977, p. 8) claimed that photography came along to memorialize, to restate symbolically, the 'imperilled continuity and vanishing extendedness of family life'. Spence and Holland (1991) also ask whether we 'strive to remember, perceive or portray the family group as 'cohesive' (p. 7).

A study of professional photographers (Cronin, 1996) indicated that studio photographers felt that one of the pre-eminent functions of family photographs was to communicate an image of family unity to the extended family. This use of photographs is supported by more theoretical accounts of photography. For example, Bourdieu (1965) sees photos as having social functions which are wholly connected to the structure of the family in a modern world, with the family photograph as an index or proof of family unity, and, at the same time, and instrument or tool to *effect* that unity. He discusses the process by which this is achieved in detail: citing Durkheim (1970), he says the taking of photographs immortalizes and reaffirms the sense of unity engendered by the family's festivals and rituals.

In a study of the photographic collections of ten families (Cronin, 1996), it was suggested that if family photographs are primarily used to illustrate family togetherness, then there would be more photographs of nuclear family members and close kin than of extended family members and non-relatives. This was indeed the case in the collections which I examined. However, within this manifestation of group cohesiveness, children most frequently appeared on their own in photographs. There was a higher proportion of photographs of rituals than might be expected given the relative infrequency of their occurrence in family life relative to other, more mundane, activities. Children were more likely to appear with nuclear family members than with non-related significant others.

As well as the co-occurrence of family members in photographs, family intimacy, as indexed by their spatial behaviour in relation to each other, was also predicted to be intimate if family photographs were used to depict unity. Parents were more likely to be touching each other and touching their children, whereas siblings tended not to be depicted as touching each other. However, the results indicate that touching as an index of intimacy should be treated with caution, as touching can also be used to assert power. The results could also be interpreted as demonstrating that family members in a powerful role tend to touch those in a less powerful position. Family members were more likely to be smiling in photographs, and this helps to boost the idea of a unified, happy family.

At the very least, this study provided evidence for Hirsch's (1981) claim that there are cultural conventions governing the representation of families in photographs, in terms of who appears in the photographs, the depiction of affect, power and intimacy in photographs, the depiction of family roles and boundaries, when photographs are taken, and the events they depict. However, it is important to note that this study makes no claims whatsoever regarding whether 'actual' family dynamics are depicted in photographs. Rather, it indicates that the 'interpretation' of photographs should be approached with extreme caution by researchers and therapists, and recommends that due consideration be given to the cultural patterning of photographic images, particularly those produced for private consumption by photographers who consider themselves neither hobbyists nor artists.

Our Personal Histories are not only Contained in Family Albums, but They are Created by Them

Phototherapists have made much use of photographs to explore personal histories and identities of clients. Re-enactment of personal photographs is used to help the client to explore different perspectives of themselves and their past. The therapist (or, in the case of Martin and Spence, e.g., 1987, the co-counsellor) discusses the person's choices of photographic subject matter to explore their personality (Weiser, 1985).

Photographs are also used to change the self-image of the client by using them to provide feedback and to confront distorted self-images. Typically, adolescents with low self esteem, poor body image and a variety of emotional problems obtain feedback from photographs, sometimes taking photographs of each other in groups. In some studies, psychotic behaviour is reduced through self-confrontation (Amerikaner, Shauble and Ziller, 1980; Ammerman and Fryrear, 1975; Aronson and Graziano, 1976; Combs and Ziller, 1977; Cornelison and Arsenian, 1960; Diamond, 1856; Hunsberger, 1984; Miller, 1962; Spire, 1973; Zwick, 1978).

The formulation of the above assumption is derived from Milgram's (1977) query regarding whether 'photographs may act on the real world and begin to shape it' (p. 32). It is a stronger, more constructionist version of Beloff's claim (1985) that our personal histories are validated by our photographic collection. Beloff states that we do not represent the more mundane aspects of our quotidian lives, such as work, argument, boredom, sadness, in photographs, but rather present universally positive and/or idealised versions of family life. This is achieved by photographing a very narrow range of events, and by the photographer's exhortations to the subject to smile. Beloff (1993) points out that the 'face-work' (Goffman, 1967) which is carried out in photographs enables them to be 'texts of identity' which are scripted by the photographer and the sitter together. This is similar to Hirsch's (1981) thesis that decisions made regarding the retention and discarding of family photographs are made not in the name of 'historical accuracy' but for the sake of a standard of meaning which the images either uphold or betray. Holland, Spence and Watney (1986) also talk about the use of photographs to create and validate the image of the family. Their thesis is couched in far more political terms: they state that

> From our most seemingly 'private' family albums . . . we are positioned and organised, according to the photographic conventions which sort out and handle differences of race, class, age, sexuality and so on. . . . In all its dominant versions, across the largely spurious barrier between amateur and professional, photography works to position us as sexed individuals within a network of unequal power relationships which it validates, with its ideology of photographic 'truthfulness', as natural and immutable. At the heart of this network lies the image of the family — one of the central units by which photography makes sense of the world. Into this image are dissolved all the complexities of wage labour, domestic labour, gendering patterns, child raising, householding, education, leisure, entertainment, holidays and so on, which photography organises, circulates and, most importantly, validates. (Holland, Spence and Watney, 1986, p. 1)

Williamson (1984) claims that the question of what is *repressed* in family photographs is a significant one. He states that the family, besides being used as a unit of social cement, is also an extremely oppressive thing to be in. Photography, he claims, erases this experience not only from the outside, in adverts of happy, product-consuming families, but also from within, as angry parents, crying children and divorced spouses are systematically omitted from the album. Instead, Williamson claims, contemporary photography, in its preference for informal photos, is predominantly concerned with fun. In earlier family images, he said, it seemed enough for the family members' external appearance to be documented, but now this is not enough, and internal states of constant delight are to be revealed on film. 'Fun', he says, 'must not only be had, it must be seen to be had' (p. 21). Spence and Holland (1991) ask:

For whom is the image so carefully manufactured? Is each individual looking for their own ideal image? Are members of the group presenting themselves for each other, or for unknown others, for future generations? Is this a joint self-celebration, or is a presentation of the imagined family group for the critical scrutiny of outsiders? (Spence and Holland, 1991, p. 7)

So, the assumption that personal histories can be reflected and possibly even created by photographs makes a strong claim concerning the use of photographs to confirm our self-image or the image a family holds of itself, or to represent the idealized image of ourselves and our family and suppress negative connotations. One would think that it would be relatively easy to ascertain whether photographs represent real or idealised versions of the family. However, if one espouses a social constructionist perspective, where reality is constituted through shared meanings (and is constantly re-invented by interacting individuals), one cannot preclude the possibility that rather than photographs being a product of family life, family life is a product of photographs, i.e., photographs may be used to construct a shared reality in the family.

Conclusion

This discussion of the assumptions underpinning the therapeutic and research uses yields several recommendations for the study of photographs:

1   The 'information' which photographs seem to yield must be treated with caution: the interpersonal, social and cultural contexts in which they were taken and are used must be given some consideration.
2   Photographs shouldn't be treated as 'mirrors' held up to reality: reality itself is a product of social processes, and photographs can be part of the process, as well as a product, of reality construction.
3   When examining the story which is woven around photographs, the question '*whose* story is being told?' must always be borne in mind.
4   The purposes for which photographs are both taken and used will have an effect on their meaning.

References

AKERET, R.U. (1973) *Photoanalysis: How to Interpret the Hidden Meaning of Personal and Public Photographs*, New York: Wynden.
AMERIKANER, M., SHAUBLE, P. and ZILLER, R. (1980) 'Images: The use of photographs in personal counselling', *Personnel & Guidance Journal*, **59**, pp. 68–73.
AMMERMAN, M. and FRYREAR, J.L. (1975) 'Photographic enhancement of children's self-esteem', *Psychology in Schools*, **12**, pp. 319–25.
ANDERSON, C.M. and MALLOY, E.S. (1976) 'Family photographs: In treatment and therapy', *Family Process*, **15**, pp. 259–64.
ARONSON, D.W. and GRAZIANO, A.M. (1976) 'Improving elderly clients' attitudes through photography', *The Gerontologist*, **16**, pp. 363–476.
BARNES, M.L. and STERNBERG, R.J. (1989) 'Social intelligence and decoding of nonverbal cues', *Intelligence*, **13**, pp. 263–87.

BARTHES, R. (1980) *Camera Lucida: Reflections on Photography*, Paris: Editions du Seuil. (Translated HOWARD, R. (1988), London: Jonathan Cape Ltd).

BARTLETT, F.C. (1932) *Remembering: A Study in Experimental and Social Psychology*, Cambridge, England: Cambridge University Press.

BAZIN, A. (1967) 'The ontology of the photographic image', in BAZIN, A. (ed.) *What Is Cinema?*, vol. 1: University of California Press, pp. 9–16.

BELOFF, H. (1985) *Camera Culture*, Oxford: Basil Blackwell.

BELOFF, H. (1993) 'Les femmes de Cameron: Rhétorique visuelle de l'identité sexuelle, *Bulletin de Psychologie*, **49**, 411, pp. 580–8.

BOERDAM, J. and MARTINIUS, W.D. (1980) 'Family photographs: A sociological approach', *Netherlands Journal of Sociology*, **16**, 2, pp. 95–119.

BOURDIEU, P. (1965) *Un Art Moyen: Essai sur les Usages Sociaux de la Photographie*, Paris: Les Editions de Minuit. (Translated WHITESIDE, S. (1990), *Photography: A middle-brow Art*, Cambridge: Polity Press.)

BURGIN, V. (1982) *Thinking Photography*, London: Macmillan.

CHALFEN, R. (1987) *Snapshot Versions of Life*, Bowling Green, Ohio: Bowling Green Popular Press.

COLSON, D.B. (1979) 'Photography as an extension of the ego', *International Review of Psychoanalysis*, **6**, pp. 273–82.

COMBS, J.M. and ZILLER, R.C. (1977) 'Photographic self-concept of counsellees', *Journal of Counseling Psychology*, **24**, pp. 452–5.

CORNELISON, F.S. and ARSENIAN, J. (1960) 'A study of the response of psychotic patients to photographic self-image experience', *Psychiatric Quarterly*, **34**, pp. 1–8.

CRONIN, Ó. (1996) 'The meaning and psychological significance of family photographic collections', Unpublished PhD thesis, University of Southampton.

DIAMOND, H. (1856) 'On the application of photography to the physiognomic and mental phenomena of insanity', in GILMAN, S.L. (ed.) (1976) *The Face of Madness*, New York: Brunner Mazel.

DITTMAR, H. (1992) *The Social Psychology of Material Possessions: To Have Is to Be*, London: Harvester Wheatsheaf.

DURKHEIM, E. (1970) *Suicide*, SPALDING, J. and SIMPSON, G. (eds) London: Routledge.

EDWARDS, D. and MIDDLETON, D. (1988) 'Conversational remembering and family relationships: How children learn to remember', *Journal of Social and Personal Relationships*, **5**, pp. 3–25.

ENTIN, A.D. (1980) 'Phototherapy: Family albums and multigenerational portraits', *Camera Lucida*, **1**, pp. 39–51.

ENTIN, A.D. (1983) 'The family photo album as icon: Photographs in family therapy', in KRAUS, D.A. and FRYREAR, J.L. (eds) *Phototherapy in Mental Health*, Illinois: Thomas, pp. 117–32.

FRYER, D.M. and PAYNE, R.L. (1984) 'Proactive behaviour in the unemployed: Findings and implications', *Leisure Studies*, **3**, pp. 273–95.

FRYREAR, J.L. (1980) 'A selective, non-evaluative review of research on phototherapy', *Phototherapy Quarterly*, **2**, pp. 7–9.

GERACE, L.M. (1989) 'Using family photographs to explore life cycle changes', *Nursing and Health Care*, **10**, pp. 245–9.

GOFFMAN, E. (1967) *Interaction Rituals: Essays in Face-to-face Behaviour*, Harmondsworth: Penguin.

GOSCIEWSKI, F. (1975) 'Photo counseling', *Personnel and Guidance Journal*, **53**, pp. 600–4.

GRAHAM, J.R. (1967) 'The use of photographs in psychiatry', *Canadian Psychiatric Journal*, **12**, p. 425.

HALBWACHS, M. (1950) *La mémoire collective*, Paris: Presses Universitaires. (Translated DITTER, F.J. and DITTER, V.Y. 1980, *The Collective Memory*, London: Harper & Row.)

HEATH, S.B. (1982) 'What no bedtime story means: Narrative skills at home and school', *Language in Society*, **11**, pp. 49–76.

HIRSCH, J. (1981) '*Family Photographs: Content, Meaning and Effect*, New York: Oxford University Press.

HOLLAND, P., SPENCE, J. and WATNEY, S. (eds) (1986) *Photography/Politics: Two*, Comedia/ Photography Workshop, London: Methuen.

HUNSBERGER, P. (1984) 'Uses of instant print photography in psychotherapy', *Professional Psychology: Research and Practice*, **15**, pp. 884–90.

JUNG, C. (1968) 'The archetypes and the collective unconscious', 2nd ed., *Collected Works*, vol. 9, Part 1, London: Routledge and Kegan Paul.

'*KODACOLOR GOLD' SURVEY*, April 1990, prepared by Audience Selection, London for Kodak Ltd.

KOTKIN, A. (1978) 'The family album as a form of folklore', *Exposure*, **16**, pp. 4–8.

LESY, M. (1980) *Time Frames: The Meaning of Family Pictures*, New York: Pantheon.

LOFTUS, E.F. and LOFTUS, G.R. (1980) 'On the permanence of stored information in the human brain', *American Psychologist*, **35**, pp. 409–20.

MARTIN, R. and SPENCE, J. (1987) *Double Exposure: The Minefield of Memory*, Exhibition commentary, Photographers Gallery Touring Exhibition.

MELOCHE, M. (1973) 'Utilisation de l'album de photos dans l'évaluation clinique', *La Vie Médicale au Canada Français*, **2**, pp. 865–70.

MILGRAM, S. (1977) 'The image-freezing machine', *Psychology Today*, **10**, pp. 30–5.

MILLER, M.F. (1962) 'Responses of psychiatric patients to their photographs', *Diseases of the Nervous System*, **23**, pp. 296–8.

MUSELLO, C. (1980) 'Studying the home mode: An exploration of family photography and visual communication', *Studies in Visual Communication*, **6**, 1, pp. 23–42.

O'CONNELL, B. (1981) in LEON, W. 'Picturing the family: Photographs and paintings in the classroom', Unpublished article *Journal of Family History*, **6**, pp. 15–27.

O'CONNOR, J., BEILIN, H. and KOSE, G. (1981) 'Children's belief in photographic fidelity', *Developmental Psychology*, **17**, pp. 859–65.

RUBY, J. (1982) 'Images of the family: The symbolic implications of animal photography', *Phototherapy*, **3**, pp. 2–7.

SCHWARTZ, D. (1992) 'To tell the truth: Codes of objectivity in photojournalism', *Communication*, **13**, pp. 95–109

SEDGWICK, R. (1979) 'The use of photoanalysis and family memorabilia in the study of family interaction', *Corrective and Social Psychiatry and Journal of Behaviour Technology*, **25**, pp. 137–41.

SEKULA, A. (1975) 'On the invention of photographic meaning', *Art Forum*, **13**, pp. 37–45.

SILBER, M. (1973) *The Family Album*, Boston, Ma.: Godine.

SONTAG, S. (1977) *On Photography*, London: Penguin.

SPENCE, J. and HOLLAND, P. (eds) (1991) *Family Snaps: The Meanings of Domestic Photography*, London: Virago.

SPIRE, R.H. (1973) 'Photographic self-image confrontation', *American Journal of Nursing*, **73**, pp. 1207–10.

VIAL, C. (1988) 'Mémoire et photographie', *Bulletin de Psychologie*, **42**, pp. 375–8.

WALKER, A.L. and KIMBALL MOULTON, R. (1989) 'Photo albums: Images of time and reflections of self', *Qualitative Sociology*, **12**, pp. 155–82.

WEISER, J. (1984) 'Phototherapy — Becoming visually literate about oneself, or "Phototherapy? What's phototherapy?",' *Phototherapy*, **4**, pp. 2–7.

WEISER, J. (1985) 'Phototherapy: Using snapshots and photo-interactions in therapy with youth', in SCHAEFER, C.E. (ed.) *Innovative Interventions in Child and Adolescent Therapy*, New York: Wiley.

WETHERELL, M. and POTTER, J. (1988) 'Discourse analysis and the identification of interpretive repertoires', in ANTAKI, C. (ed.) *Analysing Everyday Explanation: A Casebook of New Methods*, London: Sage.

WILLIAMSON, J. (1984) 'Family, education and photography', *Ten*, **14**, pp. 19–22.

WOLF, R. (1976) 'The polaroid technique: Spontaneous dialogues from the unconscious', *Art Psychotherapy*, **3**, pp. 197–214.

WOLFMAN REPORT (1993) New York: Hachette Filipacci Magazines Inc., 1633 Broadway, New York, NY 10019.

ZILLER, R.C. and SMITH, D.E. (1977) 'A phenomenological utilization of photographs', *Journal of Phenomenological Psychology*, **7**, pp. 172–85.

ZWICK, D.S. (1978) 'Photography as a tool toward increased awareness of the ageing self', *Art Psychotherapy*, **5**, pp. 135–41.

Chapter 6

Visual Sociology, Documentary Photography, and Photojournalism: It's (Almost) All a Matter of Context

Howard S. Becker

Abstract

Photographs are by their nature ambiguous. This problem is compounded for the social scientist with a camera by a world that is replete with visual sociological meanings. A photograph taken by a 'visual sociologist', 'documentary photographer' or 'photojournalist' may be very similar. However, the significance and legitimization of that photograph is not to be found in attaching any a particular 'catch-all' term but in the response it generates in those who perceive it. This chapter explores the importance of 'context' in giving photographs their meaning. (Originally published in *Visual Sociology*, **10**, 1–2, pp. 5–14)

Three Kinds of Photography

People who want to use photographic materials for social science purposes — to do what is sometimes now called visual sociology — often get confused. The pictures visual sociologists make so resemble those made by others, who claim to be doing documentary photography or photojournalism, that they wonder whether they are doing anything distinctive. They try to clear up the confusion by looking for the essential differences, the defining features of each of the genres, as if it were just a matter of getting the definitions right.

Such labels do not refer to Platonic essences whose meaning we can discover by profound thought and analysis, but rather are just what people have found it useful to make them be. We can learn what people have been able to do using documentary photography or photojournalism as a cover, but we can't find out what the terms really mean. Their meaning arises in the organizations they are used in, out of the joint action of all the people involved in those organizations, and so varies from time to time and place to place. Just as paintings get their meaning in a world of painters, collectors, critics, and curators, so photographs get their meaning from the way the people involved with them understand them, use them, and thereby attribute meaning to them (see Becker, 1982).

Visual sociology, documentary photography, and photojournalism, then, are whatever they have come to mean, or been made to mean, in their daily use in worlds of photographic work. They are social constructions, pure and simple. In this they resemble all the other ways of reporting what we know, or think we have found out, about the societies we live in, such ways as ethnographic reports, statistical summaries, maps, and so on (Becker, 1986). We can raise at least two kinds of questions about this activity of naming and attributing meaning.

Organizational: When people name classes of activity, as they have named these forms of picture making, they are not just making things convenient for themselves and others by creating some shorthand tags. They almost always mean to accomplish other purposes as well: drawing boundaries around the activities, saying where they belong organizationally, establishing who is in charge, who is responsible for what, and who is entitled to what. A contemporary example can be taken from the field of drug use. Marihuana, cocaine, and heroin are drugs but alcohol and tobacco are — what? Recreational products? The terms do not reflect a chemical distinction based on the molecular structure of substances. They distinguish, rather, ways of treating substances, saying that one is to be banned and subjected, among other things, to Presidential disapproval while the other can be used for Presidential pleasure.

So we want to ask, of these different ways of talking about photography: Who is using these terms now? What are they trying to claim for the work so described? How do they thus mean to locate that work in some work organization? Conversely, what kind of work and which people do they mean to exclude? In short, what are they trying to accomplish by talking this way?

Historical: Where did these terms come from? What have they been used for in the past? How does their past use create a present context and how does that historically based context constrain what can be said and done now? 'Documentary photography' was one kind of activity around the turn of the century, when great waves of social reform swept the United States and photographers had a ready audience for images exposing evil, and plenty of sponsors to pay them to create those images. 'Visual sociology', if we can talk about such a thing in that era, consisted of much the same kind of images, but published in the American Journal of Sociology. Neither term means now what it did then. The great social reform organizations have changed in character, their use of photographs subsidiary to a host of other techniques, and sociology has become more 'scientific' and less open to reports in anything but words and numbers.

The three terms, then, have varying histories and present uses. Each is tied to and gets its meaning in a particular social context. Photojournalism is what journalists do, producing images as part of the work of getting out daily newspapers and weekly newsmagazines (probably mostly daily newspapers now, since the death in the early 1970s of *Life and Look*). What is photojournalism commonly supposed to be? Unbiased, factual, complete, attention-getting, storytelling, courageous? Our image of the photojournalist, insofar as it is based on historical figures, consists of one part Weegee, sleeping in his car, typing his stories on the typewriter stored in its trunk, smoking cigars, chasing car wrecks and fires, and photographing criminals for a New York tabloid; he said of his work 'Murders and fires, my two best sellers, my bread and butter.' A second part is Robert Capa, rushing into the midst of a war, a battle, to get a closeup shot of death and destruction (his watchword was 'If your pictures aren't good enough, you aren't close enough' (quoted in Capa, 1968) for the news magazines. The final part of the stereotype is Margaret Bourke-White in aviator's gear, camera in one hand, helmet in the other, an airplane wing and propellor behind her, flying around the world producing classic photoessays in the *Life* style. Contemporary versions of the stereotype appear in Hollywood films: Nick Nolte, standing on the hood of a tank as it lumbers into battle through enemy fire, making images of war as he risks his life.

The reality is less heroic. Photojournalism is whatever it can be, given the nature of the journalism business. As that business changed, as the age of *Life and Look* faded, as the nature of the daily newspaper changed in the face of competition from radio and television, the photographs journalists made changed too. Photojournalism is no longer what it was in the days of Weegee or the first picture magazines in Germany (Becker, 1985). Today's photojournalists are literate, college-educated, can write, and so are no longer simply illustrators of stories reporters tell. They have a coherent ideology, based on the concept of the story-telling image. Nevertheless, contemporary photojournalism is, like its earlier versions, constrained by available space and by the prejudices, blind spots, and preconceived story lines of their editorial superiors (Ericson, Baranek, and Chan, 1987). Most importantly, readers do not expect to spend any time deciphering ambiguities and complexities in the photographs that appear in their daily newspaper or news magazine. Such photographs must, therefore, be instantly readable, immediately interpretable (Hagaman, 1995).

Photojournalism is constrained, too, by the way editors hand out photographic assignments. Except for sports photographers, who sometimes become specialized in that area, photojournalists, unlike reporters, never develop a 'beat', an area of the city's life they cover continuously and know so well that they develop a serious analysis and understanding of it. Since the photographs they make inevitably reflect their understanding of what they are photographing, that job-enforced ignorance means that the resulting images will almost necessarily reflect a superficial understanding of the events and social phenomena being photographed. Heroic legends describe the few photographers — Eugene Smith, Henri Cartier-Bresson — who were brave enough or independent enough to overcome these obstacles. But the legends serve only to hearten those whose work still reflects those constraints. (A number of social scientists have studied the organization of newsgathering. See, for instance, Epstein, 1973; Hall, 1973; Molotch and Lester, 1974; Schudson, 1978; Tuchman, 1978; and Ericson, Baranek and Chan, 1987. Hagaman, 1996 gives a detailed account of the situation of newspaper photographers and of the constraints the job imposes on the pictures they make, see also Rudd, 1994).

Documentary photography was tied, historically, to both exploration and social reform. Some early documentarians worked, literally, 'documenting' features of the natural landscape, as did Timothy O'Sullivan, who accompanied the United States Geological Exploration of the Fortieth Parallel in 1867–9 and the surveys of the southwestern United States led by Lieutenant George M. Wheeler, during which he made his now famous images of the Canyon de Chelle (Horan, 1966, pp. 151–214 and 237–312). Others documented unfamiliar ways of life, as in John Thompson's photographs of street life in London (Newhall, 1964, p. 139), Eugène Atget's massive survey of Parisian people and places (Atget, 1992), or August Sander's monumental study (finally published in English in 1986) of German social types. The latter two projects were, in fact, massive and monumental and in some deep sense impractical, that is, not tied to any immediate practical use.

Others worked, like Lewis Hine (Gutman, 1967) for the great social surveys of the early part of the century or, like Jacob Riis, (1971 [1901]) for muckraking newspapers. Their work was used to expose evil and promote change. Their images were, perhaps, something like those journalists made but, less tied to illustrating a newspaper story, they had more space to breathe in. A classic example is Hine's image of 'Leo, 48 inches high, 8 years old, picks up bobbins at fifteen cents a day', in which a young boy stands next to the machines which have, we almost surely conclude, stunted his growth.

What is documentary 'supposed to do'? In the reformist version, it's supposed to dig deep, get at what Robert E. Park (a sociologist who had worked as a journalist for daily papers in Minneapolis, Denver, Detroit, Chicago and New York) called the Big News, be 'concerned' about society, play an active role in social change, be socially responsible, worry about its effects on the society in which its work is distributed. Photographers like Hine saw their work, and it has often been seen since, as having an immediate effect on citizens and legislators. A photographically chauvinistic view of history often explains the passage of laws banning child labor as the direct result of Hine's work.

In its alternative version, documentary was not supposed to be anything in particular, since the work was not made for anyone in particular who could have enforced such requirements. Sander, who hoped to sell his work by subscription, described it variously as depicting the 'existing social order' and 'a physiognomical time exposure of German man' (Sander, 1986, pp. 23–4). Atget, rather more like an archetypal naive artist, did not describe his work at all, simply made it and sold the prints to whoever would buy them. Today, we see this work as having an exploratory, investigative character, something more like social science. Contemporary documentary photographers, whose work converges more consciously with social science, have become aware, as anthropologists have, that they have to worry about, and justify, their relations to the people they photograph.

Visual sociology has barely begun (but see the collection edited by Jon Wagner, 1979, the thorough review by Chaplin, 1994, and the publications of the International Visual Sociology Association). It is almost completely a creature of professional sociology, an academic discipline, and a poor relation of visual anthropology (Collier and Collier, 1986) which has a somewhat cozier relation to its parent discipline; in the anthropological tradition, which required investigators going to faroff places to gather skulls and linguistic texts, and dig up archeological materials as well as gather conventional ethnographic materials, making photographs was just one more obligation of fieldwork. Since visual imagery has not been conventional in sociology since its beginnings, when it was more tied to social reform, most sociologists not only do not accept that obligation, they see few legitimate uses for visual materials, other than as 'teaching aids'. It is as though using photographs and films in a research report constituted pandering to the low tastes of the public or trying to persuade readers to accept shaky conclusions by using illegitimate, 'rhetorical' means. In short, using visual materials seems 'unscientific', probably because 'science' in sociology came to be defined as being objective and neutral, just the opposite of the crusading spirit which animated the early muckraking work, itself intimately tied to photography (Stasz, 1979).

The definition of visual materials as unscientific is odd, since the natural sciences routinely use visual materials (see the discussion in Latour, 1986). Contemporary biology, physics, and astronomy are unthinkable without photographic evidence. In social science, only history and anthropology, the least 'scientific' disciplines, use photographs. Economics and political science, the most 'scientific', don't. Sociology, trying to ape the supposed scientific character of the latter fields, doesn't. As a result, the few active visual sociologists are people who learned photography elsewhere and brought it to their academic work.

What is visual sociology 'supposed to do'? We can answer that by saying what visual sociologists would have to do to compel the attention and respect of their discipline. What would they have to accomplish to convince other sociologists that their work is in some sense integral to the sociological enterprise? But it's not only a matter of convincing others. They must also convince themselves that what they are doing is 'really sociology', not just making pretty or interesting pictures. To do that, they would have to show that their visual work furthers the enterprise of sociology, however the mission of the discipline is defined. Since sociologists differ on what sociology should be, the mission of visual sociology is similarly confused. At a minimum, it should help to answer questions raised in the discipline in a way acceptable to one or more disciplinary factions.

Better yet, it might add something that is now missing. Are there topics for which photography would be a particularly good research method? Douglas Harper, an important visual sociologist, suggests these possibilities: studies of interaction, the presentation of emotion, the use of photographs to elicit information in interviews, and studies of material culture (Harper, 1982). Having made these distinctions, it remains to say that the boundaries between them are increasingly blurred, as the situations in which people work and the purposes for which they make photographs increasingly blend two or more genres.

Context

Photographs get meaning, like all cultural objects, from their context. Even paintings or sculptures, which seem to exist in isolation, hanging on the wall of a museum, get their meaning from a context made up of what has been written about them, either in the label hanging beside them or elsewhere, other visual objects, physically present or just present in viewers' awareness, and from discussions going on around them and around the subject the works are about. If we think there is no context, that only means that the maker of the work has cleverly taken advantage of our willingness to provide the context for ourselves.

As opposed to much contemporary photography made in the name of art, the three photographic genres discussed here insist on giving a great deal of explicit social context for the photographs they present. (This is not the place to consider the fluidity of definitions of photographic art. But the last statement needs to be qualified to recognize that the art world has frequently incorporated into its photographic canon work made for reasons quite different from those of self-conscious art, including work made as journalism or documentary. The extreme case is Weegee, whose work now rests in many museum collections.) Contemporary art photographs (I'm thinking of the work of Nicholas Nixon as an example) often show us something that might well have been the subject of a documentary photograph (poor kids standing around a slummy street, for instance). But they seldom provide any more than the date and place of the photograph, withholding the minimal social data we ordinarily use to orient ourselves to others, leaving viewers to interpret the images as best they can from the clues of clothing, stance, demeanor and household furnishings they contain. What might seem to be artistic mystery is only ignorance created by the photographer's refusal to give us basic information (which, it is likely, the photographer doesn't have).

The genres we're considering — documentary, photojournalism, and visual sociology — routinely provide at least a minimally sufficient background to make the images intelligible. A classic example from visual anthropology is Gregory Bateson and Margaret Mead's (1942) *Balinese Character*. Each photograph is part of a two page layout, one page devoted to photographs, the other to two kinds of text: a one or two paragraph interpretive essay, describing a topic like 'The Dragon and the Fear of Space' or 'Boys' Tantrums' or 'The Surface of the Body', these essays having a further context in a long introductory theoretical essay on culture and personality, and a full paragraph of annotation for each photograph, telling when it was made, who is in it, and what they are doing (see the discussion in Hagaman, 1995).

Some works in the documentary tradition, often infuenced by the photographer's exposure to social science, provide a great deal of text, sometimes in the words of the people involved (e.g., Danny Lyon's *Bikeriders* (1968) or Susan Meisalas' *Carnival Strippers* (1976) both done as independent projects). The text may be no more than an adequate caption, in the style of Lewis Hine or Dorothea Lange, or as in Jack Delano's portrait of a railroad worker, made in Chicago for the Farm Security Administration, whose caption reads, 'Frank Williams, working on the car repair tracks at an Illinois Central Railroad yard. Mr Williams has eight children, two of whom are in the US Army, Chicago, November, 1942.' (In Reid and Viskochil, 1989, p. 192.) Photographic books often contain extensive introductions and essays setting the social and historical stage for the images.

But things aren't that simple: leaving the context implicit does not make a photograph art, while a full context makes it documentary, social science, or photojournalism. Not all good works of documentary provide this kind of context. Robert Frank's (1959) *The Americans* (to which I will devote more attention below) gives no more textual support to the images than most art photographs, but it is not vulnerable to the above criticism. Why not? Because the images themselves, sequenced, repetitive, variations on a set of themes, provide their own context, teach viewers what they need to know in order to arrive, by their own reasoning, at some conclusions about what they are looking at.

In short, context gives images meaning. If the work does not provide context in one of the ways I've just discussed, viewers will provide it, or not, from their own resources.

A Practical Demonstration

Let's pursue this line of thought by looking at images which exemplify each of the three genres and seeing how they might be interpreted as one of the others. What it would take photographs of each type to be other than what they were made as — take a documentary photograph, for instance, as a news photograph or a work of visual sociology? What happens when we read these images in ways their makers didn't intend or, at least, differently than the way they are conventionally read?

Reading a Documentary Picture As Visual Sociology or Photojournalism

In 'En route from New York to Washington, Club Car' (Frank, 1959, p. 25), three men sit in a railroad club car. Two large men sit with their backs to us, near enough to the camera to be slightly out of focus. They wear tweed jackets, have dark slick hair, lean toward each other, and occupy half the frame. Between them, in focus, we see a black-suited third man's bald head and, behind him, the bar, above which shine many small star-shaped lights. His face is jowly, his forehead lined. He isn't looking at either of the others. He seems serious, even somber.

Robert Frank made this picture, as he made all the pictures in *The Americans* with a documentary intent, as part of a larger project designed to describe American society.[1] Frank described that intent in his application for the Guggenheim fellowship that made the project possible:

What I have in mind, then, is observation and record of what one naturalized American finds to see in the United States that signifies the kind of civilization born here and spreading elsewhere. Incidentally, it is fair to assume that when an observant American travels abroad his eye will see freshly; and that the reverse may be true when a European eye looks at the United States. I speak of the things that are there, anywhere and everywhere — easily found, not easily selected and interpreted. A small catalog comes to the mind's eye: a town at night, a parking lot, a supermarket, a highway, the man who owns the three cars and the man who owns none, the farmer and his children, a new house and a warped clapboard house, the dictation of taste, the dream of grandeur, advertising, neon lights, the faces of the leaders and the faces of the followers, gas tanks and post offices and backyards . . . (Tucker and Brookman, 1986, p. 20)

In another place, he explained his project this way:

With these photographs, I have attempted to show a cross-section of the American population. My effort was to express it simply and without confusion. The view is personal and, therefore, various facets of American life and society have been ignored. . . . I have been frequently accused of deliberately twisting subject matter to my point of view. Above all, I know that life for a photographer cannot be a matter of indifference. Opinion often consists of a kind of criticism. But criticism can come out of love. It is important to see what is invisible to others. Perhaps the look of hope or the look of sadness. Also, it is always the instantaneous reactions to oneself that produces a photograph. (Reprinted from US Camera Annual 1958, US Camera Publishing Corp., New York, 1967, p. 115, in Tucker and Brookman, p. 31)

Seen in this context, we can understand the image as a statement about American politics. These men (large, physically imposing) are the kind who occupy positions of political power, who inhabit such places as the club cars of trains going between New York, the country's financial centre, and Washington, the centre of political life. What makes this image documentary, and gives it its full meaning, is its context. The image says nothing explicit about American politics. But we understand its political statement by learning, from their use elsewhere in the book, the meaning of the image's details. We learn that a big man is a powerful man (as in Frank's 'Bar — Gallup, New Mexico', in which a large man in jeans and a cowboy hat dominates a crowded bar), and that a well-dressed big man is a rich and powerful man ('Hotel lobby — Miami Beach', in which a large middle-aged man is accompanied by a woman wearing what seems to be an expensive fur). We learn that politicians are big, thus powerful, men ('City fathers — Hoboken, New Jersey', in which a group of such men fill a political platform). We see these big, well-dressed men on the train between these two power centers. The stars in the lights above the bar recall the American flags, and their use and misuse in political and everyday settings, in other photographs in the book, and suggest that we are looking at the powerful at work in some unspecified way, probably one that will not do us any good. The image functions as part of Frank's analysis — implicit, but nonetheless clear — of how the American political system works.

If the analysis were made explicit, its complexity might well qualify it as a work of visual sociology. We would probably, in that case, want to know more about what we were seeing. Who are these people? What are they actually doing? But, more importantly, we would want to know more clearly what Frank was telling us about the nature of American politics. We would want to replace the nuance of the photographic treatment of American society, as many commentators have in fact done (Brumfeld, 1980; Cook, 1982, 1986), with an explicit statement about the nature of that society, its class and political structure, its age grading, its sexual stratification, and its use of such major symbols as the flag, the cross, and the automobile. Such an explicit statement of cultural patterns and social structure would make the image speak to the kind of abstract questions about the organization of society that interest professional sociologists.

Even then, it's not likely that many sociologists would accept Frank's book as a work of scientific sociology. They would assume, correctly, that photographs are easily manipulated; the sophisticated ones would know that you need not alter the actual image, just frame the elements properly and wait for an opportune moment. They would worry, properly, about using one image as a surrogate for a larger universe of similar situations. They would not be sure, and have warrant for their uneasiness, that the images have the meaning I am imputing. They would not, however, take the next step, which would be to see that every form of social science data has exactly these problems, and that none of the commonly accepted and widely used sociological methods solves them very well either.

Set on the front page of a daily newspaper, we might read the same photograph as a news photograph. But the people in it are not named, and newspapers seldom print photographs of anonymous people. Quite the contrary. Photojournalists are trained, until it is instinctive for them, to get names and other relevant information about the people they photograph (so a student in a course in photojournalism will be warned that a misspelled name will automatically lead to failure of the course). To function as a news photograph, the image would require a quite different caption than the one Frank gave it. For instance: 'Senator John Jones of Rhode Island discusses campaign strategy with two assistants.' But even then it's unlikely that the picture would appear in the daily newspaper, because it is grainy, not in sharp focus, and the two staff aides have their backs to us. The editor would send the photographer back for a more sharply focused image of such a routine event, one that was less grainy and showed us the faces of all three men.

In fact, many conventional photographers and critics complained about Frank's work in just the way this hypothetical editor would have. The editors of *Popular Photography*, for instance, didn't like Frank's book. These comments appeared in Vol. 46, no. 5 (May, 1960):

> Frank has managed to express, through the recalcitrant medium of photography, an intense personal vision, and that's nothing to carp at. But as to the nature of that vision I found its purity too often marred by spite, bitterness, and narrow prejudices just as so many of the prints are flawed by meaningless blur, grain, muddy exposure, drunken horizons, and general sloppiness. As a photographer, Frank shows contempt for any standards of quality or discipline in technique . . . (Arthur Goldsmith, quoted in Tucker and Brookman (1986), pp. 36–7)

And another critic said:

> It seems as if he merely points the camera in the direction he wishes to shoot and doesn't worry about exposure, composition, and lesser considerations. If you dig

out-of-focus pictures, intense and unnecessary grain, converging verticals, a total absence of normal composition, and a relaxed, snapshot quality, then Robert Frank is for you. If you don't, you may find The Americans one of the most irritating photo books to make the scene. (James M. Zanutto, quoted in Tucker and Brookman (1986), p. 37)

If, however, a photojournalist had made the picture during an exposé of political corruption, an editor might well excuse such 'technical' flaws because of the importance of what was revealed. In this case, the caption might read 'James McGillicuddy, Boston political boss, talking with Senator John Jones of Rhode Island, Chairman of the Senate Armed Forces Committee, and Harry Thompson, CEO of a major defence contracting firm'. The editor might make this the basis of a strong editorial and the Senator, like so many politicians accused of wrongdoing, might want to deny he was ever there.

In fact, at least one of Frank's photographs (made at the 1956 Democratic convention) might well, in the proper context, have appeared in a daily newspaper or newsmagazine as 'news'. The caption ('Convention hall — Chicago') characteristically names no one. Here we see the crowded floor of a political convention. Again, two men have their backs to us. On either side of them, two men face us. One, wearing dark glasses, looks suave and calm. The other, jowly, looks down worriedly. The faces of these two politicians were, at the time, recognizable, and their names might have given the picture 'news value'. The troubled looking gentleman was a sociologist (from whom I took a class at the University of Chicago, which is why I recognized him) who had left academia for politics: Joseph Lohman, a well-known criminologist who became Illinois Secretary of State, made an unsuccessful try for the Democratic gubernatorial nomination, and then left politics to become Dean of the School of Criminology at the University of California at Berkeley. At the time of the photograph he was still active in Illinois politics, seen as a 'good government' type in the Adlai Stevenson tradition. He is talking, I believe (but am not sure), to Carmine DeSapio, a major New York City political figure, in the old-fashioned party boss tradition. In the context of that convention, the image of their conversation might, by indicating an unlikely and therefore interesting potential political alliance, have been 'news'.

Reading a Sociological Picture as Journalism and as Documentary

Douglas Harper did his study of tramps as a work of sociology; the original dissertation relegated the photographs he had made to a 'Volume 2', where they had no captions. But the book he turned the thesis into, *Good Company* (1981) contained a large number of photographs, not as illustrations, the way photographs appear in sociology textbooks, but as elements integral to the sociological investigation and therefore to a reader's sociological understanding. They contain, and express, ideas that are sociological in their origin and use, and thus may not be as transparent to an immediate reading as other photographs. For instance, the photograph of a man shaving needs to be seen in context, as Harper points out, as evidence that refutes the common notion that these men are bums who don't take care of themselves and don't share conventional standards of decorum. As he says, when we see these men with a a two day growth of beard we should realize that this means that they shaved two days ago.

What makes these images visual sociology is not their content alone, but their context. They appear surrounded by a sociological text, although an unconventional one, which explains their import to us. One part of the text describes the way Carl, a tramp Harper met during his fieldwork, indoctrinated him into hobo culture. A second part describes, in analytic sociological language, that hobo culture, the characteristic forms of social organization hobos are involved in, and the conditions under which such adaptations grow up and persist. The text, both the narrative of Harper's training in how to live on the road and the later explicit sociological analysis, give the pictures added substance, sociological meaning, and evidentiary value.

Try reading these same images as photojournalism. Imagine them as illustrations for a newspaper's series on the fashionable topic of 'homelessness'. Read in that context, they would get their meaning, as photojournalistic images typically do, from the stock of easily available stereotypes daily newspaper readers carry with them. We probably would never see the man shaving because, for one thing, it's unlikely that any working photojournalist would want, or be able, to spend the months on the road that allowed Harper the ease of access and, more importantly, the background of knowledge that gave him the image's meaning. As famous a photojournalist as W. Eugene Smith, at the height of his career, still had to fight with Life repeatedly to get to spend as much as three weeks in one place.

In addition, an editor would probably say to the photographer who brought such pictures in, 'These don't say "homeless" to me.' Why don't they? Because editors know, or think they know, in advance of any investigation, what their story line is going to be. Whatever a story says about 'the problem' of homelessness will be well within what readers already know and believe. An appropriate photograph will rely, for its instant readability, on readers having that knowledge. For the editor, and therefore for the photographer, what 'homelessness' is has already been decided; they are not trying to find things about it they didn't know before. The only problem is technical: how to get the image that tells the already selected story best (see Hagaman, 1996 and Rudd, 1994).

Can we read Harper's photographs as documentary? Yes, we could see them, in Lewis Hine's classic phrase, as showing us what needs to be changed or, perhaps, the other half of Hine's famous remark, what needs to be appreciated. We might, in an appropriate setting of text and other photographs, see them as part of the effort of an aroused group of professionals to straighten out the lives of these men who wandered the country. Or we might, nearer to Harper's own intention, want to celebrate the independence and way of life of these men, in just the appreciative way David Matza (1969) described the Chicago School of Sociology appreciating what was ordinarily condemned. This celebratory mode of reading shares much with the common anthropological injunction to respect the people you study.

Reading a Journalistic Picture as Visual Sociology and as Documentary

Consider this picture.[2] We see a helicopter on a lawn, in the garden of what looks like the White House. A carpet runs from the building to the helicopter. A man, head down, shoulders hunched, walks along the carpet to the plane while, on either side, people stand weeping. People who were not old enough to be interested in politics in 1974 may not know what the image shows us, but it was then instantly recognizable to anyone reading the newspaper, anywhere in the world. Richard Nixon is leaving the White House, having just resigned the Presidency of the United States, his boast that he was not a crook belied by the continuing exposure of what he knew and when he knew it. In its day, it was a classic news photograph.

Shortly after its publication, it suffered the fate of all news photographs, which is that they are soon no longer news and have 'only historical' value. Their news value depends on context, on the event being contemporary, 'now'. In fact, the pathos and emotional impact of the Nixon image required every viewer who picked up the paper and saw it to furnish that context, to know the second they saw the picture exactly what they were looking at. The image summed up a story they had followed for months in the papers and on television, the gradual and seemingly inevitable downfall of a powerful political leader, toppled by his own lies and paranoia, finally succumbing to a combination of political and journalistic attacks.

Years later the image has no such connotations. It records an event which people who did not read newspapers and magazines at the time have possibly read or heard about. But it is not news, not the end point of a story whose dénouement was, until then, unknown and in doubt. It has to be something other than news. What else could it be?

In the proper context, news photographs of continuing interest become documentary, as Erich Salomon's photographs, made between the two World Wars, of such phenomena as the Versailles Peace Conference, have become documentary (Salomon, 1967). The politicians Salomon photographed — such luminaries of the time as Gustav Streseman and Aristide Briand — are no longer news. But we might combine the Nixon image — no longer news to us — with Salomon's photographs to create a generalized document of aspects of the political process. Others, more historically minded, might like to see the Nixon image embedded in a larger consideration of the Watergate events.

Could the Nixon image be part of a sociological analysis? An analyst might be concerned, as many have been, with the way the print media deal with the generic phenomenon of political scandal (Molotch and Lester, 1974) the way the devices of photographic representation are used to indicate the political downgrading of a disgraced leader. A good sociological analysis of this problem would require comparisons of photographs of Nixon at various stages of his career. Nixon would be an excellent subject for such an analysis because his career and reputation fluctuated so widely in such a relatively short time and the photographic representations could be expected to vary correspondingly.

Other analysts of political behaviour might concern themselves with the public rituals of societies, with the use of quasi-regal paraphernalia and events to create a sort of monarchical regime within a political democracy. Photographs of Nixon, in such a research, would be surrounded by other photographs of similar rituals and by texts which revealed other devices aimed at the same result.

Conclusion

Where does this leave us? Photographers worry about what they are doing, and hope to clear their confusion up by finding the right name for what they do. But 'word magic' is no more effective in solving photographic problems than it is anywhere else. Visual workers will find their legitimation in the response their work generates in viewers, whatever name that work goes by. They will find the direction for what they do in the particular circumstances of its doing, in the combination of organizations, audiences, and peers that surround them as they do the work.

For sociologists and other social scientists, these examples provide a warning against methodological purism, an illustration of the contextual nature of all efforts to understand social life. The same examples provide material for the continuing examination of ways of telling about society, whether through words, numbers, or pictures.

Notes

1   Treating art photographs as social science has its own hazards. We were unable to procure permission from either Mr Frank or his representative, Peter McGill of the Pace-McGill Gallery in New York, to reproduce any of the images I discuss here. I have tried to provide a description in the text that is sufficiently complete to allow readers to follow the analysis. It would be better, of course, to consult a copy of Frank's *The Americans* and have the image before you as you read.
2   I have not been able to find the image I describe here, but have found others sufficiently similar as not to mar the argument. I have taken the liberty of describing the 'perfect' image I remember.

References

ATGET, E. (1992) *Atget Paris*, Paris: Hazan.
BATESON, G. and MEAD, M. (1942) *Balinese Character*, New York: New York Academy of Sciences.
BECKER, H.S. (1982) *Art Worlds*, Berkeley: University of California Press.
BECKER, H.S. (1986) 'Telling about society', *Doing Things Together*, Evanston, IL: Northwestern University Press, pp. 121–35.
BECKER, K.E. (1985) 'Forming a profession: Ethical implications of photojournalistic practice on German picture magazines, 1926–33', *Studies in Visual Communication*, **11**, 2, pp. 44–60.
BRUMFIELD, J. (1980) '"The Americans" and The Americans', *Afterimage* (Summer), pp. 8 15.
CAPA, C. (ed.) (1968) *The Concerned Photographer*, New York: Grossman.
CHAPLIN, E. (1994) *Sociology and Visual Representation*, London: Routledge.
COLLIER, J.Jr. and COLLIER, M. (1986) *Visual Anthropology: Photography as a Research Method*, Albuquerque: University of New Mexico Press.
COOK, J. (1982) 'Robert Frank's America', *Afterimage* (March), pp. 9–14.
COOK, J. (1986) 'Robert Frank', *Exposure*, **24**, 1, pp. 31–41.
EPSTEIN, E.J. (1973) *News from Nowhere*, New York: Random House.
ERICSON, R., BARANEK, P.M. and CHAN, J.B.I. (1987) *Visualizing Deviance: A Study of News Organization*, Toronto: University of Toronto Press.
FRANK, R. (1955) *The Americans*, New York: Aperture.
GUTMAN, J.M. (1967) *Lewis W. Hine and the American Social Conscience*, New York: Walker and Company.
HAGAMAN, D. (1993) 'The joy of victory, the agony of defeat: Stereotypes in newspaper sports feature photographs', *Visual Sociology*, **8**, pp. 48–66.
HAGAMAN, D. (1995) 'Connecting cultures: Balinese character and the computer', in STAR, S.L. (ed.) *The Cultures of Computing*, Keele: The Sociological Review.
HAGAMAN, D. (1996) *How I Learned not to Be a Photojournalist*, Lexington: University Press of Kentucky.
HALL, S. (1973) 'The determination of news photographs', in COHEN, S. and YOUNG, J. (eds) *The Manufacture of News: A Reader*, Beverly Hills: Sage, pp. 176–90.
HARPER, D. (1981) *Good Company*, Chicago: University of Chicago Press.
HARPER, D. (1982) 'Visual sociology: Expanding sociological vision', *The American Sociologist*, **19**, 1, pp. 54–70.

HORAN, J. (1966) *Timothy O'Sullivan: America's Forgotten Photographer*, New York: Bonanza Books.

LATOUR, B. (1986) 'Visualization and cognition: Thinking with eyes and hands', *Knowledge and Society*, **6**, pp. 1–40.

LYON, D. (1968) *The Bikeriders*, New York: MacMillan.

MATZA, D. (1969) *Becoming Deviant*, Englewood Cliffs, N.J.: Prentice-Hall.

MEISALAS, S. (1976) *Carnival Strippers*, New York: Farrar, Straus, and Giroux.

MOLOTCH, H. and LESTER, M. (1974) 'News as purposive behavior: On the strategic use of routine events, accidents, and scandals', *American Sociological Review*, **39**, pp. 101–12.

NEWHALL, B. (1964) *The History of Photography*, New York: Museum of Modern Art.

REID, R.L. and VISKOCHIL, L.A. (eds) (1989) *Chicago and Downstate: Illinois as Seen by the Farm Security Administration Photographers, 1936–43*, Chicago and Urbana: Chicago Historical Society and University of Illinois Press.

RIIS, J. (1971 [1901]) *How the Other Half Lives*, New York: Dover.

RUDD, J. (1994) 'Picture possibilities: An ethnographic study of newspaper photojournalism', M.A. thesis, Department of Sociology, University of Washington.

SALOMON, E. (1967) *Portrait of an Age*, Collier Books: New York.

SANDER, A. (1986) *Citizens of the Twentieth Century*, Cambridge: The MIT Press.

SCHUDSON, M. (1978) *Discovering the News*, New York: Basic Books.

STASZ, C. (1979) 'The early history of visual sociology', in WAGNER, *Images of Information: Still Photography in the Social Sciences*, Beverly Hills: Sage, pp. 119–36.

TUCHMAN, G. (1978) *Making News*, New York: Free Press.

TUCKER, A.W. and BROOKMAN, P. (eds) (1986) *Robert Frank: New York to Nova Scotia*, Boston: Little Brown.

WAGNER, J. (ed.) (1979) *Images of Information: Still Photography in the Social Sciences*, Beverly Hills: Sage.

Chapter 7

The Status of Image-based Research

Jon Prosser

Abstract

Image-based Research plays a relatively minor role in qualitative research. This chapter begins by asking what informs qualitative researchers' views on Image-based Research? The remaining sections briefly explore historical reasons for the limited status of Image-based Research and methodological concerns of 'orthodox' word-orientated researchers. The central theme is understanding *why* Image-based Research has limited status. Ways of overcoming limited status are not considered.

Introduction

Social research, for nearly 100 years, endeavoured to establish its research credentials by adopting an objective or 'scientific' approach that, to a significant degree, has indirectly marginalized Image-based Research. This marginalization is further compounded by an academic community working within the qualitative paradigm who have devised a methodology which places emphasis on words, limiting the role played by images. I believe that the status of Image-based Research relative to word-based research is disproportionately low. This belief is based on two fundamental assumptions which underpin the *polemic* that follows: Image-based Research is

1   undervalued and under applied by the orthodox qualitative research community; and
2   that it can make a proportionately greater contribution to research.

The territory covered in this chapter is considerable and hence significant topics are missed or treated superficially. The aim is to identify issues common to Image-based Research and not necessarily to cover in depth how different types of this generic group respond to limited status. I recognize and acknowledge that naive universalism, *à priori* assumptions, and notions of commonality, are barriers to generating knowledge in all Image-based Research and that visual anthropologists, visual sociologists, visual ethnographers, and visual documentarists etc. will find their own solutions to the problem of limited status. What follows may seem rather assertive but this too is purposeful since the object is to stimulate debate and encourage others to react to ideas put forward.

The issue of the poor relative status of Image-based Research — an issue not on the agenda of word-orientated researchers — is widely recognized and acknowledged by those who work in film, video, photographs, cartoons, signs, symbols and drawings. How did I come to be aware of the obvious? In the 1980s I was involved in a study of how child abuse is investigated. Although I had been interested in photography and film for some time my interest in visual aspects of research was triggered when during one case an investigator decided that a small drawing of a bunch of flowers by the alleged perpetrator was indicative of ritualistic abuse. My academic training was incompatible with the need to understand others visual creations — videos, photographs, drawings, signs, symbols and drawings — and the meanings applied to these by significant others (and I suggest this is not uncommon). My study of child abuse investigation would have been enriched if I had been able to draw on an image-based methodology. However, I hold fast to that temporal state of naiveté, and I can distinctly remember on turning to classical qualitative methodological literature at the time for initial guidance on the conduct and application of image-based approach being spectacularly disappointed. The impression I gained from mainstream methodological texts was that images were a pleasant distraction to the real (i.e., word-orientated) work that constituted 'proper' research.

An arbitrary selection of ethnographic textbooks on library shelves today, probed simply for their film and photographic content, suggests that the status of images is low and that normative methodological textbooks give little credence to Image-based Research: Agar (1986) in *Speaking Ethnographically* contains no images and does not discuss photography or film; Fetterman (1989) in *Ethnography: Step by Step* includes two photographs and 3.2 per cent of the content is given over to a discussion of photography or film; Ellen (1984) in *Ethnographic Research* has no images and 0.6 per cent of the content is given over to image discussion; Stocking (1992) in *The Ethnographer's Magic* uses seventeen photographs and 0.1 per cent of the content is given over to a discussion of photographs or film; Clifford (1988) in *The Predicament of Culture* uses three photographs and 0.8 per cent of the content is given over to images; and Hammersley and Atkinson (1987) in *Ethnography: Principles in Practice* has no images and give just over 1 per cent of their content to a discussion of photographs or film.

If the above simple content analysis of textbooks is indicative of the status of Image-based Research relative to word-orientated traditional qualitative research then the *manner* images are used and the *tone* by which they are discussed is even more illuminating. In terms of *manner* the range of images used is very restrictive being almost always either line drawings or black and white photographs. In addition the photographs are used predominantly merely to illustrate what the author, high status researchers, or the object of research look like and are almost inevitably of the 'individual' or 'group portrait' genre being in a frontal standing or sitting mode.

A common theme in general methodological textbooks appears to be an enthusiasm to describe the drawbacks and limitations of using images in a qualitative enquiry and an unwillingness to celebrate their strengths. Silverman (1993) for example, a respected UK methodologist who in past work has shown support in principal for image-based work, begins 'Images are another neglected source of data for field research' before stating 'The analysis of images raises complex methodological and theoretical issues . . . Moreover, the theoretical basis for the analysis of images is complex.' The *tone* of texts also contain a common thread in that they suggest that: the act of image making (in photographic and filmic terms of aiming, framing, manipulating light and camera angle etc.) unacceptably alters the object in the frame and therefore objective content and subjective meaning of the image; images are, by their nature, ambiguous and do not in themselves convey meanings which are supplied serendipitaly by those who perceive them; contextual and reflexive data which are central to the interpretation of images is insufficiently presented; and analysis of images raises complex methodological and theoretical issues. The general message, perhaps unwittingly, is that: films, videos and photographs are acceptable only as means to record data or as illustration and subservient to that of the central narrative; they are unacceptable as a way of 'knowing' because they distort that which they claim to illuminate; and images being socially created and mediated are skewed by the socio-context of 'making', 'taking' and 'reading'; and summatively images are so complex that analysis is untenable. There is little attempt to point to solutions to these issues or identify parallel problems within word-orientated research. Even taking into account that the above textbook sample is haphazard the implication is that images should play only a minor role, or very occasionally a supporting role (for example as a way of collecting and recording data) but only very rarely as evidence or to represent findings in mainstream qualitative research.

The tenuous relationship between traditional (mainstream) ways of working and image-based researchers' working practices, will be experienced differentially and relative to the myriad contexts in which the latter work. It is probable, for example, that North American researchers who use images are more able than others around the globe to create and maintain their own academic community which is sufficiently robust to support journals and special interest groups within esteemed research associations. In addition to 'cushioning' the influence of limited status, this provides for a comparatively rich intellectual climate relative to other image-based researchers around the world. However, the remainder of this chapter will focus on the context of academic disciplines rather than a geographical context, whilst recognizing that this will provide only a partial and particular insight into reasons that underpin the limited status of Image-based Research. I will contrast anthropology with sociology and consider their relationship to their subdisciplines 'visual anthropology' and 'visual sociology', and consider the relationship between the subdisciplines.

What Informs Qualitative Researchers' Views on Image-based Research?

Image-based researchers are aware of their limited status not because of the quality of their work nor especially the focus of their work but because of the nature of their work. There is a recognition by workers from different disciplines that the parameters of those limitations are in part determined by the academic disciplines in which they work:

> Visual anthropology has never been completely incorporated into the mainstream of anthropology. It is trivialised by some anthropologists as being mainly concerned with audio-visual aids for teaching. The anthropological establishment has yet to acknowledge the centrality of the mass media in the formation of cultural identity in the second half of the twentieth century. Consequently, visual anthropologists sometimes find themselves involved with the research and thinking of professional image makers and scholars from other disciplines — visual sociology, cultural studies, film theory, photo-history, dance and performance studies, and architectural theory — rather than work with other cultural anthropologists. (Ruby, 1996, p. 1345)

> Even though most sociologists are sighted, even though much sociology depends upon observation, sociology has not derived from, nor has it reflected a visual

record of the world . . . For many of us this has been unsatisfactory. Sociology we believed ought to include a new kind of epistemology, based on knowledge represented in imagery rather than words. (Harper, 1996, p. 69)

Sociologists behave as though they were sightless. The visual is repressed by the verbal . . . should sociologists be wedded to the written word? (Chaplin, 1994)

The limited acceptance of Image-based Research can be traced back to the epistemological roots of the various academic disciplines. The two basic strands are recognized as 'quantitative' and 'qualitative'. Quantitative has its roots in the works of Compte and particularly Durkheim and his work on causal relationships; qualitative has its beginnings in the work of Weber and of understanding social or human problems based on building a complex interpretative and holistic picture of a multi-layered social world. The lack of status of images appears to have its roots in

1   the continuing influence of quantitative epistemology and an empiricist view of science on qualitative research; and perhaps consequentially
2   the qualitative paradigm uses words or occasionally numbers and only very rarely images except as a representation of words and numbers.

Historical Influences

In this section I want to briefly consider the evolution of visual anthropology and visual sociology relative to their parent disciplines in order to identify some of the similarities and differences between them.

Anthropology and sociology were founded about the same time as the earliest photographic processes were being developed. Although photographs were used in early sociological journals (Stasz, 1979) visual sociology did not emerge as a substantive subdiscipline until the late 1960s (Harper, 1989). Visual anthropology can claim to have its beginnings in the nineteenth century but changed its form according to methodological trends and fieldwork practice. Early anthropologists were often armchair theorists. Sir James Frazer, for example, an eminent eighteenth-century British anthropologist, never conducted fieldwork himself yet was able to produce studies, based on notes and images brought back by travellers, that were viewed positively by academics of the time (Pinney, Wright and Poignant, 1996). Early anthropologists also used photographs as a record of peoples' physical characteristics, their built environment, rituals and artefacts, within a 'scientific' framework (Edwards, 1992). Sociologists at the turn of the century, on the other hand, used photographs as visual documentaries or as 'reportage' of people's lives and living conditions (Riis, 1971; Hine, 1932).

Towards the end of the nineteenth century the distinction between armchair anthropologist and traveller with a notebook had diminished. Subsequently a 'fieldwork' tradition became prominent and by about 1920 the photograph had lost its hold as a prime source of data. Technology and methodology made an impact early on in the twentieth century and visual anthropology adapted and evolved, carving out a niche for itself, whereas visual sociology disappeared from the intellectual 'map'. Sociologists drew on the refined fieldwork practices of anthropology. In the 1920s and 1930s sociologists (the Chicago School) adopted ethnographic practice and a 'participant observer' role became commonplace. This could have been an important period for visual sociology but was not (this will be discussed later).

Visual records as part of anthropological field diaries were much more in evidence than in the sociological equivalent. From 1900 to the present day it is clear that even a basic visual approach to research has been more central in anthropology (as 'accurate' records of the exotic, to capture fast disappearing native rituals, the capacity to return from far off places with data that could be leisurely perused, and to 'tell a story') than in sociology (visual sociology emerged as a subdiscipline around 1970). Indeed, it could be said that the sociological images early in this period damaged any hope of academic integrity because Riis and Hine were seen by many as 'muck-raking' Stasz (1979, p. 134). Equally, it is possible that documentary photographers of this period (themselves lacking a methodological framework) where associated with photojournalists by orthodox sociologists thereby tainting, by association, visual sociology in the eyes of orthodox researchers.

There have been important milestones for visual anthropology and visual sociology. One such milestone was the considered and rigorous use of photography by anthropologists Bateson and Mead (1942). In producing *Balinese Character* they demonstrated the potential of Image-based Research to the wider research community by combining a carefully argued analytical framework, and a credible research design, photographs and words. That the study is so often referred to in the literature is testimony enough to its significance. One would have thought that the combination of a 'ground-breaking' study conducted by two authoritative (and traditional) figures in the parent discipline would enhance the case for an image-based approach but this was not the case. Becker (1974) a major figure in orthodox sociology, played a similar role by establishing guidelines for a visual sociology within the sociological discipline but again an upsurge of interest from word-oriented researchers was not forthcoming. Becker's legacy is not so much that he inspired others (which he did) but that he produced a 'legacy' of ideas that underpin present visual sociology and which can be drawn upon by future visual sociologists.

The Society for the Anthropology of Visual Communication provided many significant studies using film and photographs. Worth and Adair (1972), for example, produced the well-known *Through Navajo Eyes*, instructing the Navajo in the mechanics of camera operation not on what constituted a 'proper' film of their culture. This cross-cultural project was creative and experimental but again did not have the impact one would have expected.[1] The sum of these works in terms of their influence on mainstream disciplines is disappointing, suggesting that although key methodological models have been devised and major personalities have played a role in potentially enhancing the status of Image-based Research, other, more significant forces, have been in place which have undercut their endeavours.

Present day Image-based Research theory is changing rapidly. There have also been significant developments in the storage, accessing (for example, the Haddon project at Oxford University) and interpretation of historical images (see, for example, Ruby, 1988; and Scherer, 1990) and the work of individuals who have contributed to the visual. In addition, photographs and other media of visual anthropology have mostly been superseded by film as *the modus operandi* of present day researchers (but see Banks and Morphy, 1997). Contemporary visual sociologists, on the other hand, despite retaining an affinity for documentary and illustrative photographs, are drawing on a wider range of visual media including film, video, cartoons and drawings and encompass a wider range of topics.

Over the past two decades, there has been a move by critical and interpretative visual anthropologists, visual ethnographers, and visual sociologists, to reflexively *engage* with those they study. This initially emerged out of classical criticism of Image-based Research and the need to take account of procedural and personal reactivity but expanded and diversified as critical theory, postcolonial and cultural studies gained momentum across a range of disciplines. There has been an increase in types of documentary films (mostly without an underpinning theory) possibly out of the belief that they are moving closer to legitimating their claim on reality. A more substantive trend among both visual sociologists and visual anthropologists over the last twenty years has been the need to take into account of the way images are contextually bound and mediated by socio-cultural settings. I believe there remain problematic aspects of visual anthropology and visual sociology: many anthropological films, whilst refined in terms of filmic strategies are overly concerned with content and lacking in concern for representation or reflexivity; on the other hand visual sociology lacks an overarching, cohesive, theoretical and methodological framework (although in the past Harper, and latterly Grady, 1996, have provided incisive overviews).

Within and across visual anthropology and visual sociology there is a hierarchy of credibility in terms of methodology and visual media. Both subdisciplines believe they should play a more central role in their respective disciplines, but both also need to attend to the problems of an evolving methodology. Solutions to important long-running problems in Image-based Research such as the theoretical divide between 'formalist' and realist' theory (Ruby, 1980) bridging the gap between critical theory and empirical research, and providing encompassing yet penetrative theoretical frameworks of visual communication (although important texts exist such as Tomaselli's *Appropriating Images*, 1996).

Traditional Methodological Arguments against Image-based Research

Contemporary orthodox qualitative researchers are very limited in what they count as an acceptable use of images. For them an image is useful: as a way of breaking the boredom of the written text; as illustration of an object, place, person or event that are fully (and 'more properly') explained by language or via traditional visuals namely tables, graphs and diagrams; and as a 'record' (for as Berger, 1978, p. 51 explains, 'Photographs preserve instant appearances') allowing the researcher the luxury of post event viewing and reviewing. These applications which mirror the beliefs of many researchers in social research, have their place in the research process, but are narrow, limited, and do not do justice to the full potential of images.

Generally speaking, in the past, anthropologists and sociologists have seen their visual colleagues as working peripherally to mainstream academia. This perception is slowly changing and there is a growing interest in 'visual' aspects of research. There remains a strong belief that to include images would serve to undermine social research as a science. Ruby (1996) states a key argument for visual anthropology playing a more central role in anthropology (this argument could equally apply to visual sociology):

> Anthropology is a word-driven discipline. It has tended to ignore the visual-pictorial world perhaps because of distrust of the ability of images to convey abstract ideas. When engaged in ethnography, the researcher must convert the complex experience of fieldwork to words in a notebook and then transform those words onto other

words shifted through analytic methods and theories. This logocentric approach to understanding denies much of the multisensory experience of trying to know another culture. The promise of visual anthropology is that it might provide an alternative way of perceiving culture-perception constructed through the lens. (Ruby, 1996, p. 1351)

What are the reasons for a narrow and limited take-up of images by traditional 'word' orientated research? Alfred Shultz (1964) reminds us that academics are trammelled by history and, like most people, each:

. . . Accepts the ready-made standardised scheme of pattern handed down to him by ancestors, teachers and authors as an unquestioned and unquestionable guide in all the situations that normally occur within the social world. (Shultz, 1964, p. 238)

This raises the question of to what extent historical factors have played a part in determining status of visual subdisciplines. An ongoing and evolving relationship between anthropology and visual anthropology means that the latter has a relatively close relationship to the former. Even in within a scientific framework anthropologists have used images (for example photographs for anthropometrical studies). Visual sociology, on the other hand does not have such a 'cosy' relationship. Harper (1989) in an historical analysis, provides a sound explanation why this is the case:

Sociology . . . found little place for a visual approach. It is fair to say that from the 1920s to the 1960s there was no visual sociology. One can ponder the reasons for such a complete rejection of an information-gathering technology during a discipline's formative years. I think that there are several reasons. The field research tradition developed at the University of Chicago did not include photographic methods, this I believe, cast the original definition of a major methodology in terms of excluding a meaningful visual component. In addition, by the post world war era, survey methods and other approaches that distanced the researcher from the subject, had come to dominate American sociology. The research program of sociology became the examination of statistical patterns among variables rather than the description of social life woven so convincingly into the earlier community studies and fieldwork traditions. With the growing importance of photojournalism, particularly during the 1930s, sociologists appeared to relegate photography to the lesser status of mass communication. Indeed it is impossible to know how the sociologists of the day viewed the medium; there is simply little, if any mention of it. (Harper, 1989, pp. 85–6)

It is odd that Robert E. Park, a 'concerned' journalist by profession interested in social change (see Becker, Chapter 6), and a founding member of the Chicago School, did not foresee the potential of photojournalism in the newly evolving qualitative tradition. It is reported that Park became interested developing a qualitative approach following a particular event:

. . . he was walking through the Polish ghetto one day, he pulled back to avoid being struck by garbage hurled from a window. He saw a pack of letters in the pile and, since he could read Polish, he looked through them. He found an insider's perspective on immigrant life. (Bogban and Biklen, 1982, p. 10)

What a pity for visual sociology that a family photographic album was not thrown out of the window instead of pile of letters. What if he had used the family album as an interview device to explore their specific contexts and their meanings to the immigrant family? Would Park have made visuals more central to the paradigm that emerged from Chicago? Of course this is a whimsical notion. Forces greater than one individual shaped the Chicago school of thought and besides the sum of ones autobiography is greater than any individual act.

The points made by Ruby and Harper provide a historical explanation for the relatively limited status of Image-based Research which were translated into methodological reasons by orthodox researchers. Perhaps *the* main publicly stated methodological argument against Image-based Research by other researchers, is with images' perceived lack of 'trustworthiness' (see Chapter 4). This is judged by orthodox researchers, despite new paradigm trends, in such terms as 'objectivity/subjectivity', 'reliability/validity', 'reflexivity' and 'interpretation'. There is insufficient space here to discuss the relationship between methodological concerns of orthodox qualitative research and the approaches taken by Image-based Research. Instead I will briefly unpack some of the more pragmatic aspects of 'reflexivity' and relate these to Image-based Research.

Reflexivity

Validity in sociological and anthropological field studies has been focused essentially on methods rather than on people and human processes; hence the emphasis on multiple methods as way of overcoming the limitations of a single method rather than the *relationship* between what is to be known and the knower. This construct and application of validity is now seen by many to be limited if not inadequate for human enquiry, particularly studies of culture which are better supported by notions of validity based on an interactive, dialectical, collaborative logic. However, it is the discussion of 'contextual validity' — the contexts of 'making' and 'interpreting' images that orthodox researchers find difficult to attach credence in visual research.

Judgments and claims of contextual validity are best made essentially via *reflexive accounts* but also through *representation*. Reflexive accounts attempt to render explicit the process by which data and findings were produced. Representation for image-based researchers, reflects not only the sources of information in terms of pictorial codes but also the mode of communicating findings to recipients of research (Chaplin, 1994, p. 1). However, there are two major methodological arguments used against image-based research.

1   Traditional researchers often state that film and photography in the form of naturalistic enquiry are problematic (if not impossible) due to problems arising out of *procedural reactivity* (arising from the very issue of procedures themselves, irrespective of the researcher). The most often cited example of procedural reactivity is also the most obvious — because cameras, equipment and the act of 'shooting' etc. make the researcher more 'visible' thereby damaging rapport and inhibiting participant's everyday behaviour and activities;

2   There are also deep reservations about access to the research site because of *personal reactivity* (the impact of idiosyncratic behaviour and personal characteristics of the researcher on the findings). In addition there is an implicit concern

that the image-based researcher is insufficiently *self-conscious* since the act of creating an image requires a combination personal awareness of knowledge selection (as a basis for making decisions) technical, and artistic judgments.

Orthodox researchers perceive the complexity of this combination as a barrier to a filmic or photographic approach. Moreover, they suggest that summatively these problems make for intellectually 'thin' research and which methodologically under theorized, whereas written research is seen as intellectually 'rich' and methodologically refined.

Orthodox researchers have a valid point with regard to reflexivity where anthropological films are concerned. Reflexive accounts are not a strong feature of anthropological and visual anthropological studies despite encouragement by early theoretical protagonists such as Malinowski (1922).[2] It is clear that until recently anthropological film has been insufficiently reflexive or integrated (usually reflexive accounts, where they do exist, are provided as an adjunct to the film) that are acceptable to orthodox researchers (see Ruby, 1980). Even where a reflexive account is provided these have been partial and have not encompassed reflexivity in a broad sense. Let us consider *The Ax Fight* (1975) as an example of this. Anthropological films are often a collaboration between a filmmaker and an anthropologist.[3] *The Ax Fight* is the work of Napoleon Chagnon (an anthropologist) and Timothy Asch (an ethnographic filmmaker).[4] The film uses voice-overs and sections edited in strategically different ways to explore alternative ways of considering filmic evidence of a fight among the Yanomamo of southern Venezuela. Whilst the film is concerned with reflexivity of 'process' it misses out on the potential reflexive insights of discussing the triangulation of inter-personal reactivity (i.e., between Chagnon and Asch and the Yanomamo) which is generic to all such collaborations. There may be good reasons for this. The reflexivity was post event, which is problematic itself (see Latour, 1988) perhaps because Asch only had time to pick up his camera, rush to the site of the fight and start filming (see Chapter 4). It would have been interesting to know more about their relative values, theories, techniques, relative power status, and their capacity to relate to the Yanamomo (it is known, for example, that Asch felt he was anthropologically and linguistically ill prepared and lacked the skills for cross-cultural film-making: Asch, 1979). An understanding of their personal and intellectual relationship may have provided an insight into notions of the 'science' and 'art' of anthropological film, and, more importantly, with the interactive aspects of the research process for as Usher (1993) explains:

> . . . reflexive understanding which is always potentially present in doing research is not primarily the gaining of an awareness of one's subjectivity, one's personality, temperament, values and standpoints. The desire that structures research is not the produce of a psychology which is made 'public' through honest introspection. Rather it is the effect of the sociality and the inscription of self in social practices, language and discourses which constitute the research process. (Usher, 1993, p. 9)

Trustworthiness of visual sociological studies is equally problematic for orthodox researchers. Documentary film (for example the work of Dziga Vertov) has demonstrated greater interest in reflexivity than anthropological film (see Ruby, 1977).[5] Nonetheless, even in the case of a reflexive documentary account traditional researchers will find fundamental faults since there is widely held belief that 'reality' is distorted by artistic convention and for artistic reasons. This argument is also applied to all forms of the realist mode of communication including the 'photographic essay' and 'documentary photography'.

Because visual sociologists work mostly with still rather than moving images additional reflexive problems arise. Contextual validity is easier to achieve in film than in still images because potentially they contain continuity, movement, and contextual speech, whereas the photograph, for example, may contain a single transitory one sixtieth of a second worth of information. Since visual sociologists work mainly with photographs, cartoons, drawings, symbols or signs, there is a recognition that support for the relative trustworthiness is best achieved via multiple images in conjunction with words. There are few good examples of reflexive visual sociology that are sufficient to pacify traditional sociologists. In his study of tramps Harper (1982) successfully adopted an often-attempted strategy. He used fifty-two strong yet what appear to purposefully ambiguous photographs in a way that allows the 'reader' to provide a meaning and then juxtaposing these with written information allowing for a second 'alternative' reading, yet without supplying a definitive answer. The lack of direction by the producer of the images and the text, combined with a sufficiency of appropriate information, allow for multi-level interpretation at a distance. Harper (1987) also provides a second good example of a responsive and reflexive visual ethnography in his case study of 'Willie'. He emphasizes personal reactivity rather than procedural reactivity in his methodological discussion; his description of his relationship with Willie is empathetic with a hint of what could be called postmodern in that it is collaborative; and he makes insightful and informative self-reflective remarks airing the dilemma of acting either from a formal social scientist stance or an artistic/aesthetic stance that is part and parcel of being a visual sociologist. What is more Harper covers much reflexive ground with minimal narration — hence the avoidance of 'navel gazing'.

Researchers Do Not Live in a Vacuum

So far I have considered influences stemming from orthodox researchers' professional lives. Researchers are as much part of the social world as other people and absorb communication innovations, new fashions, political trends, economic shifts, and marketing ploys that are part of evolving cultures. The absorption of this 'wider culture' impacts on and influences academics' thinking as it does on others in the community. Consider, for example, the case of 'communication'. There is a belief that the cause of Image-based Research will be aided by the communication revolution — innovations such as multimedia, video conferencing, computer super highways, multi-channel/terrestrial television etc. I have argued elsewhere that this may not be the case:

> . . . image-based researchers and image makers underestimate the increase in text, statistics, interviews, debates and, most importantly, the influence of social organisation and market forces that permeate our society. This means that language, spoken and written will remain pre-eminent. Whilst it can be argued that television, video, computers and film are omnipresent and manifestations of changes in the presentation of data, researchers with a visual concern over-estimate such influence on and within social research. (Prosser, 1996, p. 25)

Furthermore, whereas some aspects of the new communication such as World Wide Web sites may make positive contributions to the acceptance of Image-based Research, other aspects of the revolution may work against that acceptance. Let us briefly reflect on how, for example, a rapidly growing information system — UK television — may act on orthodox anthropologists.

Consider the scenario of a tired orthodox anthropologist flopping in front of the TV to watch an 'ethnographic' film after a hard day at the 'office'. They sit and watch still wearing their professional 'hats' and 'reading' a visual representation of a subject they themselves use words to report on. The film will not have a detailed methodological explanation, provide evidence in the form of quotes, documents, structured observation, or numerical data, and even its context will most likely be hidden, sitting implicitly within the visual presentation itself. Perhaps our tired anthropologist will come away with view similar to that of Professor Bloch's (a professor at the top of the academic 'tree' in the UK, described by Marcus Banks, 1994, p. 24): 'I think there is great scope for anthropology on television, but for a *discursive* intellectual form of anthropology.' This comment tentatively implies that ethnographic films made for TV have the normative intrinsic value of a *found object* and is of discursive value only. This may be the case but it is *a* case and such a view precludes the possibility, for example, that there is a distinction between an ethnographic film made for mass consumption minimally supported by either research or anthropologists, and an ethnographic film made by a collaboration between an anthropologist and a film-maker based upon a structured investigation which is shown on television. If our 'flopped' academic was watching the former type of film and was a historian, sociologist or a non-visual anthropologist and unaware of visual anthropologist's constructive critique of UK films (Loizos, 1980; Henley, 1985; Banks, 1994) they may well argue that 'televised ethnographic film reflects a hankering after imperialistic hegemony, translated as it were through consumerist visual presentation' (Banks, 1994, p. 39).

However, informed interpretation of this medium should not be partisan. Clearly there is a need to balance the potential contribution of ethnographic film to anthropological knowledge with their drawbacks and potential dangers as Banks (1994) explains:

> Above all, anthropologists must be wary of succumbing to the spirit of the age, the market place ethic, which sees the transition of TV ethnography as good because it attracts more students into our departments, which makes us consumers of culture, our jaded palates titillated by the display of world cultures on sale in television's supermarket. (Banks, 1994, p. 40)

Alas, unlike Banks, our 'flopped' orthodox anthropologist will probably only take away from a night's viewing the inadequacies of a television documentary, of the exotic masquerading as an ethnographic film. A naive 'reader', unable to distinguish the strengths and weaknesses of different forms of ethnographic film on television, like that of a naive reader of anthropological text, may take away a limited, partial and possibly inadequate interpretation. My concern is that Professor Bloch's view is representative of the majority of orthodox social scientists who do not see 'film' as an acceptable medium for the representation or transition of academic knowledge and, what is more, their beliefs are confirmed by television ethnography. He will see ethnographic film as entertainment and 'opposite of what one tries to do in anthropology' (Houtman, 1988, p. 20). Until orthodox anthropologists are able to differentiate between documentary films of the exotic made for television and ethnographic films produced by, or in collaboration with anthropologists (see Ruby, 1975), or until visual anthropologists improve in terms of representation, little growth in the status of visual anthropology with be achieved via this medium.

Contemporary documentary films can be viewed as: the quintessential postmodernist media — in that they attempt to depict reality, they champion relativism, and place little store in objective standards of truth; equally, and this can be said of the 'fly-on-the-wall' documentary genre, they are influenced by standards dictated by television, its audience and programme controllers (and the need for spectacle) which brings into question their status as 'research'. Hence, the television documentary (similarly the television ethnography) may been damaging to visual sociology by their content, format and historical association.[6] Too many contemporary television documentaries will undermine the case for film as an informed documentary because they usually attempt, like some present day sociology and autobiography, to demonstrate that things are anything but what they appear to be — and the more shocking and revelatory the better. In the UK at least they have lost their 'trustworthiness factor' among the populous and academia.

Winston (1995) in his cleverly titled book *Claiming the Real*, in examining the principles, ethics, epistemology and practices of documentary work, offers an important insight into the essential differences between film as documentary, and the documentary as fiction. However, what is apparent to the casual observer, and I caste the orthodox researcher in this mould, television documentaries are about audience sizes not serious epistemological principles. It appears to most who watch too much television that the 'fly-on-the-wall' documentary has escaped reality and flown off into a sunset of the Hollywood sort.

Both the television ethnographic film and the documentary film serve mainly to confirm the prejudices of non image-based researchers and consequently undermine the acceptance of Image-based Research in the eyes of the intellectual 'establishment'. I wonder what other influences, apart from images in the mass media, are acting on anthropologists and sociologists in their everyday lives, and either supporting or negating the case for Image-based Research? One obvious possibility is that whilst a few academic journals do not question (within reason) the number of images (for example *Visual Sociology*) the majority of journals limit or suppress the number of images on economic grounds. Journals, if they are designed for the World Wide Web rather than for a traditional hard copy format, may overcome this problem.

Conclusion

I have contended that Image-based Research has limited status. That limited status is illustrated by lack of penetrative discussion of Image-based Research in mainstream methodological textbooks (although there are other indicators such as the paucity of teaching visual research).[7] There are convincing arguments for claiming that for historical reasons Image-based Research has a disproportionately low status.

Thoughts at this point naturally turn to considering ways of improving the status of Image-based Research. There are no political moves, no general strategies, no overarching methodology, that will alter that status. Visual anthropologists and visual sociologists will follow their separate courses in an attempt to evoke increased status: visual anthropologists, because of their close affinity with their anthropology, will choose to work within their parent discipline;[8] visual sociologists, aware of substantial differences with their parent discipline may choose to ally themselves with evolving disciplines such as cultural studies or new methodologies. Neither strategy will resolve the problem of limited status whose root cause is *fragmentation*. Despite a large and growing body of visual researchers they have no single 'voice' because they are compartmentalized and divided by their disciplines, the media in which they work, and by a changing intellectual landscape. There is no *Gestalt*, no totality that encompasses and unifies Image-based Research other than the 'visual'.

Fragmentation in Image-based Research works on two basic levels: On one level there is a substantial and growing body of image-based researchers many of whom work in very particular fields and on very isolated topics. They do not associate with other major visually orientated disciplines. The second level of fragmentation occurs within the major subdisciplines of visual sociology and visual anthropology. Visual sociologists comprise of broad and eclectic groups of workers who have tenuous methodological links. Even within visual anthropology there are various models whose thinking centres around modes of production being either 'filmic anthropology' (includes various modes of filmmaking), or 'image-based anthropology' (encompassing film, video, and photographs), or modes of interpretation being 'semiotic anthropology' (semiotics and communication theory).

Although there is a significant body of active image-based researchers working within the qualitative paradigm, because they are fragmented they do not constitute a 'collective'. Image-based researchers do not see themselves, and neither do orthodox researchers, as a 'collective'. As a result image-based researchers have no 'voice' sufficient to have an impact on orthodox qualitative research. Fragmentation is not necessarily bad for research but it is rife and part of the shifting landscape of contemporary qualitative research. The one unifying theme of Image-based Research is the belief that research should be more visual. Walker (1994) speculates:

> A question that intrigues me is how we might stand outside of our own use of language, even if only for a moment during the research process, to catch ourselves unawares. The fact that this is probably an impossible achievement does not diminish its attraction as an inspiration. How can we use language as a basis from which to develop a degree of reflexivity about our use of language? One possibility is to find forms of communication that offer the possibility of triangulation on the use of language itself. I believe that still photographs hold this promise. (Walker, 1994, p. 73)

This idealistic notion is a wolf in sheep's clothing for if it were enacted in principle it would strike at the heart of relativist sociology. It is asking qualitative researchers to act reflexively by perceiving visually and that would alter the status of the visual. The question remains — if we believe that Image-based Research is undervalued by the orthodox qualitative research community and that it can make a proportionately greater contribution to research, how is this to be achieved?[9]

Notes

1   There is a growing interest in 'backward mapping', to revisit significant works of the past. A new edition of *Through Navajo Eyes*, published by the University of New Mexico Press, appeared in June 1997, with additional commentary, a new forward, afterword and illustrations by Richard Chalfen. In addition some of Sol Worth's writing can be found at http://www.temple.edu/anthro/worth.html

2   There is disagreement on the extent to which Malinowski was reflexive (see Woolgar, 1988; Latour, 1988).
3   Collaborations between anthropologists and filmmakers are problematic perhaps due to a conflict of interests and knowledge. Collaborations appear to be more successful in the UK than in the USA.
4   Asch was a filmmaker interested in ethnographic description. He had studied anthropology with Mead but this knowledge played a minor role in his films (see Ruby, 1995).
5   From the early 1920s Vertov was producing reflexively innovative films of which *The Man with the Movie Camera* is the most referenced work.
6   Early sociological journals and books used photographs as illustrations and to stimulate readers' awareness for the 'ills of society'. But this form of documentary work is probably perceived by orthodox sociologists as ideologically based (e.g., the work of Lewis Hine and Jacob Riis) and having as its aim social change rather than social knowledge. Since the 1940s in-depth, long-term, 'considered' documentary photography, for example, the Smiths and the Minamata study (1974) is seen as a long way short of being 'research'. Consequently the serious and analytical visual documentary worker, even one applying a qualitative methodology approach, will find an uphill struggle for acceptance by the academic community.
7   I am not aware of any graduate or postgraduate programmes in visual sociology in the UK, although some units within degree programmes are available. Banks (1994, p. 22) reports 'At the end of 1991 eight departments of anthropology in Britain (out of approximately twenty) ran undergraduate or graduate courses [i.e., units] in visual anthropology'. Ruby (1996, p. 1349) reported 'Graduate-study programmes currently exist in the University of California, New York University, and Temple University in the United States and at the University of Manchester in England. Numerous other institutions offer single courses.'
8   Visual anthropology places a major emphasis on film, limiting the status of other media. In addition Winston (1995, p. 196) makes the point 'Because such film-making [handheld sync. Cameras] made the strongest claims to science, stronger than implied sociology of most documentary, this failure was most grievous. The evidential pretensions of the new equipment fell harder and further in anthropology' suggesting that filmic anthropology is flawed in the eyes of orthodox anthropologists causing significant problems for contemporary visual anthropologists.
9   I would like to thank Dr Elizabeth Chaplin for her critical comments on an earlier draft of this chapter. The weaknesses that remain are mine.

References

AGAR, M.H. (1986) *Speaking Ethnographically*, Beverly Hills: Sage.
ASCH, T. (1979) 'Making a film record of the Yanomamo Indians of southern Venuezela', *Perspectives on Film*, **2**, pp. 4–9, 44–9.
BANKS, M. (1994) 'Television and anthropology: An unhappy marriage?', *Visual Anthropology*, **7**, 1, pp. 21–45.
BANKS, M. and MORPHY, H. (1997) *Rethinking Visual Anthropology*, London: Yale University Press.
BATESON, G. and MEAD, M. (1942) *Balinese Character: A Photographic Analysis*, New York: New York Academy of Sciences.
BECKER, H.S. (1974) 'Photography and sociology', *Studies in the Anthropology of Visual Communication*, **1**, 1, pp. 3–26.
BERGER, J. (1978) 'Ways of remembering', *Camerawork*, **10**, London.
BOGDAN, R.C. and BIKLEN, S.N. (1982) *Qualitative Research for Education*, Boston: Allyn and Bacon.
CHAPLIN, E. (1994) *Sociology and Visual Representation*, London: Routledge.

CLIFFORD, J. (1988) *The Predicament of Culture: Twentieth-century Ethnography, Literature and Art*, Cambridge, Massachusetts, London: Harvard University Press.

EDWARDS, E. (1992) (ed.) *Anthropology and Photography: 1860–1920*, New Haven, Conn.: Yale University Press.

ELLEN, R.F. (1984) *Ethnography Research: A Guide to General Conduct*, London: Academic Press.

FETTERMAN, D.H. (1989) *Ethnography: Step by Step*, Newbury Park, California, Sage.

GRADY, J. (1996) 'The scope of visual sociology', in *Visual Sociology*, International Visual sociology Association, **11**, 2, pp. 10–24.

HAMMERLEY, M. and ATKINSON, P. (1987) *Ethnography: Principles in Practice*, London: Routledge.

HARPER, D. (1982) *Good Company*, Chicago: University of Chicago Press.

HARPER, D. (1987) *Working Knowledge: Skill and Community in a Small Shop*, Chicago: University of Chicago Press.

HARPER, D. (1989) 'Visual sociology: Expanding the sociological vision', in BLANK, G., McCARTNEY, J. and BRENT, E. (eds) *New Technology in Sociology*, New Brunswick: Transaction Publishers.

HARPER, D. (1996) 'Seeing sociology', in *The American Sociologist*, **37**, 3, pp. 69–78.

HENLEY, P. (1985) 'British ethnographic film: Recent developments', *Anthropology Today*, **1**, 1, pp. 5–17.

HINE, L. (1932) *Men at Work*, New York: Macmillan.

HOUTMAN, G. (1988) 'Interview with Maurice Block', *Anthropology Today*, **4**, 1, pp. 18–21.

LATOUR, B. (1988) 'The politics of explanation: An alternative', in *Knowledge and Reflexivity: New Frontiers in the Sociology of Knowledge*, London: Sage.

LOIZOS, P. (1980) 'Granada television's disappearing world series: An appraisal', *American Anthropologist*, **82**, pp. 573–94.

MALINOWSKI, B. (1922) *The Argonauts of the Western Pacific*, New York: Dutton.

PINNEY, C., WRIGHT, C. and POIGNANT, R. (1996) *The Impossible Science of Being*, London: The Photographers' Gallery.

PROSSER, J. (1996) 'What constitutes an image-based methodology?', *Visual Sociology*, **11**, 2, pp. 25–34.

RIIS, J.A. (1971) *How the Other Half Lives*, New York. Dover.

RUBY, J. (1975) 'Is an ethnographic film a filmic ethnography?', *Studies in the Anthropology of Visual Communication*, **2**, pp. 104–11.

RUBY, J. (1977) 'The image mirrored: Reflexivity and the documentary film', *Journal of the University Film Association*.

RUBY, J. (1980) 'Exposing yourself: Reflexivity, anthropology, and Film', *Semiotica*, **30**, 1, pp. 153–79.

RUBY, J. (1988) 'Images of rural America', *History of Photography*, **12**, pp. 327–43.

RUBY, J. (1995) 'Out of sync: The cinema of Tim Asch,' in *Visual Anthropology Review*, **11**, 1, pp. 19–37.

RUBY, J. (1996) 'Visual anthropology', in LEVINSON, D. and EMBER, M. (eds) *Encyclopedia of Cultural Anthropology*, vol. 4, New York: Henry Holt and Co, pp. 1345–51.

SCHERER, J.C. (1990) 'Picturing cultures: Historical photographs in anthropological inquiry', *Visual Anthropology*, **3**, 2–3.

SHULTZ, A. (1964) *Collected Papers*, The Hague: Martinus Nijhoff.

SILVERMAN, D. (1993) *Interpreting Qualitative Data*, London: Sage.

SMITH, W.E. and SMITH, A. (1974) *Minamata*, New York: Holt, Rinehart and Winston.

STASZ, C. (1979) 'The early history of visual sociology', in WAGNER, J. (ed.) *Images of Information: Still Photography in the Social Sciences*, Beverly Hills and London: Sage.

STOCKING, G.W. (1992) *The Ethnographer's Magic and Other Essays in the History of Anthropology*, Madison: University of Wisconsin Press.

TOMASELLI, K.G. (1996) *Appropriating Images: The Semiotics of Visual Representation*, Hojbjerg (Denmark): Intervention Press.

USHER, R. (1993) *Reflexivity*, Occasional papers in education as interdisciplinary studies, 3, Southampton: School of Education, University of Southampton.

WALKER, R. (1994) 'Finding a silent voice for the researcher: Using photographs in evaluation and research', in SCHRATZ, M. (ed.) *Qualitative Voices in Educational Research*, London: Falmer Press.

WINSTON, B. (1995) *Claiming the Real: The Grierson Documentary and Its Legitimations*, London: The British Film Institute.

WOOLGAR, S. (1988) 'Reflexivity is the ethnographer of the text', in *Knowledge and Reflexivity: New Frontiers in the Sociology of Knowledge*, London: Sage.

WORTH, S. and ADAIR, J. (1972) *Through Navajo Eyes*, Bloomington: Indiana University Press.

Part 2

Images in the Research Process

Editor's note

In Part 2, the chapters focus on the role of images in the research process. Hence they are essentially concerned with methodology. The chapters are quite diverse and cover: the use of images throughout the research process; how images are used to advantage in particular research contexts; the problematic aspects of visual research such as the context of creating an image; and the possibilities of changes to the research process as a result of technological change. However, each chapter applies a structure, a terminology, and explores themes and concepts, that are recognisable and accessible to orthodox qualitative researchers.

Chapter 8

Photographs within the Sociological Research Process

Jon Prosser and Dona Schwartz

Abstract

This chapter considers the use of photographs within the sociological research process. In particular it explores issues of research design, data collection and data analysis. Theoretical and practical considerations are discussed within a traditional qualitative framework rather than adopt ideas emanating from post-modern critique. A central theme throughout is how different phases of the research process require the deployment of different photographic strategies.

Any discussion of using photographs in the research process should begin by considering researchers' underlying epistemological and methodological assumptions, since they orientate the way we conduct our studies. How research proceeds also depends on the orientation provided by: an academic discipline e.g., sociology, anthropology, psychology; the theoretical framework guiding the study e.g., material culture, phenomenology, symbolic interaction, and feminist theory; the researcher's role i.e., ethnographer, historian, advocate, biographer, evaluator and interpreter; and personal attributes such as skills, experiences, values and beliefs. These many variables shape the way we design our studies, our views of what constitutes data, and the kinds of conclusions we draw. Uncertainty surrounding the research act, a consequence of recent critiques launched by post-modernists and exponents of new approaches to ethnography, compounds the problems posed by these complex contextual issues. Debates regarding the appropriate relationship of theory to practice, a quandary inherent in any research process, reflect the difficult times in which qualitative researchers work. While recent discussions usefully foreground critical issues facing social scientists, they sometimes threaten to undermine the entire research enterprise and seem to suggest that we surrender our efforts to the truths put forth by fiction.

Discussions of these underpinning issues rarely encompass the use of images, unsurprisingly, since so little has been written regarding the role photographs can play in the research process. In addition, widespread assumptions that photographic images offer a transparent 'window on the world' has discouraged critical analysis of the medium. Just as recent debates have raised questions about the neutral status of data collected by social scientists and the conclusions they yield, so too has photography come under closer scrutiny. Even among practitioners whose livelihood hinges upon the factuality of the photographic image — photojournalists, documentarians, and many scientists — the malleability of photographs has injected formerly secure fields with a healthy dose of circumspection. We take heed of the ongoing dialogues and the arguments put forward by different factions from a variety of fields of endeavour, but, rather than throw out the baby with the bath water, our purpose here is to suggest productive approaches to using photographs in social science research, while simultaneously acknowledging the contingent nature of the empirical research we ourselves conduct. We have elected to discuss a selection of issues that help us do field work, building on an empirical tradition within Image-based Research initially espoused in the 1960s and 1970s by Sol Worth, Howard Becker, John Collier Jr., and Jay Ruby.

We undertake this task because, as image-based researchers, we have discovered the valuable contribution photographs can make, both in the practice and presentation of our work. Like our field notes and other forms of empirical data, photographs may not provide us with unbiased, objective documentation of the social and material world, but they can show characteristic attributes of people, objects, and events that often elude even the most skilled wordsmiths. Through our use of photographs we can discover and demonstrate relationships that may be subtle or easily overlooked. We can communicate the feeling or suggest the emotion imparted by activities, environments, and interactions. And we can provide a degree of tangible detail, a sense of being there and a way of knowing that may not readily translate into other symbolic modes of communication. So, despite the irksome complexity of travelling through contested territory, the new knowledge yielded by the innovative methods we suggest makes the journey beneficial.

Consider this:

> I am walking along a city street. In one pocket I have a camera and a notebook and in the other two lenses and extra rolls of film. A young couple are peering into a jeweller's shop. I take out the camera and begin shooting, using the wide angle lens and a slow shutter speed to freeze the couple and turn other shoppers into a blur, suggesting and emphasising the couple's stillness and intimacy. I change to a short telephoto, shift position, and shoot against the light to accentuate their intimacy and body language. The couple's reflection in the window catches my eye and I switch to a standard lens and shoot some more, aware that the image is analogous to a theoretical concept derived from interviews with other couples conducted earlier in the study. I put the camera away, take out my notebook and . . .

No doubt you could, whatever your discipline or theoretical persuasion (but assuming some experience in conducting qualitative research), provide a reasonable account of the *processes* and *techniques* preceding the activity, which were used during the event described, and also those following the 'shoot'. You will be aware that a research focus, a flexible research design and an understanding of theoretical sampling provide me with a rationale to be doing what I'm doing in the place I'm doing it; you will also be aware that I made three different types of photographs, perhaps for different applications; you recognize that I collected interview data prior to taking photographs and that further data based on an analysis of these and other data may lead to further, more focused data collection; and you correctly surmise that this will lead to a formal report — a case study perhaps — in which the photographs, presented in the form of visual quotes, will be used in conjunction with other evidence to support a particular theory or working hypothesis. You are aware of this because there are certain elements commonly applied to a wide range of qualitative studies. Researchers using photographs span multifarious disciplines but share common understandings about what constitutes a 'qualitative' study and that the overall aim is to contribute to a body of knowledge by marshalling evidence to answer research questions. The defining characteristics which shape the way we design and conduct our studies could be described as holistic, contextually well defined, field-orientated, design is emergent and progressively focused, naturalistic and non-interventionist, interpretative, working hypotheses emerge from the data, interpretations are validated by triangulation, multiple realities or single view (adapted from Stake, 1995, p. 48).

In this chapter we aim to 'unpack', explore and refine the meanings of such terms with regard to Image-based Research with one important caveat described earlier: we will focus attention on methodology and the ways in which theory informs and legitimates practice. The remainder of the chapter will, therefore, consider key facets of conducting research involving photography: research design, data collection, and briefly, analysis.

Research Design

Research design makes explicit a plan for conducting a study, proffers a model and justification for establishing the validity of data and inferences drawn from them, and implicitly indicates a researcher's ability to successfully conduct a study. Research design should be made explicit so that others may gain insight into how the study was conducted and, more importantly, judge its worth. Any design of research operates within a discipline or across disciplines, takes into account the purpose of the study and deploys a particular set of research strategies.

Orthodox qualitative research design offers a 'blueprint' for the conduct of research, incorporating, according to Marshall and Grossman (1995, p. 38): the overall approach and rationale; site and sample collection; the researcher's role; data collection methods; data management; analysis strategy; trustworthiness features; and the time management plan. The future status and acceptability of Image-based Research may depend on working within a relatively conservative framework whilst exploring alternative modes of enquiry which are image-orientated yet sensitive to orthodox researchers, methodological concerns. Researchers using photographs in their work lack alternative over-arching research designs that provide models of good or innovative practice and a rich 'menu' of alternatives. Other more established approaches, for example designs for auto/biographical studies, historical research, or case studies, are sufficiently well rehearsed to indicate potential variations of strategy and probable data collection methods. Image-based researchers have not routinely explicated their research designs and few models of good practice exist outside of anthropology and ethnography.

Bateson and Mead (1942), Byers (1964), Collier (1979), and Collier and Collier (1986) among others, provide models and insights into research design for anthropological and ethnographic studies. Good examples of research design within visual sociology are more difficult to find. An interesting discussion of how to conduct a study, however, is given by Rieger (1996) in a paper which reflects on the relationship between visual change and social change. He uses examples of changes in peoples' lives and to the landscape of small towns in the USA over an extended period to illustrate the ways in which various photographic strategies, combined with traditional qualitative and quantitative data, are able to provide a robust research design. He provides, for example, 'picture portraits' of changes to a mining town over a 100 year period, and juxtaposes Dorothea

Lange's famous 'Migrant Mother' image of 1936 with an image exhibiting a similar structure taken in 1979. Within Rieger's paper are features important to the design of a sociological study: theoretical underpinnings (such as the relationship between visual change and social change) are employed and act as a framework within which the study 'sits'; there is a rationale for combining research strategies; various visual methods are discussed (for example repeating photographs of the same site over time, repeating photographs of participants in the change process, and re-photographing activities, processes or functions); complementary non-visual methods are applied (for example examining statistics on changes in population and employment); the use of triangulation of various indicative data to add trustworthiness of findings is discussed; and the problems (such as determining what constitutes an indicator of social change) and limitations of data and findings are aired. An image-based approach, as Rieger points out, 'must adhere to the same standards of evidence and inference' (p. 45) demanded of traditional non Image-based Research and it should make logical connections that start with a study's initial research questions and extend through to its conclusions.

Not all research designs follow the kind of structured approach Rieger describes. If research design is 'colloquially . . . an action plan for getting from here to there' (Yin, 1994, p. 19), as long as important methodological signposts are present many paths can be travelled. Some designs emphasize the flexibility that distinguishes qualitative research from other approaches. Harper (1992), in a case study of 'Willie', an auto mechanic living in New York's 'Northern County', takes a more responsive and reflexive stance than Rieger. Through Willie Harper he explores the decline of skilled manual labour and the kinds of knowledge lost in the process. As the study unfolds the reader senses a degree of empathy between the researcher and his subject that exceeds the norm in traditional participant observation and we are left with the feeling that the study is as much a statement about Harper as Willie.

One key signpost in research design is how and by what criteria data are to be interpreted. Here Harper draws on grounded theory (Glaser and Straus, 1967) to allow theory to emerge from the data but he adds commentary distinguishing Willie's 'emic', or insider understandings, from the 'etic' sociological framework he uses to characterize that world in terms that have resonance and significance for social scientists.

> I have studied Willie's work from several angles, but the categories I have ended up with are my own. In naming and classifying its elements, I have separated out aspects of Willie's taken-for-granted world, presented them back to him in discussions we have recorded, and finally used them to translate Willie's experienced world in terms that those unfamiliar with the culture can understand. (Harper, 1992, p. 9)

Rieger and Harper offer two quite different but legitimate approaches to research design. However, the outcomes are similar in that they instil a level of confidence in the veracity of their images that is missing in many visual sociologists' work. Whatever research design is put forward as a methodological 'blueprint' of conduct during the research process, the overarching concern must be with enhancing the trustworthiness of findings and the scope and clarity of the constructs developed. Research design translates epistemological principles into pragmatic decisions and explains the choices we make.

Data Collection

Important steps in formulating any study involve identifying, locating, and gaining access to an appropriate research site and the sources of data it can yield. Before qualitative researchers begin to mine a site for the data it holds, we need to consider how we present ourselves to our subjects. Many qualitative methods texts examine the relative advantages and disadvantages of assuming an overt or covert role, of participant observation or observation alone (Bogdan and Taylor, 1984; Lincoln and Guba, 1985), but we consider these dichotomies overly abstract simplifications of the complex relationships formed in the field. The choices we make regarding the roles we play in the field raise a host of procedural and ethical issues, many of which have been outlined in recent critiques of qualitative work. These issues become even more salient when considered within the context of visual research strategies.

Cameras in hand, visual researchers generally take a more pragmatic stance than other fieldworkers, because we need to employ methods that enable us to produce images capable of generating useful data. Recognizing the added complexity introduced when making images in the course of conducting research, we also feel compelled to consider issues regarding 'empowerment' (of subjects) and 'ownership' (of data and findings), especially in regard to photographs. We accept that making pictures can be a threatening act (amply demonstrated by the metaphors photography invokes: we 'load', 'aim' and 'shoot') that yields an artificial product, an artefact of the idiosyncratic relationship among photographers and subjects, the medium, and the cultural expectations it generates. We also make the assumption that the appearances of naturally occurring objects, events and behaviours provide a gateway to the taken-for-granted and reflects deeply embedded and therefore unquestioned aspects of culture which are critical to studies of society. Therefore, it is incumbent upon us to devise multiple strategies and roles for photographers that allow us to produce images that further our attempts to study the everyday world. While we cannot envision methods that guarantee photographs uncontaminated by reactivity between photographers and subjects, unbiased by cultural expectations shaping the act of making pictures, or unmediated by the characteristics of the technology itself, we do propose to build upon the uniquely iconic capacity of photography to usefully represent the particularities of a specific moment in time and space.

There is a hierarchy of questions to pose when considering the issues of access and role. The nature of the research question, even taken at a pragmatic level, is of paramount importance. A mature female researcher photographing a young man's world or a white middle class academic making a video of low income Hispanics may both claim that as 'outsiders' they have 'critical distance' on the problem at hand. This approach has credibility since 'critical distance' allows them to treat as problematic that which is taken-for-granted — as did Robert Frank (1955) in *The Americans*. Conversely, outsider status may prevent researchers from penetrating a protected domain. We must consider and make explicit the benefits and disadvantages our own positions engender, and the ways in which cameras hinder or help our attempts to gain access.

An alternative to maintaining a distinct separation between 'outsider' researchers and their subjects is to build a bridge between them. Worth and Adair (1972) adopted this approach when they taught the technology of filmmaking to Navajo Indians so that they themselves could represent their traditions and rituals. Worth and Adair hoped that by offering them the means to visually depict their own culture the Navajo would provide an emic account offering the insider's perspective. Worth and Adair did encounter and acknowledge problems with their approach. Since film was not an indigenous representational medium available to the Navajo prior to their study, the researchers attempted to teach film production from a neutral perspective, unbiased by the cultural codes and conventions Worth and Adair themselves had internalized. The Navajo were asked to narrate their culture using an alien communicative medium. Nevertheless, *Through Navajo Eyes* presents an innovative research model that has been imitated in both academic and professional milieus.

Data can be collected covertly, 'under cover'. Photographers may hide themselves from public view, or choose a telephoto lens that allows shooting a scene from a distant berth. Some research questions encourage such a strategy. For example, time samples can be compiled at a particular locale in order to establish patterns of use or activity. But researchers who hope to gain access and be welcomed by members of communities may place future relationships at risk if they begin by employing what appear to be surveillance techniques. What happens further down the line when the 'spy' is discovered? Such revelations can compromise researchers' credibility and, consequently, trust may be impossible to cultivate. In most instances surveillance photography provides only superficial data which can be easily construed the result of 'outsider arrogance'. Covert photography more often reveals researchers' discomfort with their own photographic activity than it does insights into the daily lives of their subjects.

The nature of the research question should determine strategies for gaining access to subjects and constructing the researcher/photographer's role but subjects' own social positions factor into the equation. When qualitative researchers make their agendas explicit they often depend on subjects' willingness to be studied, and members of different social groups may view the research process (and the researcher) with varying degrees of scepticism. And different populations have unequal defence mechanisms to ward off the intrusions researchers inevitably introduce. In some situations, the power differential between the researcher and the researched may make an overt approach untenable as Taylor (1989) points out:

> You will find many ethnographic studies of relatively powerless groups, such as school-children, the sick and handicapped, gays or dope smokers, but very few, if any, of powerful groups such as leading politicians, senior civil servants or military chiefs. This is not because sociologists are not interested in power and how it is used. They are. It is simply because sociologists (and other potential observers) are not normally granted access to centres of power. The only knowledge we have of what goes on in some powerful groups comes when one of the participants makes disclosures and even then, in the UK at least, there are problems in getting such revelations published. The problem of access illustrates that what can be achieved through participant observation is strictly limited. (Taylor, 1989, pp. 66–7)

This scenario repeats itself in many guises and encourages visual researchers to use covert and devious means to gain access to data. While we acknowledge that elites wield greater power to limit outsiders' access to their social domains, we must also recognize valid ethical and moral restrictions, like religious proscriptions, individuals' and groups' rights to privacy, or threats to security, health or safety. For example, in a comparative study of the daily lives of mothers of different US social classes, Schwartz spent several months locating and interviewing wealthy women, most of whom declined to participate in a photographic study, or were later urged to decline by their husbands. Among the more compelling reasons cited was one couple's genuine fear that publishing photographs of their children could conceivably lead to a kidnapping attempt. It bears noting, however, that economically disadvantaged mothers were equally hesitant to be photographed, although they harboured quite different anxieties. The knowledge that powerful groups are likely to deny access to qualitative researchers, especially camera-toting fieldworkers, increases the likelihood that visual sociologists will adopt a covert stance and employ hidden cameras or craft personae resembling despised paparazzi who stalk celebrities in search of valuable photo opportunities. While going covert may yield usable photographic data, it undermines possibilities for participant observation, an important check on whether the researcher has captured participants' experiences. The flip side of the coin is, of course, the inability of powerless groups and individuals to protect themselves from intrusion. Researchers too often tend to shirk these moral dilemmas; the concrete issues they raise should be addressed in the design and implementation of research strategies so that we do not infringe upon the rights of our subjects.

Deciding on an appropriate role is only the beginning of 'getting in and staying in' the field. All qualitative researchers confront the process of establishing rapport with subjects, but cameras present additional complexities for subjects and researchers alike. Because photography is a popular hobby and photographs pervade western industrialized societies, our subjects are likely to be familiar with both making and viewing photographic images. Snapshooting provides a template for subjects' ability to understand what visual sociologists do and the equipment they use. But as visual sociologists, we often present ourselves as professionally trained camera users and because we photograph a variety of objects, people, and events in the course of research, subjects may implicitly compare visual sociologists with photojournalists as part of their own process of classifying and thereby understanding what is taking place. In the course of our field experiences, the authors have been initially construed curious amateurs, professional freelance photographers, journalists, and artists. While none of these classifications accurately reflect the role we intend to play, these common sense understandings provide a useful starting point for conversation, in the course of which we can clarify our goals and procedures. Whatever the opening, whether discussions of our activities, our equipment, or the weather, these first encounters with community members can (and should) be used to lay the groundwork for future data collection. Our identity as friend or foe is often established during these initial exchanges.

The introduction of the camera to participants can take place on the first day as a 'can opener' (Collier and Collier, 1986; Schwartz, 1989a) or over a period of time using a 'softly softly' approach (Prosser, 1992). The 'softly softly' approach, in this case, initially entailed walking around the sampling site with a camera in its 'out of the case over the shoulder like a piece of jewellery' mode, followed by 'safe' photography of buildings, and only much later was 'serious' photography attempted when participants were accustomed to photography taking place. Whether the camera comes out immediately or gradually, visual sociologists need to confidently perform the tasks necessary to make pictures and they should handle equipment with apparent ease. Photographers who act nervous or lack self-confidence usually convey those feelings to the people around them and, consequently, their activities may become suspect. In the initial stages of a research project qualitative researchers with little photographic experience do well to begin by mapping the physical surround. This accomplishes several tasks simultaneously: it allows the photographer to ease into the new setting and role; it makes the photographer visible to community members, opening opportunities for interaction; and it provides a visual catalogue of the physical setting in which the fieldwork take place. Not only must visual sociologists feel comfortable with themselves as photographers, they must also be attuned to the comfort levels displayed by subjects. Insensitive photographers who lack the ability act and react to significant 'others' as they themselves act and react to them, will damage the quality of their data and compromise their ability to maintain rapport, a necessity if the researcher hopes to remain in the field.

Both the camera and the photograph are flexible tools used to collect data in various ways. In this section we will explore a small range of possibilities. Found photographs, like found or historical documents, are useful for 'backward mapping' but often lack important contextual information such as the relationship between the photographer and the subject, why a photograph survived when others did not; and the photographer's intention in making the image. How can we interpret an image or assess its significance without its context? Alternative forms of data and methods which illuminate, confirm or disconfirm, are used to complement initial interpretation of found images. Found photographs, whatever their age and history, may be enlightening or misleading if viewed without an 'encompassing structure' (Trachtenberg, 1989). The 'encompassing structure' may come in the form of an analytical framework or constituent data, i.e., from contemporary writings, field notes, auto/biographical details about the photographer or participants. Historical, political, social, and cultural information often aid our interpretation by elaborating the milieu from which a found photograph emerged. But, as in any qualitative study, all data have their limitations and there is danger in over extrapolation, of claiming what cannot be justified. The skills of the historian and archivist extend to us the possibility of judging the significance of found photographs. For example an important icon of the Spanish Civil war that had been reproduced in *Life* magazine in 1936, 'Death of a Loyalist Soldier' by Robert Capa, was thought to be a 'set up' during the 1970s. However, an amateur historian found evidence that suggested the photograph was authentic and subsequent 'police work' re-established the trustworthiness not only of the icon but also of Capa himself.[1]

Researcher generated images are widely used as a 'visual record' or as a 'visual diary'. While these two terms may seem synonymous we see an important, if fine-grained, distinction between them, a distinction that reflects differing positions with regard to the capacities of photography to provide an 'unbiased' record of a reality. When viewed as visual records, researchers depend upon photography's capacity to provide extra-somatic 'memory'. The ability of the camera to record visual detail without fatigue suggests that 'camera notes' may be superior to the fieldnotes recorded by tired social scientists. Even when we become weary or muddled the camera can continue, so long as film and batteries are refreshed. The visual records produced by the indefatigable camera can be organized, catalogued and analysed at a later date. Thus, the camera's reproductive and mimetic qualities can be used in two basic ways, first as an adjunct or complement to an ethnographic field diary (see Ball, Chapter 8), or, second, to systematically record visual detail with emphasis on reproducing objects, events, places, signs and symbols, or behavioural interactions.

Creating a so-called 'visual diary' carries a somewhat different set of connotations that build upon an alternative conceptualization of the photographic medium itself. As Paul Byers (1966) asserted early in the game, 'cameras don't take pictures', people do.

Even though cameras don't tire, the social scientists pressing the shutter release do, and the degree of perspicacity we marshal by the end of a field encounter may affect both what we include or omit, and the way in which we render the activities in front of the lens. Besides the person/machine issue looms a larger critique of factual uses of photography. Choices of types of supplies and equipment make a difference in the view of the world photography can offer. Large or medium format cameras depict the world differently than a thirty-five millimetre; the lens we choose to employ may either collapse or expand space and impart a different feeling to the viewer. The use of natural or artificial light, colour or black and white film stocks, and a myriad other choices shape the nature of the depictions we create. Add to this laundry list such concerns as the aesthetic predisposition of the photographer, his or her own level of sensitivity to objects and events before the lens, and degree of facility with the medium, and the sanctity of the photographic image as a visual record is assailed. All of these factors contribute to the production of photographic images.

The notion of photographs as visual diary reintroduce the researcher and the qualities of the medium into the research process. That is, a diary is a self-reflexive and media-literate chronicle of the researcher's entry, participation in, and departure from, the field. The images generated within this paradigm are acknowledged to be the unique result of the interaction of a certain researcher with a specific population using a particular medium at a precise moment in space and time. Reviewing these many variables in the photographic process more clearly distinguishes the notion of a visual record from that of visual diary. Consonant with these different views, when considered and constructed as visual records, photographs may offer greater potential as comparative data, uncontaminated by the idiosyncrasies different photographers might introduce. On the other hand, photographs intended as diaries of field experiences may better encode researchers' inferences (see Schwartz, 1993 for an example of the visual diary approach). Whatever belief qualitative researchers espouse regarding the medium, whether they make visual records or visual diaries, we advocate researchers making their approach explicit so that colleagues can better judge the conclusions they present. The argument we are making parallels a distinction made by Worth (1980) between 'records of' and 'records about' culture. Records of culture are the documents made by members of a culture themselves, while records about culture are the documents made by outsiders. Taking this point a step further, Ruby (1976) suggests that the images made by anthropologists may be usefully viewed as records of the culture of visual anthropologists, while simultaneously considered records about the culture of so-called others.

Researcher generated photographs are commonly used during data collection as an interview device. This is commonly referred to as 'photo-elicitation' and takes many differing forms including interviews with individuals, with groups, with children, and those who respond more easily to visual, rather than lexical, prompts. We have described elsewhere (Schwartz, 1989b) an important addendum to the use of photographs as an interview device:

> Viewing photographic imagery is a patterned social activity shaped by social context, cultural conventions, and group norms. In order to present photographs to informants for purposes of photo-elicitation, some foreknowledge of the respondents group's use of photographs is required so that methodological strategies can be planned, and the resulting data assessed within the context of informants' shared meanings. (Schwartz, 1989b, pp. 120–1)

Although not a homogeneous set of practices, in its conventional form (see Harper, 1988; Schwartz, 1989a; Walker and Weidel, 1985) photo-elicitation can be described as a single or sets of photographs assembled by the researcher on the basis of prior analysis and selected with the assumption that the chosen images will have some significance for interviewees. The photographs are shown to individuals or groups with the express aim of exploring participants' values, beliefs, attitudes, and meanings, and in order to trigger memories, or to explore group dynamics or systems. Of course researchers in different disciplines, with distinct epistemological assumptions may approach photo-elicitation differently (for psychology see Cronin, Chapter 5). A less conventional use of photo-elicitation in sociology draws its inspiration from psychology, using photographs as a projective technique similar to that of incomplete sentences or inkblots. This approach, however, does not draw on the ambiguous nature of an image but is purposefully provocative and disruptive and is intended to elicit suppressed views. Prosser (1992) provides an example of this approach in an educational setting. Figure 8.1 'Pupil Graffiti' was shown to staff in a secondary school. The photograph is of a book whose title was altered form its original *Nine Modern Poets, An Anthology* to *Nine Nude Puffs in an Orgy*. As anticipated, when shown the photograph, staff reacted and reacted differently providing insights that other, more passive means, may not have achieved.[2] The aim was to stimulate comment not on the content of the photograph but what is intimate to the interviewees that is 'triggered' by the photograph. Photo-elicitation used in this way can be provocative but is not necessarily aggressive.

Figure 8.1 Pupil Graffiti

Regardless of the strategy the researcher adopts, the chosen approach must be consistent with the way in which photography has been conceptualized at the outset. Photographs conceived and constructed as records will most likely be used according to a different logic than photographs made as part of the researcher's self-reflexive visual diary. While either approach can yield useful interview prompts, visual researchers need to understand both the processes of encoding meaning in which he or she has engaged, and informants' approaches to decoding photographic meaning. Researchers are often clear about their intentions as they go about constructing a set of images to use in the course of interviews, but they may just as often be surprised (pleasantly or disappointingly) by the nature of the responses their photographs generate. Confessions regarding serendipitous or disastrous interchanges rarely make there way into research narratives. Since many people spend time looking at photographs — in the press, in advertising, in family albums, in galleries — researchers need to carefully explain the similarities or differences between the interview setting and these other familiar viewing events so that subjects can be better informed about the task at hand. It is then the researcher's respons- ibility to interpret and assess the nature of respondents' interactions with the photographs used for elicitation, and to incorporate those conclusions into the data to be analysed.

Analysis

Analysing photographic data in qualitative research, as with textual data, is a series of inductive and formative acts carried out throughout the research process. As with other qualitative research strategies, visual researchers begin the task of analysis in the course of field research so that new inferences can be exploited before the fieldwork ends. Caldarola (1985) elaborates a plan for integrating photography into ethnographic research that includes regular viewing sessions with informants. In this way visual data can be validated as research proceeds and used to generate new inferences that inform future data gathering. All data have strengths and limitations but poor data, that is data that are invalid, implausible, or untrustworthy, are not worth analysing. The initial problem for the interpreter of photographs is how to ensure their plausibility and believability. Because cameras do not take pictures (Byers, 1966) the fallibility and selectivity of the picture maker must be scrutinized. Full contextual detail (if this is ever possible) enables the trustworthiness and limitations of photographs to be assessed and this means having an understanding of both the external (see Chapter 6) and internal (see Chapter 10) photo- context. Such contexts are multi-faceted, reflecting: the academic discipline, research paradigm and theoretical framework the researcher works within; the extent of disparity between the picture taker's culture (and the interpreter's) ethnicity, religion, gender, class, and values and the object of the photograph; and the micro-context that shapes the particular dynamic relationship between 'taker' and 'taken';[3] and picture theory. Picture theory is of growing importance to visual sociologists because it takes repres- entation as problematic. It investigates the differences and relationship between images and words, or as Mitchell (1994, p. 5) explains 'the interactions of visual and verbal representation in a variety of media, principally literature and the visual arts'; and ques- tions the relationship between representations on two-dimensional surfaces and their con- nection with issues of power, values and social influences (see, for example Chapter 18 which discusses a famous picture — the Cornfield by John Constable). Any analysis of photographs without information elaborating the macro and micro contexts is generally unacceptable since image production and image reception informs our understanding of those photographs.

There are numerous theoretical and practical approaches to analysing photographs. One approach is the 'doctrine of signs' which draws on the work of Barthes' *Elements of Semiology* (1964) and denotation-connotation pairing, the semiotics of Peirce, or more recently socio-semiotics (Gottdiener, 1995). At the opposite end of the spectrum Collier (1979) suggests:

> We should first approach photographs *openly* (Hall, 1974) in order to respond to their holistic content. We could call this initial experience 'listening to the visual voice of imagery'; the researchers respond with all their senses open so that they may be more deeply affected by documentary realism. (Collier, 1979)

Between structuralist and hermeneutical investigation are more specific approaches to interpretation. In addition to Caldarola (1985), Ruby (1976) critiques how anthropologists derive meaning from photographs, suggesting new and innovative approaches to visual anthropology; Collier and Collier (1986, p. 178) provide a four stage generic analytical model applicable to a wide range of research topics; Ball and Smith (1992) describe general theoretical approaches to interpreting images; Collier (1979) suggests three broad approaches to interpreting photographs depending on the nature of the enquiry — macro analysis and open enquiry, structured and micro analytical study, and micro image analysis of behaviour; and Chalfen (Chapter 14) provides a good example of an analytical framework within a substantive area. A common thread running through each approach is the way they move the analyst toward theory generation (substantive rather than grand theory) and the testing of emergent ideas.

Interpretation of any photographic data requires a theoretical framework. A framework aids management of large amounts of (visual) data by providing logic for sorting, organizing, indexing and categorization. The interpretative process begins well before viewing a photograph, and takes place, for example, when decisions are made as to *what* and *how* the photographs are to be taken Harper (1992) honestly describes these early faltering analytical steps that are part and parcel of any photographic study:

> The first photographs I took at the shop lacked any coherence from Willie's perspective. They were really photos by an interested outsider, seeing the exotic forms in the routine of the shop. Howard Becker would say I lacked a theory, which in his terms is 'a set of ideas with which you can make sense of a situation while you photograph it. The theory tells you when an image contains information of value, when it communicates something worth communicating. It furnishes the criteria by which worthwhile data and statements can be separated from those that contain nothing of value, that do not increase our knowledge of society.' (Harper, 1992, p. 12)

Harper adapts, realigns and refines his approach and moves on, illustrating the flexibility and non-linearity of analytic induction required in qualitative studies.

Making sense of photographs is also dependent on what sort of social explanation or intellectual puzzle is to be resolved. Consider, for example, Figures 8.2 and 8.3 of two deputy principals of similar status and carrying out similar roles in an English secondary school.

Figure 8.2   Deputy principal's room

Figure 8.3   Deputy principal's room

The photographs were taken to provide data for a *comparative* study of working practices, to explore the similarities and differences in the deputy principals' working practices. They are two 'slices' of constituent data (constituent in that they require separate interpretation informed by the context in which the images were made, and the particular questions being asked of them) which were contrasted with each other and other data sets. A starting point for analysis would be to consider the photographs in terms of what Collier and Collier (1986, p. 47) call a 'cultural inventory': 'The spatial configuration of otherwise ordinary objects, common to a mass society, may often reflect or express the cultural patterns and values of distinct cultural groups.' Each office contains proxemic information (measurements of space), numerical information, information on the level of technology available, and information on décor aesthetics. The layout of objects in space is not arbitrary but tells us a great deal about the deputy principals, about who they are, what they do, and how they behave in their rooms.

Choosing an analytical framework must be guided by the same logic that undergirds the visual researcher's overall approach. We reiterate that researchers must themselves be clear about the way they conceptualize photographs and their role in research so that methodological strategies can be consistently employed throughout. Photographs prepared as visual records will trigger a different analytic strategy than will photographs intended as visual diaries. Worth's (1980) distinction between records *of* and records *about* culture, which built upon his and John Adair's *Through Navajo Eyes*, exemplifies the kind of theoretical clarity and circumspection we advocate, both for visual researchers in particular and qualitative researchers in general. These same concerns must govern the use of photographs in the presentation of research. While detailed discussion of this issue remains beyond the scope of the present chapter, suffice it to say that the agenda set forth by Ruby in 1976 has yet to be completed. Visual researchers need to attend closely to the ways in which their images are used in the display and/or publication of their findings.

Conclusion

As with any overview we have been both selective and brief in our outline of research procedures, resulting in some important omissions. We have not discussed, for example, notions of 'sampling', 'representation' or 'ethics'. In this chapter we elected to focus on a narrow set of issues that have helped us conduct fieldwork: research design; data collection, and analysis. Nevertheless these issues are crucial to planning and implementing visual research and our discussion will inform, if not enable, new researchers to enter the field. Image-based Research as social enquiry is developing and refining both its theory and methodology. In this chapter we have discussed key methodological issues and we have tried to balance theoretical frameworks with practical insights. A central theme throughout has been to illustrate how different theoretical assumptions and different phases of the research process require the deployment of distinct photographic strategies in order to provide a visual orientation to qualitative research.

Notes

1 Jay Ruby circulated, via the Visual Communications Discussion Group <VISCOM@ TEMPLE.EDU, the following message taken from the *New York Times*, Sunday, September 1996: 'The decisive moment, when it was taken in 1936, it was called one of the great war

photographs ever. In the mid-70s it was called a great fake. Now Robert Capa's spectacular image of the Spanish Civil War, a picture of a Loyalist militiaman falling as he is fatally shot in the head, is being rehabilitated. The picture was supposed to have been taken in Cerro Muriano on 5 September. So, an amateur historian named Mario Brotons went to the military archives in Madrid and Salamanca and found that only one man died at Cerro Muriano on September 5: Frederico Borrell, a mill worker from Alcoy. From there Rita Grosvenor picked up the pieces. She tracked down Frederico's brother's widow, who confirmed that the picture was of Frederico. Richard Whelen, Mr Capa's biographer, said, "It has the ring of truth"'.

2 Principal of the school, on seeing the photograph took a stance commensurate with his role, said he 'felt threatened' and believed showing it to pupils would lead to further 'vandalism', whilst the art teacher (taking a similar 'role' orientated stance) thought it most 'creative' and wished more pupils demonstrated such talent. It is interesting but peripheral that to Prosser the graffiti represented the darker unpleasant side of pupil culture and their perception of sexuality. Any member of the staff who saw the photograph did not raise this interpretation.

3 Because people make pictures, not cameras, personal reactivity needs to be considered. Researchers bring to any study, skills, knowledge, past experiences, abilities, personal values, beliefs, enthusiasms, which are embedded in a culture which directs not only their visual perception and what they study, but the way they conduct that study. Hagaman (1996), in *How I Learned Not to Be a Photojournalist* offers a rare but valuable insight into how she (a photojournalist) produced images useful for sociological purposes. She describes how she put to one side her journalistic skills that produced images with the required impact and drama and learned to be a visual sociologist.

References

BALL, M.S. and SMITH, G.W.H. (1992) *Analysing Visual Data*, Newbury Park: Sage.

BATESON, G. and MEAD, M. (1942) *Balinese Character*, Special Publications of the New York Academy of Sciences, Vol. II.

BARTHES, R. (1964) *Elements of Semiology*, New York, The Noonday Press.

BOGDAN, R. and TAYLOR, S. (1984) *Introduction to Qualitative Research Methods*, New York: John Wiley.

BYERS, P. (1964) 'Still photography in the systematic recording and analysis of behavioural data', *Human Organisation*, **23**, pp. 78–84.

BYERS, P. (1966) 'Cameras don't take pictures', *Columbia University Forumieal* 9, pp. 27–31.

CALDAROLA, V. (1985) 'Visual contexts: A photographic research method in anthropology', *Studies in Visual Communication*, **11**, 3, pp. 33–53.

COLLIER, J. (1979) 'Evaluating visual data', in WAGNER, J. (ed.) *Images of Information*, Beverly Hills: Sage Publications.

COLLIER, J. and COLLIER, M. (1986) *Visual Anthropology: Photography As a Research Method*, Albuquerque: University of New Mexico Press.

FRANK, R. (1955) *The Americans*, New York: Aperture.

GLASER, B.G. and STRAUSS, A.L. (1967) *The Discovery of Grounded Theory*, Chicago: Aldine.

GOTTDIENER, M. (1995) *Postmodern Semiotics: Material Culture and the Forms of Postmodern Life*, Oxford: Basil Blackwell.

HAGAMAN, D. (1996) *How I Learned Not to Be a Photojournalist*, Kentucky: University Press of Kentucky.

HARPER, D. (1988) 'Visual sociology: Expanding the sociological vision', *The American Sociologist*, **19**, 1, pp. 54–70.

HARPER, D. (1992) *Working Knowledge: Skill and Community in a Small Shop*, Oxford: University of California Press.

LINCOLN, Y.S. and GUBA, E.G. (1985) *Naturalistic Enquiry*, Newbury Park: Sage.

MARSHALL, C. and GROSSMAN, G.B. (1995) *Designing Qualitative Research*, London: Sage.

MITCHELL, W.J.T. (1994) *Picture Theory: Essays on Verbal and Visual Representation*, Chicago: University of Chicago Press.

PROSSER, J. (1992) 'Personal reflections on the use of photography in an ethnographic case study', *British Educational Research Journal*, **18**, 4, pp. 397–411.

RIEGER, J.H. (1996) 'Photographing social change', *Visual Sociology*, **11**, 1, pp. 5–49.

RUBY, J. (1976) 'In a pic's eye: Interpretive strategies for deriving significance and meaning from photographs', in *Afterimage* (March), pp. 5–7.

SCHWARTZ, D. (1989a) 'Legion post 189: Continuity and change in a rural community', *Visual Anthropology*, **2**, pp. 103–33.

SCHWARTZ, D. (1989b) 'Visual ethnography: Using photography in qualitative research', *Qualitative Sociology*, **12**, 2.

SCHWARTZ, D. (1993) 'Superbowl XXVI: Reflections on the manufacture of appearance', *Visual Sociology*, **8**, 1, pp. 23–33.

STAKE, R.E. (1995) *The Art of Case Study Research*, Thousand Oaks: Sage.

TAYLOR, R. (1989) 'Research in child abuse', in BURGESS, R. (ed.) *Investigating Society*, London: Longman Educational.

TRACHTENBERG, A. (1989) *Reading American Photographs: Images as History Mathew Brady to Walker Evans*, New York: Hill and Wang, The Noonday Press.

WALKER, R. and WEIDEL, J. (1985) 'Using photographs in a discipline of words', in BURGESS, R. (ed.) *Field Methods in the Study of Education*, Lewes: Falmer Press, pp. 191–216.

WORTH, S. (1980) 'Margaret mead and the shift from visual anthropology to the anthropology of visual communication', *Studies in Visual Communication*, **6**, 1, pp. 15–22.

WORTH, S. and ADAIR, J. (1972) *Through Navajo Eyes: Explorations in Film Communication and Anthropology*, Bloomington: Indiana University Press.

YIN, R.K. (1994) Case Study Research: Design and Methods, Beverly Hills: Sage.

Chapter 9

Remarks on Visual Competence as an Integral Part of Ethnographic Fieldwork Practice: The Visual Availability of Culture

Michael Ball

Abstract

As a research method, ethnographic fieldwork is organized around participation in, and observation of, socio-cultural arrangements and behaviour. In practice, whilst ethnographic fieldwork is being carried out, it is embedded in an environment which is powerfully visual, and exhibits a distinct visual availability. A case study of Himalayan fieldwork is explored to illustrate aspects of the visual availability of culture. As a research product, ethnography adopts primarily a textual form of representation. A programmatic argument fashioned within this chapter is that an ethnographic variant could be sponsored which makes an investigative topic of cultures' visual availability.

Introduction

This chapter exhibits the following organization. It commences with a consideration of the analytical status of ethnographic description. It is argued that in its various forms, a central attraction of ethnography inheres in its descriptive and qualitative analytical potential. The visual availability of a collection of cultural arrangements is introduced, and it is suggested that visual competence is at the core of fieldwork practice. A case study of the ethnographic analysis of stored visual materials is presented. The case study is based around a visual research problem, and has potential as an ethnographic variant.

Ethnography as Description

It is somewhat ironic to report that in recent years, whilst the ethnographic method has enjoyed something of a vogue in a range of social sciences, within anthropology the discipline which pioneered it and which is widely credited as the originator of ethnography as a fieldwork technique, the method has received considerable criticism (Ball, 1996; Grimshaw and Hart, 1994). Practioners in disciplines as epistemologically diverse as computer science and cultural theory have taken on the apparent qualitative mantel of ethnography, frequently as a perceived haven from various of the excesses of quantification and positivism. The extent to which practioners in these disparate disciplines share a common understanding of ethnography, is of course something of a debatable methodological point, but nonetheless they all pay lip service to the enterprise. As Spencer has however made plain, in anthropological usage ethnography is traditionally methodologically eclectic, blending where appropriate qualitative and quantitative elements (Spencer, 1989). Whilst the early forms of ethnographic fieldwork as developed by Malinowski and others made claims to being potentially descriptively all embracing of a culture, in practice they of course fell considerably short of this goal, except in some quasi functionalist sense (Malinowski, 1922). Early in the ethnographic tradition Evans-Pritchard, a student of Malinowski's, came into conflict with the master's stated preference for an all encompassing ethnography. Tinkering with the method, Evans-Pritchard fashioned a limited problem centred form of research, and his student Gluckman in turn developed a form of case study, whereas Bateson became somewhat more fundamentally critical of the potential of ethnographic description, licensing a form of experimental ethnography long before anthropological post-modernism (Evans-Pritchard, 1937; Bateson, 1936). Thus, after a relatively short period of time within accepted anthropological practice, a range of styles of ethnography were employed, with different levels of analysis, foci and concerns.

In common use, the term ethnography has two distinct senses attributed to it. It serves firstly as a description of a research method for investigating a cultural phenomena, and secondly as a written report or representation which is the standard textual product of the fieldwork, and covers elements from within it. A consideration of the descriptive potential of language has the same relevance for ethnography as it has for all academic and lay analytic activities. Indeed, description is germane to most areas of human activity.

Part of ethnography's attraction inheres in the status and apparent potential veracity of its descriptions of aspects of the fieldwork context. In the competent and imaginative textual products of a Malinowski or an Evans-Pritchard, ethnographies can be fashioned into very readable accounts of cultural arrangements, whereas other ethnographies can be dry or technical. The apparent observational and descriptive veracity and efficacy of the ethnographic method accounts for its current attraction beyond anthropology. The social scientific status of ethnographic description arises from its taken for granted observational foundations. As Malinowski made plain in his classic ethnography of Trobriand, and never tired of reminding us, he had 'been there' as a professional anthropologist, and had seen the arrangements described. In his ethnographic reports, Malinowski displays photographs of himself and his tent in the fieldwork context, as palpable visual evidence, and he also weaves himself into the ethnographic text by the use of the pronoun I. As in I went on a kula expedition and the like, even though in practice it was an aborted one. In a consideration of Levi-Strauss, Sontag romantically characterizes the anthropologist as hero, but as Malinowski's personal diaries attest however, fieldwork can be a lonely, tiresome business, and one clearly pays an emotional and physical price for 'being there' (Malinowski, 1967; Geertz, 1988; Sontag, 1979). Thus, Malinowski guided by the epistemological canon of natural and social science, places a premium on demonstrating the empirical observational foundations of his descriptions. By so doing, Malinowski distinguishes anthropological descriptions from those of others who had also 'been there', including missionaries and traders.

The scientific credentials of anthropological ethnographic analysis and description is in large part wedded to, and suggestive of, a scientific heuristic model in which one collects data and generates theories from the data, a variant of what Popper and others have referred to as the hypothetico-deductive model (Popper, 1963). Research practice is of course neither that simple nor that mechanical and tied to a formula, indeed, as Feyerabend has perceptively advocated, 'anything goes' (Feyerabend, 1975). As Evans-Pritchard and others were only too aware, one can not engage in research without theories to guide the investigation. Without theory, there is no means of distinguishing and ordering observations and in practice, all research includes a mix of theory and data, as indeed do all human activities (Ball and Smith, 1992). In terms of a model of science, possibly the best one can hope for is a variant of what Glazer and Strauss have referred to as grounded theory, but even that is in practice somewhat idealized (Glazer and Strauss, 1967).

At one significant level, ethnographic products tend to be characterized by the quality of their description, what Geertz following Ryle has termed thick description, and are apparently distinct from thinner more 'scientific' modes of description (Geertz, 1973). Ryle's illustrative visualist metaphor for thick description hinges around distinguishing a mechanical bodily motion from its powerfully symbolic sense when embedded in cultural arrangements. The contraction of an eyelid, is contrasted to a symbolic wink of an eye. Whilst Geertz's employment of Ryle is in a scholarly manner engaging and entertaining, by drawing our attention to certain matters, it tends to gloss and obfuscate others. In one sense, Geertz constructs almost an ideal type opposition of scientific description and its constraints, comparing it to the apparent descriptive freedom offered by certain paradigms within the social sciences and humanities. Such freedom however comes with an analytical and terminological price tag attached. Description is always of something in time and space, whether real or fictive developmental or static.

The classic ethnomethodologists were fascinated with the problem of description. Equipped with a reading of the later Wittgenstein, the apparently rule based ethnographic products of cognitive anthropology, Husserlian phenomenology, and a desire to construct a Weberian and Parsonian inspired theory of social action, ethnomethodology offers a powerful and sophisticated treatment of the problem of description. Axiomatic to ethnomethodology's position on description is the view that cultural members through their talk and accounts of what they do, make the very properties of their behaviour and arrangements observable, reportable and palpable in so many words, members methods. Thus, the problem of description is treated as central to all human endeavours (Garfinkel, 1967). In a consideration of the limitations and lack of rigour exhibited by conventional sociological description, Sacks employs the powerful visualist metaphor of a self narrating machine, a 'commentator machine', which whilst carrying out mechanical actions simultaneously describes them. This is a fascinating metaphor which raised the issue of what Sacks termed literal description (Sacks, 1963). Can something be described in so many words adequately and completely, or can we only ever achieve description for all practical purposes?

Sacks's consideration of description is revealing when set against Geertz's discussion of thick and thin description. Whilst Geertz draws attention to the enabling aspects of thick description, Sacks alerts us to certain of its constraints and shortcomings. Geerz's use of Ryle's metaphor hinges on a duality, thick and thin, whereas Sacks focuses on the act of description as a unitary phenomena, which everyone does within both lay and scientific communities. For Sacks, in all instances, description exhibits ethno methods in its artful cultural construction. Ethnomethodology thus equates the practice of science to lay practices as members methods, and thus the professional scientist natural or social is ascribed an unprivileged status of cultural member. Ethnomethodology goes on to argue that rather than language comprising a fine instrument for descriptive purposes, that it is indexical, thus opening a can of worms which is never to be closed however hard we might try (Garfinkel, 1967). Logicians had noted that a range of indexical expressions such as 'this', 'here', and the like amount to ambiguous formulations which only acquire a sense within context. Ethnomethodology extends this by arguing that all language use is contingent on contextual particulars, and that all descriptions are indexical, and index-icality cannot be repaired however 'thick' the description might become. Indeed, whilst 'thick' description might prove qualitatively rich, symbolically suggestive and more directly metaphorical in orientation, it certainly has no more likelihood of accurately fixing a phenomena in language than does the thin descriptions of science, as in Ryle's char-acterization of the contraction of an eyelid. Somewhat perversely, it may prove to be the case that descriptions founded in some professional argot or other, such as a frame-work within physics, which devises specialist concepts with a precise and limited sense attached to them, may be employed to more efficiently and accurately describe phe-nomena. In Wittgensteins sense, it is all a matter of language use and language games (Wittgenstein, 1953).

Ethnomethodology fashioned certain systematic and philosophically rigorous criti-cisms of the ethnographic method, approximately twenty years prior to those of anthro-pological post-modernism. Ethnomethodology steeped in Wittgenstein and phenomenology was for qualitative analysis epistemologically radical. Whilst expressing general support for ethnographic and qualitative orientations, ethnomethodology nonetheless had certain critical points to make about them (Sacks, 1992, p. 26). Central to the ethnomethodological criticism of ethnography, was the methodological observation that many ethnographies amount to 'just so' anecdotal accounts of cultural arrangements in which the reader does not share with the ethnographer the rich data on which the account is founded. Garfinkel and Sacks refer to this practice as an anthropological gloss, the transformation of data collection and field notes into a professional ethnographic report, 'writing culture' (Garfinkel, 1986, p. 187). The products of cognitive anthropology were deemed to com-prise an exception insofar as they were based around collected linguistic materials, which were presented in the body of the report, typically taxonomies of cultural phenomena, such as categories for disease, plants, food and persons (Tyler, 1969).

From the radical ethnomethodological vantage, most conventional ethnographies were considered to be far too unaccountable in terms of the data they employ and the versions and interpretations they fashion from it. For ethnomethodology, ethnographic practice is of interest insofar as the ethnographer employs members methods for making sense of culture. Stoddart, invoking a variant of the topic resource debate informs us how ethnographers appropriate and make a resource of the natives conceptual apparatus for their own professional analytical descriptive purposes, whilst rarely treating it as a topic in its own right (Turner, 1974, p. 173). Conversation analysis, a technical product of ethnomethodology, sets out to make a topic of language use, treating it as social action, whilst offering rich descriptive treatments of stored audio materials, which the writer shares with the reader (Button and Lee, 1987). The reader thus has the ability to agree or disagree with the analysts' version, add to it and the like, a potential which arises from sharing the data on which the descriptions are based. This model is worthy of emulation with visual materials, as it is potentially productive. In much the spirit that conversation analysis modelled its data-based analysis on cognitive anthropology and certain philo-sophical traditions, whilst differing from them, similarly, our suggestions for visual analysis differ from conversation analysis, but draw on certain of its strengths. The purpose being to fashion a form of ethnographic qualitatively informed inquiry of visual materials. A form of enquiry is being advocated which is tied to visual data sources, and presents them alongside the analysis and is thus accountable as the reader or viewer can agree or disagree with the presented analysis. Analytical descriptions based upon shared stored data and accountable through that data, amount to a worthwhile if somewhat ambitious undertaking.

Ethnography and the Visual Domain: Cultures Visual Availability

Ethnographic fieldwork involves the direct observation of people in culture, and the observational metaphor is central to an understanding of the method, of how the ethnographer witnesses cultural arrangements. To this extent, the fieldworker is finely intertwined with the arrangements described. Much as Cicourel has observed, the interactional behaviour of the researcher conducting the fieldwork can significantly affect the data observed and collected, as it is an active and reactive mode of enquiry (Cicourel, 1964, p. 39). Ethnography is thus a study of cultural arrangements and practices, which is engaged in for the purpose of fashioning a descriptive analysis. In conducting fieldwork, the ethnographer engages all the senses, they hear, see, talk, smell, feel and taste culture. When as can be the case for anthropologists, they carry out fieldwork in an exotic culture, then many of the senses but particularly the sounds, smells and visual aspects of the culture can be noticeably in evidence, sharp and distinctly different.

As Garfinkel and Sacks have accurately pointed out, anthropological research in an exotic culture can involve the fieldworker being in a situation in which to different degrees for months and possibly even for the entire stay, the spoken language of the natives may not in any full sense, ever be under their complete control (Garfinkel, 1986, p. 186). The visual domain also comprises a form of 'language' which is however coded somewhat differently, and a cultures 'visual availability' is an area the ethnographer must engage with and acquire competence in from the start of fieldwork (Ball and Smith, 1986). In part, this is the domain Hall was concerned with in his study of the 'silent language' (Hall, 1959). The fieldworker is engaged in making observational sense of a powerfully visual environment, and we are advocating that this commonsense visual component of fieldwork practice, requires to be investigated and understood. Simmel has indicated something of the immense significance of the visual domain to socio-cultural arrangements, when he argued that of our senses, 'the eye has a uniquely sociological function' (Simmel, 1921, p. 358). Within our culture and others, a number of arrangements have a distinct 'visual availability', and fieldworkers must acquire the competence to both recognize and employ it.

For people with sight, the majority of humankind, vision comprises a fundamental sense of occupancy in a shared cultural world. For most persons including of course ethnographers, aspects of the environment they inhabit are 'visually available'. The natural and cultural worlds exhibit a visual availability. The world of nature and other species, and the culturally fashioned built environment including items of material culture, persons and social actions, all are visually available and symbolically significant when making visual sense of the seen world. For most cultural members, observational competence is an elementary foundation for existence and participation in a shared world of appearances in time and space (Heidegger, 1962). The ethnographer of necessity makes copious use of the visual domain when carrying out fieldwork, and it is notable that not all cultures are visually identical.

Anthropologists carrying out fieldwork in exotic cultures are confronted with the visual availability of this difference on a daily basis, as it oozes out of various aspects of cultural life, but surprisingly little of this filters through in the research reports. Anthropologists have however been inclined to include evidence of the cultural difference, and indirectly the visual availability of culture within their ethnographic reports, by adding photographs to the text to serve largely illustrative purposes. The photographs which anthropologists include within their ethnographic reports range from inanimate items of material culture, such as buildings, modes of transport, symbolic items for employment in rituals or whatever, to persons both with and without items of material culture. In all of these types of photographs, the visual availability of culture is both apparent and implicit. For example, photographs of women in Islamic cultures dressed in yashmak or chador, indicates and exhibits something of the visual availability of an abstract matter, a belief system and its consequences for the visual presentation of persons. Examples from Islamic culture, might be usefully contrasted to the visual availability of the presentation of gender in European and north American cultures as revealed in for instance advertising practice (Goffman, 1979).

The powerfully symbolic visual availability of the person in culture is evident in styles of clothing and self decoration, as revealed in for example body and facial art, tattooing, body piercing and clothing fashions (Strathern and Strathern, 1971; Polhemus, 1978). Aspects of rituals and ceremonies and certain scenes and arrangements located within everyday life are also powerfully visually available. For instance, in ritual and ceremony status can often be indicated and visually available in terms of the relative position of one person to another. A person of higher status can be ritually above another person, as in for example a curtsy or bow to a king or queen by a subject, what Goffman has termed the ritualization of subordination (Goffman, 1979). In addition, certain mundane social arrangements such as turn taking systems as occurs with queuing behaviours are visually available (Ball and Smith, 1986). All cultures thus exhibit a rich visual character which is visually available. When carrying out anthropological fieldwork in another culture, the researcher is inescapably bound up in that cultures visual availability, and they must become sufficiently competent to operate within its parameters. In short, the ethnographer is immersed in a world, which includes a powerfully visual component and it is notable that only rarely do even glimpses of this find a formulation in ethnographic reports.

Ethnographic Analysis and the Visual Availability of Cultural Arrangements

In the 1936 epilogue to Naven, Bateson informs us that after carrying out his fieldwork and returning to England, he was confronted with a visual interpretative enigma which in part arose from his inspection of a collection of photographs he had taken of Naven ceremonial amongst the Iatmul people of New Guinea (Bateson, 1936). Bateson implies that by reference to these photographs and his background knowledge acquired from fieldwork, that he was able to make sense of an aspect of Iatmul culture whilst in England, an aspect which from our point of view can be characterized as visually available. Germane to Batesons analytical reasoning, is a reliance on the 'realistic' 'factual' 'documenting' character of photographs in contrast to their aesthetic potential. It must be made plain, that even if it is presumed of photographs that they comprise 'realistic' 'factual' photo chemical 'documentary' representations of some state of affairs such as the Naven ceremonial, and if the interpretative and aesthetic aspects of camera use are primarily glossed, the information encoded in photographs is still far from transparent (Sontag, 1979). As a form of data, photographs are not capable of talking for themselves, the information has to be teased out of them, interpreted and decoded, the visual availability of the phenomena has to be unpacked. Just as language is ambiguous through indexicality, so visual materials and photographs as stored representations are likewise ambiguous insofar as they are polysemic. Stored visual materials such as photographs have been described by Goffman as essentially heterogeneous in character and ambiguously polysemic, in that it is possible to make a number of senses of them, and Barthes has gone further by arguing that the 'denotation' of visual materials renders them polysemic and beyond description (Barthes, 1977; Goffman, 1979). To this extent, the inherent ambiguity of visual materials is fundamental to their character.

Bateson was able to employ his visual materials to assist in the solution of an analytical problem by reference to a range of theories he had fashioned concerning the phenomena of Naven. Bateson's concerns were not arbitrary, they arose from the magnitude of analytical questions he addressed and the combination of theories he employed for explanatory purposes, furnishing him with 'A composite picture' — 'From three points of view'. Thus, in the 1930s Bateson engaged in a form of ethnography which would now likely warrant or earn the title experimental, as a consequence of it exhibiting certain features in common with post-modern and post-structuralist thinking, namely the exploration of a unit of data from a range of theoretical perspectives (Clifford and Marcus, 1986). Navens subtitle, 'A survey of the problems suggested by a composite picture of the culture of a New Guinea tribe drawn from three points of view', makes extensive active use of visual metaphors. Thus, prior to his pioneering visual analytical work with Mead, Bateson made use of the visual in his explanation of the Naven ceremonial, which involved recourse to the fully public visual availability of displays of ritual transvestitism and homosexuality (Bateson and Mead, 1942). Aspects of Bateson's radical epistemological orientation in Naven serve as an exemplar for an analysis of a problem associated with data obtained from our own fieldwork.

A Case Study in the Ethnographic Analysis of Stored Visual Materials

The Ethnographic Context

The case study arose from a period of preliminary fieldwork in Manali in the Kulu valley in Himalayan India, an essentially Hindu area. Manali is the gateway to a collection of high mountain passes into Tibet and other parts of India, areas whose culture is primarily Tibetan. Following China's occupation of Tibet Manali has a large community of Tibetan Buddhist refugees. Manali boasts two notable Buddhist monasteries (gompas). The ethno graphic research project was organized around an investigation of certain Tibetan Buddhist meditation practices, a limited problem-centred form of ethnography. As part of the research, although not linked directly into the study of meditation practice, collections of photographs of the Tibetan Buddhist community and items from its material culture were taken, focusing around their visual availability. Aspects of Tibetan Buddhist culture which through their visual availability, serve to distinguish it from the indigenous Hindu culture of which collections of thematized photographs were also taken. Visually exotic aspects of Tibetan Buddhist material culture can be found displayed in a number of standard textbooks. An early work, is Waddell's, which although deficient and wrong on certain aspects of the culture, is non the less interesting for its visual representations and artwork (Waddell, 1895).

After returning to England and having numerous reels of photographic film developed, in common with Bateson, a significant post-fieldwork interpretive dilemma was experienced. This arose from the inspection of visual materials when away from the fieldwork context, a dilemma which had nothing to do with Tibetan culture in particular, and was indeed more a feature of the visual availability of an aspect of the indigenous Indian culture. As part of the research, collection of thematically related photographs of items of material culture and aspects of daily life in Manali were taken, with no particular purpose in mind, except for them to serve as forms of visual fieldnotes. Within the corpus, a small collection of thematically linked photographs posed a problem (see Figures 9.1 to 9.5). It needs to be made plain that whilst this collection of photographs are not fully random, neither are they part of some grand systematic research plan, although an after the fact rationalization of fieldwork practice could display them as such. As with all photographs however, certain images have been consciously selected, whilst other visually available features have been ignored, thus a purpose and no purpose. Figures 9.1 and 9.2 reveal two buildings, one of brick the other of wood. Figures 9.3 and 9.4 focus on the written signs which each building displays, whilst Figure 9.5 reveals a type of courtyard area between the buildings, indicating something of the spatial arrangement they display.

Figure 9.1

Figure 9.2

Figure 9.3

Figure 9.4

Figure 9.5

After the photographs had been developed, a close inspection of Figures 9.1 to 9.5, when back in England, distant in time, some six months or so after having taken them, and space, thousands of miles away revealed an interpretative dilemma. Figure 9.3, of the sign displayed in front of the smaller wooden building was plainly out of focus and effectively unreadable. To what extent can the visual availability displayed collectively by the photographs, which are themselves visual fragments, be explored adequately without this information? Being thousands of miles away from Manali, with no immediate possibility of returning, the enigma was not resolvable except by treating the photographs as visual data, and engaging in practical reasoning about the information encoded within them. Equipped with Ruby's argument that photographs amount to culturally informed representations for 'Establishing pictorial systems of inference which are based upon anthropological or scientific paradigms', it is possible to set about exploring the materials (Ruby, 1976, p. 7). Photographs are a relatively accurate two-dimensional record or representation of a three dimensional phenomena.

To engage in analytical textual descriptions founded on photographs, is to construct representations of representations. It is to move from the visual domain into the textual, but to do so based upon photographs as a form of fixed stored and accountable data, which can be repeatedly reviewed and also shared with the reader of the text. In this type of analysis, the photographic data which displays its particulars visually, is given centre stage, and its analysis is accountable at every turn. As a practice, this is far from common place within the social sciences, where data tends to be alluded to rather than revealed as a component part of analysis.

The form of accountability offered by this ethnographic variant is subtle and sophisticated, insofar as the reader can actively follow analytical developments within the text and actively agree or disagree with the analyst's version. The reader thus has reflexively available the relationship of the data to its analysis, as it is assembled, and the authority of the author and text can be at all stages accounted for and challenged by the reader. The reader is no longer a passenger in an analytical vehicle fashioned by the author, and in one sense, they have also 'been there' and viewed the materials. Having emphasized these positive dimensions of this mode of analysis, something of the status of the data and of visual representations as a class of phenomena needs to be placed in context. Figures 9.1 to 9.5 comprise data fragments, all photographs are visual fragments. Photographs do not and could not comprise a complete or fully systematic record of the scene or scenes depicted. Indeed, to fashion something even loosely approximating to such an analytic design, to fully record the visual availability of a phenomena, would necessitate taking reels and reels of still photographs of the same visual phenomena from every conceivable angle and vantage. An inspection of Figures 9.1 to 9.5 reveals that they were taken from roughly one vantage, the roadside, and at best they can be said to represent a partial version of that view. As a photographic corpus, they are thematically loosely related one to the other. Sharing these photographs with the reader is in one sense analogous to sharing with them pages of 'raw' field notes, before they are interpreted and fashioned into a written report for publishing. In another sense, it is to share, with the reader something of the messy processual and fragmentary character of how analysis is always fashioned and arrived at.

It has already been noted that photographs and all visual materials are polysemic. Within the limited visual frames offered by Figures 9.1 to 9.5 a range of items and information are visually available, and it is always possible to speculate and infer about the relationship of the depicted items one to the other. Thus, whilst a photograph might be intentionally focused and taken to reveal a particular aspect or item within a visual field, in pursuit of one analytical theme, it will automatically and inescapably always reveal others. Figures 9.1 to 9.5, reveal buildings, walls, signs a motorcycle and scooter as items of material culture, persons, Himalayan mountains, plants and shrubs as items of the natural environment, culture nature.

Employed as sources of stored visual materials, photographs enable if not encourage the eye to rest for an extended period of time on the scenes depicted, and to unnaturally subject these scenes to close inspection and scrutiny. In contrast, when routinely or 'naturally' encountering the scenes depicted in Figures 9.1 to 9.5, as part of daily life, people would likely pay no more attention to them than that of an observational glance. Much as Sudnow has argued, in daily life the fleeting glance is an observational device which is sufficient for making rapid sense of a setting and negotiating oneself through environments of persons and things efficiently for the practical purposes at hand (Sudnow, 1972, p. 259). Plainly, an extended analytical inspection of stored visual materials has the potential to furnish more elaborate information than a fleeting glance, in much the manner that conversation analysis does for brief utterances recorded from everyday conversations. It is however unlikely in daily life that the scenes shown in Figures 9.1 to 9.5, would receive anything like the observational interest lavished on them in our analysis. As a principal, this applies equally to other analogous modes of scholarly analysis. For example, whilst conversation analysis, can subject an utterance to close scrutiny, in the conversation it is naturally embedded within, it would likely be rapidly passed over by the participants (Button and Lee, 1987). That said, the analytical advantages conferred by the relatively permanent stored photographic record are immense. It facilitates continuous access to its version or vantage of the particulars of the photographed scene, within the context of an analytical enterprise. A temporally extensive inspection of a photograph has the potential to furnish more information and enable greater analytical conjecture about the recorded scene than it is possible to fashion from a brief observational glance.

Preliminary Observations on the Data

Foundational to the current analytical enterprise is the assumption that what we see in the visual materials is also readily seen by others, and that the commonsense practical reasoning we employ is employed by others in these and analogous situations. This is not an attempt to fashion an account of how sense is made of built environments in general, but of how sense can be made of this data, to explore something of the particulars of this built environment. To borrow a phrase from Garfinkel, our data is not being treated as the 'poor relatives' of the elegant properties of some formal model or other (Garfinkel, 1967). An inspection of Figures 9.1 to 9.5 reveals two single-storey buildings which at the level of visual availability differ from each other significantly on relative size, architectural style, the construction materials used and the ambience they exude. The spatial relationship between the two buildings as revealed from the vantage of the road which passes them is illustrated in Figure 9.5. To the left behind the motorcycle is a building of largely timber construction with an essentially run-down appearance, whereas to the right is a a building of newish appearance, of largely brick construction. The buildings are sited along one of the main roads around the northern edge of Manali. There is no obvious boundary either between the two buildings or jointly around them, although on one side the road and low brick walls operate as a perimeter. Between the two buildings as revealed in Figures 9.1 and 9.2, but particularly by Figure 9.5, a type of joint courtyard area is visually available from which paths radiate effectively connecting the buildings, and tyre marks suggest that vehicles have been either parked in or driven across the area. As Hall informs us, 'space speaks' (Hall, 1959).

The two buildings are observably adjacent, and their closeness indicates that a relationship likely exists between them. Buildings in close proximity to each other are frequently seen as in some sense belonging together, in the same manner that co-present people such as the two males in the courtyard in Figure 9.5, would for Goffman comprise a 'with' (Goffman, 1971). Juxtaposition and close location are very suggestive in this respect. Collections of buildings can hence be seen as linked together, comprising a school, motel, factory, or whatever. Proximity thus affects how we interpret what we see. Sharrock and Anderson make a similar point concerning the location of and relationship between collections of directional signs in a hospital, when they argue 'Spatial organisation is a powerful aspect of social organisation, and local organisation a potent form of spatial organisation, and things found in the same locality often have a stronger association than those of juxtaposition' (Sharrock and Anderson, 1979, p. 83). Similarly, we argue that proximity coupled with how the space is used, is strongly suggestive of a relationship existing between the two buildings in the data. When the two buildings are compared in terms of their relative size, materials of construction and aesthetic matters such as style, prestigious appearance and imposing location, this suggests that the one to the left is both smaller and occupies a less commanding position than the one to the right, Figures 9.1, 9.2 and 9.5. When compared to each other, these buildings prove almost a paradigm case of Marx's perceptive observation on the relative character of impoverishment, when he commented that 'A house may be large or small, as long as the surrounding houses are equally small it satisfies all social demands for a dwelling. But let a palace arise besides the little house and it shrinks from a house to a hut' (Marx and Engels, 1968, p. 83). In Manali, buildings range from the makeshift shanty accommodation of some Tibetan refugees to the more permanent buildings of the indigenous Indian population.

Signs

Figures 9.3 and 9.4 are of the written signs each of the buildings displayed. The use of signs in public and semi-public spaces is now common place in India and other cultures. Signs can employ pictorial symbols as a communicative medium, and or linguistic information. Certain signs can be completely pictorial and non linguistic, as in internationally conventional signs indicating litter disposal, male and female toilets, or one way traffic flow. Other signs comprise information in written form only, such as those informing of Harvard University Law School or Buckingham Palace. A further type of sign comprising a mixture of the pictorial and written. Linguistic signs are informational fragments which inform about some state of affairs, social arrangement, prohibition, or direction to be followed. Signs inform that trespassers will be prosecuted, no parking, Smiths garage, and the like. In the public and semi-public domains, we inhabit a world remarkable for its visual availability, in which items of material culture such as signs are consciously designed to attract our attention and to be looked at. The purpose of all signs is to be seen, and there can be considerable competition for our visual attention. The types of signs can

range from advertisements to those indicating location, direction, information, or displaying the name of an organisation such as Safeway, or Oxford University.

In Figures 9.3 and 9.4 locating the signs prominently in the front of the buildings
invites viewers to see them as having something to say or as providing some information
about that building or context. The signs are analogous to the labels on purchased pack-
aged commodities which indicate the contents, such as Yorkshire tea or Coca Cola. They
are also analogous to captions sited next to photographs included in ethnographies, which
inform us that the photograph is of a shamanic seance. Figure 9.4 is in English, a major
public written language in India, used for advertisements and public notices. The sign
in Figure 9.4 informs us that the building is part of the H.P.S.E.B. (organization), and
that it is the office of the Executive Engineer Elect. Division Manali. The sign thus speci-
fies the occupational category of the person who has certain incumbency rights over the
building. The sign is read in context and strongly particularistic, being of application to
this building only, and not to buildings in general. Taken in the broader framework of
the information which can be cumulatively gleaned from Figures 9.1, 9.2, 9.3 and 9.5.
Figure 9.4 serves as a visually available document concerning this context. Making sense
of the visual availability displayed by Figures 9.1 to 9.5 is analogous to what Garfinkel
has referred to as the documentary method, insofar as the photographs of signs and
buildings serve as documents which stand on behalf of the circumstances they visually
depict (Garfinkel, 1967).

In all instances of making sense of written signs, the sense is context dependent,
relating to the practical concerns of the user. As Sharrock and Anderson have perceptively observed concerning directional Hospital signs, 'When we think of people using
signs it becomes obvious that the use they make of them is practical. They are not interested in the meaning of the sign but are interested in using the sign for some purpose.
They are not interested in what signs in general mean, but in the use they can make of
THIS sign HERE and NOW. Their reasoning is not theoretical and general but practical'
(Sharrock and Anderson, 1979, p. 81). As indicated, the photograph of one of the signs
Figure 9.3 was effectively out of focus and unusable for reading the sign, thus posing
a post-fieldwork interpretative dilemma. As a photograph of a sign, Figure 9.3 is almost
useless, and in its current form it hardly serves as a visual facsimile of the sign. Equipped
only with the information available in Figure 9.3, this sign could inform us of anything,
for example that it is the anthropology department of Manali University, or encourage us
to purchase an ice cream. In order to resolve our dilemma, the assistance of a professional
photographic studio was sought some months later. The negative of Figure 9.3 was repro-
cessed, enlarged and treated, in an attempt to discover the written content of the sign, the
outcome being Figure 9.6. Whilst Figure 9.6. is not perfectly clear, its message, at least
that in large English letters is generally discernible, informing us that the building is used
by the assistant engineer of the Electric. Subdivision Manali. At the bottom of the sign is
an undecipherable communication in an Asian language, likely Hindi, which is possibly
an approximate equivalent of the English. Having linguistic information available to us
from both signs, we are in a position to argue that the buildings are not only adjacent to
one and other but significantly they are also organizationally linked. Employing Goffman's
terminology, they can be seen as comprising a 'with', in this instance an inanimate one,
and are thus fully visible as being associated one with the other (Goffman, 1971). The
categories executive and assistant engineer are likely positions from within a broader organizational framework, and suggestive of hierarchical social organizational arrangements
(Handy, 1976).

Figure 9.6

The Potential to Analyse a Unit of Data from Different Theoretical Vantages

As already indicated, Bateson's *Naven* serves as a classical illustration of experimental ethnography. Early in the fieldworking tradition, Bateson set out to if not break away from the fledgling ethnographic mould, then to display certain of its limitations. Bateson's work preceded by many years the current vogue for purposefully self conscious reflexive forms of experimental ethnography. Marcus has termed this orientation 'different takes on a common object of study', and he recommends that theoretical orientations be juxtaposed (Marcus, 1989, p. 12). In the case of exploring, Figures 9.1 to 9.6, we would not promote the juxtaposing of theoretical orientations for good analytical reasons. In contrast, different but complementary comparative analytical frameworks might prove more heuristically satisfying, cumulative and useful as an approach for certain purposes when framing 'different takes on a common object of study'.

The analytical machineries of structuralism, cognitive anthropology, and ethnomethodology are each data sensitive in their own ways, and could be productively applied to the visual data in order to explore different aspects of its analytical potential, and its visual availability (Levi-Strauss, 1978; Tyler, 1969; Garfinkel, 1986). Each of the analytical machineries are distinct and in no sense interchangeable. Each is geared to its analytical purposes only, and each directs us to focus on certain concerns at the expense of others. The common thread which runs through each of the approaches is that all are cognitively focused and singularly data sensitive and in part formalistic in orientation. Data sensitivity comprises a matter of huge analytical consequence for the type of enterprise outlined above.

To conclude, it has been argued that linguistic description, ethnographic or otherwise turns out to be somewhat less than straightforward. As a fieldworking enterprise, the ethnographer trades on their general visual competence and ability to interpret culture's visual availability. This chapter places on a somewhat firmer epistemological basis the proposal that ethnographic analysis framed around aspects of a culture's visual availability and the ethnographers visual competence, might be promoted as a productive and accountable ethnographic variant.

References

BALL, M.S. (1996) *Remarks on Certain Methodological Implications of Post Modernism*, Occasional Papers Series: Staffordshire University.

BALL, M.S. and SMITH, G.W.H. (1986) 'The visual availability of queuing's local organisation', *Communication and Cognition*, **19**, 1.

BALL, M.S. and SMITH, G.W.H. (1992) *Analyzing Visual Data*, California: Sage.

BARTHES, R. (1977) *Image Music Text*, London: Fontana Press.

BATESON, G. (1936) *Naven*, Cambridge, UK: Cambridge University Press.

BATESON, G. and MEAD, M. (1942) *Balinese Character* (Special Publications, vol. 2), New York: New York Academy of Sciences.

BUTTON, G. and LEE, J.R. (eds) (1987) *Talk and Social Organisation*: Avon Multilingual Matters.

CICOUREL, A.V. (1964) *Method and Measurement in Sociology*, New York: Free Press.

CLIFFORD, J. and MARCUS, G.E. (eds) (1986) *Writing Culture*, Berkeley: University of California Press.

EVANS-PRITCHARD, E.E. (1937) *Witchcraft, Oracles and Magic Among the Azande*, Oxford, UK: Oxford University Press.

FEYERABEND, P. (1975) *Against Method*, UK: Verso.

GARFINKEL, H. (1967) *Studies in Ethnomethodology*, Englewood Cliffs, NJ: Prentice Hall.

GARFINKEL, H. (ed.) (1986) *Ethnomethodological Studies of Work*, London: Routledge & Kegan Paul.

GEERTZ, C. (1973) *The Interpretation of Cultures*, New York: Basic Books.

GEERTZ, C. (1988) *Works and Lives*, Stanford, California: Stanford University Press.

GLASER, B.G. and STRAUSS, A.L. (1967) *The Discovery of Grounded Theory*, Chicago: Aldine.

GOFFMAN, E. (1971) *Relations in Public*, New York: Basic Books.

GOFFMAN, E. (1979) *Gender Advertisements*, London: Macmillan.

GRIMSHAW, A. and HART, K. (1994) 'Anthropology and the crisis of the intellectuals', *Critique of Anthropology*, **14**, 3, p. 227.

HALL, E.T. (1959) *The Silent Language*, New York: Doubleday.

HANDY, C.B. (1976) *Understanding Organisations*, Harmondsworth, UK: Penguin.

HEIDEGGER, M. (1962) *Being and Time*, London: Macmillan.

LEVI-STRAUSS, C. (1978) *Structural Anthropology*, vol. 2, Harmondsworth, UK: Perigrine.

MALINOWSKI, B. (1922) *Argonauts of the Western Pacific*, London: Routledge.

MALINOWSKI, B. (1967) *A Diary in the Strict Sense of the Term*, London: Routledge & Kegan Paul.

MARCUS, G.E. (1989) 'Imaging the whole', *Critique of Anthropology*, **9**, 3, p. 7.

MARX, K. and ENGELS, F. (1968) *Selected Works*, London: Lawrence & Wishart.

POLHEMUS, T. (ed.) (1978) *Social Aspects of the Human Body*, Harmondsworth, UK: Penguin.

POPPER, K.R. (1963) *Conjectures and Refutations*, London: Routledge & Kegan Paul.

RUBY, J. (1976) 'In a pic's eye', *Afterimage*, **3** (March), pp. 5–7.

SACKS, H. (1963) 'Sociological descriptions', *Berkeley Journal of Sociology*, **8**, p. 1.

SACKS, H. (1992) *Lectures On Conversation* (2 vols), Oxford, UK: Basil Blackwell.

SHARROCK, W.W. and ANDERSON, D. (1979) 'Directional hospital signs as sociological data', *Information Design Journal*, **1**, 2, p. 81.

SIMMEL, G. (1921) 'Sociology of the senses: Visual interaction', in PARK, R.E. and BURGESS, E.W. (eds) *Introduction to the Science of Sociology*, Chicago: University of Chicago Press.

SONTAG, S. (1970) 'The anthropologist as hero', in HAYES, E.N. and HAYES, T. (eds) *Claude Levi-Strauss: The Anthropologist as Hero*, Cambridge, Mass.: The MIT Press.

SONTAG, S. (1979) *On Photography*, Harmondsworth, UK: Penguin.

SPENCER, J. (1989) *Anthropology As a Kind of Writing*, Man, **24**, 1, p. 145.

STRATHERN, A. and STRATHERN, M. (1971) *Self-decoration in Mount Hagan*, London: Duckworth.

SUDNOW, D. (ed.) (1972) *Studies in Social Interaction*, New York: Free Press.

TURNER, R. (ed.) (1974) *Ethnomethodology*, Harmondsworth, UK: Penguin.

TYLER, S.A. (ed.) (1969) *Cognitive Anthropology*, New York: Rinehart & Winston.

WADDEL, L.A. (1895) *The Buddhism of Tibet, or Lamaism*, London: Allen.

WITTGENSTEIN, L. (1953) *Philosophical Investigations*, Oxford, UK: Basil Blackwell.

Chapter 10

Photocontext

Clem Adelman

Abstract

In his chapter Clem Adelman considers the problem of what might be acceptable as a valid photodocument by qualitative researchers. Drawing on sources from evaluation, sociology and anthropology the author suggests criteria for claims of validity and these based on the photographers explicit awareness of social and photo contexts.

There are two contexts that yield meanings inferred about photographs. One is the context in which photographs are made; the other is the context in which they are viewed. (Templin, 1982, p. 138)

In this book the chapter by Becker concentrates on 'the context in which they are viewed', I am writing about the context of making or, as I will argue, the context of discovery rather than the context of justification of interpretation.[1] I mean that to understand the making, the photographer has to give a reflexive account of the way in which the image for the photograph was discovered. The justification is the account which gives the reasons why the photograph is significant in relation to other photographs and to one or more *à priori* social interpretations of the action, interaction, artefacts and object relations. Most photographs we see in journals and newspapers confirm our beliefs and are taken by the photographer with that rather than with discovery in mind. Ron Silvers (1988) writing about his journeys in Ladakh says:

In composing A Pause on the Path, I felt that I had to carefully reflect my experience of liminality, but to do so, I had to depart from methods of the human sciences and also from a photographic tradition based either on absenting the photographer writer, or on taking the role of a knowledgeable cultural overseer. (Silvers, 1988, p. 184)

The photograph is ultimately an extension of the photographer not of the technology and technique of photography. Even the legendary Cartier-Bresson states that too much is said of technique diverting attention from the qualities of the maker, the photographer;

a whole fetishism has grown up around the technique of photography. Technique should be so conceived and adapted as to induce a way of seeing things, preferably in essentials, excluding the effects of gratuitous virtuosity and other ineptitudes. Technique is important and we should master it . . . The real problem is one of intelligence and sensitivity. (Cartier-Bresson, 1968, p. iv)

'Intelligence' for the French means to comprehend the relationships of one part to another, which would include the photographer's awareness of the relation of prominence to context in the making of the photograph. Awareness is a prerequisite for reflexive accounts of practice. That few photographers have written reflexively about the context of making does not mean they are unaware but that they are more concerned with technique and the impact of the photo on the viewer. Cinematographers have written reflexively about context in the image and through montage for decades (Eisenstein, 1943).

Indeed no one approach to the collection of photos as documents can be claimed as the 'natural', unobtrusive way, that is without the photographer making some selection from the whole whether fortuitously ('it was the only place I could stand') or deliberately.

It is impossible to do serious social documentation with a camera without some informing theory: there are too many chances for selection, options for inclusion or exclusion, too many choices to be made. (Jackson, 1981, p. 40)

Duff (1981) concludes:

Photography, then, is a mechanical process crucially dependent on a single human decision. The process produces single images which are again, crucially dependent, on the context, in which they are seen. Photographs might appear to be self-evident but they are more often open, incomplete and ambiguous, and to make sense of them they need to be seen with words or with other images. (Duff, 1981, p. 76)

Ruby refers to the normative assumptions that have been employed to differentiate the document called self portrait as compared to that called documentary:

If you wanted to make films about people exotic to your own experience you made documentaries, and if you wanted to explore yourself, your feelings, and the known world around you, you made personal art films, which tend to be more self referential than the autobiographical or self-portrait films. In subject matter they violate the norms of traditional documentary in that they are overtly motivated by and deal with a personal interest of the film maker. Yet the look or style of these films is documentary. In other words, the subject matter is that which has been traditionally the province of the art film-maker and the style is that of the documentary. (Ruby, 1978, p. 9)

Recently Bromhead (1996) has argued that to the viewer there is often no detectable difference between 'documentary' and 'art' film. The differences are in the methodology of the making.

The Sensitive Eye

What can be said about the making of the photograph for qualitative research? What does the photographer take into account about context in the making and in subsequent technical work? I will begin to answer there questions and, drawing on a variety of sources, suggest some guidelines for the making of qualitative research photographs. I use the quasi-experimentalists terms 'reliablity' and 'validity' partly because they still pervade the literature of research, even qualitative research, although the positivist assertions in both qualitative and quantitative literature have long since been rejected by the very people who founded quasi-experimental work.[2] My main concern is with the problems of context and reflexivity.

We could begin by suggesting that the research photograph is a method seeking discovery, rather than a technique of documenting life instances and object relationships. Some photographs are images of instances and events taken without interfering with the action as in a public place, such as an open street with no or few 'focused encounters' (Goffman, 1963). For the photographer and 'subjects', photographs made in places with mutual gaze or surveillance with mostly focused encounters, as in prisons, law courts or hospital wards share the problem of reaction to the presence of the observers' gaze. But the presence of the gaze through a camera makes for even greater intrusion into the personal identity of others. The reaction may be for the subjects to cease their action to hurling direct abuse at the photographer. The context in these cases is not given only through the visual medium but by some prior knowledge of the social relations in the organization.

In his comments on drafts of this article, Ron Silvers (1997) wrote:

> Discovery means locating phenomena that is not conceptually determined: phenomena that emerge out of the tacit concerns and interpretative sensitivities that you bring to the occasion of research. Indeed the whole point of the 'sensitive eye', as you call it, is one in which the unconscious and conscious come together to inform us of what animates our action. You note Berger's distinction between film and still photography, the former permitting discovery of development, the latter allowing for finding conjuncture. The former emphasizes time, the latter space. (Silvers, 1997)

My suggestion of a second process level of internal validity being that of photographic selectivity is extremely important since the photographer must be positioned (the spatial dimension) in order to locate conjunction. This is really the operative feature of Cartier-Bresson's 'decisive moment'. His term seems to refer to the exact, crucial time of the operator taking the photograph, when in fact, if we look at his images, they are spatially decisive: his position as photographer in reference to subjects and the surrounding visual environment, when all three are exactly in their respective positions to offer a visual account of the action taking place.

> My own experience of photography is not to look for the right time to press the shutter, but rather to enter into rhythm of the subject's gestures so as to be a part of the flow of events without 'consciously' anticipating what gesture is to come. Once in the rhythm, I select a gesture preconsciously, since the moment that I release the shutter is temporally prior to the 'seeing' of the gesture. If we are to wait for the gesture we want to 'capture' on film, that gesture has already under-gone change: we photograph something else. This is true for all who photograph people in their everyday activities — when they are not setting a pose. We cannot work

any other way in documentary photography. Now I realize that writing about the presence of the preconscious in research may be heretical, but I believe there is no way around this issue of photographic documentation and the evaluation of such research. All methodology, as I see it, must submit to accountability. Part of that accountability is to acknowledge the limits of what we can make explicitly available to ourselves and to others. It is also to recognize the limits of our control within research. I can say more about entering gestural rhythms and what is operative, but that, I think, is to go outside of your paper. (ibid.)

The research photograph would desirably be a documenting of a spontaneous rather than contrived instance but the reactivity of 'subjects' eliminates spontaneity of subjects social relations. The photographer's sensitivity and intelligence in relation to context and instance is challenged by such a threat to claims of validity.

Documenting Instances

For the researcher the pursuit of internal validity for the photo document entails; informed selection of what to document, being systematic through reflection in the taking of photographs whether one approves or disapproves of the action being recorded, justified sampling, low reactivity of the subjects to the presence of the photographer, 'normal' printing, no editing, argued inclusion as evidence in a research report/and or presentation — whether the medium is photo, slide, film, video, CD ROM and so on.

Here we are considering not only what criteria a photographer employs to take a valid photograph but whether those criteria are employed consistently. In psychostatistical research reliability (consistency) is related to sampling and sampling to hypotheses. The reliability of data has to be demonstrated before internal validity is sought. Without reliable data, claims of external validity would be discounted whatever the interpreter's credence. A similar methodology; informed guess, tested by sampling, consistency and then to validity is claimed by few photodocumentarists. Templin's excellent 1982 article mentions this point and but she goes further to she ask the question; to what extent are photographers reflexive about the criteria they are employing in taking the photo? She notes the extent that many single and series photo documents (rather than a case study or 'thick description') are taken without either research methodological criteria or method ical reflexivity.

Internal Validity and Reflexivity

In social documentary photography, there is a need to have prior theory to pose questions and direct the study and to have some assurance about the photographic practice that follows it. Yet perhaps the greatest threat validity is not the danger of being guided by an unfruitful line of theorising, but, rather, having to account for photographic data that 'just happened' and that cannot be shown to have arisen from the rules of sampling or data collection. This serendipitous quality of photography has a powerful influence over the place of theory in the interpretative process taking place, and requires continuous searching for new information that may contest or modify the interpretation. (Templin, 1982, p. 137)

The crucial problem for those who seek validity of photo document as evidence seems to me to be able to account for the inclusion of particular context at the point of taking the photo. In this chapter I am more concerned with the criteria for what used to be called (see Note 1) 'internal validity' of the photo document; but more so with the reflexive problems of context for meaning for the person recording the event, the instant. As researchers we are obsessed with meaning of data for ourselves and others and if we claim to conduct our qualitative research by interpretative means then we allow anyone to make interpretations of our data. Would we only present those photo documents that we considered internally valid? 'Insufficient' context would logically prompt demands from viewers for more context before some meaning could be given to the photo document. If the context demanded were not forthcoming would the photo document be classed having dubious 'external validity' or generalizability from the instance to an inclusive class or even none at all if few or no viewers agreed on the social meaning rather than just the signification of the photograph?

The important and testing question for the photodocumentarist is what additional context is required for similar social meaning to be given by viewers. Does the viewer need to know more? Will demographic detail suffice? In which case include details of age, gender, class, ethnicity, occupation, geographical location and date of taking.

Becker (1974) argues that making sense of a situation is prior to taking valid (rather than arbitrary or intuitive) photographs. To 'make sense' the photographer draws on his or her own ideas about how individual actions relate to social practices. Becker is saying that the photodocumentarist has to have more than an itemised knowledge of a society and its cultures; a reflexive understanding is required. But social theorists are not necessarily able to capture the instants of the social action as a visual image. The seeing of the relationships and the essential context at the moment of self revelation is one ability; taking the photograph at that instant seems to often elude many professional photographers.

When social documentary photography is not analytically dense the reason may be that photographers use theories that are overly simple. They do not acquire a deep, differentiated and sophisticated knowledge of the people and activities they investigate. Conversely, when their work gives a satisfyingly complex understanding of a subject, it is because they have acquired a sufficiently elaborate theory to alert them to the visual manifestations of that complexity. In short, the way to change and improve photographic images lies less in technical considerations than in improving your comprehension of what you are photographing — your theory. (Becker, 1974, p. 11)

My experience of working from awareness towards the methodological reflexivity required by a photodocumenarist suggests that the person with the camera 'follows' and 'captures' the significant action only by prior observation and understanding of the culture. The point at which to take a photo in the process of action and interaction is one where the membership and context exemplify the theory, not as a 'one off' but as a contiguous series. This is the indicator that the photographer-theorist has been in the right place at the right time with the right line up of actors. In Kenneth Burke's (1945) terms the setting, scene, action, act and agency were all taken into account by the reflexive photographer to be included as context for taking a photo which pertains to a known hypothesis, null or positive. If this seems hypothetico-deductive and too neatly rational a process then I must add that the social hypotheses and the enactment context only inform when then photodocument may be taken. The images collected are often 'discoveries' to the qualitative researcher, being 'more than' and 'different to' that expected. Such 'discrepancies' should be pursued by reflection on the hypotheses and the case, by going back to the scene/setting/action matrix over time and trying to find other examples in other places. By this methodology of analytic induction (Robinson, 1951) higher level contrastive categories are constructed from internally valid photographs and this process continues until categories are saturated and 'deviant' photos accounted for. This is one means of adding to the photographers claims that the photo document is valid rather than random or accidental.

Another perspective on the conscious context of the photographer is to ask why, to the viewer, few photographs 'tell their own story'. John Berger (1971) writes:

> It has often been said that no good photograph requires a caption . . . The photograph itself demonstrates why the photographer chose to take the picture at exactly that moment. It was the moment when what was visible made sense of itself. A photograph which preserves the original uniqueness of the event or person it depicts are very rare. (Berger, 1971, p. ii)

Berger suggests that Walker Evans and Cartier-Bresson have been able to take such 'internally valid' photographs, fulfilling the four criteria embodied in the above quotation. The majority of photographers, he implies give meaning, or in the researchers term external validity, through confirming our knowledge of the world, caption, explanatory text as in a research report and by montage. If we were teaching the history of the second part of this century the well-known photo of the Vietnamese child on fire, running towards the photographer (you and me) would be sufficient to prompt meanings of cruelty, devastation and peril but would prompt questions about where and when and what war that would require the teacher to discuss the Vietnam war and its ramifications. The photo of a helicopter on a lawn with a person huddled under a jacket being assisted into the helicopter has only one additional clue and only for those who recognize the building as the White House. That photo document as a representation is unremarkable; when we are told that the person is President Nixon fleeing after Watergate we may be given meaning.

But this apparent external validity is false if we do not have surety of the internal validity; why was the photo taken in that way? I suggest that one off photo documents like this are rarely the stuff of internally valid qualitative research and whilst agreeing with Berger have some doubts about his exemplars as photodocumentarists as compared to art photographers. Walker-Evans (Curtis, 1986) is said to have set up his scenes to suit his aesthetic preferences rather like O'Flaherty in what is now contested to be authentic documentary film. But as Ruby (1978) and Bromhead (1996) as with many other authors observe, in appearance the 'documentary' and the 'art film' are now indistinguishable.

But I am not suggesting that researchers have ever accepted that the label documentary means that the record is internally valid. Qualitative researchers, I suggest, should work towards agreement on criteria for what could be called 'image research records'. Fred Erickson and Jan Wilson (1982), suggest a differentiation into 'ethnographic film', cinema verity and microethnograpic film:

> The purposes of the microethnographic approach are to identify the fundamental principles of social organisation, and to identify the cultural patterning of that organisation, according to which people make sense of the actions of others and take in the conduct of everyday life. . . . While the main purpose of ethnographic film [and *cinéma vérité* — this author] is to tell a story, and do so in a selective way, the main criteria for film or tape that is to be used as a primary data source is that it contain as complete a record as possible of the continuous sequence of action as it occurs in real time. Such records permit systematic analysis of verbal and non-verbal behaviour in the event recorded. (Erickson and Wilson, 1982, p. 43)

I think that the single photo cannot fulfil the reflexive and internal validity criteria for the research photodocumentarist. However the montage by Euan Duff from which the Berger quote is extracted does fulfil many of the criteria and this without any written text from Duff. But the external validity is limited to those who know the culture he has photographed; the affiliations and affections at home and at work of the 1950–60s urban working class.

Accounts of Reflexive Photographers

The montage of Euan Duff is made possible by his long-term photographic project and his reflexivity on it. There are few photographic montage volumes which satisfy qualitative research criteria; Ron Silver's *A Pause on the Path*, Berger and Mohr's *A Seventh Man* (1975) about migrant workers and probably the pioneer work, Bateson and Mead's photodocumentary montage *Balinese Character* (1942).

The work of Mead, Bateson and Belo on Bali may be considered as explicitly seeking internal validity through analytic induction. Mead and Bateson had a number of agendas to fulfil; they were to seeking to record and investigate the aetiology of types of behaviours which seemed akin to those called schizophrenia in the West and, incidentally, Mead wanted to bring back a visual record which would vindicate her written accounts in her earlier ethnographies. Some social scientists did not and to this day do not accept her ethnographies as internally valid. Jane Belo had been taking photographs of Balinese life during a residence with her musicologist spouse (Mead, 1977). To record the complexity of some of the Balinese events Belo photographed the wider view, Bateson kept a view of the fine features by movie close frames whilst Mead and one of the three Balinese secretaries, equipped with chronometers, took notes. 'Bateson was an experienced photographer, and Mead had developed a technique of writing in a notebook while hardly looking at what she was doing, so that she cold at the same time focus on what was going on in the field in order to select and direct Bateson's next shot' (Chaplin, 1994, p. 210 fn). They were without tape recorders.

We tried to use the still and the moving picture cameras to get a record of Balinese behaviour, and this is a very different matter from the preparation of a 'documentary' film or photograph. We tried to shoot what happened normally and spontaneously, rather than to decide upon the norms and then get the Balinese to go through these behaviours in suitable lighting. (Bateson and Mead, 1942, p. 49)

Bateson deliberately included parents in his systematic record of small babies and this is another indication of the testing of the 'hypotheses' (Mead, 1977) about the formation of 'character' that guided the collection and selection of data. Hypotheses were developed and tested as they arose out of interpretations through comparative methods. 'As the corpus of photographic data grew, it was used consciously to compensate for the changing sophistication of the viewer' (Mead, 1963, p. 174). This was accomplished mainly by comparing photographs taken before a hypothesis was formulated with those made afterwards. 22000 feet of movie and 25,000 stills were shot (Mead, 1977; Harris, 1969). Bateson and Mead chose and arranged 759 of the stills in 100 plates, thematically juxtaposing related details without 'violating the context and the integrity of any one event' (Mead, 1972, p. 235).

What to Frame and Questions of Validity

I have already suggested what quickly becomes clear to still photographers in their initial attempts to make a video or movie for the record; that in moving pictures a context has to be included for the viewer to gain a sense of time and space, objects and people. I draw on my experience as that allows me to say how I began to learn about photocontext. I had taught film studies and made 8mm films with students prior to working as a photographer and film maker in science education. Whilst at the Centre for Science Education, London, Rob Walker told me of his long term research on classroom teaching. He said that although he was using a radio microphone as well as note taking the conversations between teacher and small groups of students in a very large room were full of prepositional references to — such as 'look here, what's that' which could not be understood by the researcher without a visual record. Rob had taken some still photos but they did not provide enough detail in continuity. I suggested that we try 16mm stop frame cinematography using a wide angle lens set high on a tripod well above the visual scan of teacher and pupils. We devised a crude electromechanical circuit breaker which could be adjusted to give between about one frame every second to every eight seconds. The circuit breaker activated the camera and put a sonic pulse on the tape recording track. This provided synchronization of sound and vision on playback. On viewing the film the eight second interval frames 'lost' many visual interactions pertaining to verbal referents recorded from the radio microphone. We found on viewing the 16mm colour film on a motion analysing projector (one that will hold and project a single frame on demand) that one exposure every two seconds recorded sufficient visual information to identify who was talking to whom, about what and where. A frequency of one frame a second only repeated visual information. In this sense one exposure every two seconds was optimum. A similar technique is available with some 'hi-tech' camcorders nowadays but for the most part the redundancy of the recording can only be reduced by in-camera editing which in a sense ceases the stream of action and presumes non-significance can be anticipated — the antipathy to discovery. Walker and I were working on the classroom research in 1969–72 when video was primitive and very intrusive.

After many trials and some errors we were satisfied with two stop frame 16mm cameras set high on tripods at a viewing angle of between 90–120 degrees to each other. The two cameras were electronically synchronized with each other and with up to two radio microphone inputs to two separate tape channels. With this we could record continuously for four hours and this was required as some of the classes were of three-hour duration plus the setting up and clearing away times.

One of the two cameras had a reflex zoom lens with its own eyepiece for focusing. We called this lens the 'hypothesis' lens as with this we would follow and frame what we thought was the salient action with regard to our research interests-social interaction and its 'ripples', the resource–task relationship, teacher scanning, students' ways of gaining attention and so on.

We played the recordings back on two motion analysing projectors and could often see the initiation of an interaction which would ripple and develop elsewhere, later in the lesson. One could view the movement in most of the room with the wide angle shots, seeing the flow of interaction as a whole from that angle and then the specific relationships that were being researched in the manned camera. Visible consequences of communication in one frame could be seen affecting the interaction in the other frame. As data we had a richness and usually sufficient context to trace the interaction over time and space. Our limitation was the sound recording and this of course depended on where the mikes were located. We monitored one of the sound channels whilst working the zoom camera (Adelman and Walker, 1974) This technique was adapted for a half frame still camera later and samples of the image sequences formed parts of the book, *A Guide to Classroom Observation*. I began using the technique in other settings — notably around a London park pond to collect contextualized speech samples of adult control over children. I sought evidence, justification, for the social class differentiation of speech codes. The whole true story of our efforts to gain further grants for our research cannot be said here, let me continue with my reflections on photocontext!

Making an important distinction between still and movie photography, Berger observes;

> The fact that a film camera works with time instead of across it affects every one of its images on both a technical and metaphysical level . . . Most important of all, the eye behind the film camera is looking for development not conjuncture.

Walker and I were aware that using stop frame with set time intervals we were having to think of how to frame the conjuncture as well as include the context to include development. Looking through the naked eye we could see interactions which we hoped would last long enough to be included in the next and succeeding two seconds. In this anticipation we were aware of the interactants and the topic of their attention, we could see students looking on, getting up to see what was going on and leaving the group; in short we could see the context with the naked eye and framed the images to include all the interaction. More about this later. We used close ups rarely; when the topic was some aspect of resources materials or equipment that was visible., for instance the work sheet or laboratory kit, or to try to capture the expression on the teacher or a student's face when they were alone reacting to the immediately ceased, but not concluded, interaction.

Subsequently I read Hymes on sociolinguistic context, in particular the distinctions about contextual dimensions that Hymes makes after Burke (1945). These are setting, scene, actor, act, agency to which we added resource and task. The aspects of interaction that we were framing for our photo documentation relied on those dimensions for their context and it was these that we tried to consistently include. In stop frame or taking sequences of still photos our framing and taking cues were these contextual markers:

1   any change in participants-number, substitution, spatial arrangement;
2   any change in the resources being used;
3   any change in the location of the interaction around the target, for instance the teacher or a piece of equipment; and
4   intervals, breaks and transitions in the proceedings.

What was hidden from one camera was often recorded by the other given the angular difference. For instance with the zoom the students were seen attending to the teacher whilst the wide angle showed them passing something to each other keeping their hands behind their backs.

In subsequent research of a more participant observer-action research type I put together synchronized sound with half frame photographs. The equipment was light, silent and easy to use. The additional problem for the photographer was to keep out of eye contact and attention seeking of students and teacher, to avoid 'procedural reactivity' by reflexive awareness of self (Walker and Adelman, 1974, p. 9). Otherwise the same contextual clues were used to frame the fixed focus, automatic exposure, virtually silent Olympus Trip. One could load up to eighty half frames and if this was not sufficient for the lesson (that is more than eighty instances of contextual clue acted upon) then a second loaded camera could be used. The slides were played back on a Carousel projector of which the Kodak Ektalight was best as it did not show black between slides but it was only available in the USA! As an indication of the satisfying contextual complement between slide and sound an experience social anthropologist complimented us some years later on the 'that movie film technique'.

External Validity

For all their efforts to systematically follow an explicit set of procedures and to be take photodocuments informed by an hypothesis or theory of social action the acid test of the sense making remains whether the photos communicate to viewers much of the intended messages. Other chapters in this volume deal with this test of veracity, what I will describe briefly are the debriefing methods using photos and sound that I devised during the Ford Teaching Project of 1972–4. The director of the project gives a full account of these methods (Elliott, 1978).

The methods derived form the ethnomethodological pursuit of 'revealing the taken for granted' and from cognitive anthropologists use of question sequences which expose the labels used by the actor to name his or her realities and the taxonomic relationship between these labels. For instance eliciting six labels for a particular professional practice the researcher then searches for what is included and what is excluded from the labels. By subsequent content differentiation the labels may be arranged into the superordinate, ordinate and subordinate on the vertical axis and this set may have one or more label in common with another branch — rather like a family tree (Tyler, 1969). In this process the researcher may use photos as documentary images, asking questions like 'what is going on here', 'is this what you mean by X (label)?' The informant has to make the effort to fill in the intervening information between and inside the photo and in doing so draws on their knowledge which they often take for granted. Thus tacit knowledge becomes propositional knowledge. When conducted with a group of practitioners the stating of prepositional knowledge excites comments on fundamental difference in, approach and social values. The veracity and authenticity of the photographs is incidentally given external validity by the consistence with which the viewer informants are able to raise their taken for granted in a sustained way and the contrasts across informants.

Conclusion

I have argued that for Image-based Research particular criteria should be fulfilled in the making of the photographic record. These criteria require that each image be filled with as much contextual detail for the researcher to engage in a systematic and iterative analysis of the image record. The quest is that of case study (Adelman, Jenkins and Kemmis, 1982) and that is to discover the relationships between the parts that provides understanding of the whole. For those who seek 'internally valid' qualitative photorecords the techniques of art, documentary and cinema-verite film and still photography have to a considerable extent been set aside. The veracity of the record is not given by the quality of the images or their conventional illustrative force but by the context of discovery of the researcher image maker.

Notes

1 I thank Professors Howie Becker and Jay Ruby for encouraging and critical comments and Professor Ron Silvers for his generous sharing during the journey.
2 On the question of validity I suggest that Mark (1986) tells a convincing story, context, instance and shadows. I quote and paraphrase. 'Campbell and Stanley's (1966) classic work popularized the concept of the quasi-experiment, the typology of internal and external validity, and the concept of validity threats.' Cook and Campbell expanded both the validity typology and the discussion of quasi-experiments. Cronbach (1982; Cronbach *et al.*, 1980) critiqued Cook and Campbell's preference for designs that emphasized internal validity and proposed an alternative validity framework (Mark, 1986, p. 47). 'The concept of certainty plays a role in most validity typologies. It seems to underlie Cook and Campbell's (1979, p. 37) definition of validity as "the best available approximation to the truth" and it is part of their statistical conclusion validity.

Cronbach (1982) strongly emphasizes the role of uncertainty reduction in the selection and formulation of research questions' (Mark, 1986, p. 53).

Campbell and Stanley's (1966) and Cook and Campbell's (1979) category of internal validity can be defined clearly with the present terminology: Internal validity concerns the accuracy of inferences about the causes element when all other elements are at the lowest level of generalization. Thus, internal validity concerns the making of accurate inferences about whether the treatment that was implemented caused the effect that was measured for the specific persons observed in the particular setting under study. For internal validity, the causes element should therefore be construed in the past tense, that is, as caused. In Chapter 4 of the volume, Campbell clarifies this interpretation of internal validity as local and concerned with a particular place and time.

Cronbach (1982) has reached a similar interpretation. He notes (pp. 127–8) that Campbell and Stanley (1966) 'define internal validity as pertinent only to an interpretation of a particular historical event . . . Campbell apparently has always meant the term internal validity to refer to an inference devoid of generalization.' Cronbach (1982) and Kruglanski and Kroy (1976) criticize this understanding of internal validity on the grounds that the concept of causality implies more than an inference devoid of generalization.

The differences between Campbell and Cronbach's validity priorities seem to result largely from Campbell's emphasis on scientific inquiry and Cronbach's on more immediate applied policy concerns. They also seem to make different assumptions about how to maximize certainty. In placing the priority on internal validity (Campbell and Stanley, 1966; Cook and Campbell, 1979). Campbell seems to assume that having confident inferences at a low level of generalization (internal validity) ultimately increases the confidence about higher-level inferences. This assumes 'that the consequences of being wrong about causal connections are greater than the consequences of being wrong about other features of research design' (Cook *et al.*, 1985, p. 761).

One likely answer is that there is no simple answer. Campbell's approach seems preferable when a treatment effect is robust across variations in persons and settings, but causal inference is difficult because spurious relationships are likely. In contrast, Cronbach's approach seems preferable when spurious relationships are unlikely or can easily be ruled out, but a treatment effect is not robust. Unfortunately, the researcher is not likely to know in advance which conditions hold, at least without more substantive knowledge than we generally have. Thus, the dilemma remains.

Cook and Campbell (1979, p. 37) equate validity with an imperfect assessment of truth value: 'We shall use the concepts validity and invalidity to refer to the best available approximation to the truth or falsity of proposition.' In contrast, both Cronbach (1982) and Krathwohl (1985) equate validity with persuasion, credibility and consensus: 'Validity is subjective rather than objective' (Cronbach, 1982, p. 108).

One can acknowledge that many strands of reasoning may buttress validity claims while retaining a truth value conceptualization of validity. Validity is, however, unknown (Campbell, 1974), while consensus is more tangible — but that does not require equating the two. However, some will argue that utility — that is, the ability to solve or at least to ameliorate problems — is a more important criterion than validity (Lauden, 1977).

The work of Campbell and Stanley (1966) and the others noted in Figure 10.1 has greatly enhanced our understanding of research. Validity typologies are valuable in helping us to understand quasi-experiments and in bringing potential validity threats to our attention. However, we can move beyond traditional validity typologies in several ways: by honestly acknowledging our certainty or uncertainty in an inference, by being explicit about the reasoning underlying our inference from a low to a high level of generalization, and by studying causal process. Moreover, we can be aware that the useful lessons of a validity typology do not substitute for critical logical analysis. I understand the latter to correspond to methodological reflexivity as discussed in this article in relation to photodocumentary context.

References

ADELMAN, C.L. and WALKER, R. (1974) 'Stop frame cinematography with synchronised sound: A technique for recording in school classrooms, *The Journal of the Society of Motion Picture and Television Engineers*, Hollywood, USA.

ADELMAN, C.L., JENKINS, D. and KEMMIS, S. (1982) 'Rethinking case study', in SIMONS, H. (ed.) *Towards a Science of the Singular*, CARE Occasional Publication No. 2, Norwich: University of East Anglia.

BATESON, G. and MEAD, M. (1942) *Balinese Character: A Photographic Analysis*: New York Academy of Sciences.

BECKER, H.S. (1974) 'Visual sociology, documentary photography, and photojournalism: It's (almost) all a matter of context', *Visual Sociology*, **10**, 1–2, pp. 5–14. (see chapter 6 in this book).

BERGER, J. (1971) 'Introduction' to Euan Duff, *How we Are*, Harmonsworth: Penguin.

BROMHEAD, T. (1996) *Looking Two Ways*, Los Angeles: Intervention Press.

BURKE, K. (1945) *A Grammer of Motives*, Hemel Hempstead: Prentice-Hall.

CAMPBELL, D.T. and STANLEY, J.C. (1966) *Experimental and Quasi-experimental Designs for Research*, Chicago: Rand McNally (1966).

CARTIER-BRESSON, H. (1968) *The World of Henry Cartier-Bresson*, New York: Viking.

CHAPLIN, E. (1994) *Sociology and Visual Representation*, London and New York: Routledge.

COOK, T.D. and CAMPBELL, D.T. (1976) 'The design and conduct of quasi-experiments and true experiments in field settings', in DUNNETTE, M.D. (ed.) *Handbook of Industrial and Organizational Psychology*, Chicago: Rand McNally.

COOK, T.D. and CAMPBELL, D.T. (1979) *Quasi-experimentation: Design and Analysis Issues for Field Settings*, Chicago: Rand McNally.

COOK, T.D., LEVITON, L.C. and SHADISH, W.R.JR. (1985) 'Program evaluation', in LINDZEY, G. and ARONSON, E. (eds) *Handbook of Social Psychology* (3rd ed.), New York: Random House.

CRONBACH, L.J. (1982) *Designing Evaluations of Educational and Social Programs*, San Francisco: Jossey-Bass.

CURTIS, J. (1986) *Minds Eye, Minds Truth: FSA Photography Revisited*, Philadelphia: Temple University Press.

DUFF, E. (1981) 'Working world', in BECKER, H.S. (ed.) *Exploring Society Photographically*, Chicago: Chicago University Press

EISENSTEIN, S. (1943) *The Film Sense*, London: Faber and Faber.

ELLIOTT, J. (1978) 'Classroom accountability and the self-monitoring teacher', in HARLEN, W. *Evaluation and the Teacher's Role*, London: Macmillan Education.

ERICKSON, F. and WILSON, J. (1982) 'A resource guide to film and videotape for research and education', *Sights and Sounds of Life in Schools*.

GARDNER, R. and HEIDER, K.G. (1974) *Gardens of War: Life and Death in the New Guinea Stone Age*, Harmonsworth: Penguin.

GOFFMAN, E. (1963) *Behaviour in Public Places*, USA: Free Press of Glencoe.

HARRIS, M.C. (1969) *The Rise of Anthropological Theory*, London: Routledge and Kegan Paul.

JACKSON, B. (1981) 'Killing time: Life in the Arkansas penitentiary', in BECKER, H.S. (ed.) *Exploring Society Photographically*, Chicago: University of Chicago Press.

MEAD, M. (1977) in ANSHEN, R.N. (ed.) *Letters from the Field 1925–75*, New York: Harper and Row

ROBINSON, W. (1951) 'The logical structure of analytic induction', *American Sociological Review*, **16**, 6, pp. 812–18.

RUBY, J. (1978) 'The celluloid self, in autobiography: Film/video photography', in KATZ, J. (ed.) *Art Gallery of Ontario*, pp. 7–10.

SILVERS, R. (1988) *A Pause on the Path*, USA: Temple Press.

SILVERS, R. (1997) Personal communication by e-mail.

TEMPLIN, P.A. (1982) 'Still photography in evaluation', in SMITH, N.L. (ed.) *Communication Strategies in Evaluation*, London: Sage.

TYLER, S.A. (1969) *Cognitive Anthropology*, New York: Holt Reinhart Winston.

WALKER, R. and ADELMAN, C.L. (1974) *A Guide to Classroom Observation*, London: Methuen.

Chapter 11

Media Convergence and Social Research: The Hathaway Project

Rob Walker and Ron Lewis

Abstract

Until recently the conventions of publishing have caused us to treat photographic and video images separately from written words. The convergence of media precipitated by the digitization of practically everything make for a seamlessness which undermines these conventions and makes new forms possible: text becomes image just as image becomes text. Among the new possibilities this creates for research practice are a collapse of the conventional distinctions between 'writing down' and 'writing up' as 'fieldwork' ceases to be a discrete set of activities and 'writing' no longer bounded by the act of putting words on paper. In this chapter we will draw on our efforts to create a school case study using multimedia as part of a distance course for teachers. Our central argument is that Image-based Research is not simply the ground for methodological innovation but indicates broader shifts in the practice and politics of social research and in the nature of the university. Illustrative material, links and interactive possibilities for this chapter are provided at a website we have created for the project. This can be found at http://www2.deakin.edu.au/hathaway/

Introduction

As Nicholas Negroponte and others have pointed out (Brand, 1987), worldwide, we are currently experiencing a convergence of areas of activity that were previously separate and discrete. In everyday life, we can see that the worlds of publishing, communications and computing are becoming seamless as practically all information becomes digital in form. Overall, research may be a smaller enterprise than the mass media but similar effects are being felt. The long running debates between those advocating quantitative, and those advocating qualitative, methods have become almost meaningless now that the potential exists to move easily between the two. The conventions of print technology which require separations (on the page and in the division of labour) between pictures and words mean little in multimedia publishing; as text becomes image and image becomes text. The forms of academic organization that underline separations between teaching and research, between the face-to-face interactions of the classroom and the forms of virtual communication to be found on the internet, and which provide the basis for social control through publication and citation are becoming increasingly fluid and problematic.

The importance of the image in social research, we believe, is not that its use offers a new set of methodological tricks to be added to the existing repertoire of research instruments but that taking it seriously exposes a current of social change which has implications for the practice (and politics) of social research; for who does it, who uses it and who controls it (Schratz and Walker, 1995). In this chapter we will give an account of our experience in developing a case study of a school on CDROM but our purpose is not simply descriptive (if description can ever be called simple) but to show how some of these broader consequences of social change are changing the world of social research, the nature of university teaching and the emergence of a global educational economy.

Origins of the Project

We both work in distance education programs, directed mainly to teachers but increasingly to others with an interest in education — in industry, commerce, the 'caring professions' and the arts; in Australia, around the Pacific rim and elsewhere. At Deakin University academic staff both write and teach courses, which provides us with opportunities to collapse the distinctions between teaching and research that still exist in many other universities. Having developed a close working relationship with our in-house multi-media publishing colleagues, having direct access to our audience and frequent opportunities to adapt and rewrite our programs, we find that our teaching program is rather like running a continuing curriculum development program involving some 200 teachers each year. At least this is how we have reconstrued what some others may feel is a production-line model of teaching!

Central to our interests is a professional development course called 'Changing Classrooms', which we have taught in various forms since the late 1970s. Basically, this course aims to get teachers to adopt an action research approach to their teaching (though we almost never use the term and there is not a spiral diagram to be seen). Given the commitment of our students to spending some ten hours a week through the year on the course and the completion of three major assignments, we set out to establish and develop the view that classrooms are places of infinite interest and unrecognized potential and that good teaching involves adopting an experimental approach coupled with a developed capacity to reflect upon the complex and unexpected consequences of actions directed towards change.

Over the years we have developed the course as a three-part structure, each part having its own coherence and rationale but the three parts adding up to something more than their sum.

- The first part is in the form of a 'training program' in classroom research, consisting of thirty-two tasks which include exercises in perception and evaluation around three main themes — the classroom as a built space, language use in classrooms (the classroom as a 'language space') and the emotions of teaching and learning (the classroom as an emotional space). A key task in this sequence

involves students photographing themselves at work and exchanging commentaries on these photographs with each other.

- The second part is a more introspective and requires students to keep a reading
journal while closely studying a single book about teaching. (We change the titles
we use each year but those that have proved enduringly successful include Margaret
Clark's book, *The Great Divide*, which is about gender issues in primary schooling
and Vivien Paley's book about pre-school children, *Wally's Stories*). What is
important in this part of the course is not that the books are treated as informative
or authoritative texts (as they would be in most academic courses), but that they
provide springboards from which teachers can write about their own experience
and develop the capacity for sustained reflective writing.[1]
- In the third part of the course we provide a collection of case material which
we have built up over several years from a single primary school. This material
constitutes a 'case record' in the sense that the term was adopted by Lawrence
Stenhouse to describe 'lightly edited' texts that are edited forms of primary data
(Stenhouse, 1985). While the earlier parts of the course focus directly on the
students' own experience, perceptions and educational values, here they are asked
to project themselves into a documented but imagined space, to learn, as Robert
Stake would say, 'vicariously' (Stake, 1995).

The Hathaway Project

In what follows our focus will be on the case record of the school. This school has become
known as 'Hathaway School', following the name given to it by Susan Groundwater
Smith, whose research provided the basis for our first attempt to document it (Groundwater Smith, 1989; Groundwater Smith and Walker (in press). In the last two years we
have reworked the case record, this time reconfiguring it as a CDROM. Known as 'The
Hathaway Project', this attempt to create a multimedia school case study provides the
basis for the current discussion. It is though important to keep the context we have just
outlined in mind. While the summary of the course we have given here is condensed to
the point of being cryptic, it is important to remember that we are concerned with a
particular form of research: action research by teachers as part of the process of professional development, and that the case study was developed for use, not as a 'stand alone'
resource, but as part of a course that has other important elements. While others have
used it in other places intending different purposes, our reference points remain defined
by an image of the lone student, working late at night, at the end of the kitchen table (an
image we have developed further elsewhere, Walker, 1992).

The Nature of the Resource

If you have not looked at it already, now is a good moment to browse the Hathaway web
pages and to get some idea of the kind of material they contain. For those who do not
have immediate web access we will include some examples in this text.

Figure 11.1 Video extract with transcript

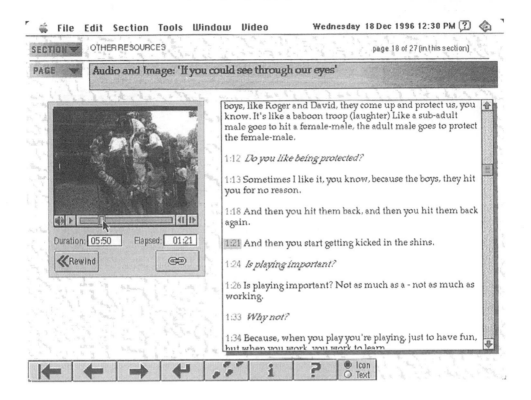

One of the enduring features of qualitative research is its reliance on fragments of transcript as crucial evidence. Direct quotes are frequently used to underline a point, illustrate an assertion or provide the starting point for the development of an argument. Necessarily, these quoted fragments are carefully framed and cropped and the reader is left to fill-in paralinguistic and prosodic features, to guess at the pretext and the context to the text as is it is quoted and to trust the researcher not to have misunderstood, misinterpreted or cheated. Since the purpose of the case record is in part to take the reader behind the scenes of the case study we have provided on the disc material that is less closely edited and interpreted. This is not to say it is not some degree removed from the raw state but it does exist in a frame that is less tightly strung than is usual in research publications. To use Stenhouse's term, it is 'lightly edited'.

In Figure 11.1 we see an instance which exemplifies the point. Here we are given a video image plus an audio track and a linked transcript. This extract is taken from a film made by Susan Groundwater Smith ('If you could see through our eyes') in which she gave students 35mm cameras and asked them to record a day at school. In the film they talk about their pictures, many of which (as here) concern life in the school playground.

The CDROM provides 'tools' which allow us to manage this material in different ways. We can pause and replay the video. We can follow suggested links to other sources (including a glossary). We can use a word-search function to link to other documents and

Figure 11.2 Photographs of the school exterior

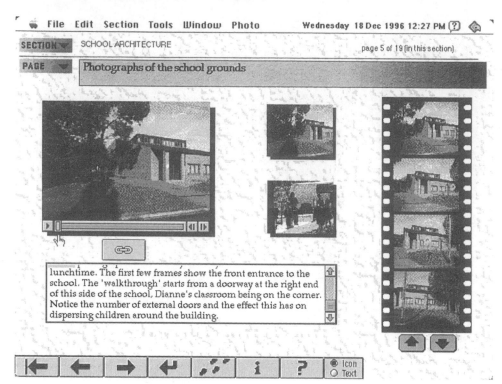

File Edit Section Tools Window Photo
Wednesday 18 Dec 1996 12:27 PM
SECTION
SCHOOL ARCHITECTURE
page 5 of 19 (in this section)
PAGE
Photographs of the school grounds
lunchtime. The first few frames show the front entrance to the school. The 'walkthrough' starts from a doorway at the right end of this side of the school, Dianne's classroom being on the corner. Notice the number of external doors and the effect this has on dispersing children around the building.
Icon
Text

Figure 11.3 Dianne's class, grade 5/6

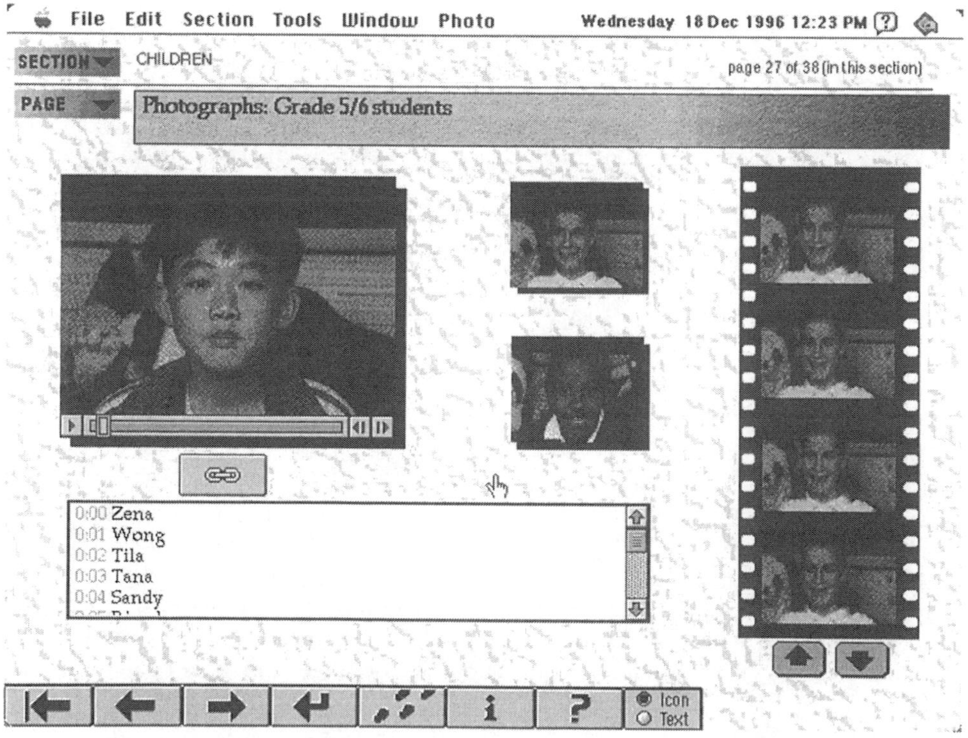

File Edit Section Tools Window Photo
Wednesday 18 Dec 1996 12:23 PM
SECTION
CHILDREN
page 27 of 38 (in this section)
PAGE
Photographs: Grade 5/6 students
0:00 Zena
0:01 Wong
0:02 Tila
0:03 Tana
0:04 Sandy
Icon
Text

interviews. We can cut and paste from the text into a document we might create (just as we have done here) and we can 'bookmark' moments from the video into hypertext 'commentaries'. In short, where the conventional qualitative research text leaves us with many questions about the accuracy and versimilitude of the fragment we are given, in this medium we have many more opportunities to check accuracy, judge fairness and assess relevance. Much of what the author may want us to take on trust in a conventional text is here open to question and to scrutiny and not only in ways which the authors themselves can predetermine or control.

This might be described in terms of 'image plus sound plus text' but we argue that it is not simply 'multimedia' in the sense of being fragments of different media linked together, but that the functions added to the material create a form which in itself constitutes a new medium. The film from which this frame is taken is 'multimedia' too, but there are important differences between the film and the way it is presented here. There is more to the whole than the sum of the parts. This is not to claim it is more 'real' so much as to claim that there is more you can do with it. It is in Mcluhan's terms a 'cool medium' for it only comes to life — it only becomes meaningful — when you interact with it, and the nature of that interaction, while it is constrained by the functional possibilities scripted into the case, is not predetermined, sequenced or programmed. Educationally this is significant, for as we have argued elsewhere (Walker, Lewis and Laskey, 1996), it implicitly undermines those assumptions about instructional design which underlie most attempts to make use of educational technology.

Of course all those questions that are frequently raised in media studies and in research about the selection and framing of images and quotes still apply. Why this video clip? What was happening off-camera? How was this sequence set up? What purposes and intentions did/do we have in mind? What did people say when the camera stopped? When they saw the replay? But while not every question can answered, some can. There is the capability for the user/viewer to construct their own interpretation of the case in a way that emulates rather than replicates the field experience. For this is not a field-work simulator but more of training device. Our intention is to provoke the user to think rather than to replicate the overwhelming rush of perceptive input that is characteristic of the here-and-now of classrooms, corridors, the playground or the staff room. Using the CDROM calls on the user's capacity for analysis and synthesis, rather than for field skills.

Perhaps a photographic analogy is most appropriate. Working with this material is most like working with contact sheets and trying to create a finished print. The raw material exists, with all its constraints and possibilities. It is not possible to go back and collect more or different images, to change the lighting, the focus or the angles, but there is still a lot that can be done. In fact there is an infinite range of possibilities with which to work.

In Figure 11.2 we took the darkroom image literally. The strips here are not real contact strips, they derive from video images, but in providing photographs of the school building and site we have mimicked the contact sheet so that users can select and enlarge chosen images so creating their own 'Gallery'.

Figure 11.3 is a different example of the same format. On this page there are photographs of each child in the grade 5/6 class which provides the central focus for the case study. The blue font is used to indicate links to other pages, so a mouse click on each child's name takes the user to a short video in which the student talks about themselves, both in English and in their first language.

Rob Walker and Ron Lewis

Figure 11.4   Video with notes

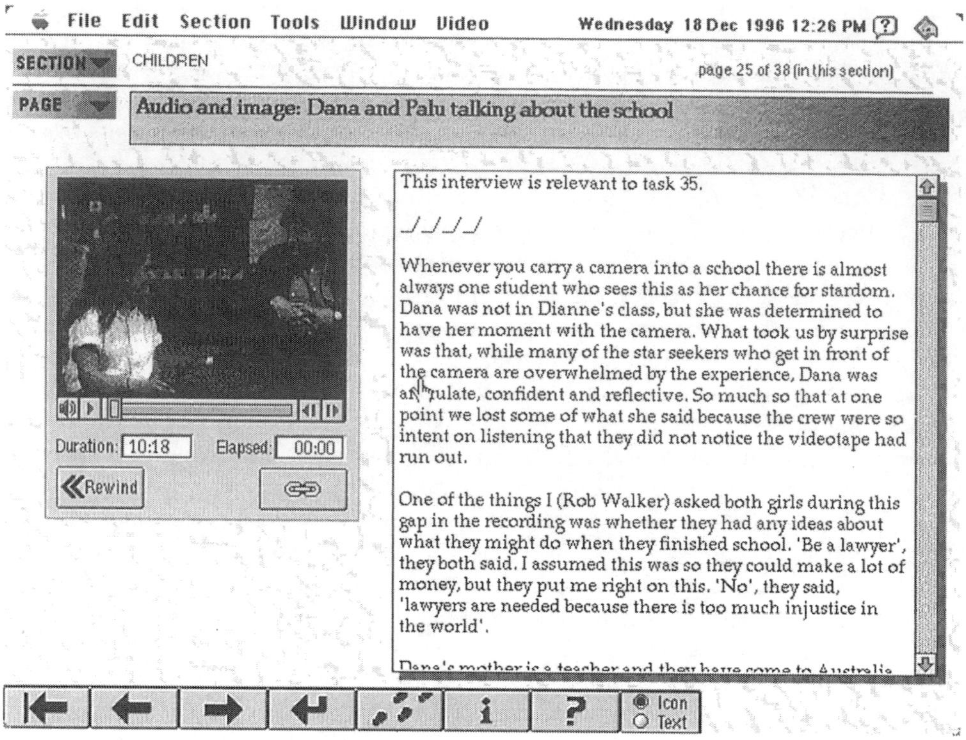

File   Edit   Section   Tools   Window   Video   Wednesday 18 Dec 1996 12:26 PM ?

SECTION ▼   CHILDREN   page 25 of 38 (in this section)

PAGE   ▼   **Audio and image: Dana and Palu talking about the school**

This interview is relevant to task 35.

_/ _/ _/ _/

Whenever you carry a camera into a school there is almost always one student who sees this as her chance for stardom. Dana was not in Dianne's class, but she was determined to have her moment with the camera. What took us by surprise was that, while many of the star seekers who get in front of the camera are overwhelmed by the experience, Dana was articulate, confident and reflective. So much so that at one point we lost some of what she said because the crew were so intent on listening that they did not notice the videotape had run out.

One of the things I (Rob Walker) asked both girls during this gap in the recording was whether they had any ideas about what they might do when they finished school. 'Be a lawyer', they both said. I assumed this was so they could make a lot of money, but they put me right on this. 'No', they said, 'lawyers are needed because there is too much injustice in the world'.

Dana's mother is a teacher and they have come to Australia

Duration: 10:18   Elapsed: 00:00

◀◀ Rewind   ⊂⊃

|←   ←   →   ↵   •'   i   ?   ● Icon   ○ Text

We said earlier that one of the features of the format is its capacity for interactivity and the nature of the demands it makes on the user. In looking through these pages you can maintain a commentary by calling up a commentary screen. This allows you to make notes and also to 'bookmark' pages. The next screen shows how this would appear on the previous page (the commentary itself is blank!). Of course commentaries can be saved and added to the resource, so that in future users may use the record to argue or debate with previous commentaries.

In the first screen we showed how video and film can be displayed alongside a transcript. This has proved a useful research device, especially when linked to word searching tools which can take the user straight to moments when words are being used, But the 'box' set up to display the transcript can also be used to add notes and commentaries by the author and participants. In Figure 11.4 we provide an introduction to an interview with some methodological background. There is an element of judgment creeping into our editing here, for we think many users will find this a significant interview and will need a little more background to the interview itself to help them interpret what is said, the role of the interviewer and the broader context of the interview.

One of the advantages with multimedia is that it is possible to build sequences of images and words. For instance in describing and documenting the context of the school we have a set of pages which help the user orientate themselves in relation to the school. These pages include census data from the Sydney region and from the post code area and also some visuals. For instance we have an aerial photograph of the school site (Figure 11.5):

Figure 11.5   Ariel photograph of the Hathaway School site

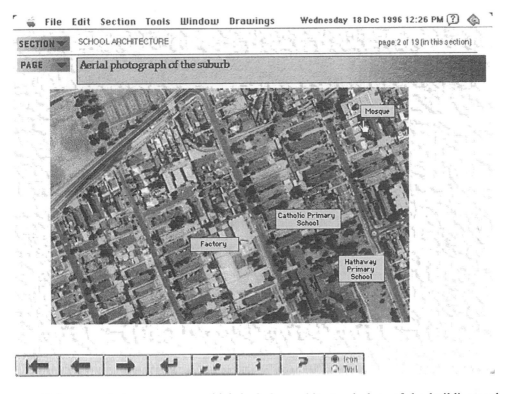

This screen is in a sequence which includes architectural plans of the building and the site, a street map and a 'drive through' — a video taken from a car driving around the neighbourhood and showing housing types, shopping areas and streetscapes. In developing this sequence we commissioned an architectural student to produce some 3D drawings of the school building. The school building is somewhat unconventional and complex in design, it has a series of linked semi-open plan classrooms located around meeting spaces and wet areas, each classroom has outside access and in the roof space there is a series of lofts designed as 'child spaces' and intended to be used by children as a retreat from classrooms. Explaining this, or seeing drawings and photographs, it is not always easy to see how the separate spaces inter-relate. The diagrams help (Figure 11.6):

Figure 11.6 'Lift off' 3D plan of the classroom

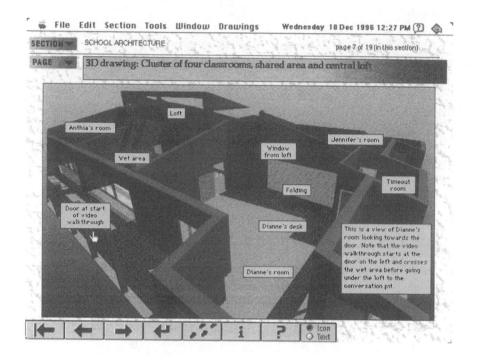

In this version of the CD this screen is presented as a single image. In later versions it would be possible, by incorporating the relevant software, to allow the user to display an image from any viewpoint, to change the lighting according to the time of the day or season and to add or subtract furniture to scale. Since this version was produced for teachers, rather than for architects, we thought this might be confusing, but one of the features of CDROM is that users need only use what tools they choose and can leave the rest. In future we would attempt to be a little more ambitious! It is also possible now to display how buildings look to the viewer in a 'stitched' panoramic image assembled from photographs (using Quicktime VR). You can choose a spot and view the building from any angle, scanning around a full 360 degrees. As with all software of this type, getting it to work within a particular case is time consuming and inevitably raises a host of difficulties to be solved and eventually some balance has to be struck between the cost of achieving what is possible as against what is likely to be used or needed.

One of the reasons we took some care in reconstructing the building on screen was that during development of the CD the school burnt to the ground. We had a difficult decision to make about whether to include this fact in the resource itself, but decided to do so. This meant that we could not return to the school to capture images we might have missed. We had to work with what we had got. But also it created an opportunity to document the fire itself and to begin looking at the ways in which it was reported by the media, and the response of the community to the loss of 'their school'. We have plans to make this the subject of a later project!

Another 'sequence' we developed in the materials involves a staff planning meeting in which teachers plan their curriculum and other activities, This meeting included how to work around religious education lessons conducted by volunteer teachers from the

Figure 11.7   Newspaper photograph taken immediately after the fire

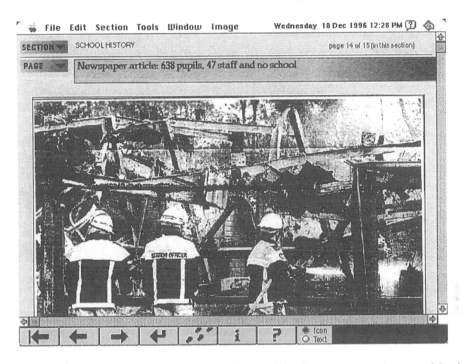

Figure 11.8   Newspaper report; one of the office staff is given a community award for her work after the fire

community, and the planning of an event to be part of a sequence of work on dinosaurs, which included viewing the film *Jurassic Park* and the visit to the school of some 'life' sized dinosaur models.

We were able to show the teachers' meeting (Figure 11.9):

Figure 11.9 Teachers' Planning Meeting

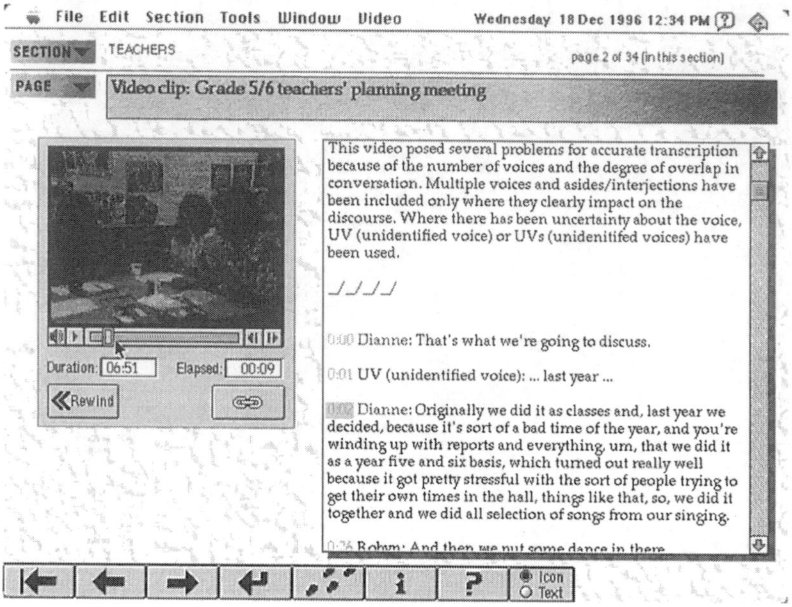

We were able to record the religous education lesson (Figure 11.10):

Figure 11.10 Religious Education lesson

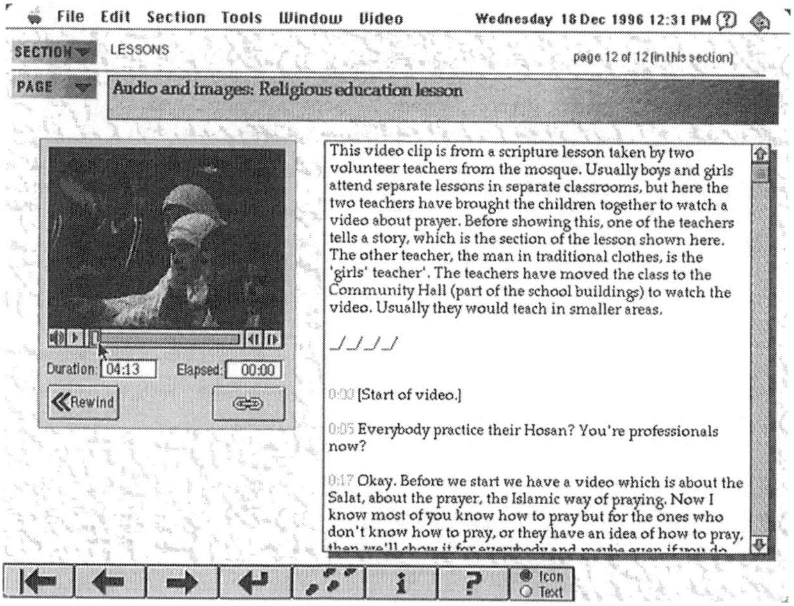

And we were able to collect photographs of the day when the dinosaurs arrived in school (as well as such documents as the letters sent home to parents) (Figure 11.11).

Figure 11.11 'Dinosaurs At Large'

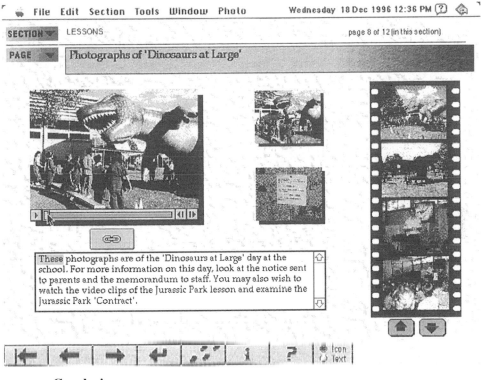

Conclusion

In these extracted screens/pages we have been able to show something of the range of material it possible to include in a resource of this kind. We can also give some idea of the way images, sounds and texts of different kinds can be integrated. What we cannot easily do is convey the dynamic nature of the material and the different role required of the user/reader. We tend to talk somewhat glibly about multimedia being 'interactive'. Just what interaction means in this context is something we are experimenting with, and this forms a key element in the way we plan and conduct our courses. Clearly, to use a resource like this is different from reading a case study in a book, and even from watching a video, but what educational potential lies in these differences is less obvious.

In our introduction we made the claim that this 'interactivity' also provided the basis for rethinking the way we conceive, conduct and report research. This is perhaps not immediately clear from the examples we have provided, but we have given some indication of the way we have organized material around branching sequences. These are not prescriptive, or like chapter headings, but are more like nature trails. They attempt to provide information directly relevant to what the user sees in front of them at any moment. When they work well they provide cues to push the observer into seeing things they might not otherwise see and suggest ways that they might take from here. But, unlike a nature trail, these cues are open-ended and the trail has multiple branches at any point. This makes a big difference to the nature of the medium as a form of reporting because, in the way we have used it, it does not direct the reader, does not make clear expositions or arguments, but proceeds more subtley and with less control, in many ways more like fiction than documentary.

This has implications for data collection. We began with data from a well-worked case study and at first thought we could simply transfer this to CDROM. In the event we used little of the original data and looked increasingly to collect new information, not because it was new so much as because the medium demanded information in a different, 'less processed' form. For example, in the earlier version we had some interview material from the principal and assistant principal in which they talked about the information demands of the system in a recently devolved system. In the written case it seemed adequate simply to report what they said, for their perception that system demands for information was increasing was as much as we needed to claim. In the CDROM such claims seem thin unless they are backed-up empirically. So we asked the principal to keep a diary of meetings and events for a day and a log of phone calls through one morning and we asked one of the office staff to keep copies of all the fax messages that came into the office for a day. And there were suprises, Bev Dunbar, our research assistant in the school discovered that the accident book was a fascinating source of cross-cultural misunderstandings. These records all appear as 'pages' on the CDROM for those who want to look at them, as do various 'found' documents that were being discussed at the time — a survey of computers and peripheral equipment in the school, the current rules and procedures for playgrounds, various letters and notices sent to teachers and to parents.

In a written case study these things would probably remain in the case study researcher's file and only be used if they provided vital information; on the CDROM they can be included for anyone who seeks them out. There is of course a next step, one we have yet to take, which is to reassemble these bits and pieces into a virtual reality. We would like to have recreated the principal's office (somewhat as Barry Harper has created a field study centre at 'Lake Ileuka' and on the 'Nardoo River'). Perhaps the user could 'enter' the principal's office, look in the in-tray, open files, look at the diary for the day. The phone might ring, and if answered someone might ask questions calling for a hurried report on a child. Files would have to be found, the accident records checked, the child located, the nature of the problem assessed and a judgment formed. While this is in progress, the press might call, or an estranged parent: crises headed off, redirected or resolved.

The difficult decisions involve deciding how much programming/scripting work is worth investing in the resource given its likely uses. The work can expand at a frightening rate! But the point is that the kind of content structures that work best are different from the kind of structures we are used to finding in a research report or a book. As curriculum they are more like what we might find in an art gallery (particularly in an installation), in a museum, on a National Park trail, in attending a sporting event, in a theatre, in a film or in music. They demand different kinds of attention (a different gaze), different forms of engagement, and require different forms of production. If we are to advance intelligently in using multimedia in social research we might need to investigate more closely the educational nature of the engagement, attention and interaction demanded by a range of cultural events of this kind.

Note

1 This part of the course has been developed by Helen Modra. who has written about the approach elsewhere (Modra, 1989).

References

BRAND, S. (1987) *The Media Lab: Inventing the Future at MIT*, New York: Viking/Penguin.

CLARK, M. (1989) *The Great Divide*, CDC, Canberra ACT.

DEAKIN UNIVERSITY (1996) *EAE411/601 Changing Classrooms*, Learning Resource Services, Victoria, Australia: Deakin University.

GROUNDWATER SMITH, S. (1989) 'A process of critical enquiry: The evolution of curriculum learning in pre-service teacher education', Unpublished PhD thesis University of Sydney.

GROUNDWATER SMITH, S. and WALKER, R. (in press) 'Case study and case records: A conversation about the hathaway project', in ALTRICHTER, H. and ELLIOTT, J. (eds) *Images of Educational Research*, Buckingham: Open University Press.

HARPER, B. (ed.) *Lake Iluka* and *Discovering the Nardoo* are CDROM resources developed by the University of Wollongong, NSW.

MODRA, H. (1989) 'Using journals to encourage critical thinking at a distance', in EVANS, T. and NATION, D. (eds) *Critical Reflections on Distance Education*, London: Falmer.

PALEY, V.G. (1981) *Wally's Stories: Conversations in the Kindergarten,* Cambridge, Mass: Harvard University Press.

SCHRATZ, M. and WALKER, R. (1995) *Research as Social Change*, London: Routledge.

STAKE, R.E. (1995) *The Art of Case Study Research*, Beverley Hills Ca: Sage.

STENHOUSE, L. (1985) *Research as a Basis for Teaching*, RUDDUCK, J. and HOPKINS, D. (eds) London: Heinemann.

WALKER, R. (1992) 'The transformation of education in times of change', in EVANS, T. and NATION, D. (eds) *Critical Research in Distance Education*, London: Kogan Paul.

WALKER, R., LEWIS, R. and LASLEY, I. (1996) 'Flying in the face of instructional deign: Rationale for the case study', *Australian Educational Research Journal*, **23**, 3, pp. 29–44.

Chapter 12

The Application of Images in Child Abuse Investigations

Hollida Wakefield and Ralph Underwager

Abstract

Mental health professionals use a variety of image-based techniques when interviewing children about sexual abuse allegations. These include anatomical dolls, books, puppets, drawings, projective cards, play dough, games, and toys. Many of these lack acceptable validity or reliability for the ways they are used, whereas others appear helpful in obtaining forensically useful information from young children. The history and current status of research concerning the child witness is the background for a discussion of these practices. It is argued that interviewers should only use techniques that can be defended in terms of their reliability and validity.

From ancient cave drawings, to archeological artefacts ranging from royal jewelry to household objects, to thousands of clay Chinese warriors, to today's computer screen, images and symbols show the richness and complexity of human life. Human cognition often depends upon the use of images and symbols to represent or stand for something other than itself. This ability separates us from all other creatures and has enabled humanity to transcend space and time. Science makes great use of models, symbols, and number systems to advance our human capacities.

The use of images and symbols is so much a part of human cognition that adults often completely overlook the fact that children are not born with a capacity to represent one thing by another thing. This is a cognitive capacity that must be learned during the developmental process of the individual from infant to adult (DeLoache, 1995a). A longitudinal study of this process in seven distinct symbol systems (Gardner and Wolf, 1987) shows developmental changes both within and across the seven systems. From ages 5 to 7 the symbolic process begins to develop and notational literacy is acquired in early school years.

Unfortunately, during early developmental stages when children are difficult to communicate with, adults who want to elicit information from children may attempt to use images and symbols in an effort to break through the limitations. But the child may not have the capacity to use one object to represent another. If adults are not familiar with this developmental process, they may miss opportunities to accurately understand children and may then introduce unnecessary error into the interaction.

Mental health professionals use a variety of techniques employing images when interviewing children about sexual abuse allegations. These include anatomical dolls, books, puppets, drawings, projective cards, play dough, games, and toys (Conte, Sorenson, Fogarty and Rosa, 1991; Kendall-Tackett, 1992). Many of these are controversial and do not show acceptable validity or reliability for the ways they are used (Underwager and Wakefield, 1995); others appear valuable for assisting young children to provide forensically useful information. A crucial factor is how the image-based techniques are used by the interviewer. The history and current status of research concerning the child witness is the background for a discussion of these practices.

Brief History of Research on Child Witnesses

In the early part of the twentieth century, research on children's memory focused on children as witnesses in court. Most of this research was in Europe, especially Germany and France; there was very little in the United States until the 1920s and even then there were only a few studies on the child witness until the 1980s (Ceci and Bruck, 1993, 1995). Although children in Canada, America, and Great Britain were rarely permitted to testify, their testimony was allowed in some other European countries, hence the interest in performing research that dealt directly with children's court testimony. The general conclusion from this research was that young children were suggestible and vulnerable to making serious errors in their court testimony (Ceci and Bruck, 1993, 1995; Goodman, 1984; Wakefield and Underwager, 1988).

Following this early period, little research was done for years and laboratory studies of children as witnesses were rare until the 1970s. But then the increases in reports and allegations of sexual and physical abuse led to changes in the legal system regarding the admissibility of child witnesses' testimony (Ceci and Bruck, 1993, 1995; Goodman, 1984). In most countries the requirement for corroboration of children's statements alleging sexual abuse was dropped. Therefore, children's credibility, their reliability as witnesses, and their susceptibility to leading questions quickly became salient issues. Over the past few years interest in this issue has proliferated and there are now hundreds of articles in the literature addressing these topics.

During the beginning of this recent period, the testimony of young children was often accepted in the Justice system as truthful and false allegations were believed to be extremely rare (i.e., Faller, 1984; Summit and Kryso, 1978). A number of unsupported dogmas, such as children cannot lie about sexual abuse and children cannot be 'coached' to make erroneous statements about abuse, gained acceptance in the legal and mental health communities. Although some researchers acknowledged that suggestive interviews might cause children to make unimportant errors about peripheral details, it was claimed that children could not be led to make statements about important, central events. Several highly publicized cases during this period involving satanic, ritual abuse allegations resulted in convictions (Nathan and Snedeker, 1995).

To our knowledge, the first time expert opinion on the impact of leading interrogations was given in a court of law was when Dr Underwager testified in a sex abuse trial in Winner, South Dakota, in the winter of 1983. The next year we were the experts in the first of the highly publicized Scott County cases to go to trial where Dr Underwager provided similar testimony. In these cases twenty-five adults were accused of abusing forty children in two interlocking sex rings. The alleged abuse involved animals, ritual abuse, and murder. This trial resulted in an acquittal and charges were dropped against all but the first defendant, who had confessed. A later state attorney general's report (Humphrey, 1985) concluded that the repeated suggestive interrogations of the children made it impossible to sort out what may have happened.

Following this, a few forensic psychologists and psychiatrists began to report on their analyses of actual real world interrogations (Coleman, 1986; McIver, 1986; Underwager, Wakefield, Legrand, Bartz and Erickson, 1986). These early reports of actual real world interrogations suggested coercive questioning could produce serious errors in a child's statements. Then, as academic researchers became involved in actual cases and reviewed videotapes of actual interviews, they began conducting studies that more closely approximate what happens in the real world. These studies demonstrated that children who are interviewed suggestively can produce false narratives about fictitious events, including central events (see Ceci and Bruck, 1995 for a review of this research). These erroneous narratives were often coherent and detailed and could not be detected as false by professionals. As a result, the current consensus of scientific opinion has revived the initial caution and concern about children's reliability and suggestibility. The justice system now recognizes these data and several of the highly publicized convictions in the United States and Canada from the 1980s have been overturned.

It is now acknowledged that persistent suggestive questioning can lead children to provide accounts of events that never occurred, even when they first denied them. Sometimes the questioning results in the child developing a subjectively real memory for an event that never happened. (Bruck and Ceci, 1995; Ceci, 1994; Ceci and Bruck, 1993, 1995; Ceci, Loftus, Leichtman and Bruck, 1994). Several conclusions are now generally accepted in the scientific community (Ceci and Bruck, 1993):

- First and foremost, contrary to the claims made by some . . . there do appear to be significant age differences in suggestibility, with pre-school aged children being disproportionately more vulnerable to suggestion than either school-aged children or adults (p. 431).
- Our review of the literature indicates that children can indeed be led to make false or inaccurate reports about very crucial, personally experienced, central events (p. 432).
- The second major conclusion is that contrary to the claims of some, children sometimes lie when the motivational structure is tilted toward lying (p. 433).
- Third, notwithstanding the aforementioned two points, it is clear that children — even pre-schoolers — are capable of recalling much that is forensically relevant (p. 433).

It is extremely important to examine the conditions prevalent at the time of the child's original report. The way the child was interviewed, including the use of image-based techniques, must be carefully examined. The conclusions from the current research are clear — when children are interviewed skillfully and appropriately and supported and encouraged to tell their story in their own words, they can provide accurate and forensically useful information. But when interviewers use suggestive, leading, specific, and coercive questioning to get the child to confirm pre-existing biases about abuse, they risk eliciting false statements. Therefore, if image-based techniques are used, it must be in a nonsuggestive way that encourages children to provide details and a narrative account from their free recall of events.

The Use of Images in Interviews

Techniques using images vary greatly as to whether they introduce potential error into the investigation or whether they are useful aids to accurate recall. Unfortunately, despite growing knowledge about how interviews should be done to increase the reliability of the information elicited, many interviews in actual cases continue to be suggestive and contaminating (Underwager and Wakefield, 1990; Warren, Woodall, Hunt and Perry, 1996).

Anatomically Detailed Dolls

Anatomically-detailed dolls are routinely used in interviewing children suspected of being abused. The dolls are made of plastic or cotton and come dressed with easily removable clothing. There are several commercial manufacturers who sell the dolls but they are also sometimes hand made. The mature female dolls have representations of breasts that protrude and the boy and mature male dolls have penises. There are holes in the dolls representing the mouth, anus, and vagina. The penis is able to fit into these openings. Often, the dolls have fingers that also fit into the openings. The mature male and female dolls have pubic hair. Although some early versions of the dolls appeared to have genitals that were disproportionately large, a survey of seventeen sets of anatomical dolls (Bays, 1990) indicated that the genitals were not exaggerated in size. The design of the dolls is not standardized (see Figure 12.1).

Anatomical dolls are used by many different types of professionals (Boat and Everson, 1988, 1996; Conte *et al.*, 1991; Kendall-Tackett and Watson, 1992), many of whom may have little or no training in their use. Despite their widespread use, these dolls are extremely controversial and there is disagreement in the professional community as to whether they should be used (e.g., Koocher *et al.*, 1995; Yates and Terr, 1988). However, all agree that they have no demonstrated validity and reliability.

The dolls are sometimes used in ways that can induce serious error into the interview. In one videotape we reviewed, the mother, who was part of the interview, took the dolls, put them in the intercourse position, and then asked the child to do this. In another, the interviewer pointed to and touched the genitals of a doll that had been labelled 'daddy' and told the child, 'Show me where daddy touched you.' Boat and Everson (1996) describe an example of a young child putting the doll's penis in her mouth but not responding when asked about it. Later, the interviewer asked, 'You put [the doll's] wienie in your mouth. Whose wienie have you had in your mouth?' Boat and Everson (1996) also note that in 28 per cent of the interviews with 2- to 5-year-olds and 9 per cent of the interviews with 6- to 12-year-olds, the terms 'play' or 'pretend' were used as part of the doll interview. To invite a young child to play or pretend as a part of an interview about real events can be very confusing. This is compounded if the adult then assumes the pretend behaviour reflects actual events.

We believe the dolls should not be used. There are no accepted standards for their or normative data on them (APA Council of Representatives, 1991; Koocher *et al.*, 1995; Levy, Markovic, Kalinowski, Ahart and Torres, 1995). The dolls, in the way they are often used, may become learning experiences for a child (Wakefield and Underwager, 1988; Underwager and Wakefield, 1990). Interviewers may model handling the dolls, undress them, or name them for the child. They may ask the child to show with the dolls

Figure 12.1a

Figure 12.1b

what the accused person did. They may place the dolls in sexually explicit positions. Although some researchers claim the dolls are not necessarily suggestive (e.g., Everson and Boat, 1994), some non-abused children engage the dolls in representations of sexual play (Dawson and Geddie, 1991; Dawson, Vaughan and Wagner, 1992; Everson and Boat, 1990; Gabriel, 1985; Glaser and Collins, 1989; McIver, Wakefield and Underwager, 1989).

Studies that claim to show differences between the doll play of sexually abused and non-abused children have major methodological shortcomings which limit any conclusions that can be drawn from them (Ceci and Bruck, 1993; Skinner and Berry, 1993; Underwager and Wakefield, 1990; Wakefield and Underwager, 1988, 1989, 1994; Wolfner, Faust and Dawes, 1993). DeLoache (1995b) notes that the basic reason for using anatomical dolls is the belief that the dolls will elicit information from children who are unable or unwilling to verbally describe the abuse. She observes, however, that not only is there no good evidence that dolls help in interviews with young children, but the presence of the dolls might result in the youngest children providing *less* information. Younger children cannot understand the basic self–doll relation assumed by interviewers. They cannot use dolls as symbols or representations for themselves and therefore cannot use the dolls to enact their own experiences. DeLoache concludes that the presence of an anatomical doll might even interfere with the memory reports of younger children.

Wolfner *et al.* (1993) point out that the necessary research to determine whether the dolls provide any incremental validity in establishing abuse would involve a group of children who were all *suspected* of being abused who, based on subsequent evidence, could be definitely divided into those who have and have not been abused. The doll interviews would have to take place prior to the children undergoing the standard procedures for investigating sexual abuse, since the process of being questioned about abuse could affect their reactions to the dolls. Such research has not been done — the studies that are claimed to support the use of the dolls only compare children suspected of abuse to those who are not suspected.

In summary, anatomical dolls are controversial, with some professionals claiming they are useful and others contending that they are too suggestive. Their use is especially problematical if the child's interaction with the dolls forms the basis for a conclusion about sexual abuse. Some professionals maintain that the dolls can be used if great care is taken not to be suggestive, if the child's interaction with the dolls is not the basis for an opinion about sexual abuse, and if they are not be used with very young children (e.g., Boat and Everson, 1996; Koocher, *et al.*, 1995; Simkins and Renier, 1996).

Others believe the dolls should not be used, even with great care (e.g., Fisher and Whiting, in press; Underwager and Wakefield, 1995; Wolfner *et al.*, 1993). They are unnecessary for older children and risk introducing error into the accounts of younger children. There is no empirical evidence that doll interviews are a valid and reliable method for getting accurate information. The use of the dolls as an assessment or investigatory technique is not generally accepted within the scientific community, rather, their use remains highly controversial.

Puppets

Although puppets are used as interview aids (Kendall-Tackett, 1992) we found no research concerning them. The way they are used in videotapes we have seen is highly suggestive. When a child is not responding to questions or is saying, 'I don't remember', the interviewer may give the child one puppet, place another on her own hand, and have the puppets talk to each other. The child sometimes interprets this as a pretend game and begins saying all sorts of things. The interviewer, however, fails to recognize this and responds to the child-puppet's statements as though the child were telling about actual, real-life events. In our opinion, puppets have no place in an investigatory interview.

Books

Books for younger children can provide cues for eliciting spontaneous information or they can be suggestive and potentially contaminating, depending upon the book and how it is used. We often read books to very young children, both as an ice breaker and rapport builder and as a possible cue for children to provide spontaneous information about their families and their concerns. The books, which can be bought at the children's department at any bookstore, are on topics such as bathing, nap time, parents who are divorcing, bedtime, dreams, the birth of a new brother or sister, etc. These are environments in which abuse may occur and reading about them may permit a child to naturally and spontaneously speak about events in these circumstances. Such books, although providing possible cues for spontaneous information, are not suggestive in terms of sexual abuse.

Other books directly deal with sexual abuse. Children may be taught about 'good' and 'bad' touches and told that they can tell others not to touch them if they don't want it. For example, *Red Flag Green Flag People* (Rape and Crisis Abuse Center, 1985) leads children through a series of pages that present good touch and bad touch and instructs them to colour portions of a figure where they were touched. *My Feelings* (Morgan, 1984) tells children to 'trust your feelings' and tell an adult when a touch makes them feel 'creepy and icky and such'. *No More Secrets for Me* (Wachter, 1983) contains short stories about children who are touched 'in a way you don't like'. A *Very Special Person* (Nelson, 1985) informs children that they can choose who can touch them and that they should tell 'yucky secrets' to someone they trust. The research evidence on prevention programs using the same concepts as these books suggests they are both ineffective and may increase false accusations (Krivacska, 1990). Since such books deal directly with sexual abuse, the use of them in an investigatory interview is suggestive.

One of the better books is *A Touching Book* by Hindman (1985), who uses 'secret touching to refer to sexual abuse. This book, which contains many humorous cartoon-type drawings and clever examples, treats bodies and adult sexuality positively and lacks the anti-sexuality found in many of the books. But all books of this type may be suggestive if used as part of an assessment for suspected sexual abuse.

A completely inappropriate book is *Don't Make Me Go Back Mommy: A Child's Book About Satanic Ritual Abuse* (Sanford, 1990). This book contains explicit full-colour pictures illustrating satanic rituals and is used to encourage the child to describe ritual abuse. One of the illustrations contains naked children in a ritual circle, black-robed figures and a noose. This book presumes the reality of widespread satanic ritual abuse, despite the fact that there is no evidence suggesting organized satanic, ritual abuse actually occurs (Bottoms, Shaver and Goodman, 1996). Using it to get information from children cannot produce reliable statements.

Drawings

Children's drawings may be interpreted in a variety of ways. Tests such as the Bender-Gestalt and the House-Tree-Person provide information about perceptual-motor abilities and developmental level and can be useful for this purpose. But children's drawings are also used to assess possible sexual abuse (Conte *et al.*, 1991; Kendall-Tackett, 1992). This latter use lacks empirical support.

The assumption underlying this use is that, since emotionally disturbed children are believed to reflect their problems in their drawings (e.g., Di Leo, 1973, 1996; Handler, 1996; Koppitz, 1968; Myers, 1978; Yates, Beutler and Crago, 1985), the drawings of children who have been abused will differ from those of non-abused children. Free drawings, as well as the House-Tree-Person, Draw-A-Person, and Kinetic Family Drawings are used and qualitative features of the drawings, such as the colours used, the size and detail of body parts, and the shape of the figures may be interpreted in terms of the presence or absence of sexual abuse.

Burgess, McCausland and Wolbert (1981) claim that drawings in which a child exhibits a shift from age-appropriate figures to more disorganized objects or drawings with repeated stylized, sexualized figures indicate suspected sexual abuse. Sahd (1980) recommends using drawings as part of the evaluative interview of the sexual abuse victims and gives several examples of drawings that reflect abuse histories. Kelley (1984, 1985) believes that human figure drawings can be analyzed for 'emotional indicators' (signs) in young children who are unable to verbalize their trauma.

Cantlay (1996) claims that distress and trauma, including sexual abuse, is reflected in drawings that include such signs as large heads, large, empty eyes, abundant hair, shaded clouds, knotholes in trees, large hands, large heads, large pointed teeth, abnormally tiny eyes, eyes without pupils, crossed eyes, excessive details, box-shaped bodies, poorly integrated body parts, lack of gender differentiation, hair that is long at the sides or thinning at the crown, wedge-shaped windows, extraneous circles, and large smoke trails coming out of the chimney. She cautions, however, that trauma can only be determined from a series of drawings which contain a number of these signs and that a single characteristic is not enough to indicate abuse.

The presence of genitalia is often considered a sign of sexual abuse because it is considered rare for normal, non-abused children to include genitals in their drawings (Di Leo, 1973, 1996). Cantlay (1996), Hibbard, Roghmann and Hoekelman (1987), and Kelley (1984, 1985) claim that the presence of genitalia in drawings means possible sexual abuse, Yates *et al.* (1985) believe that incest victims either exaggerate or minimize sexual features in their drawings, and Miller, Veltkamp and Janson (1987) state that sexualized drawings indicate sexual knowledge beyond a child's years.

Empirical support for all these claims is extremely weak. In addition, a major difficulty with these assumptions is that sexually abused children are likely to have been interviewed about sexual abuse, have perhaps undergone a distressing genital examination, and/or have been placed into sexual abuse therapy. They are likely to have been shown undressed anatomical dolls where their attention is focused on the genitals. They may have been asked repeatedly to describe the details of the abuse. Therefore, genitalia may well become salient and it is not surprising that some of these children will include genitals in their drawings. In addition, other factors, such as family nudity, the birth of a sibling, or viewing an X-rated video may affect the tendency of a child to include sexual details in a drawing.

Figure 12.2

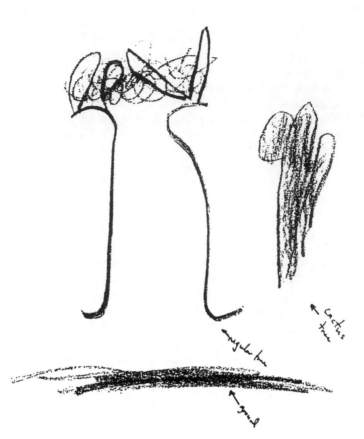

Figure 12.3

We have seen many examples of drawings by children that are erroneously inter-preted as bolstering a conclusion of sexual abuse. For instance:

1   A 4-year-old girl drew nothing but circles which she called 'caves'. One of the drawings looked to the psychologist like male genitalia — when asked what it was, the child said it was 'a ball rolling into a lion's cave'. The psychologist said this meant the child has been subjected to some type of traumatic experience. But when we saw and evaluated the child, now age 5, we found that she was of borderline intelligence and could not do any kind of drawing task. All she could do was make scribbled circles.

2   The child, when asked to draw a tree, also drew a cactus (Figure 12.2). This was interpreted in terms of 'unconscious expression of danger and fearfulness'. However, the child was not asked if she had a cactus in her yard (this was in Texas).

3   The 7-year-old girl drew a picture of herself and her sister with their hands up in the air with the father standing next to them and smiling (Figure 12.3). She told the psychologist that she and her sister were 'cheering at a show'. But the psychologist claimed that this really signified a 'helpless posture'. She saw it as significant that there were no fingers drawn on the hands and that the hands were large on the father — she claimed that abused children put large hands on the drawings of their perpetrators. She also said that the thick lines in the crotch in the picture of the father meant an emphasis on genitals, was probably a penis, and showed anxiety about the father. She concluded that the girl, who continued to deny allegations of sexual abuse by the father, had, in fact, been sexually abused by the him.

4   Hundreds of drawings over two years were interpreted by a psychologist who saw two girls in a day care case with allegations of ritualistic satanic abuse complete with costumes, masks, dead animals, sacrificed babies, blood, faeces, skeletons, and monsters. These allegations only surfaced during therapy. The psychologist depended heavily upon the children's drawings in forming conclu-sions about satanic ritual abuse. But all of the drawings were typical of the types of scribbles and rudimentary figures drawn by 3- and 4-year-olds. In her deposi-tion the psychologist said that what she believed was significant included prac-tically every characteristic she believed she saw in the drawings:

- shapes that are untypical for 3- and 4-year-old children;
- shapes that are phallic symbols;
- jiggly lines that indicate anxiety;
- straight mouths that mean people can't say anything;
- jagged mouths that mean anxiety;
- a mouth that is open and oval shaped;
- darkened eyes;
- eyeballs that are scribbled around;
- eyes that are two different colours;
- drawing something and then covering it up;
- drawing something and not talking about it;
- colours are very important and significant: black means the child is frightened or distressed; black is a morbid down colour; red means angry, unless the child

is drawing a pretty red flower, when it is healthy; if everything in the picture is red or red and black, this is very suspicious; blue, brown, and orange mean fear, anger, and depression; pink, red, and green are healthy colours.

There are no empirical data to support these types of interpretations. Despite their frequent use in child abuse investigations, drawings are subject to the same criticisms as the anatomical dolls (Underwager and Wakefield, 1990; Wakefield and Underwager, 1988, 1989, 1994). Interpretations of drawings lack validity and reliability as projective assessment devices. In a review of the Draw-A-Person test in the Seventh Mental Measurements Yearbook, Harris (1972) states that there is little evidence for the use of 'signs' as valid indicators of personality characteristics. In fact, there is so much variability from drawing to drawing that particular features of any one drawing are too unreliable to say anything about them. Reviews by Cundick (1989) and Weinberg (1989) in the Tenth Mental Measurements Yearbook note that there are no normative data establishing reliability and validity of the Kinetic Drawing System. Smith and Dumont (1995) state that four decades of research have failed to support the validity of human figure drawings in assessing personality, behaviour, or intelligence. They observe that the confirmatory biases expressed in anchoring errors predispose clinicians to find support for their initial opinions in whatever material the client provides.

There are serious methodological problems with the few studies that claim to find differences between sexually abused and non-abused children. As with the anatomical dolls, studies with drawings with children suspected of being abused would have to take place before children underwent physical examinations, interviews, or therapy since these could affect their drawings. The persons who rated the drawings would have to be blind concerning the child's status regarding abuse. Ideally, a study would involve children who were all suspected of being abused who, based on subsequent evidence, could be divided into those who have and have not been abused. None of the studies meet these criteria.

Another common drawing technique is an outline of the back and the front of a naked male or a female. These cards are ostensibly used to enable the interviewer to learn what terms the child uses for body parts. However, this suggests that the purpose of the interview is to talk about sexual matters. The interviewer also may also tell the child to put an X where he or she was touched, which gives the message, 'You were touched, now show me where'. A recent New Zealand research report questions whether this constitutes a prompt or priming technique and states that drawings increased errors and confabulation in children's accounts (Rawls, 1996).

Nevertheless, drawings may be useful evaluation aids. They can provide information about possible perceptual-motor difficulties and developmental delays. They can help build rapport and encourage narrative accounts. Goodwin (1982) had children complete the Draw-A-Person task and the Kinetic Family Drawing and also asked them to draw whatever they wanted, to draw the whole family doing something together, and then to draw a picture of the alleged perpetrator. She reports that drawings were helpful in understanding the child's fears and anxieties, her view of the family, and her self-image, and in opening up a workable line of communication between the evaluator and the child. She cautions, however, that by themselves drawings are not sufficient to form diagnostic conclusions. Miller *et al.* (1987) report that, once a child has drawn a picture, he or she becomes highly verbal regarding the contents of the drawing. They believe that drawings are less threatening to a child who is hesitant to talk.

But drawings must not be used suggestively or the child's description of the drawing selectively reinforced. It inappropriate to tell a child who has not mentioned anything about abuse to 'draw me a picture of what daddy did to you'. Any useful information about possible abuse will come from the child's explanations of the drawing and spontaneous narratives that this elicits. Details and signs in the drawings itself cannot be projectively interpreted. Drawings may be valuable in building rapport and in facilitating communication but they cannot be used in the absence of a description from the child to draw conclusions about abuse.

Other Projective Techniques

Other image-based projective techniques are often used in child abuse assessment. The Rorschach Ink Blot Test, which can be used with children as young as 5, consists of ten inkblots on white backgrounds (Rorschach, 1921). The child is asked what the inkblot 'looks like' and asked to explain the response. Although the responses are believed to reflect personality characteristics, there are serious doubts about the Rorschach's validity, and hence usefulness, as a diagnostic technique (Dawes, 1994; Wakefield and Underwager, 1993; Ziskin, 1995).

Another well-known projective test is the Thematic Apperception Test (TAT). The TAT consists of thirty-one ambiguous pictures depicting a variety of situations or dramatic events and the person is asked to tell a story about the characters (Murray, 1943). Although scoring systems have been developed for analyzing the responses, none have received widespread acceptance. Practitioners are likely to use different systems, idiosyncratic systems, or no systems at all; therefore, despite its popularity, the TAT lacks reliability and validity (Ryan, 1985). A similar test intended for children ages 3 to 10 is the Children's Apperception Test (CAT) (Bellak and Bellak, 1980). The CAT, which consists of ten pictures depicting anthropomorphic animals in a variety of situations, also lacks norms and data on reliability and validity.

The Storytelling Card Game (Gardner, 1988) consists of twenty-four different scene cards and fifteen figurines, ranging in age from infancy to old age. The child is asked to select one or more figurines, place them on the card, and tell a story. This technique is not suggestive in terms of sexual abuse and may be used as a rapport builder or interview aid. There are no data on its reliability or validity and it cannot be considered a psychological test.

The Projective Story Telling Cards (Caruso, 1990) consist of a series of cards with drawings on them depicting a wide variety of situations. There are no standard instructions for administration and the evaluator is instructed to select cards that represent particular concerns. The manual gives the example of choosing cards that may represent circumstances of sexual abuse when evaluating a child where child protection believes the child may have been abused by a live-in boyfriend.

Many of the cards are relatively neutral or ambiguous, and may serve the same function as does a carefully chosen book. But other cards are highly suggestive. Some depict adults and children in bed wearing only underwear with cameras prominently displayed. One depicts a young child with his mouth open standing a few inches in front of the open fly of an adult male. Several show graphic satanic ritual abuse scenes, including one in a graveyard with robed adults standing around a fire, holding a baby with its head cut off. Although the publisher claims that these cards represent 'a relevant, meaningful, and useful tool' for assessment, there are no data concerning reliability and validity.

Play Therapy Toys

In play therapy, the assumption is that the child expresses and works out conflicts and problems through play. There are many different toys to choose from and the toy chosen along with the child's play with these may be interpreted in terms of suspected sexual abuse. For example, in one case, the child made long rolls out of play dough, which were interpreted as penises by the therapist. When the child then cut the play dough into pieces, this was interpreted as reflecting anger at the alleged perpetrator (the father).

The symbolic interpretation of play behaviours as images representing something else is a psychoanalytic concept. In 1905 Freud used the case of Little Hans to suggest the play of little children represents conscious and unconscious wishes and fears. Psycho-analytic therapists take for granted that children's behaviours can reveal troubling unconscious factors otherwise not available to either the child or the observer (Slade and Wolf, 1994).

Play therapy for sexual abuse is sometimes called 'disclosure-based' and the sessions focus on re-enactments in play, expressing feelings, and talking repeatedly about the alleged abuse. Although there is no evidence that play therapy is an effective therapeutic procedure (Campbell, 1992b; Underwager and Wakefield, 1990; Wakefield and Underwager, 1988, 1994; Weisz and Weiss, 1993), children are frequently given therapy for sexual abuse before there has been any legal determination that sexual abuse has occurred.

There is no support, however, for the supposition that specific interactions with toys in play therapy can be used as signs to establish the truth of past events. The same objections raised earlier about the projective 'sign' interpretation of drawings are relevant here. Also, disclosure-based play therapy can influence children to accept the beliefs of the therapist and can be a contributing factor in cases of false allegations (Campbell, 1992a).

Image-based Techniques in the Cognitive Interview

Children's reports of events based on their free recall are quite accurate, but young children provide very limited amounts of information. Therefore, the task of the interviewer is to encourage children to provide more information without asking leading questions which risks increasing error. The cognitive interview involves techniques designed to elicit from a child as complete a narrative report of the event as possible. Although much in the cognitive interview is similar to other suggestions about how to conduct an effective and non-suggestive interview, the cognitive interview is distinguished by its memory-joggling strategies.

Several research studies on the cognitive interview indicate that it does improve the accuracy and increase the amount of information (Fisher and McCauley, 1995; Powell and Thomson, 1994). Studies with children also suggest that, in comparison with a standard interview, the cognitive interview results in more correct facts recalled without an increase in errors (Fisher, 1995; Fisher and McCauley, 1995; Saywitz, Geiselman and Bornstein, 1992). There are limitations in generalizing from this research since none of the children were younger than 7 and the events have not involved personally experienced, traumatic events. In addition, the interviews in the research studies took place shortly after the event, but in the real world, investigatory interviews may take place months later.

Nevertheless, several of the image-based suggestions may be useful in interviewing children about alleged abuse. Modifications of the techniques are necessary with young children since some of the specific techniques are not appropriate with children. For example, before a certain age, children do not appear to understand some of the memory strategies (Bekerian and Dennett, 1995).

One memory retrieval technique involves attempts to recreate the original context or circumstances. The witness is instructed to mentally recreate the environmental, cognitive, physiological, and affective states that existed at the time of the original event (Fisher and McCauley, 1995). We have used family photographs, favourite toys, and familiar objects to help young children picture the circumstances, persons, and feelings surrounding the alleged events. We then encourage free narrative recall by asking them to tell everything that happened that they can remember.

For example, a father who had not seen his 4-year-old son in over a year provided a favourite toy that had been left with him. The child remembered the toy with affection and began talking about playing with his father. Another child, who initially recalled very little about life with her father, recalled several relatives and incidents when looking at family photographs. A child was able to talk about when he was in day care after looking at several photographs of the day care centre. The value in such objects lies in tapping into the child's free recall. If suggestive and leading questions are asked about the objects, the risk of error is greatly increased.

Another way of reinstating the context is by imaging. The child can be asked to close her eyes and try to picture the event and the circumstances surrounding it. She can be asked to report everything she pictures in her mind about it, no matter how small. With children, however, it is important to stress that they should only describe actual events that have happened.

Children who are old enough to understand the instruction can be asked to describe the incident from a different perspective, that is, as if someone else were watching, what they would have seen. They can be asked what the incident would have looked like from the doorway or from the ceiling. Since the words 'imagine' or 'pretend' may be perceived as an instruction to fantasize these terms should be avoided with young children. For children who are old enough, backward order recall may allow increased information to be produced. The child can be asked to picture the events in backward order beginning with the end, then the middle, and then the beginning. After each response, the child is asked, 'What happened right before that?' This technique, however, will be confusing to younger children who have not developed the necessary knowledge about time and sequencing.

Conclusion

Given the lack of demonstrated validity and reliability for many image-based techniques used in obtaining information from children, there are serious questions about the ethical quality of their use. The use of invalid techniques and techniques when there are questions about competency is proscribed by the 1992 American Psychological Association's Ethical Principles and Code of Conduct (Bersoff, 1995; Smith and Dumont, 1995; Dumont and Smith, 1996). Since it is not possible to be competent in doing something that nobody knows how to do to produce outcomes at a better than chance level (Underwager and Wakefield, 1989), until there is sufficient research to show a technique can meet the requirements for validity and reliability, it is best to remain cautious and use only those which can be defended adequately. Knowledge and understanding of the developmental capacities of children to use one object to represent another must also be demonstrated. Whatever techniques are used, any limitations or qualifications to any opinion based on the use of images must be clearly stated.

References

APA COUNCIL OF REPRESENTATIVES (1991) 8 February. *Statement on the Use of Anatomically Detailed Dolls in Forensic Evaluations*, Washington, DC: American Psychological Association.

BAYS, J. (1990) 'Are the genitalia of anatomical dolls distorted?', *Child Abuse and Neglect*, **14**, pp. 171–5.

BEKERIAN, D.A. and DENNETT, J.L. (1995) 'An introduction to the cognitive interview technique', in NEY, T. (ed.) *True and False Allegations of Child Sexual Abuse: Assessment and Case Management*, New York: Brunner/Mazel, pp. 192–206.

BELLAK, L. and BELLAK, S.S. (1980) *A Manual for the Children's Apperception Test* (7th ed.), Larchmont, NY: CPS, Inc.

BERSOFF, D.N. (1995) *Ethical Conflicts in Psychology*, Washington, DC: American Psychological Association.

BOAT, B.W. and EVERSON, M.D. (1988) 'Use of anatomical dolls among professionals in sexual abuse evaluations', *Child Abuse and Neglect*, **12**, pp. 171–9.

BOAT, B.W. and EVERSON, M.D. (1996) 'Concerning practices of interviewers using dolls in child protective services investigations', *Child Maltreatment*, **1**, pp. 96–104.

BOAT, B.W., EVERSON, M.D. and HOLLAND, J. (1990) 'Maternal perceptions of non-abused young children's behaviours after the exposure to anatomical dolls', *Child Welfare*, **69**, pp. 389–400.

BOTTOMS, B.L., SHAVER, P.R. and GOODMAN, G.S. (1996) 'An analysis of ritualistic and religion related child abuse allegations', *Law and Human Behaviour*, **20**, pp. 1–34.

BRUCK, M. and CECI, S.J. (1995) 'Amicus brief for the case of State of New Jersey v. Michaels presented by committee of concerned social scientists', *Psychology, Public Policy, and Law*, **1**, pp. 272–322.

BURGESS, A.W., MCCAUSLAND, M.P. and WOLBERT, W.A. (1981) 'Children's drawings as indicators of sexual trauma', *Perspectives in Psychiatric Care*, **19**, 2, pp. 50–8.

CAMPBELL, T.W. (1992a) 'False allegations of sexual abuse and the persuasiveness of play therapy', *Issues in Child Abuse Accusations*, **4**, pp. 118–24.

CAMPBELL, T.W. (1992b) 'Promoting play therapy: Marketing dream or empirical nightmare?', *Issues in Child Abuse Accusations*, **4**, pp. 111–17.

CANTLAY, L. (1996) *Detecting Child Abuse: Recognising Children at Risk through Drawings*, Santa Barbara: Holly Press.

CARUSO, K.R. (1990) *Projective Story Telling Cards*, Redding, CA: Northwest Psychological Publishers, Inc.

CECI, S.J. (1994) 'Cognitive and social factors in children's testimony', in SALES, B.D. and VANDENBOS, C.R. (eds) *Psychology in Litigation and Legislation*, Washington, DC: American Psychological Association, pp. 11–54.

CECI, S.J. and BRUCK, M. (1993) 'The suggestibility of the child witness: A historical review and synthesis', *Psychological Bulletin*, **113**, pp. 403–39.

CECI, S.J. and BRUCK, M. (1995) *Jeopardy in the Courtroom: A Scientific Analysis of Children's Testimony*, Washington, DC: American Psychological Association.

CECI, S.J., LOFTUS, E.F., LEICHTMAN, M.D. and BRUCK, M. (1994) 'The possible role of source misattributions in the creation of false beliefs among pre-schoolers', *International Journal of Clinical and Experimental Hypnosis*, **42**, pp. 304–20.

COLEMAN, L. (1986) Jan-Feb, 'False allegations of child sexual abuse: Have the experts been caught with their pants down', *Forum*, pp. 12–20.

CONTE, J.R., SORENSON, E., FOGARTY, L. and ROSA, J.D. (1991) 'Evaluating children's reports of sexual abuse: Results from a survey of professionals', *American Journal of Orthopsychiatry*, **61**, pp. 428–37.

CUNDICK, B.P. (1989) 'Review of the kinetic drawing system for family and school: A handbook', in BUROS, O.K. *The Tenth Mental Measurements Yearbook*, Highland Park, NJ: Gryphon Press, pp. 422–3.

DAWES, R.M. (1994) *House of Cards: Psychology and Psychotherapy Built on Myth*, New York: The Free Press.

DAWSON, B. and GEDDIE, L. (1991) August, *Low Income, Minority Pre-schoolers' Behaviour with Sexually Anatomically Detailed Dolls*, Paper presented at the American Psychological Association in San Francisco, CA.

DAWSON, B., VAUGHAN, A.R. and WAGNER, W.G. (1992) 'Normal responses to sexually anatomically detailed dolls', *Journal of Family Violence*, **7**, pp. 135–52.

DELOACHE, J.S. (1995a) 'Early understanding and use of symbols: The model model', *Current Directions in Psychological Science*, **4**, pp. 109–13.

DELOACHE, J.S. (1995b) 'The use of dolls in interviewing young children', in ZARAGOZA, M.S., GRAHAM, J.R., HALL, G.C.N., HIRSCHMAN, R. and BEN-PORATH, Y.S. *Improving Children's Testimony*, Thousand Oaks, CA: Sage, pp. 160–78.

DI LEO, J.H. (1973) *Children's Drawings as Diagnostic Aids*, New York: Bruner/Mazel.

DI LEO, J.H. (1996) *Young Children and Their Drawings*, New York: Brunner/Mazel.

DUMONT, F. and SMITH, D. (1996) 'Projectives and their infirm research base', *Professional Psychology: Research and Practice*, **27**, pp. 419–21.

EVERSON, M.D. and BOAT, B.W. (1990) 'Sexualised doll play among young children: Implications for the use of anatomical dolls in sexual abuse evaluations', *Journal of the American Academy of Child and Adolescent Psychiatry*, **29**, pp. 736–42.

EVERSON, M.D. and BOAT, B.W. (1994) 'Putting the anatomical doll controversy in perspective: An examination of the major uses and criticisms of the dolls in child sexual abuse evaluations', *Child Abuse and Neglect*, **18**, pp. 13–29.

FALLER, K.C. (1984) 'Is the child victim of sexual abuse telling the truth?', *Child Abuse and Neglect*, **8**, pp. 473–81.

FISHER, R.P. (1995) 'Interviewing victims and witnesses of crime: Psychology, public policy, and law', **1**, pp. 732–64.

FISHER, C.B. and WHITING, K.A. (in press) 'How valid are child sexual abuse validations?', in CECI, S.J. and HEMBROOKE, H. (eds) *What Can (and Should) an Expert Tell the Court*, Washington, DC: American Psychological Association.

FISHER, R.P. and McCAULEY, M.R. (1995) 'Improving eyewitness testimony with the cognitive interview', in ZARAGOZA, M.S., GRAHAM, J.R., HALL, G.C.N., HIRSCHMAN, R. and BEN-PORATH, Y.S. (eds) *Applied Psychology, Individual, Social, and Community Issues: Vol. I. Memory and Testimony in the Child Witness*, Thousands Oaks, CA: Sage Publications, pp. 141–59.

GABRIEL, R. (1985) 'Anatomically correct dolls in the diagnosis of sexual abuse of children', *The Journal of the Melanie Klein Society*, **3**, 2, pp. 40–51.

GARDNER, H. and WOLF, D. (1987) 'The symbolic products of early childhood', in GÖRLITZ, D. and WOHLWILL, J.F. (eds) *Curiosity, Imagination, and Play: On the Development of Spontaneous Cognitive and Motivational Processes*, Hillsdale, NJ: Lawrence Erlbaum Associates, pp. 305–25.

GARDNER, R.A. (1988) *The Storytelling Card Game*, Cresskill, NJ: Creative Therapeutics.

GLASER, D. and COLLINS, C. (1989) 'The response of young, non-sexually abused children to anatomically correct dolls', *Journal of Child Psychology and Psychiatry*, **30**, pp. 547–60.

GOODMAN, G.S. (1984) 'Children's testimony in historical perspective', *Journal of Social Issues*, **40**, 2, pp. 9–31.

GOODWIN, J. (1982) 'Use of drawings on evaluating children who may be incest victims', *Children and Youth Service Review*, **4**, pp. 269–78.

HANDLER, L. (1996) 'The clinical use of drawings: Draw-A-Person, House-Tree-Person, and Kinetic Family Drawings', in NEWMARK, C.S. (ed.) *Major Psychological Assessment Instruments*, Boston: Allyn and Bacon, pp. 206–93.

HARRIS, D.B. (1972) 'Review of the Draw-A-Person', in BUROS, O.K. *The Seventh Mental Measurements Yearbook*, Highland Park, NJ: Gryphon Press, pp. 401–4.

HIBBARD, R., ROGHMANN, K. and HOEKELMAN, R. (1987) 'Genitalia in children's drawings: An association with sexual abuse', *Pediatrics*, **79**, 1, pp. 129–37.

HINDMAN, J. (1985) *A Very Touching Book . . . for Little People and for Big People*, Durkee, OR: McClure-Hindman Associates. Ontario, OR: AlexAndria Associates.

HUMPHREY, H.J., III (1985) February, *Report on Scott County Investigations*, Office of the Attorney General, St Paul, Minnesota, Author.

KELLEY, S. (1984) 'The use of art therapy with sexually abused children', *Journal of Psychological Nursing and Mental Health Services*, **22**, 12, pp. 12–18.

KELLEY, S. (1985) 'Drawings: Critical communications for sexually abused children', *Pediatric Nursing*, **11**, pp. 421–6.

KENDALL-TACKETT, K.A. (1992) 'Beyond anatomical dolls: Professionals' use of other play therapy techniques', *Child Abuse and Neglect*, **16**, pp. 139–42.

KENDALL-TACKETT, K.A. and WATSON, M.W. (1992) 'Use of anatomical dolls by Boston-area professionals', *Child Abuse and Neglect*, **16**, pp. 423–8.

KOOCHER, G.P., GOODMAN, G.S., WHITE, C.S., FRIEDRICH, W.N., SIVAN, A.B. and REYNOLD, C.R. (1995) 'Psychological science and the use of anatomically detailed dolls in child sexual-abuse assessments', *Psychological Bulletin*, **118**, pp. 199–222.

KOPPITZ, E.M. (1968) *Psychological Evaluation of Children's Human Figure Drawings*, New York: Grune & Stratton.

KRIVACSKA, J.J. (1990) *Designing Child Sexual Abuse Prevention Programs: Current Approaches and a Proposal for the Prevention, Reduction, and Identification of Sexual Misuse*, Springfield, IL: C.C. Thomas.

LEVY, H.B., MARKOVIC, J., KALINOWSKI, M.N., AHART, S. and TORRES, H. (1995) 'Child sexual abuse interviews: The use of anatomic dolls and the reliability of information', *Journal of Interpersonal Violence*, **10**, pp. 334–53.

MCIVER, W.F. (1986) *The Case for a Therapeutic Interview in Situations of Alleged Sexual Molestation: Champion*, **10**, 1, pp. 11–13.

MCIVER, W., WAKEFIELD, H. and UNDERWAGER, R. (1989) 'Behavior of abused and non-abused children in interviews with anatomically-correct dolls', *Issues in Child Abuse Accusations*, **1**, 1, pp. 39–48.

MILLER, T.W., VELTKAMP, L.J. and JANSON, D. (1987) 'Projective measures in the clinical evaluation of sexually abused children', *Child Psychiatry and Human Development*, **18**, 1, pp. 47–57.

MORGAN, M.K. (1984) *My Feelings*, Eugene, Oregon: Equal Justice Consultants & Education Products.

MURRAY, H.A. (1943) *Thematic Apperception Test manual*, Cambridge, MA: Harvard University Press.

MYERS, D.V. (1978) 'Toward an objective evaluation procedure of the kinetic family drawings (KFD): An interpretive manual', *Journal of Personality Assessment*, **42**, pp. 358–65.

NATHAN, D. and SNEDEKER, M. (1995) *Satan's Silence: Ritual Abuse and the Making of a Modern American Witch Hunt*, New York: Basic Books.

NELSON, C.S. (1985) *A Very Special Person*, Grand Junction, CO: Pyramid Printing.

POWELL, M.B. and THOMSON, D.M. (1994 April) 'Children's eyewitness-memory research: Implications for practice', *Families in Society: The Journal of Contemporary Human Services*, pp. 204–16.

RAPE AND CRISIS ABUSE CENTER (1985) *Red Flag Green Flag People*, Fargo, ND: Red Flag Green Flag Resources.

RAWLS, J.M. (1996) 'How questions and body parts diagrams could affect the content of young children's disclosures', *Law Talk*, **452**, pp. 28–9.

RORSCHACH, H. (1921) *Psychodiagnostik*, Bern: Bircher (Trans. Hans Huber Verlag, 1942).

RYAN, R.M. (1985) 'Thematic apperception test', in KEYER, D.J. and SWEETLAND, R.C. *Test Critiques: Volume II*, Kansas City, MO: Westport Publishers, Inc, pp. 799–814.

SAHD, D. (1980) 'Psychological assessment of sexually abusing families and treatment implications', in HOLDER, W. (ed.) *Sexual Abuse of Children*, Englewood, CO: The American Humane Association, pp. 71–86.

SANFORD, D. (1990) 'Don't make me go back mommy', Portland, OR: Multnomah Press.

SAYWITZ, K.J., GEISELMAN, R.E. and BORNSTEIN, G.K. (1992) 'Effects of cognitive interviewing and practice on children's recall performance', *Journal of Applied Psychology*, **77**, pp. 744–56.

SIMKINS, L. and RENIER, A. (1996) 'An analytical review of the empirical literature on children's play with anatomically detailed dolls', *Journal of Child Sexual Abuse*, **5**, 1, pp. 21–45.

SKINNER, L.J. and BERRY, K.K. (1993) 'Anatomically detailed dolls and the evaluation of child sexual abuse allegations: Psychometric considerations', *Law and Human Behavior*, **17**, pp. 399–421.

SLADE, A. and WOLF, D.P. (1994) *Children at Play: Clinical and Developmental Approaches to Meaning and Representation*, New York: Oxford University Press.

SMITH, D. and DUMONT, F. (1995) 'A cautionary study: Unwarranted interpretations of the draw-a-person test', *Professional Psychology: Research and Practice*, **26**, pp. 298–303.

SUMMIT, R. and KRYSO, J. (1978) 'Sexual abuse of children: A clinical spectrum', *American Journal of Orthopsychiatry*, **40**, pp. 237–51.

UNDERWAGER, R. and WAKEFIELD, H. (1989) Response by Ralph Underwager, Ph.D. and Hollida Wakefield, M.A. in the matter of the proposed adoption of the rule amendments of the Minnesota Board of Psychology governing licensure and professional conduct.

UNDERWAGER, R. and WAKEFIELD, H. (1990) *The Real World of Child Interrogations*, Springfield, IL: C.C. Thomas.

UNDERWAGER, R. and WAKEFIELD, H. (1995) 'Special problems with sexual abuse cases', in ZISKIN, J. *Coping with Psychiatric and Psychological Testimony*, 5th ed., Venice, CA: Law and Psychology Press, pp. 1315–70.

UNDERWAGER, R., WAKEFIELD, H., LEGRAND, R., BARTZ, C.S. and ERICKSON, J. (1986 August) *The Role of the Psychologist in the Assessment of Cases of Alleged Sexual Abuse of Children*, Presented at the 94th annual convention of the American Psychological Association, Washington, DC.

WACHTER, O. (1983) *No More Secrets for Me*, Boston, MA: Little Brown and Company.

WAKEFIELD, H. and UNDERWAGER, R. (1988) *Accusations of Child Sexual Abuse*, Springfield, IL: C.C. Thomas.

WAKEFIELD, H. and UNDERWAGER, R. (1989) 'Evaluating the child witness in sexual abuse cases: Interview or inquisition?', *American Journal of Forensic Psychology*, **7**, 3, pp. 43–69.

WAKEFIELD, H. and UNDERWAGER, R. (1993) 'Misuse of psychological tests in forensic settings: Some horrible examples', *American Journal of Forensic Psychology*, **11**, 1, pp. 55–75.

WAKEFIELD, H. and UNDERWAGER, R. (1994) 'The alleged child victim and real victims', in KRIVACSKA, J.J. and MONEY, J. (eds) *Handbook of Forensic Sexology*, Buffalo, NY: Prometheus Books, pp. 223–64.

WARREN, A.R., WOODALL, C.E., HUNT, J.S. and PERRY, N.W. (1996) 'It sounds good in theory, but . . . : Do investigative interviewers follow guidelines based on memory research?', *Child Maltreatment*, **1**, pp. 231–45.

WEINBERG, R.A. (1989) 'Review of the kinetic drawing system for family and school: A handbook', in BUROS, O.K. *The Tenth Mental Measurements Yearbook*, Highland Park, NJ: Gryphon Press, pp. 423–25.

WEISZ, J.R. and WEISS, B. (1993) *Effects of Psychotherapy with Children and Adolescents*, Newbury Park, CA: Sage.

WOLFNER, G., FAUST, D. and DAWES, R.M. (1993) 'The use of anatomically detailed dolls in sexual abuse evaluations: The state of the science', *Applied and Preventive Psychology*, **2**, pp. 1–11.

YATES, A., BEUTLER, L. and CRAGO, M. (1985) 'Drawings by child victims of incest', *Child Abuse and Neglect*, **9**, pp. 183–9.

YATES, A. and TERR, L.C. (1988) 'Debate forum: Anatomically correct dolls: Should they be used as a basis for expert testimony', *Journal of the American Academy of Child and Adolescent Psychiatry*, **27**, 2, pp. 254–7.

ZISKIN, J. (1995) *Coping with Psychiatric and Psychological Testimony*, 5th ed., Venice, CA: Law and Psychology Press.

Part 3

Image-based Research in Practice

Editor's note
The chapters in this section provide an insight into the possibilities for Image-based Research in practice. Authors from different backgrounds and differing disciplines illustrate, via a series of studies, how visual theory and method are applied in practice. What is noticeable in these chapters is the range of media used in visual research — photography, cartoons, drawings and paintings. They serve as exemplars of good practice and the potential of an image-based approach.

Chapter 13

Picture This! Class Line-ups, Vernacular Portraits and Lasting Impressions of School

Claudia Mitchell and Sandra Weber

Abstract

This chapter focuses on photographs, in this case school photographs, as both phenomenon and method. In so doing, it looks at the rich possibilities that school photographs offer for Image-based Research within work on professional identity in teacher education. Such possibilities range from considerations of the role of the 'outsider' photographer, to the resulting products and the memories of school that are evoked by such images, to using these memories to go beyond nostalgia so that the images can be used to inform and transform professional practice.[1]

Introduction

Portrait photographs are invested with a routine deception. Normally one thinks of them as the result of a moment that has been taken out of time to exhibit the face. For such images all psychological slack has been pulled taut to assert the prepared, immobile display of the person or persons. The characterizing process should look stable, with details consistently presented throughout the frame. A subject may appear self-absorbed or unconcerned about a later audience, but this is only a device that masks the fact that he or she is primed and ready for inspection. (Kozloff, 1994, 3)

In the same text Kozloff goes on to observe that still portraiture 'is one cultural index of how people are *schooled* to regard themselves . . .' (our italics) (1994, p. 76). Kozloff's use of the term 'schooled' in relation to posing for a portrait is an interesting one since one of the most regularized and routinized practices in portraiture in many western countries is the taking of the school photograph. These 'vernacular portraits', as they might be called, being not unlike department store poses, as opposed to say the portraits of a Karsh or a Cartier-Bresson, are hardly 'high art'. If they are to have a public showing, this is less likely to be on the wall of an art gallery. Rather, often years after they were taken school photographs are often displayed — usually much to the embarrassment of the subject who is no longer a schoolgirl or schoolboy — on someone's television set or piano. In spite of, or perhaps because of, the ordinariness of school photographs there has been relatively little attention paid to them — either in the literature of domestic photography, or in the professional literature of schooling and teacher education. And yet, because these artefacts provide some of the most lasting impressions of school, we believe they deserve to be studied — as cultural phenomenon in an of themselves — particularly in relation to the fact that it is 'outsiders' — those outside the teaching profession, notably school photographers, who construct and maintain certain images of schooling. Indeed, in this regard they are not unlike the images of schooling constructed by Hollywood producers, television producers and directors in the various teacher movies and school-related television sit-coms that we explore elsewhere (Mitchell and Weber, 1995; Weber and Mitchell, 1995; Weber and Mitchell, 1996a, 1996b). Equally, however, school photographs merit investigation in the context of research on image-making and professional identity in teacher education. Indeed, as we note in our previous work on professional identity and the images of teachers in popular culture, the term 'image' is often taken to be synonymous with 'snapshot' visual memories (Eraut, 1985):

> Quick! Think of 'teacher'. What do you see? What does what you see mean? Where does what you see come from? (Weber and Mitchell, 1995, p. 20)

In this chapter we examine school photographs as indices of how people — teachers, in particular — have been 'schooled' to regard themselves in relation to school, focusing on the ways that the images contained within these photographs can serve as both method, particularly as prompts to memory, and as phenomenon. What influenced our investigation of school photographs as being both method and phenomenon was Jean Bach's documentary film on jazz musicians in New York: *A Great Day in Harlem*. The film is organized around a photograph that was taken for *Esquire* magazine in 1959 of a number of jazz musicians such as Dizzie Gillespie in New York who were invited to show up at a particular address in Harlem to be part of a group photo. Drawing from film footage of the taking of the photo, the film-makers of *A Great Day in Harlem* concentrate both on the 'taking of the picture' and the picture taken, so that more than thirty-five years later the subjects who are interviewed for the film are still talking about 'that day' — and those interview segments of the film are very much the kind of oral history, memory-work, memory-in-action that is something that we have been exploring in our work with teachers. While such events have been immortalized in country and western songs (as in the 'The class of 57 had its dreams'), and the snapshot is a widely used literary device, we began to ask ourselves questions about how the images contained within school photographs might contribute to Image-based Research: what happens when people, especially teachers, go back to their school photographs? What insights might we gain about teaching and schools by looking with teachers at the nature of class line-ups themselves?

Constucted Images

We discovered in our work with a group of 10- and 11-year-old girls who were in the process of 'revisiting' their school photographs that they already had a strong sense of being 'schooled' to regard themselves a certain way as schoolgirls. When we asked these girls who had all been in the same school since kindergarten to talk about their school photographs from the last couple of years, we were struck by how aware they were — already — of the ways in which images of schooling are constructed and perpetuated by school photographers. The following episode which we entitle 'Constructed Literacy' arose in response to their second grade photos, the year that the photographer had them each pose in front of a book.

Participants: Abby, Norah, Dana, Gretchen

Abby Oh Grade 2 — they made us sit at the desks with the open book — a geography book! (shrieks and screams)

Norah Oh no — mine was a dictionary,

Interviewer A dictionary?

Gretchen Mine was an encyclopaedia!

Norah Mine was a Larousse dictionary.

Gretchen That year I had forgotten it was picture day and I remember I was wearing a mickey dress.

Interviewer What's that?

Everyone A mickey dress — it has Mickey at the front and Minnie at the back.

Gretchen It was so awful, plus I had to sit at this desk . . . uh . . . in front of this book that I would *never* read. I looked a bit stupid reading this book.

Norah I remember my hair was going all over and I had these little strings attached . . .

Norah I guess they wanted to make us feel like we looked so smart.

Interviewer Do you think that's why they put you in front of a book which you probably couldn't even read? Hmm — was it a difficult book? Was it a French book?

Gretchen Uh yes some of them.

Norah Some of them were English.

Abby I remember my book was English plus they made me do this (demonstrates how she had to look down at the book and point)

Interviewer Oh you're kidding. You mean they actually made you point your finger like they do in kindergarten.

Abby (does another demonstration.)

Interviewer And is that what you were doing in the photograph?

Abby (nods head.)

Norah You wouldn't believe what I was reading — because to make me look like I was reading they made me read it. I was reading the definition in French and the word was 'alphabet' (laughter all round) . . . and the next word was . . . uh acqua . . . and it was all these weird definitions.

Interviewer Imagine reading the definition of the word alphabet while you get your picture taken in front of a book so you look like you can read.

Norah I remember they used these books for the kindergarten kids too and they couldn't even read!

Interviewer Oh you're kidding. Did they make them look at the page with their finger?

Norah (nods.)

Gretchen Well, they didn't do that for me. They just made me look at a weird book . . . Then they made me hold the book like this (holds out her hands in the book reading position.) and then I had to go like this (demonstrates the way in which her eyes had to land on the page.).

Interviewer Why do you think they made you do that?

Figure 13.1

Gretchen I think they were trying something out that year.
Norah Maybe it's because it was supposed to look like a school so they wanted . . . I feel like it was kind of like to make the parents think we are really smart or something (Figure 13.1).

At a later point, Abby draws our attention to the fact that part of the posing is 'to look good' but much of this is determined not only by the photographer who insists 'on making you smile with your mouth open even though you've practised a more serious look' or point to words on a page, but also 'by your classmates who are all standing there waiting for their turn and wondering why you're taking so long because everybody knows you aren't going to look that great anyway'.

This same kind of 'constructedness' can be read in Claudia's recollection of how she had posed a certain way so as to construct a particular sense of herself in her first year of teaching:

When I look upon this photograph I have no difficulty remembering the circumstances of the picture. It was taken by my brother at Christmas-time during my first teaching assignment which was to teach English to 13-, 14- and 15-year-olds. It was the first time that I had gone home in some sort of professional capacity. I had just turned 22 and I wanted to look intellectual, and somewhat literary or artistic — hence the octagonal horn rimmed glasses and dark turtle neck sweater — taken in black and white. The year was 1970 and I remember choosing very carefully the very short jumper/dress that I am wearing — as some sort of statement about who

Figure 13.2

I thought I was (young and radical) and who I thought I was not (conservative and part of the status quo) (Figure 13.2).

A point that is made in some of the literature on family photographs is that in many respects everyone's family photos look the same — and it is only in the narrativization that there are differences (Holland and Spence, 1991). As Holland writes in her introduction to *Family Snaps: The Meaning of Domestic Photograph*,

> Everyone's family album contains a set of pictures which, at first glance, are familiar and predictable, beginning with the careful monochromatic poses of the turn of the century, then bursting from the covers under the sheer volume of informal snaps which tumble through today's letter boxes. Yet our 'own' family pictures, however ordinary, remain endlessly fascinating as we scrutinize them for exclusive information about ourselves. The images of relatives we never knew but whose influence is felt, reminders of the optimistic youth of our parents and their parents, these things seem to throw light on our present condition. (Holland and Spence, 1991)

In this regard, the same might be said of school photographs: 6- and 7-year-olds are missing their two front teeth, 12-year-olds often have a certain detached and cool look, graduation photos are distinctively graduation photos, even allowing for the obvious in the addition of academic gowns or diplomas, and so on. Similarly, group photos of the whole class have a particular look — and viewers who see a class photo in a newspaper or magazine immediately 'read in' certain details according to the conventions of the 'look'. The potency of this look is taken up by one of our participants (Sarah) in her construction of what might be described as 'the generic class photo'. This generic, yet, particularized nature of class photos was brought home to us by Sarah's photo project in which she plays with an impressionistic quality through her use of drawings in the darkroom. She writes:

> I've always had trouble remembering the events and images surrounding photographs which no longer exist. I have almost no memories from the third and fifth grades, also years I haven't school photos for. Without them, I have nothing to remind me of my teachers or the people in my classes.

> I began to think about this a few months ago while immersed in a photography class and far away from the pictures of home. I decided to try and recreate the ghosts and missing pictures from our photo box at home. Originally, I was just messing around in the darkroom, experimenting with the various effects of shining light through simple drawings onto light sensitive photo paper.

> The technical premise is similar to that of a film negative. The dark images in the negative, as well as the dark pencil lines of the drawing, show up on developed photo paper as the light areas. Clear patches develop into black. Without having had any preconceptions about my photos, the results I found compelling. Lines blurred, the graphite lines became a mottled grey, and images seemed to appear out of the random. Absentmindedly thinking of those lost class pictures, I sketched out a quick approximation of the shape and layout of a generic class picture, with three rows of students and the teacher standing to the right.

> The pictures which appeared were eerie and unsettling for me. What were previously mere scribbles and shapes became almost, but not quite, faces, and arms, and the personalities I began to remember from those years.

> As I looked at them, I saw Adam's perennial plaid shirt, the way 'those two' always stayed together, and then that girl in the front row who seemed to sit always the same, in a dress, with white socks and shoes, and who was yet every year a different girl (Figure 13.3).

In Sarah's description we are particularly taken with her reference to 'ghosts' such as the girl in the front row in her white socks, the perennial plaid shirt and so on. Her description resonates with an observation made by bell hooks (1995) in her description of a favourite affirming childhood snapshot of herself as a cowgirl that had been lost:

> I remember giving her [her cousin's wife] the snapshot for safekeeping; only when it was time for me to return home, it could not be found. This was for me a terrible loss, an irreconcilable grief. Gone was the image of myself I could love. Losing that snapshot, I lost the proof of my worthiness — that I had ever been a bright-eyed child capable of wonder — the proof that there was a 'me of me'. The image in this snapshot has lingered in my mind's eye for years. It has lingered there to remind me of the power of snapshots, of the image. (hooks, 1995, p. 57)

Figure 13.3

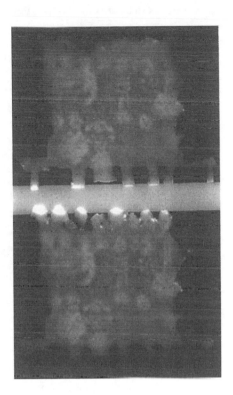

Photography and Narrative

These ghosts may be part of what Andrew Dewdney (1991) describes as the process of 'narrativizing' photographs — a point that challenges the old saying 'one picture is worth a thousand words'. What might be more accurate is that one picture evokes a thousand (or more) words! He talks about a family album project that he and a group of associates in Australia were involved in — an anti-racist project where people brought in their family snapshots and began to (re)order them — engaging in the process of relating photos to each other — 'ordering them and comparing and contrasting them' (p. 119), and discussing the role photography played for immigrant families:

> We then took the next step of trying to locate our families in a broader social and political history to see if we could find points of connection between them . . . As people struggled with this broadening of their family album, other narratives began to emerge within those already established of colonialism, imperialism, migration and dispossession . . . The process of narrativizing photographs through the project was one which continually surprised people. However familiar individual photos were, ordering them according to a narrative concept continually brought with it unexpected elements. The familiar was made strange by its insertion into a socially shared context. The narrativization of parental histories required the speaking of what was absent from or hidden behind photographs. (Dewdney, 1991, p. 120)

Applied to the film mentioned earlier *A Great Day in Harlem*, the use of the group portrait is a good example of a conscious (as opposed to a spontaneous) form of narrativization.

The work of Jo Spence (1986, 1991, 1995) on the private and social uses of photography, and the memory project work of Janet Zandy (1995) and of Frigga Haug and others (1987) also draw on photography and narrativization. Chalfen (1987) in *Snapshot Versions of Life* points out the significance of the verbal interpretation and stories that accompany the showing/viewing of photographs As Chalfen notes:

> Visual renditions of life experiences that appear in family albums, slide shows, or home movies are inevitably accompanied by parallel verbal accounts. Comments in the form of storytelling and various recountings, serve to expand and complement minimal identifications common to other kinds of written captions. Complete silence during a home mode exhibition event is socially inappropriate behaviour — viewers and exhibitors are expected and conditioned to say something. These accompanying remarks appear to be as conventionalized as the imagery itself. (Chalfen, 1987, p. 129)

Interestingly, even though bell hooks (1995) describes these visual texts as narratives 'without words', she too goes on to describe the verbal accounts that come out of doing 'recuperative memory' work with photographs:

> Drawing from the past, from those walls of images I grew up with, I gather snapshots and lay them out, to see what narratives the images tell, what they say without words. Together a black male friend and I lay out the snapshots of his boyhood, to see when he began to lose his openness, to discern at what age he began to shut down, to close himself away. With these images he hopes to find a way back to the self he once was. We are awed by what our snapshots reveal, what they enable us to remember. (hooks, 1995, p. 64)

The reference here to remembering is an important one for us in our work with teachers whose memories of schooling we are interested in as reference points for engaging in what bell hooks describes as 'illuminating' the present and 'transforming' the future. How do teachers read themselves as learners and teachers through their school photographs? What themes can be found in their revisitings? How do photographs figure in the lives of teachers-as-photographers? How might inscriptions also contribute to Image-based Research?

Revisiting the Family Album

As with the work of Rosy Martin, Jo Spence and Annette Kuhn, we have provided some very straightforward protocols for eliciting responses to the photographs. Very simply, we have asked teachers to gather together their school photographs. Where they might have a large collection we ask them to assemble them in some way that makes sense for them and to begin to write about what they see and what they recall. In the case of teachers we have met who have no photographs we simply ask them to try to recollect memories of a particular photograph. Following this, we ask participants to simply describe their photograph: What grade was it? What was happening? Can they recall the actual taking of the photograph? Can they remember preparing for the photograph? Finally, we ask them to consider what the photograph means to them now?

Consider the written response of Patricia, a beginning teacher, to this prompt. Patricia, like several of the women in the class (and unlike most of the male teachers), had managed to pull together her entire school career in pictures. We include Patricia's narrative as a whole to give some flavour of how one person would continue certain themes throughout their revisitings:

> The following pages include some of my school photographs from elementary school. These are the only pictures I have, the pictures from high school are in the yearbook. We were not given a copy of our class picture because we did not have a home room class. Getting our picture taken in elementary school was a big deal for everyone. I remember everyone being so excited to get their picture taken. The girls came to school with their prettiest outfits and some boys actually wore suits. If I remember correctly, our parents were sent a letter from the administration reminding them that we were to have our pictures taken.
>
> There is one thing I especially remember about having our class pictures taken. The photographer always made the short people sit on the bench and the rest were allowed to stand. I remember hating that. I wanted to stand too! I also remember once we were given our many copies of our pictures, we all exchanged individual pictures with our classmates and had them signed by the person who gave it to us. The rest of the copies are just sitting in a box somewhere. My mother didn't give our relatives any of the pictures. My grandmother may have one or two, but that's about it.
>
> Grade 3 — My grade 3 teacher was Miss Boileau. She was probably the kindest teacher I had in elementary school. This picture is really strange because of the division of the sexes. It's such a typical picture — boys on one side and girls on the other. I'm the first one seated on the left-hand side.
>
> Grade 4 — It was the worst year of my life. We all look like happy little kids, but the truth was that we were all miserable. Everyone was terrified of Miss Perry. She was very strict and naturally we all feared her. I'll never forget this picture. Everyone laughed about it for weeks. Everyone knew that Ronnie had a crush on Linda. But we actually got it on print. Notice the way Ronnie (the boy sitting on the far right) is looking at Linda!
>
> Grade 5 — This was my favourite class. I was in the same class with eight of my best friends. This is probably the picture I hated most. I had my hair cut short for the first time and everyone said that I looked like a boy. I can't believe I chose to wear such an ugly outfit. I'm the funny looking one with the red and white striped knickers.
>
> Grade 6 — Once again I'm sitting! The only reason I can think of is that I probably didn't grow enough to stand with the taller kids. This was also the year I wore braces on my teeth. I refused to smile when I had my individual picture taken, but the photographer managed to get a smile out of me. At least my braces matched my long silver earrings!

In many of the recollections, teachers referred to recurring concerns: being the shortest, being the tallest, being the one who is always in the front row or back row, being the one who is forced to comply with what the parents have decided is the appropriate look, although it is important to note with regard to this last point that at least one participant observed that the actual facial expression that was adopted was the one thing that parents couldn't control!

Beyond our work with beginning teachers, a number of colleagues and graduate students around us reflected on their memories of school photographs. Rae, an experienced teacher writes:

> My favourite picture might be Grade 8; I see it is our first year out of uniform. I have on that purple blouse that I wore into the rag barrel, and a necklace of love beads. That year I'm sure I must have made all my friends beads (well it was the 1970s). It's also the first one where my bangs [fringe] aren't cut too short and my hair's not too greasy! I do remember the next two years well from their photos; the years of longer hair and of course, the grade 10 bleached blond look! Well, at least I wasn't still wearing the peace sign on my choker like the year before.

We were also interested in how teachers might look back at certain photographs of themselves as teachers — either as part of a class photo with one or more of the classes, or in individualized pictures of themselves 'as teachers'. Rae, in writing about her gaze on her gaze notes:

> As I look upon these [photos] now, I am thinking back to what I thought and the idealism, naivete, and dreams that I had. I can't really say that I don't still have some of this; maybe rather than looking wistfully at this time, I instead feel that I'm glad that I held on to a lot of that. But I can't help thinking, as I gaze upon myself, could you ever have imagined then what the world would be like now and what your place in it would be? I guess this exercise, in causing me to reflect . . .

Like Rae other teachers have often spontaneously begun to reminisce about earlier photos, commenting on how they used to look and how this look linked to their professional identity as teachers. Other teachers refer to the ways in which their own memories of schooling led them to want to contribute to the lasting memories of the students in their classes by becoming class photographers.

Teachers as Photographers

Our interest in teachers as photographers was inspired by an essay by Anne Krisman (1986) 'You shout at us one minute, you take photographs the next . . .' In the essay, Krisman (1986) briefly describes her own obsession with taking snapshots of the students in her classes:

> I have always taken photographs of the children I have taught. In the past, they have been 'special occasions' ones, at parties, school trips, the Annual Fête. I must have had problems with these children in lessons but the photographs give none of this away. The children smile, pose as a united group, offering Miss as a photographer a great deal more respect than they gave her in class. When I took photographs inside school, after the initial queries about my camera and the fears that Darin would drop it as he told me about his Dad's superior Canon AE1, I was often heard to say, 'Look, I'm not taking a photo of you until you look as if you're working.' I was amazed at how this threat worked, and the willingness of the

children to co-operate as we set up photographs that indicated either that they were swots (signified by top buttons done up, arms folded, head erect) or rough kids (signified by lunch on the table, feet up, laid back posture). The photographs were displayed on my wall, created a mass of interest and often minor stirs. One girl ripped a photograph from my wall display as it had her on it (her face = her possession). Someone drew a moustache on the Head of Music and some children on the photos were pricked with compass points. I still took photographs and from time to time allowed the children to use my SLR when we were banned from using the school's as a child dropped it. (p. 122)

She then goes on to talk about why she has taken pictures over the years, and how taking these pictures has contributed to her teaching:

When my photographs were developed, I showed them, in no real order, to people who weren't teachers at my own school. I found myself explaining the images, making sense of them . . . I was more aware of the children I was teaching. My eyesight had sharpened. I felt as if I knew them better, after coming to terms with them in their second form and in their developing, alive, vibrant state. Schools as institutions still rile me, but by restating it for myself in terms other than anger or bitterness, I feel better equipped to survive to fight again. (p. 124)

In part, our initial interest in this essay came out of the fact that it was one of the few references we could find anywhere to school photographs, and in this way it served to validate what otherwise might have seemed to be idiosyncratic obsession on our part. When we showed the article by Krisman (1986) to some of the teachers we knew, several of them noted that they were always taken pictures of their classes. Consider, for example, Carolyn's comments:

There are not many pictures of my students reading and writing. I used the camera mostly for trips and special days, Halloween, Christmas, end of year. I was able to see how I've changed classroom setup. For the first three years I had the students sit in pairs and I moved from there to having the students in groups of four. Mostly all the pictures are posed and the children are smiling. I've always realized that pictures were an effective way of making the children feel they belong. At the beginning of every year I take individual pictures of each student and make three copies. I use one picture for a class book, one for outside our room, and one to use when a child is the 'special person'. In the last two years, I have taken more pictures when creations are completed. Does that send the message that the product is more important than the process? Hmmm. Right now, I'm thinking I should take pictures of the children when they're mad, crying, etc. so that they have a 'complete' picture of who they are and perhaps they will then be able to understand more about being 'fully aware' of themselves. . . . When I look at my own pictures, I have very few pictures of me alone. I was the fifth of seven children. My parents obviously had their hands full. My identity was always that of being one of the seven and I fit into the group of 'the three little kids'. There's no damage, I would say done to me, though it might explain why I like working in groups. I've worked in groups all my life. I can stand up on my own, though, and I think that's important too. It may be for that reason that I take the individual pictures at the beginning of the year. The students are a part of a group, but first and foremost they are a person unto themselves and they hold responsibility to themselves.

Similarly, Mary talks about how she used photographs even as part of her student teaching:

> The first time I took a camera with me to school was when I was student teaching. I went on a field trip, *une cabane à sucre* in Mont St-Grégoire. I remember being so excited to have pictures of my first students. About seven years later I went on *une autre cabane à sucre* with a different group of students. Again, I was very excited to have pictures. I was pregnant with my second daughter and I knew I wouldn't be back teaching for a while. When I look at the pictures, I can no longer remember the names, but the personalities are fresh in my mind. It was important for me to have those pictures. When I taught, I loved being a part of the lives of the students. I guess I could say I took my job 'seriously'. I would often talk about my students at home, so it was nice to put faces to the names. I also liked having my daughter's picture over my desk. The students would often ask questions about my daughter, and I was always happy to share anecdotes about her. It seemed to make the classroom a more real place to me. While Anne Krisman talks about teachers taking pictures, it made me think about the power of photography, in general. Students taking pictures of teachers, students taking pictures of other students . . . as usual there is no end of things to study. Handing over a roll of film and a camera to students . . . this sounds like something that has probably already been done. Has it? It seems to me that doing so is like giving the students 'a voice'. It might also help them to examine their world — from where they stand.

Mary's references to the 'power of photography' and the 'handing over a roll of film and a camera to students' are interesting ones in that they suggest an association with agency and taking charge. In this regard her work is similar to the photography project of Wendy Ewald (1985) as described in *Portraits and Dreams: Photographs and Stories by Children of the Appalachians.*

But we are also intrigued by the 'flipside' of these photographs — both figuratively as well as literally. In a figurative way, the anecdotes that these teachers provide about the taking of the pictures — and the sense of belonging that they hope the students will feel — suggest a relationship between photo-subject and photographer that goes beyond representation. This is not unlike the relationship between the photographer and subject noted by Annette Kuhn in her essay 'She'll always be your little girl . . .' In this essay she analyzes a snapshot of herself posed with a budgie bird, focusing in her analysis on the ways that her mother is both invisible and excluded from the photograph. Her father, the photographer, she observes, is an 'absent presence', not visible but very much in evidence:

> He is not in the picture, you cannot see him . . . In another sense, however, my father is very much 'in' the picture . . . The child in the photograph is absorbed with her pet bird, a gift from her father, who also took the picture. The relay of looks — father/daughter/father's gift to daughter — has a trajectory and an endpoint that miss the mother entirely. (pp. 13–14)

Chalfen (1987) points out the significance of the verbal interpretation that accompanies much of the visual in photographs — through the addition of captions and inscriptions such as 'To my darling Ann', and the messages written on the backs of snapshots such as the cryptic 'Taken from our balcony'. Inscriptions then, on the flipside of photographs — literally — provoked us to think further about teachers-as-photographers — and the meaning of snapshots to the student.

Figure 13.4

On the back of a photo taken of a young girl in the early 1920s is written is the following: 'This is a snap of Elsie taken by her teacher the morning we left Belmont' (Figures 13.4 and 13.5). Elsie, now looking at the inscription and the snapshot of herself some seventy or more years later struggles to remember exactly which year it could have been, and where it was that she and her family left for. Because her father worked for the railway, they moved often and it was not at all uncommon for the family to have to be uprooted in the middle of a school year. So the destination could have been one of several small prairie towns on the Canadian prairies. Elsie looks again at the snapshot and thinks that the coat she is wearing was probably cut-down from a larger coat, something that would have been a common occurrence given the shortage of money and the fact that she had two older sisters and several younger ones coming along. Aside from these 'bits' she has no memory of the photo being taken, the name of the teacher, or why her father wrote on it. She does recall that she was never a very good student so that her recollections of her childhood are rarely about school. In a conversation about the photograph we speculate about a teacher — *the* teacher — taking the time (and having the resources) to photograph one of her departing pupils, and mailing it to Elsie's family after it was developed. Elsie speculates about what it must have meant to the family for a teacher to bother to send the snapshot. But she is also curious about the author of the inscription. According to the family graphologists it was written by Elsie's father, someone who worked long hours and who normally paid little attention to such domestic matters. Taking the time to inscribe the photo, then, raises questions about the relation of the inscriber to the event, something that Kuhn also explores in relation to the budgie photo

Figure 13.5

where her mother attempts to lay claim to the event by inscribing the photo with her own explanation 'Just back from Bournemouth (Convalescent) [sic]'. As Kuhn notes 'In my own handwriting "Bournemouth" has been crossed out and replaced with "Broadstairs", and a note added "but I suspect the photo is earlier than this"' (p. 13). Kuhn's point is that a photograph can be a site of conflicting memories, and of power relations within the family.

Inscriptions like the one on the back of Elsie's snapshot — along with captions and cryptic messages — might be also be read as narrative or verbal interpretations of the visual. Consider the inscription: 'To my two bestest teachers Mr and Mrs M. From me. Twenty years from now you may forget my name so, Cathy Banks' was inscribed on the back of an individual picture which had been taken well over the requisite twenty years, by an eighth grade student and given to the two teachers. The person who now possesses the photograph, Claudia, one of the two teachers, has had the photograph for over twenty-five years. Not only has she not forgotten the student, who of course, is no longer a student but is an adult who is now twenty-five years older than she was at the time of the inscription, but in fact they have kept up a regular correspondence and friendship over the twenty-five years. It was a surprise then when Claudia was going through her box of photographs and found this snapshot, along with many others of former students — twenty-five years later with its almost eerie inscription, eerie because it was discovered so far into the future — past the twenty years; eerie because of the projection of a 13-year-old into a 'twenty years from now' future as a type of time travel; and eerie because of the way it futuristically anticipates looking back.

School Photography in Image-based Research

Through our examples we have focused on the ways that school photographs and the images of schooling contained within them might serve as prompts to memory in approaching research on professional identity in teacher education. Our examples also draw attention to the various meanings contained within school photographs so that we have provided some indication of the range of issues and topics that school photographs might spark in Image-based Research.

In addition to those that we mention in relation to 'reading' the family photo album or in relation to teachers as photographers, we have been struck by the significance of such factors as age in school memories as evoked by school photographs. While there is no shortage of research on the significance of memory in childhood (Kotre, 1995) there is often an ageist sense that it is only older people who have memories of schooling, or that it is the memories of those who have been around for a long time which are the memories which count. Indeed, we have occasionally heard critics of reflective practitioner and autobiographical approaches to teacher preparation lament the fact that beginning teachers have so little to reflect upon. Earlier in the chapter, however, we cite examples of 10-year-olds who already are able to look back at their school experiences at the age of 6 and 7 years old as memory-laden. Beginning teachers such as Patricia with whom we work, many of whom are in their early 20s clearly also bring rich memories of school.

In this chapter we have also said little about the contribution of outsiders to constructing particular images of schooling. In the same way that tourists and *National Geographic* photographers construct particular images of the place visited, the school photographer, as outsider, might be seen to contribute to shaping the world of the insiders, teachers and students. Thus, we suggest that there is a need to consider the ways in which post colonial theory within visual anthropology (Lutz and Collins, 1994) might inform an insider outsider analysis of school photography.

School photographs offer rich possibilities for Image-based Research within work on professional identity in teacher education. Such possibilities range from considerations of the role of the outsider photographer, usually an employee of some national photography company who arrives at the school armed with a camera and a backdrop scene of a sky and forest or some other photo-innocuous background, and some snappy repartee with the subjects who are directed to 'cheese' 'sex' or 'my father has smelly socks', to the resulting products, which are likely to be traded off according to the popularity of the subjects, finding their way into the clear plasticized section of other people's wallets and photo albums, to a consideration of the memories of school that are evoked by such images, to using these memories to go beyond nostalgia so that the images can be used to inform professional practice. In so doing, school photography can be seen as both method and phenomenon, as involving both the setting of the pose and posing for the picture, and as examining both the taking the picture and the picture taken.

Note

1   We are grateful to the Social Sciences and Humanities Research Council of Canada for their continued financial support. We are also grateful to Laurin Ashley, Faith Butler and Sarah Mitchell for their technical assistance on this project.

References

CHALFEN, R. (1987) *Snapshot Versions of Life*, Bowling Green, Ohio: Bowling Green State University Popular Press.

DEWDNEY, A. (1991) 'More than black and white: The extended and shared family album', in HOLLAND, P. and SPENCE, J. (eds) *Family Snaps: The Meaning of Domestic Photograph*, London: Virago.

ERAUT, M. (1985) 'Knowledge creation and knowledge use in professional contexts', *Studies in Higher Education*, pp. 117–33.

EWALD, W. (1985) *Portraits and Dreams: Photographs and Stories by Children of the Appalachians*, London: Writers and Readers Publishing Cooperative Society Ltd.

HAUG, F. (1987) *Female Sexualisation: A Collective Work of Memory*, CARTER, E. (ed.), London: Verso.

HOLLAND, P. (1991) 'Introduction: Memory and the family album', in HOLLAND, P. and SPENCE, J. (eds) *Family Snaps: The Meaning of Domestic Photograph*, London: Virago.

HOLLAND, P. and SPENCE, J. (eds) (1991) *Family Snaps: The Meaning of Domestic Photograph*, London: Virago.

HOLLAND, P., SPENCE, J. and WATNEY, S. (eds) (1986) *Photography/Politics: Two*, London: Comedia/Photography Workshop.

hooks, b. (1995) *Art on My Mind: Visual Politics*, New York: The New Press.

KOTRE, J. (1995) *White Gloves: How We Create Ourselves through Memory*, New York: Free Press.

KOZLOFF, M. (1994) *Lone Visions: Crowded Frames. Essays on Photography*, Albuquerque: University of New Mexico Press.

KRISMAN, A. (1986) 'You shout at us one minute, you take photographs the next . . .', in HOLLAND, P., SPENCE, J. and WATNEY, S. (eds) *Photography/Politics: Two*, London: Comedia/Photography Workshop.

KUHN, A. (1995) *Family Secrets: Acts of Memory and Imagination*, London and New York: Verso.

LUTZ, C. and COLLINS, J. (1994) 'The photograph as an intersection of gazes: The example of National Geographic', in TAYLOR, L. (ed.) *Visualizing Theory: Selected Essays from V.A.R. 1990–4*, London: Routledge.

MARTIN, R. (1986) 'Phototherapy: The school photograph (Happy days are here again)', in HOLLAND, P., SPENCE, J. and WATNEY, S. (eds) *Photography/Politics: Two*, London: Comedia/Photography Workshop.

MITCHELL, C. and WEBER, S. (1995) 'He draws, she draws: Texts of interrogation', *Textual Studies in Canada: Canadian Journal of Cultural Literacy*, 7, pp. 132–43.

MITCHELL, C. and WEBER, S. (in progress) *Beyond Nostalgia: Reinventing Ourselves as Teachers*, London: Falmer Press.

SPENCE, J. (1986) *Putting Myself in the Picture: A Political Personal and Photographic Autobiography*, London: Camden Press.

SPENCE, J. (1991) 'Shame-work: Thoughts on family snaps and fractured identities', in HOLLAND, P. and SPENCE, J. (eds) *Family Snaps: The Meaning of Domestic Photograph*, London: Virago.

SPENCE, J. (1995) *Cultural Sniping: The Art of Transgression*, London: Routledge.

WALKERDINE, V. (1990) *Schoolgirl Fictions*, London: Verso.

WEBER, S. and MITCHELL, C. (1995) *That's Funny, You Don't Look Like a Teacher: Interrogating Images of Identity in Popular Culture*, London: Falmer Press.

WEBER, S. and MITCHELL, C. (1996a) 'Drawing ourselves into teaching: Studying the images that shape and distort teacher education', *Teaching and Teacher Education*, 12, 3, pp. 303–13.

WEBER, S. and MITCHELL, C. (1996b) 'Using drawings to interrogate professional identity and the popular culture of teaching', in GOODSON, I. and HARGREAVES, A. (eds) *Teachers' Professional Lives*, London: Falmer Press, pp. 151–78.

WILLIS, D. (ed.) (1994) *Picturing Us: African American Identity in Photography*, New York: The New York Press.

ZANDY, J. (ed.) (1995) *Liberating Memory: Our Work and Our Working-class Consciousness*, New Brunswick, New Jersey: Rutgers.

Chapter 14

Interpreting Family Photography as Pictorial Communication

Richard Chalfen

Abstract

This chapter suggests a descriptive framework for the qualitative study of collections of snapshots in contexts of family photography. One objective is to develop a cultural appreciation of amateur/vernacular photography as a ubiquitous form of visual communication, specifically home mode communication. The descriptive model — a series of events and components drawn from sociolinguistics and the ethnography of speaking — is used to examine what family photographs represent and how these images serve as representations of a particular version of the human condition. Discussion includes how the construction, organization and consumption of family photographs can be understood as social activity.

Introduction

The purpose of this chapter is to suggest an approach to an assemblage of generally taken-for-granted pictorial artifacts — specifically, the realm of snapshot photography. The central concern is with collections of personal family photographs. My objectives include

1   developing ties between an intellectual curiosity about amateur photography and a cultural appreciation for collections of ubiquitous snapshots;
2   suggesting a model for the critical examination of snapshot photography in conjunction with appropriate methods of fieldwork; and
3   understanding better how the construction, organization and consumption of family photographs can be understood as social activity. Though I stress issues of communication throughout, the qualitative approach I suggest is intimately connected to past and ongoing studies in visual sociology and visual anthropology.

A Social Approach to the Pictorial World

Ordinary people have never had as many images of themselves — whether we are talking about drawings, sketches, paintings, prints, etchings, or photographs. Mass consumer cameras have helped people see themselves and their private lives in ways that were previously reserved for the wealthy or the elite — people in political, religious, or even entertainment components of society. Virtually everyone can now have pictures of themselves, and ordinary people can document their lives in more complete ways. No longer do ordinary people have to rely on professional photographers or other 'outsiders' to produce their pictures — they 'take' them for themselves.[1] These circumstances are relatively new in the history of imagemaking and have opened up rich areas of visual research.

In broad terms, systematic studies of snapshot collections in particular and home photo-media in general are largely neglected. Academics more routinely study the content of mass media, the organizational structure of mass communication, and the use of mass media channels and impersonal message forms. In short, we have been drawn to (or seduced by) the study of professionally produced renditions of the world — but, in general, we have ignored the vast 'tradition' of personally made images, and we know very little about relationships of photo-media and private symbolic worlds.

Important questions fundamental to the social sciences and the humanities lie buried in our home media. What are ordinary people saying about themselves and their conditions of human existence? What can we learn about ourselves as social and cultural beings through studies of photographs we make *about* and *for* ourselves? How does the social structure and political order of the family coincide or conflict with the politics of this symbolic form?[2] What roles are played by different family members? How is the 'head of household' related to who takes the pictures, who gets 'in' these pictures, or who takes charge of making the photograph albums? On a broader scale, how important are such variables as historical period, technological developments, regional and cultural variation to what appears in these portraits of family life and in snapshot photography in general? What roles do social class, gender and age play? These questions are equally important to studying social process and the pictorial content of home media.

Locating the Home Mode of Communication

I have called the snapshot, as well as events surrounding its making and use, the 'home mode' of visual/pictorial communication.[3] I coined the term 'home mode' in 1969 when working on a study of home movies in a graduate seminar directed by the late Erving Goffman.[4] The seminar focused us on how humans construct different presentations of themselves in alternative social contexts. I noted that people using relatively inexpensive cameras were adding to this repertoire of presentations-of-self; people and their personal camera-use were generating what Goffman referred to as a 'key of reality'. In short, transformation and representation became central themes to the performance and appearance of 'normal' behaviour.

An emphasis on *communication process* distinguishes this analytic approach from others.[5] First, the snapshot is understood as a symbolic form embedded in a communication process that necessarily includes making (encoding), interpreting (decoding), and a multi-faceted use of pictures. Second, in comparison to mass modes of communication, the home mode is a process of interpersonal and small group communication that focuses on *family life* mostly at home but occasionally away from home.[6] The home mode includes verbal forms, such as letters, birthday and Christmas cards as well as postcards and most recently, e-mail messages. In a larger context, spoken home mode forms include telephone calls, tape recordings sent through the mail, and messages left on telephone answering machines. The key here is that messages are produced for personal uses, to be shared between family members, friends or people with at least a passing personal knowledge of one another. There is no overt intention to 'publish' or 'broadcast' these mediated message forms.[7]

However, the focus of this chapter is on visual/pictorial forms of home mode communication. These include the wallet and locket photos, the family album snapshot, the photo booth picture, the framed graduation portrait, the posterized personal photograph, photo cube pictures, framed snapshot collages, photo-stickers, among others. Photograph albums devoted to such topics as weddings, vacations, births, confirmations, Bar Mitzvahs, senior proms, graduations, family reunions, and to a much lesser extent, military service and funerals are also important elements. Motion picture variations include the home movie and the home videotape.[8] Very frequently, of course, pictorial and written/spoken forms are combined, as when people include recent snapshots with a hand-written letter, when people 'talk over' the screening of their slide shows, and now, listen to the sound-track on their home videotapes. Thus verbal-visual integrations remain central to this ubiquitous mode of communication and require attention.

Searching for an Orienting Question

How does one address the questions and study the problems suggested in this chapter? How do we begin to describe a home mode collection of images and what descriptive models can we draw upon? In an attempt to claiming or disclaiming a patterned structure of behaviour, consider the following statement:

> While it is the case that we can take a picture of anyone, under any circumstances (light conditions, personal or social settings), for any reason, and subsequently show that picture to anyone, under any circumstances, for any reason — it appears that we do *not* behave in this manner.

If we accept this premise — one that claims non-random behaviour — then we must seek a way to explicate the *selective qualities of snapshot photography*. Said differently, we need to (1) specify patterns of what usually happens and does not happen in the *social construction* of snapshot photographs *and* in the entire process of snapshot communication, and we need to (2) make some claims for why specific groups of people organize their thinking and their behaviour in specific ways.

Proposing a Descriptive Framework

Central problems must now be addressed: How can we discover, reveal, or otherwise get at the structure of the pictorial product as well as the social process of home mode communication? How can we make comparisons across alternative examples from either the same social collective, or across social classes, ethnic groups, subcultures or cultures? Are different cultures creating different messages about themselves? Or, how can we compare what people are doing with different kinds of cameras as they make snapshots, home movies, or home videotapes. Are different media predisposed to communicating different messages?

One answer to these problems is to use a framework that helps us describe the communication process and the content of images.[9] Processes of pictorial communication consist of five kinds of 'communication events', namely: (1) *planning* events, (2,3) *shooting* events (on camera and behind camera), (4) *editing* events, and (5) *exhibition* events. In addition, five kinds of 'components' can be used to describe the operation of each event. Components include (1) *participants*, (2) *settings*, (3) *topics*, (4) *message form*, and (5) *code*.[10] When these two lists are cross-referenced, we produce a grid of twenty-five cells, as appears in the following illustration:

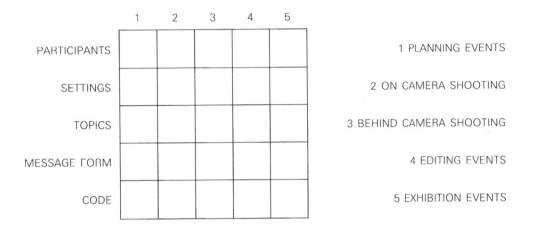

Each of these twenty-five cells represents a relationship between a specific event and a specific component and can be used to generate certain kinds of questions that are useful in both describing and comparing specific examples of image communication.[11] For example, when we look at Cell P-1 (participants-planning events) we are asking who generally takes charge of some form of preparation for snapshot photography? Relevant questions include: Who decides that pictures should be made? Who is responsible for buying the film, remembering to get out the camera, and so on? Many other questions and examples will be given in the following pages.

When we reference each component with each event, a pattern of activity and behaviour emerges that is characteristic of a specific group's pictorial communication. The framework should be helpful in clarifying *specific* questions and research problems. Not all of the event-component cells are relevant to each problem. For example, we would not have much to say for Cell P-4 (participants-editing events) if we were doing a study of home movies because home movies are so seldom edited by family members.

This framework should be treated as a starting point and as a heuristic tool. It is subject to change as new findings come from new studies. Cross-cultural research and cross-medium studies may point to important inadequacies in this beginning formulation. For instance, Musello feels that 'processing events' ('all methods and activity through which photographs are developed and/or printed') should be added (1979, p. 105) — but I have included this activity within 'editing'; and different types of 'amateur' photographers may be treating the significance of editing events in different ways.[12]

The central task is to elicit *patterns of appropriate behaviour* — that which happens without causing much personal disturbance or social disruption. For example: Most of us would agree that it is perfectly appropriate for Dad (participant) to take snapshots (message form) of his children (participants) as they open their presents (topic) by the tree on Christmas morning (setting). But, would we also agree that it is equally appropriate for a daughter (participant) to take portrait photographs (message form) of her dead uncle in his coffin (topic) in a funeral parlor (setting)? Atypical examples and 'problem cases', as when norms are broken, can teach us a lot about what is expected and treated as 'normal'. In addition *patterns of exclusion* (e.g., topics that are never photographed or settings where cameras are seldom or never used) are as significant to this approach as are patterns of inclusion. The following discussion and a few examples will clarify the meaning and use of the descriptive grid.

Image Communication Events

The first dimension of the framework — five communication events — emphasizes attention to parts of the social process inherent to any form pictorial communication.

Planning Events

A Planning Event consist of any action(s) in which there is a formal or informal decision regarding the production of a photographic image(s). In all cases, some form of planning must occur before proceeding to the next category — shooting events.

The following questions are relevant to the study and description of planning events: What kinds of social preparation are seen to occur before someone takes a snapshot? For instance, who decides when pictures should be made, and who is asked to use the camera? Who promotes or discourages the idea? What kinds of equipment or supplies must be borrowed or purchased? How important are technical preparations to the success of making snapshots? Is there any kind of specialized learning or training necessary? Will the production require a shooting plan or some form of script? What kinds of personal or social cooperation are needed?

An example of planning in the home mode is mentioned in the following etiquette column letter:[13]

> Dear Ann Landers,
> Would it be considered improper to take a photograph of a deceased friend or relative in the slumber room during viewing hours? I would like such pictures as final remembrances, but am reluctant to go ahead and take them. Of course, I would be discreet and wait until I was alone. Please give me your opinion.
> (Want to Do What's Right)

> Dear W.T.D.W.R.,
> It is perfectly proper to photograph the deceased. In fact, according to the executives of two mortuaries with whom I checked, it is done frequently.
> (*Philadelphia Inquirer*, n.d.)

In this example and others to follow, we shall see how these events interact with communications components, in this case, setting and participants.

Shooting Events

A Shooting Event consists of any action(s) in which an image is put on film by using some form of camera technology. Shooting events occur in two forms, related either to the action that occurs *in front of* the camera, or to the action that occurs *behind* the camera.

On-camera Shooting Events consist of any action(s) that in some way structures the person(s) or thing(s) that 'happens' in front of an operating camera. In all cases, something has to appear or be placed in front of a loaded camera and be recorded on light sensitive material. In this case relevant questions include the following: What kinds of actions and behaviours occur when people are taking snapshots? Who is regularly included, who is likely to be neglected or eliminated, and who is never included? What kinds of settings, environments, activities, or events are likely to be included in snapshots on a regular basis? What kinds of systematic rearrangements or transformations are made of people's appearances, of scenery, or of events when snapshots are made? Do people insist on 'posing' or 'acting' in special ways for snapshot recording? Are conventions or standards for posing recognised, criticized, or otherwise commented on?

A somewhat unusual example of a problem surrounding an on-camera event — although no one knows how uncommon or common it may really be — appeared in another column letter:

Dear Abby,
I am approaching 40 and so is my wife. We've been married for twenty-two years Like most couples our age, our sex life isn't what it used to be. My wife can take it or leave it. I'm no sex maniac, but I'm not exactly dead yet. Last Christmas the wife gave me a Polaroid camera, and just for the heck of it, she let me take some pictures of her in the bedroom, unclothed. That's when I discovered those pictures really turned me on. Now, all of a sudden the wife tells me she is no striptease model, and she doesn't want to pose for any more pornography. I say it's not pornography as long as we're married because I'm the only one who sees those pictures. We are both born-again Christians. I'd like your opinion. Am I kooky or not?

Shutterbug

Dear Shutter,
Not Kooky, just a little far out. Whatever you do behind closed doors that is mutually agreeable is all right. I'm sold. Now all you have to do is sell the wife.
(*Philadelphia Evening Bulletin*, June 13, 1974)

As a second kind of shooting event, *Behind Camera Shooting Events* consist of any action(s) not in front of a camera but which in some way structures the use and operation of it. Here we are studying what people do while they are taking the snapshot rather than what happens 'in' the picture. In all cases, someone (or group of people) must make a series of decisions regarding how, when, where, and why a camera is being used. For this category of event, the following questions are relevant: Is there a recognized behavioural routine or style of using a camera to make a snapshot? Who, more likely than others, will be asked to use the camera? Are there specific times and places that seem to require the making of snapshots? What is the social relationship between people behind and in front of the camera? Are verbal instructions required, optional, or never heard? Are any kinds of 'directing' part of this activity? Is much, if any, attention given to 'setting up' the shots, arranging the scenery, or use of 'props'?

An illustration of this event appeared in a letter from a pastor:

Dear Abby,
I am a clergyman, and as such, I perform many marriage ceremonies. My pet peeve is the well-meaning shutterbug who insists on flashing his camera during the wedding service. One such photographer actually kept crawling around on the altar, adjusting the bride's veil and the groom's coat. He even asked me to please 'lean in' a little more toward the couple. And all this while I was performing the ceremony! Please say something in your column to discourage this type of thing.
                                                                    Distracted Pastor

Dear Distracted,
Seems to me that a pastor performing a marriage is, or should be, in command. He should lay down conditions for photography, and if the client couple dislikes the conditions, let them hunt up another pastor.
(*Philadelphia Evening Bulletin*, September 30, 1975)

In summary, by observing and accounting for behaviours on both sides of the camera, we gain a much stronger feeling for 'managed presentations' that serve, in turn, to alter our notions of snapshots as constructions rather than as copies of reality.

Editing Events

An Editing Event consists of any action(s) which transforms, accumulates, arranges, or rearranges images. Editing events occur after film has been exposed but before the pictures have been shown to a group of people. This category of event may include processing and/or retouching film or sequencing a series of prints or slides. Editing events are better understood when the following questions are asked: what kinds of editing are likely to be done on snapshots as soon as they are returned from processing and printing? Are any pictures regarded as 'bad' and, if so, what criterion are used for judgments of 'goodness' or 'badness'? Do good pictures receive special treatment e.g., being framed, duplicated, enlarged? Are bad images changed in some way (with scissors, written or painted on), or never shown, thrown away, hidden?

Editing events come in many forms. One example of an image replacement appears below:

Dear Ann Landers,
Can I get in my two cents' worth in response to the man who had a picture of his deceased wife hanging in the bedroom? My husband had a small photograph of his dead wife on a shelf in the kitchen. I dusted it every day for six months. One day, my son-in-law took a great snapshot of my husband and me. I took out the wife's picture and replaced it with the one of us. When he noticed, he said, 'Why did you remove my wife's picture?' I replied, 'I thought I was your wife.' What followed was an unusually long period of silence. Then he scratched his head and grunted something that sounded like, 'Uh . . . er . . . ah.' He never said a word on the subject after that.
(*Philadelphia Inquirer*, December 30, 1983)

In the future, editing events may take on added significance when people begin to integrate snapshots and video into multi-media presentations using scanners and their home computer technology.[14]

Exhibition Events

An Exhibition Event consists of any action(s) which occurs after shooting, in which snapshots are shown to groups of people. These viewings are considered more 'public' than private instances when editing can take place. In the home mode context, public means any audience of more than the picture-taker or editor (if any editing is done). This may include one or two member audiences — as when an individual or two children look at a photograph album or tray of slides, perhaps without the rest of the family.

Clarification of this event occurs when the following set of questions are used: How is the viewing of snapshots or albums socially organized? For instance, who initiates, promotes, or restricts this activity? When do these events take place? What other kinds of behaviour or social activity are likely to accompany the showing personal pictures? What are the social relationships between people who plan the snapshots, people who take or appear in them, and the people who subsequently show (or are invited to see) these pictures?

Occasionally we find exhibition events closely tied to the suggestion of editing as in the following problematic situation:

Dear Ann Landers,
Last weekend my husband and I went to visit his parents. We had a nice time until Sunday. His parents were at church and 'Ted' was fishing. While looking for something to read I ran across a photo album. I opened it up and discovered it was the wedding album from my husband's first marriage. I cannot describe my feelings of rage.

Ted divorced this woman four years ago but she has made a career of keeping in close touch with every member of his family except the dog (he died). It galls me that Ted's parents continue to keep his old wedding picture hanging in the recreation room with all the other family photos.

I had a huge fight with my mother-in-law about the album when she returned from church. I asked her to please throw it out. She said, 'This is my house. Don't tell me what to keep and what to throw out.' The argument got pretty hot, and then

she said, 'If you don't like it, you can leave.' My husband and I left. Now what?
I'd like some advice.

Second Wife in Chicago

Now you can tell your mother-in-law that you are ashamed of yourself for acting
like a spoiled brat and that you hope she will forgive you.

You were completely out of line, toots. Her son's first marriage is part of the
family history and she has every right to keep the pictures. Sorry, I can't think of
a single thing to say in your defense.
(*The Boston Globe*, July 31, 1990)

We shall soon see that virtually any description of event is necessarily based on
inclusion of elements that I have chosen to call 'components'. These are discussed next.

Image Communication Components

The second dimension of this descriptive framework consists of five communication
components.[15] Here the objective is to break down each of the events described above
to clarify further how each is structured. By using this list of components, a researcher
is again coerced to ask certain questions about organization, structure and variation in a
systematic way. The *Participant* component focuses on anyone who participates in any
activity for which the central organizing concern is snapshot communication. The main
objective is to identify people who take, appear in, and/or look at snapshots. For instance,
we want to know if one person is in charge of each event; if the personnel changes from
event to event; and how participants are known or related to one another in each event.
Is it the case that anyone can play any role in this process? Who is accepted as an
'audience' member? Or must certain people participate in specific roles for an event to
be deemed 'successful'?

The appropriateness of certain on-camera appearances can be a problem — not every
family friend or person who comes to the house counts or qualifies for inclusion.[16] In one
example that juxtaposes questions of appropriate participants with snapshot exhibition
events, we read of the following problem and solution:

Dear Ann Landers,
What should I do about a friend who insists on showing snapshots and clippings
to anyone who will look at them? When she had guests in her home, she drags out
albums and letters . . . and takes over the entire evening bragging about her family.
The same thing happens when she visits others . . . The latest was a wedding reception to which she carried pictures. I don't mean six or seven. I'm talking fifty or
sixty. I have grandchildren, too, but I wouldn't dream of collaring acquaintances
and handing them a fistful of photos . . .

Overexposed in Pennsylvania

Dear Overexposed,
. . . The best approach is to look at the first five or six pictures, make some pleasant
comment and whiz through the rest of the photos lickety-split, hand them back and
say, 'How nice.'
(*Philadelphia Inquirer* July 25, 1989)

Figure 14.1 The state of *participants* also plays a role in any analysis of the snapshot view of life. An adult male sleeping near a dog house is unusual (and suggests an in-house family joke). For instance, a happy person is preferred to a sad one, smiling to crying, awake to asleep, healthy to sick, and, of course, alive is preferred to dead. 'Catching-people-unaware' (as when asleep) is occasionally favored as a behind-camera strategy in snapshot photography

In snapshot communication, smiling and awake participants are generally preferred to dour, sad, crying or sleeping ones (see Figure 14.1). The living or deceased quality of the on-camera participant may be in question, as in the previous letter questioning the appropriateness of taking snapshots of 'a deceased friend or relative'. In other instances, non-human participants must also be considered, as in the frequent inclusion of family pets (see Figure 14.2). Or, how many people feel it appropriate to take snapshots of their dead pets?

The *Topic* component describes image content in terms of the subject matter, activities, events, and themes that are represented in snapshots. Relevant information on topic will be elicited in responses to the general question, 'What is this snapshot of?'

Interestingly, this question may be answered in different ways by different participants; not every viewer will agree on the central topic, and some viewers may disclose 'behind-the-scenes' topics that would not be recognized by people less familiar with the material. When looking at a snapshot of a daughter and her date standing in front of a white limousine hired for the senior prom, different family members might express the central topic in different ways: how grown up the daughter looked, the ridiculous expense of the prom dress, the bad job the hairdresser did the day before, the less-than-enthusiastic look on the young man's face, how Mom and Dad didn't know where the couple was until 6 PM the next day, etc. Also, identification of topic may change through time (see Figure 14.3). The male escort in the above snapshot might have been considered 'a hunk' when the picture was taken but 'a creep' one year (or less) later.

Figure 14.2 Non-human *participants* play meaningful roles in the snapshot version of family life and offer evidence for the existence of the canine/feline extended family

What may be seen as the central topic when one is 20 years old may have changed when one is 60.

The *Setting* component, in most cases, refers to when and where a particular communication event takes place. The time and place of planning, editing, and exhibition events are easily described. For instance, how appropriate is it to exhibit personal photographs in a bathroom?

> Dear Abby,
> Here's a new one for you. My daughter-in-law has my wedding picture hanging directly over the toilet in her bathroom. She has 'honoured' her parents' wedding picture in this fashion by hanging it next to ours. This must be a new fad because my daughter hung the wedding picture of her grandparents (my beloved mother and father) over the 'throne' in her bathroom! I am tempted to ask for those pictures back. I would rather see them destroyed than hanging there. They should be in an album. I treasure those pictures and wanted my family to have them after I'm gone. I'm 82.
>
> Hurt in Arizona

> Dear Hurt,
> Please don't judge your daughter and daughter-in-law too harshly. I'm sure they meant no offence. Many contemporary decorators suggest hanging heirloom pictures

Figure 14.3 *Topic* would be: 'Neighborhood friend — always borrowing our bicycle.' But through time, the significance or meaning of photograph can change. In this case: 'Who would have guessed? Three years later Jimmy dropped out of high school, joined the Army, and was never seen alive again — poor kid.'

in the bathroom, powder room or dressing area. Though the idea may not appeal to you, the pictures will be enjoyed far more where they are seen every day, rather than placed in an album that's seldom opened.
(*Philadelphia Daily News*, November 12, 1987)

The task here is to inventory the places and times that people select as appropriate for either the making or showing of snapshots. Notions of social prescription and proscription become important. Social psychologist Stanley Milgram has stated that, 'Any place is considered appropriate for taking a picture, unless the photographs violate the sanctity or privacy as a funeral parlour or brothel' (1977, p. 54). However this general notion of what people 'can do' tends to overlook the possibility that appropriateness may change according to individual social context and identity of the photographer, e.g., snap-shooter vs. photojournalist vs. fine artist. In yet other cases, the selection of appropriate settings away-from-home may differ from at-home. Tourists make snapshots in settings that they would not consider in either their own homes or their own communities — and sometimes get in trouble for their selection of setting, participants, and topic.[17]

The component *Message Form*, meaning the physical form, shape or kind of picture, is central to all other components. Home mode examples of message form include 'snapshot', wallet photo, photo booth picture, passport photo, framed wedding portrait. One objective here is to determine how both camera technology and other components relate to and structure the message form. Interestingly, much can be learned from the

A

B

D

C

Figure 14.4 Four examples of *code* that are appropriate for the snapshot message form. Snapshot photographers do not attend to background features, resulting in pictures of things growing out of peoples' heads (as in A and B). In other cases, details of composition become code items, as in C when the result is the segmentation of body parts, or as in D when only one-quarter of the image carries the meaningful information

stereotypic characteristics of the 'snapshot' message form as published in commercial contexts such as advertisements, magazine exposes, short stories and other examples of mass media. For example, photographers like Emmet Gowin, associated with the 'snapshot chic' or 'snapshot aesthetic' schools of fine art photography, will play with forms of facsimile snapshots. Their gallery shows and publications include pictures of family members doing things at home, 'around the house', but they have been made for professional presentation in public settings.

Fifth, and last, the *Code* component includes characteristics that define the compositional 'style' of the snapshot message form. Description of code includes information on habits, conventions, and/or routines that have structured shooting and/or editing events that, in turn, give a certain 'look' to individual snapshot images or organized collections of snapshots. For instance, we may find a tendency to place a person's head in the centre of a picture, leaving a lot of empty space in the top half of the snapshot, to frame a picture that segments body parts, or to take snapshots on a diagonal, producing diamond shaped pictures (see Figure 14.4).

Code also describes the pattern of social habits and conventions responsible for what people do in snapshots.[18] Here, we include giving instructions on posing — describing such habits as saying, 'ready?', having all people looking at the camera lens, smiling (possibly saying 'cheese'), and perhaps waving at the photographer (see Figure 14.5).

Figure 14.5 Components *code* and *participant* find an integration in this snapshot. We see how the shadow of the photographer (as behind-camera participant) is included — as a code item serving as a stereotypic marker of the snapshot message form, in what would be regarded as a mistake in most forms of professional photography

Other examples might include an insistence that subjects be clean or even wearing new clothes, or that the setting (backyard, living room) be cleaned up before snapshot recording. In all these code descriptions, we are discussing conventions of pictorial representation — the details of how some events, activities, or people are 'translated' from ongoing life situations to symbolic form, and the choices, decisions, rules, techniques used to make these transformations in accepted ways.

I have suggested that an inventory of certain components may be helpful, implying the need for some form of content analysis — but only in an informal sense of formal content analytic methods.[19] Frequency counts and 'values' assigned to individual elements are optional, again depending on specific questions being addressed. Issues of coding and coder reliability are given less attention fully realizing that manifest content can be interpreted by home mode participants in different ways. In most cases, qualitative issues take precedence over quantitative ones.

Personal, Social, and Cultural Functions

In addition to asking what people *do with* their abilities to create home mode images as well as their pictures *per se*, it is instructive to study what home mode collections *do for* their creators and custodians. On the one hand, people will speak of such functions as having fun, documentation, and 'evidence', they also mention memorabilia — and how their pictures serve to jog and trigger their memories. Sometimes a financial metaphor is invoked. This kind of photography is seen as an investment — pictures are stored in a 'memory bank' earning new interest through time, effort that will 'pay off' in the future. In one example about home movies that could easily be applied to snapshots, a mother writes:

> Dear Killing Me Softly,
> . . . A bizarre and tragic accident took the life of my eldest daughter, 27, last summer. She left a husband and three young children, two boys, 8 and 6, and a new baby daughter, only 5 weeks old. . . . I don't think our memories should be let go, unless they keep us from functioning among the living. I have some marvelous movies of my daughter, starting when she was 4 years old. This is the only way her little girl will ever know the kind of person her mother was. I am extremely thankful that I stuck to my movie-making so faithfully. It comforts me to bring back the happy memories.
>
> Signed — Can't Help Singing
>
> (*The Boston Globe*, June 6, 1975)

Other functions are less easy to articulate, but every bit as significant. Snapshot collections, and the home mode in general, offer people chances to make personal statements of social and cultural conformity. Photographers and family members can acknowledge the significance of individuality within contexts of group and cultural membership. In addition, people can display their knowledge of a culture's value system, and profess beliefs in what's good, what counts, and what's right.

In summary, makers of snapshots and family albums seem to be devoted to producing a special kind of truth about life, a particular biased view of human existence. This use of cameras develops one of our photographic versions of life — one of the many symbolic renditions that comprise our everyday symbolic environment.

Fieldwork Methods for Home Mode Projects

Protocols for fieldwork will vary from study to study. Methods must follow specific research problems and thus can vary considerably. However virtually all methods will include a need to locate appropriate research subjects and subject matter,[20] the development of general and specific questions sometimes in the forms of questionnaires,[21] and personal and/or small group interviews.

Questionnaires can be very useful for getting a project started and providing some quantitative data for qualitative issues that will be studied later. After introductory inventory-like questions, a schedule of open-ended questions is usually better than closed ones. In turn, different projects will suggest the need for different types of individual and group interviews. 'Photo-interviews' should then be done with family members as they review examples from their own photograph collections and/or concentrate on specific pictures in their family albums. This information on content can be learned in no other way because these images are 'high context' artefacts. The personal significance of snapshot images lies in the minds and voices of their custodians — pieces of information that are known and remembered by family members, perhaps by the original photographer, the maker of the family album or someone in a specific photograph.

In turn, questions and answers in these interviews will stimulate the telling of family stories and many related anecdotes. Viewers will be provoked into a variety of emotional reactions to specific photographs and their memories — joking, laughing as well as crying. Thus photographs are used as an elicitation device, as described best by Collier and Collier (1986).[22] These interviews are very important because they surface personal meanings that family members attach to their own photographs — the ideas *they* interpret as significant in *their* own photographs. In short, the construction process continues. We get a first hand view of how people make meanings *with* and *from* pictures, and how the construction process is indebted to the knowledge that viewers bring to the making of their interpretations. Information gathered on 'local knowledge' from 'the native's point of view' and the 'beholder's share' clearly makes a difference — 'outsiders' would never get it.

Conclusion

I end this chapter with three statements from social scientists that tie studies of home mode communication into larger concerns. Projects suggested in this chapter shed new light on the communication habits that are central to what it means to be human, specifically in the domain of our symbolic support systems. For instance, anthropologist Christie Kiefer has written about the ways that:

> people maintain the illusion of inner continuity and consistency. For one thing, people construct and reconstruct their biographies and their histories, explaining to themselves and others in the process how they came to be who they are. This process appears to be largely unconscious and haphazard in the most part most of the time. It is stimulated by the discontinuities in one's environment, and depending on the individual's education and belief system, it takes the form of folklore, religious cosmology, historicism, or private introspection. . . . Furthermore, most people make at least a little effort to anticipate and prepare for the future stages of

their lives. In relatively stable societies, there tends to be a well-developed lore at hand for this task . . . (Kiefer, 1974, pp. 232–33)

The home mode finds a comfortable place in this statement. The construction and use of home media are central to a communication system that allows for and, indeed, promotes the same kinds of psychological, social, and cultural functions. In a sense, the availability of modern image-making apparatus provides the latest chapter in allowing humans to keep track of themselves and communicate their existence in the present and into the future.

When discussing the 'organization of experience' Erving Goffman contributes a comment that addresses the internal consistency of the self-reports we produce in home mode formats:

> What people understand to be the organisation of their experience, they buttress, and perforce, self-fulfillingly. They develop a corpus of cautionary tales, games, riddles, experiments, newsy stories, and other scenarios, which elegantly confirm a frame-relevant view of the workings of the world. . . . And the human nature that fits with this view of viewings does so in part because its possessors have learned to comport themselves so as to render this analysis true to them. Indeed, in count-less ways and ceaselessly, social life takes up and freezes into itself the understandings we have of it. (Goffman, 1974, p. 563)

Throughout this chapter we have been addressing questions of how 'real life' experience can be transformed and reproduced in personal snapshot photography. Home mode images can be understood as an organization of experience, one, like all others, that is selectively organized for some form of replay. Home mode images contribute another dimension — they provide us with pictorial forms. These picture collections are similar to 'newsy stories and other scenarios' that comprise our repertoire of life renditions. And, as Goffman claims, they seem to operate as a 'frame-relevant view of the workings of the world' — one that is repeated and duplicated with remarkable consistency.

Studies suggested in this chapter lie at the heart of doing research on our symbolic environment, on our methods of creative 'worldmaking,'[23] and on structuring a view of the world. When Howard Gardner comments on the work of philosopher Nelson Goodman, he notes:

> . . . It is misleading to speak of the world as it is, or even of a single world. It makes more sense to think of various versions of the world that individuals may entertain, various characterisations of reality that might be presented in words, pictures, diagrams, logical propositions, or even musical compositions. Each of these symbol systems captures different kinds of information and hence presents different ver-sions of reality. All we have, really, are such versions; only through them do we gain access to what we casually term 'our world'. (1980, pp. 92–4)

The making of snapshots and family albums falls within this domain of human activity, and, in fact, can be treated as the construction of a symbolic world. This world of representation both reflects and promotes a particular look at life, a preferred version of life that will outlive us all.

Notes

1   Statistics which detail the frequency of still photography suggest the popularity and indeed power of this medium. Figures compiled by the Photo Marketing Association and The Wolfman Report indicate that amateur photographers shot over 19 billion still pictures in 1995 in the US alone.

2   Sol Worth's (1969) *Toward an Anthropological Politics of Symbolic Forms* suggests many unexplored topics, from macro to micro contexts of this notion.

3   'Pictorial' is added here since not all forms of visual communication are strictly pictorial e.g., kinesic and proxemic behaviours as well as matters directly related to the built environment, all of which are subsumed in the notion of visual communication. In addition, I have paid most attention to camera-generated pictures and less to sketches, drawings, paintings, murals, graffiti, among other image forms.

4   A revised version of this paper appeared in *the PIEF (Program in Ethnographic Film) Newsletter* under the title 'Cinéma naïveté: A socividistic approach to the home mode of visual communication' (1973).

5   Other approaches emphasize technological history (see Coe and Gates, 1977; and Jenkins, 1975), aesthetic features (see King, 1984), literary analysis (see Hirsch, 1981), family folklore (see Graves and Payne, 1977; and Kotkin, 1978), social semiotics (see Hodge and Kress, 1988), Jungian analysis (see Lesy, 1980), etc.

6   The personal and private features of home mode forms stand in dramatic contrast to more frequently referenced mass modes of communication — forms that are characterized by impersonal relationships between producers and anonymous audiences, and by public message systems that are broadcast through methods of mass distribution.

7   For many examples of when inadvertent publication of home mode materials does occur, see Chapter 8 of the author's *Snapshot Versions of Life* (1987). More recently, home videotapes are finding their ways into the national evening news, as in the case of the San Francisco earthquake in 1990, and into court cases as in the 1991 amateur-made tapes of the Rodney King beating. Perhaps the most famous example is the Abraham Zapruder home movie footage of President Kennedy's assassination.

8   See Chalfen, (1988) 'Home video versions of life — Anything new?', *SVA Newsletter*, 4, 1, pp. 1–5, for initial observations and speculations on the future.

9   Much of the following section comes from Chapter 2 of the author's 1987 book, *Snapshot Versions of Life*.

10 The linguistic and sociolinguistic foundations of this scheme are described in Chalfen, 1987, pp. 17–19.

11 For an illustration of how this framework has been used to study films made by different groups of teenagers, see Chalfen, 1981 'A socividistic approach to children's filmmaking: The Philadelphia Project', *Studies in Visual Communication*, 7, 1, pp. 2–32.

12 For a good description of the problematic term, 'amateur photographer', see Schwartz and Griffin (1987).

13 Readers will see that I have quoted several letters written to etiquette columnists published daily in national newspapers. Rather than debating the relative truth qualities of these comments, I prefer to use these letters to illustrate situations and circumstances relevant to the proposed framework. For a more complete treatment of how etiquette columns can be used, see Chalfen's 1984 article, 'The socividistic wisdom of Abby and Ann: Toward an etiquette of home mode photography', *Journal of American Culture*, 71, 1–2, pp. 22–31.

14 Chet Raymo writing a 'Science Musings' newspaper column (1991) entitled 'Cameras don't lie but a photograph might' describes a time when people will be able to put their pictures into a digital scanner, transform them into a array of pixels, import them into a graphics program and modify the image like any other computer graphic.

15 The notion of 'component' is borrowed from a model of socio-linguistics developed by Dell Hymes to be used in ethnographies of speaking. Elsewhere I have proposed several parallels for doing ethnographies of pictorial communication under the rubric 'sociovidistics'. The foundations of this scheme are described in Chalfen, 1987, pp. 17–18.

16 For example, snapshot collections seldom if ever include pictures of the daily mailman or delivery people or repair personnel e.g., plumbers, electricians, etc.

17 See Chalfen, 1979 in *Annals of Tourism Research* for many examples.

18 Boerdam and Martinius discuss the component as 'arranging, directing, and posing' (1980, pp. 111–15).

19 A standard and time-tested reference is *Content Analysis in Communication Research* by B. Berelson (1952) (New York: Free Press).

20 One method is seldom appropriate for all projects. For instance, research subjects can be recruited by placing notices in local newspapers, in photography stores, or on bulletin boards in local libraries. I have had most success with 'snowball' methods of recruitment when your first interviewees recommend other people for participation in the project; subjects may suggest relatives who, in turn, may suggest friends, neighbours, colleagues at work, etc. Care must be taken when making generalizations from research using self-selected samples.

21 For one example, readers may want to consult the 'Home Mode Questionnaire' found in the Appendix of the author's 1987 book, *Snapshot Versions of Life*.

22 Collier and Collier (1986) describe many instances of interviewing their informants with photographs that the researchers have taken specifically for their fieldwork. The main difference in home mode research is that informants are asked to talk about photographs that they have made themselves.

23 Reference here is to two important books by philosopher Nelson Goodman, specifically *Languages of Art* (1968) and *Ways of Worldmaking* (1978).

References

BERELSON, B. (1952) *Content Analysis in Communication Research*, New York: Free Press.

BOERDAM, J. and WARNA OOSTERBAAN MARTINIS (1980) 'Family photographs: A sociological approach', in *The Netherlands' Journal of Sociology*, **16**, pp. 95–119.

BOURDIEU, P. (1965) *Un Art Moyen: Essai sur les Usages de la Photographie*, Paris: Les Editions de Minuit.

BOURDIEU, P. (1991) 'Towards a sociology of photography', in the *Visual Anthropology Review*, **7**, 1, pp. 129–33.

CHALFEN, R. (1973) 'Cinema naïveté: A sociovidistic approach to the home mode of visual communication', *PIEF (Program In Ethnographic Film) Newsletter*, **4**, 3, pp. 7–11.

CHALFEN, R. (1979) 'Photography's role in tourism', in *Annals of Tourism Research*, **6**, 4, pp. 435–47.

CHALFEN, R. (1981) 'A sociovidistic approach to children's filmmaking: The Philadelphia project', in *Studies in Visual Communication*, **7**, 1, pp. 2–32.

CHALFEN, R. (1984) 'The sociovidistic wisdom of Abby and Ann: Toward an etiquette of home mode photography', in the *Journal of American Culture*, **71**, 1–2, pp. 22–31.

CHALFEN, R. (1987) *Snapshot Versions of Life*, Bowling Green State University: Popular Press.

CHALFEN, R. (1988) 'Video versions of life: Anything new?', in *SVA (Society for Visual Anthropology) Newsletter*, **4**, 1, pp. 1–5.

CHALFEN, R. (1988) 'Japanese American family photography: A brief report of research on home mode communication in cross-cultural contexts', in *Visual Sociology Review*, **3**, 2, pp. 12–16.

CHALFEN, R. (1989) 'Review of *Family Gathering*', in the *American Anthropologist*, **91**, 2, pp. 525–7.

CHALFEN, R. (1991) *Turning Leaves: The Photograph Collections of Two Japanese American Families*, Albuquerque, NM: The University of New Mexico Press.

COE, B. and GATES, P. (1977) *The Snapshot Photograph: The Rise of Popular Photography*, London: Ash and Grant Ltd.

COLLIER, J.Jr. and COLLIER, M. (1986) *Visual Anthropology: Photography As a Research Method*, Albuquerque: University of New Mexico Press.

CONNIFF, R. (1988) 'When "friends" pressed the button, there was nowhere to hide', in *The Smithsonian*, **19**, 3, pp. 106–16 (June).

ENTIN, A.D. (1981) 'The use of photographs and family albums in family therapy', in GURMAN, A. (ed.) *Questions and Answers in the Practice of Family Therapy*, New York: Brunner Mazel.

FREUND, G. (1974) *Photography and Society*, Boston: David R. Godine.

GALLOWAY, D. (1978) *A Family Album*, New York: Harcourt, Brace, Jovanovich.

GARDNER, H. (1980) 'Gifted worldmakers', in *Psychology Today* (September).

GARDNER, S. (1990) 'Images of family life over the lifecycle', in *The Sociology Quarterly*, **31**, 1, pp. 77–92.

GEFFROY, Y. (1990) 'Family photographs: A visual heritage', in *Visual Anthropology*, **3**, 4, pp. 367–410.

GOFFMAN, E. (1974) *Frame Analysis: An Essay in the Organization of Experience*, New York: Harper Colophon Books.

GOMBRICH, E.H. (1972) 'The visual image', in *Scientific American*, **277**, 3, pp. 82–96.

GOODMAN, N. (1968) *Languages of Art*, Indianapolis: Bobbs-Merrill Co., Inc.

GOODMAN, N. (1978) *Ways of Worldmaking*, Indianapolis: Hackett Publishing Company.

GRAVES, K. and PAYNE, M. (1977) *American Snapshots*, Oakland, CA: The Scrimshaw Press.

HIRSCH, J. (1981) *Family Photographs: Content, Meaning, and Effects*, New York: Oxford University Press.

HODGE, R. and KRESS, G. (1988) 'Transformations of love and power: The social meaning of narrative', in *Social Semiotics*, Ithaca: Cornell University Press, pp. 204–39.

HOPPAL, M. (1986) 'Ethnic symbolism and images of identity: Family photography of the American Hungarian', Paper prepared for the 1987 Conference on Family Photography and Cross Cultural Comparison, Utrecht, NL.

JENKINS, R.V. (1976) *Images and Enterprise: Technology and the American Photographic Industry 1839–1925*, Baltimore:

KAUFMANN, J. (1980) 'Learning from the fotomat', in the *American Scholar*, **49**, 2, pp. 244–6.

KIEFER, C. (1974) *Changing Cultures, Changing Lives*, San Francisco: Jossey-Bass.

KING, G. (1984) *Saying 'Cheese!': Looking at Snapshots in a New Way*, New York: Dodd, Mead & Company.

KOTKIN, A. (1978) 'The family album as a form of folklore', in *Exposure*, **16**, 1, pp. 4–8.

KUNT, E. (1983) 'Photography and the peasant', *New Hungarian Quarterly*, **24**, 96, pp. 13 20.

LESY, M. (1980) *Time Frames: The Meaning of Family Photographs*, New York: Pantheon.

MILGRAM, S. (1977) 'The image freezing machine', *Psychology Today*, January, pp. 50–4, 108.

MUSELLO, C. (1979) 'Family photography', in WAGNER, J. (ed.) *Images of Information*, Beverly Hills, CA: Sage, pp. 101–18.

OHRN, K.B. (1975) 'The photoflow of family life: A family's photography collection', in *Folklore Forum*, **13**, 8.

RAYMO, C. (1991) 'Cameras don't lie but a photograph might', *The Boston Globe*, 22 June.

SCHWARTZ, D. (1990) 'Review of family gathering', in *Visual Anthropology*, **3**, 4, pp. 495–99.

SCHWARTZ, D.B. and GRIFFIN, M. (1987) 'Amateur photography: The organizational maintenance of an aesthetic code', in LINDLOF, T.R. (ed.) *Natural Audiences: Qualitative Studies of Media Uses and Effects*, Norwood, N.J.: Ablex.

STEIGER, R. (1987) 'You look just like Elsa: A father photographs his daughter in the early twentieth-century', Unpublished manuscript, files of the author.

Richard Chalfen

THOMAS, A. (1977) 'The family chronicle', in *Time in a Frame: Photography and the Nineteenth Century Mind*, New York: Schocken Books.

WEISER, J. (1988) 'See what I mean?: Photography as nonverbal communication in cross-cultural psychology', in *Cross-cultural Perspectives in Nonverbal Communication*, POYATOS, F. (ed.): Hogrefe Publishers.

WORTH, S. (1969) 'Toward an anthropological politics of symbolic forms', in HYMES, D. (ed.) *Reinventing Anthropology*, New York: Pantheon, pp. 335–64.

WORTH, S. and GROSS, L. (1974) 'Symbolic strategies', in *Journal of Communication*, **24**, pp. 27–39.

Chapter 15

Pupils Using Photographs in School Self-evaluation

Michael Schratz and Ulrike Steiner-Löffler

Abstract

Pupils, especially at a younger age, are rarely integrated as active participants in school evaluation and development, as they especially at that age find it very difficult to react to standardized forms of feedback or to write elaborate reports. Photography gives pupils the chance to research into the 'inner world' of school life without a lot of verbal argumentation. This paper shows the power of pupils' photographic images when they are asked to take pictures of places they like or dislike in school. They are the result of their effort to evaluate the climate of the school through their eyes' view, and the discussion of the processed photographs offers valuable insights into how young people experience school life through their eyes. The practical part of the paper does not only give a clear breakdown of the necessary steps introducing photo evaluation in the classroom but also gives an insight into the workings of such an evaluation approach through practical examples

What's the Use of Taking Photographs in Evaluation?

'What's the use of all this?' Lisa asked. We had just explained to the pupils how the photo-project should take place. While we were wondering how to reply, another girl answered: 'Oh, Lisa, it's wonderful, you see, you can explain clearly your reason for liking and not liking certain things in school!' We were impressed and listened carefully to the negotiation processes among the five boys and nineteen girls of a second form of a Viennese primary school, who worked towards a consensus of which places they liked or disliked in their school. We had suggested they should take photographs of those places, discuss their choices and think of improvements of their dislikes.

We have experimented with photographs in school self-evaluation with different age groups, but not yet with children of primary school age. Would they be able to handle this instrument too? Claudia Stehndl, the teacher of this second year class, was fascinated by the idea and offered us to try it out with her pupils.[1]

Well, in order to set the scene and make things clear for our readers we'd better leave the children alone for some time now and turn to the roots of our photo-project.

Figure 15.1 A girl taking a photograph of her classroom

Why Not Think of Life as a Chain of Photographs?

Why not think of life as a chain of photographs and reading its text as if turning over the pages in a photo album: People's movements set the direction and speed for how many photos are thought necessary by the author . . . (Arno Schmidt) [our translation]

Fascinated by the ideas of the German author Arno Schmidt who developed this snap shots technique of rebuilding human memory and inspired by the metaphoric use of the photo session, we got more and more drawn into the idea of making use of the visual image in our research life. Research in general and evaluation in particular are dominated by methods based on the spoken or written word. Culturally and historically this has to do with the tradition of academia, which has built its foundations on the written word. When we started experimenting with different activities including pupils and students in school developmental work, we soon realized that traditional research methods cannot easily be put into practice, as pupils especially at that age find it very difficult to react to standardized forms of feedback or to write elaborate reports on this matter. Using such methods, we suffered from the fact that the power relationship proved to be too much in favour of the adults when pupils were confronted with verbal arguments.

Therefore we set out to find other possibilities of looking into the 'inner world' of schools from the pupils' perspective. It was particularly important to get an idea of how they experience their school, yet very little literature has been available in the area of research methods which pupils can be in control of. Even if action research, where practitioners set the research agenda, is used in schools, it is usually not the pupils who research their own situation in their workplace.

We were attracted by Rob Walker's suggestions on the use of photographs in evaluation and research, who argues 'it touches on the limitations of language, especially language used for descriptive purposes. In using photographs the potential exists, however elusive the achievement, to find ways of thinking about social life that escape the traps set by language' (Walker, 1993, p. 72). His aspiration in using black and white photographs was to find a silent voice for the researcher. Thus, looking at photographs creates a tension between what one expects to observe and what one actually sees. Therefore, images 'are not just adjuncts to print, but carry heavy cultural traffic on their own account' (Walker, 1993, p. 91).

These ideas have been further developed in Schratz and Walker, 1995, who write that there has been a curious neglect of the visual imagination in the social sciences. 'Despite an enormous research literature that argues the contrary, researchers have trusted words (especially their own) as much as they have mistrusted pictures' (1995, p. 72). For them the use of pictures in research raises the continuing question of the relationship between public and private knowledge and the role of research in tracing and transgressing this boundary. 'In social research pictures have the capacity to short circuit the insulation between action and interpretation, between practice and theory, perhaps because they provide a somewhat less sharply sensitive instrument than words and certainly because we treat them less defensively. Our use of language, because it is so close to who we are, is surrounded by layers of defence, by false signals, pre-emptive attack, counteractive responses, imitations, parodies, blinds and double blinds so that most of the time we confuse even (perhaps, especially) ourselves' (Schratz and Walker, 1995, p 76).

After our first steps into exploring the use of photography in research practice we became convinced of the power of pictures and ventured further into the theoretical background of using photographs in evaluation. Then we decided to try out how photo-evaluation works as a research method if the camera is given into the hands of the pupils. Moreover, we were particularly fascinated by the idea of choosing this approach as a way of researching into school culture. This lead us to the idea of confronting the pupils with the question 'Where in school do you feel good, where not and why (not)?', since we regard well-being as an important criteria for the quality of school culture seen through the pupils' eyes.

How to Do Photo-evaluation

In the following we give a short breakdown of the procedure we used when experimenting with this photographic approach and suggest two different ways of how to implement it as a means of self evaluation.

A Short Guide to Photo-evaluation

- Self-selected groups of four or five pupils are formed into teams.
- First each team discusses the places in school where they feel good and where not, then they find consensus on three or four places of both categories to be banned on photographs.

Figure 15.2 Documenting work in the computer room

- The teams decide on the details of what they want to photograph (e.g., people 'in camera' or not).
- The teams go and take the photographs as planned.
- When the pictures have been developed, each team produces a poster presenting their photos in the two categories (+/–) and writes comments to give reasons for their choices.
- Each group presents their poster to the class. (At this instance, the pupils usually get involved in heated discussions about their situation in school in general!)
- A possible next step: The teams organize themselves with a view to getting changed what they consider necessary and possible.

Ways of Implementing Photo-evaluation

There are (at least) two ways of how photo-evaluation can be used in school. Either photo-evaluation is introduced like any other classroom project. In the end nobody might be interested in changing anything as a result. However, the project might serve as a starting point for change as well. Or photo-evaluation is introduced as part of a wider self-evaluation which the school decides on. This will only happen when a school is convinced that the pupils' voices are to be taken seriously. Since pupils have rarely been involved in self-evaluation processes, it has to be considered that the ones not involved in the photo-evaluation might be opposed to giving the pupils a 'photographic voice'. For example, once a teacher reacted by saying 'They should first do their learning before they start demanding changes.' We believe that schools will increasingly need evaluation methods that give pupils more say.

Photo-evaluation in the Making

In the following we present key situations of photo-evaluation by taking authentic scenes from its practical application.

Teamwork Observed

The following conversation took place between a boy and two girls in one of the groups doing photo-evaluation in the primary school mentioned above.

> What's a place we don't like?
> Let's take our classroom! There we have to write at the blackboard.
> Hm, that's a good idea.
> No, we can't.
> But why?
> Because we have agreed the bookshelf in our classroom to be a place we do like!
> Perhaps we can write down 'at the blackboard' to be negative, otherwise it would
>   not fit together with what we have decided before

This dialogue shows that children of that age are generally able to handle the team task on their own. If one of the groups had problems, Claudia, the teacher, joined them giving special support. But on the whole we got the impression that there were hardly any problems arising during this phase of the project. When Ulrike used photo-evaluation with older children in her school, which is located in an area largely inhabited by working class children and children whose first language is not German, she had a similar experience. Here, the pupils called the photo project *Im Dschungel der Gefühle* (In the Jungle of Feelings).

First Findings

Often the positive or negative 'appreciation' depends on the experiences the pupils have had with certain people in certain places. The older ones, for example, consider the handicraft room a 'minus place' because the group members do not like their handicraft teacher. We noticed that the connection between places and persons they can relate to was particularly strong in the decision-making process of primary school children, as the following example shows.

Figure 15.3 Positive and negative 'appreciation' depends on experience

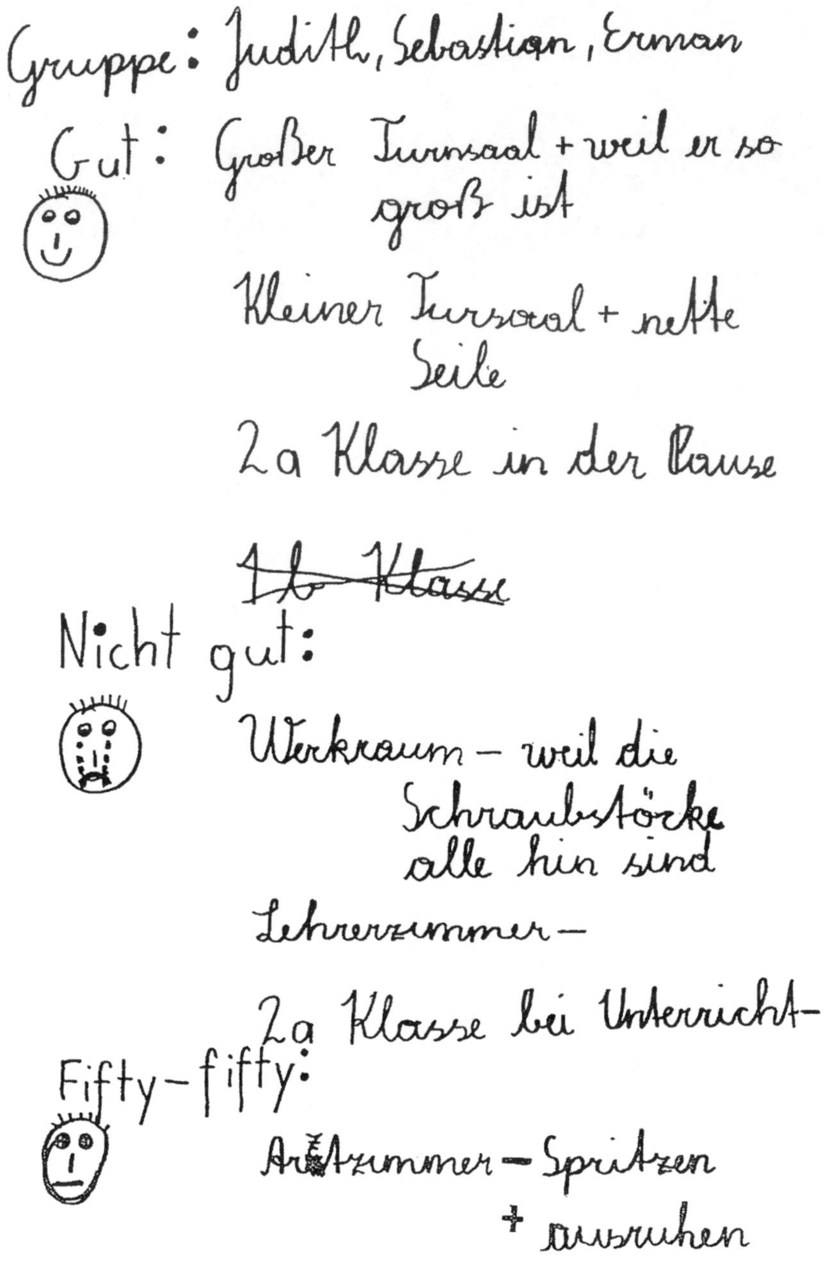

Gruppe: Judith, Sebastian, Erman

Gut: Großer Turnsaal + weil er so groß ist

Kleiner Turnsaal + nette Seile

2a Klasse in der Pause

~~1b Klasse~~

Nicht gut:

Werkraum — weil die Schraubstöcke alle hin sind

Lehrerzimmer —

2a Klasse bei Unterricht-

Fifty-fifty:

Arztzimmer — Spritzen + ausruhen

group:	Judith, Sebastian, Erman
good:	big gymnasium + because it is so big
	small gymnastic hall + nice ropes
	2A class during break
not good:	woodwork room — because all the vices are out of order
	staff room
	2A during lessons
fifty-fifty:	medical room: – syringes
	+ resting

What place do you like very much in school?
The classroom of 1B.
Why?
Because I know many children there.

Therefore it is not surprising that Claudia, their teacher, is the focus of their attention. When we asked one group why they had chosen the staff room as a positive place, one girl answered:

> Because Claudia can take a rest there now and then, and afterwards she is in a good mood again. First I wanted to write down the staff room being a minus place because whenever Claudia is there she is not with us. But we voted and it was three to one against me in the group, and so I thought it is o.k. In the end I agree with the others that it is good for her that she can relax there!

Older pupils too cannot easily agree how to judge the staffroom, but for different reasons. For them it belongs to the category 'hidden and forbidden places' (like the head-master's office), which are very attractive on the one hand because they are taboo places, but on the other hand the pupils sometimes expect 'boring lessons' or even punishment originating from there. Another example is the *Tagesschulheim* (afternoon care), where pupils can stay in the afternoon supervised by teachers. The girls love this place, they obviously enjoy being there together with their girlfriends, but they also like to be together with their teachers, who have more time to talk to them personally and play games with them in the afternoon than during morning lessons. The boys consider it a terrible place, because 'Everything is forbidden!' The same place — entirely different views!

When some groups were confronted with opposition, they had to realize that certain people felt irritated by their activities. One 8-year old girl told us:

> Afterwards we wanted to take photos of the 3A, but Susi (teacher of the 3A) snapped on us. 'Keep out of this room', she said, 'some other children were here one minute ago!' She seemed frustrated, so we tried to explain to her what we wanted to do . . . and after a few minutes we came back secretly and took a photo of the room without stepping inside so that she didn't notice us at all . . .

In contrast to the choices of the primary school children, pupils in secondary school use to look at their school with a more critical eye. For example, they often prefer places in school which symbolize a 'way out', such as windows or the front door. One group in year six commented on a photograph of the front door: *Wir haben den Ausgang gewählt, weil sich dahinter die Freiheit verbirgt!* (We have chosen the exit because freedom lies behind it!). Similarly, often pictures of the small school yard were taken by the children, who called it their most beloved place in the whole school.

Pupils of all ages would choose places where they are allowed to move freely or do manual work (e.g., gym). There the usual predominance of academic work is weakened in favour of contrastive experiences.

Another important aspect of photo-evaluation turns out to be the fact that it offers the pupils the chance to deal with taboo places, for example with the toilets. They are usually the only place in school where children are unsupervised, which makes them very attractive places to be taken photographs of. Besides, it might be exciting to test how the teacher will react.

Figure 15.4 A place the pupils are not sure about: The handicraft room

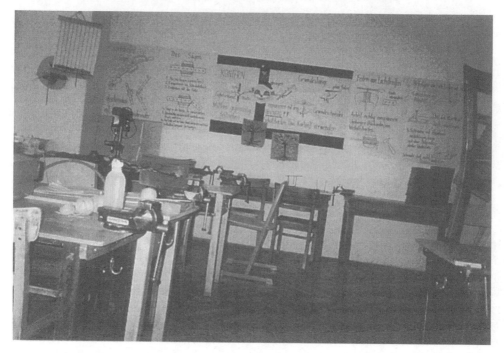

Figure 15.5 A positive place: The school yard

Figure 15.6 Another ambiguous place: The medical room

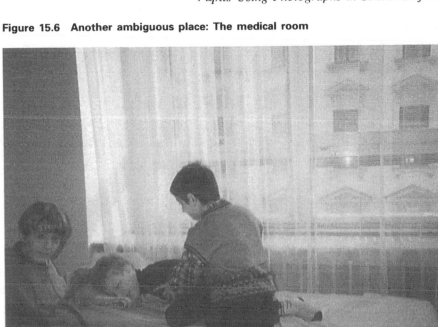

Figure 15.7 A negative place: 'Here it stinks!'

Figure 15.8   Pupils creating posters

Figure 15.9   A group working on their poster

What We Have Learned from Observing Discussion, Decision Making and Presentations

The processes of discussing, decision making and presenting depend very much on the age of the pupils involved. Even though the basic decisions between 'positive places' and 'negative places' had been made before the pictures had been taken, usually the groups have to go through an intensive phase of discussion when they write down their reasons on the poster. The younger children, however, concentrate on the artistic aspects of the posters, the older ones often deal with the consequences they expect from their presentation.

There is one result that we consider especially important: Pupils — and, of course, teachers, start to talk about a topic they had never spoken about so clearly before: they talk about their individual perspective of school life. In this sense evaluation takes place and as we have experienced, often initiatives are started by the pupils to change things they dislike (e.g., a group of 6th graders started a campain to get a second 'long break').

Hints and Warnings

The following hints and warnings can be useful when putting photo-evaluation into practice.

- Make sure that the setting gives everybody a fair chance to participate, for instance by watching the process of decision-making in the groups. Look for the opinion leaders and outsiders.
- Watch your time resources. One lesson will not be sufficient for doing the photo-project. Take into account that all groups should be able to take their pictures without time pressure. On the other hand it makes no sense to allow too many shots with the camera or to provide too much time for each group. An important part of the learning process is to deal with the limited time available within the school setting.
- Consider the pupils' age. It might be an advantage to have an extra person to help the pupils while working in groups.
- Use only one camera and have the pupils prepare a list with an exact plan of the procedure: Who is going to take which photos? (If some of the pupils are allowed to use their own camera you will hardly ever get all the photographs in the classroom at the same time, because they might not be developed in time. It is necessary to have all the photos ready for the further steps of the project.)
- Photo-evaluation can evoke strong emotions, since the message of the question 'Where do you feel good in school and where not?' for the pupils is the following: 'It is of importance what *you* think and feel about things, your view is even worth being documented and made public.' Therefore, it is easy to understand that the pupils can get deeply involved in their 'jungle of feelings'.
- Decision-making in the groups needs communication skills and conflict management. Photo evaluation offers the opportunity to deal with communication and conflict-resolution learning by doing. The whole project may even develop into a lesson on how to handle conflicts and emotions for pupils and teachers!
- Identification with their school can be stimulated among the pupils if they take responsibility for the consequences of what they have found out in the photo-evaluation. The teachers can make use of this positive energy towards enhancing social skills.

Getting Hold of the Invisible: Theoretical Annotations

Islands of Agreement

Evaluating (certain aspects of) education always means dealing with a very complex social structure, and breaking down reality into photographic images is always an act of constructing new realities in our conceptual world. It is the study of the social significance, that is how things, events, and rules of interactions become meaningful within the overall framework of reference, which signifies the changes of the overall system and structures of the system (Simon, 1993, p. 26). Since organizational life is always constituted by multiple realities, taking photographs offers a challenging opportunity to bring to the fore the different layers of reality. To do so, the camera forms a special lens which can be focused on the single elements of organizational life by changing between the foreground and the background and thus enabling 'unimportant details' to become the main focus of interest.

Through photography, parts of the micro system of a school can be de-ranged by isolating elements from the whole, because they can be viewed from a different perspective. Thus, in the pictures taken by the pupils, the head's office is no longer the administrative centre of the school, but commented on as 'not an enjoyable place because behind that door there are dangers lurking'. For them the staff room is not, as it is for the teachers, the only retreat to their professional community, but 'this is the place where boring lessons come from'. As there is no 'real' reality and no comprehensive human consensus, photographic images can help in finding islands of agreement in the sea of different opinions (Simon, 1993, p. 61).

In this study the pupils have used the camera as a powerful instrument to freeze some of the different views and opinions about life in an institution like school. Pierre Bourdieu (1981) sees one main function of taking photographs in an escape from the everyday world. When the pupils move through the school building taking photographs, they have not only left their classrooms but also the hidden curriculum in class which is built around the pattern I-R-E (teacher *initiates*, pupil *responds*, teacher *evaluates* 'correct' or 'incorrect') (Schratz and Mehan, 1993). They are the typical school questions, to which the correct answer is already known and which form the basis for the universal pattern of teaching. There is no authoritative 'right' or 'wrong' any more for the pictures to be taken, but the necessity to negotiate where to take it, what to depict etc.

By discussing and reflecting on which pictures to take 'in the jungle of feelings', as the students called the situation, this fine distinction between learning questions and life questions is partially compensated. They are trying to find the unknown in the known and to sense where relationships exist between their school world and their world of feelings: it is *their own* appreciation that counts; what is important is how *they* feel. In the course of the project they are asked to articulate those feelings and make them accessible, which brings in another element Bourdieu sees constitutive for photography: the expressions of feelings.

By doing this kind of action research through taking photos pupils (and teachers) have the opportunity to interrupt the teaching routine according to the I-R-E pattern described above. The pupils start asking questions to which the teachers do not have answers. There is no evaluation referring to 'correct' or 'incorrect', no prescribed curriculum, and the pupils' opinions have to be respected. This can mean a first step towards a *learning school*, a school which organizes its own process of development through a social architecture which involves teachers, pupils, heads, parents, non-teaching staff etc.

Control and Liberation

Freezing the situation at a critical time should not only be an occasion for beginning to reflect and exchange experiences of different feelings in order to be put to rest as a frozen picture in the school chronicle. More than that, the photos depict school as an institution in which the social rules of behaviour and the moral codex are emphasized more strongly than the feelings, wishes and thoughts of the subjects. That is why Bordieu asks 'How under such conditions, how could the representation of society be something different from the presentation of a society which represents itself?' (Bourdieu, 1981, p. 95 [our translation]).

Foucault (1976) argues that schools are organizations which are built according to the principle of 'closed institutions' using 'control' and 'punishment' as typical mechanisms of sanctioning. Therefore schools are included among institutions which are usually regarded as organizations of mistrust, in which a permanent surveillance of the pupils takes place. To them, taking photographs means a temporary liberation from this control of teacher surveillance, which they may use according to their own imaginations within the school premises. Therefore, it is not surprising that several photos depict ways out of this surveillance situation (e.g., windows into the open, doors leading towards the street, toilets).

In an action research context the photographs become an instrument for change because the photo documents are harder 'facts' than individual expressions by pupils which often do not even reach the ears of the person in charge. In this form they become important pieces of testimony for living out forgotten (or suppressed?) reasoning. Talking about change is no longer a learning question but a question of survival — in a time when the identity of the individual has become more and more absorbed by the process of civilization (Elias, 1969). Although the steps taken by the pupils are only timid, as trace elements they can gain momentum through the photos taken and initiate further steps.

Although it is often difficult to influence changes regarding the building site within the state school system, there are different ways of reacting to pupils' wishes, which, in our experience, range from the local educational authorities not allowing ugly concrete walls to be painted to providing the pupils with a common room of their own which they could declare off limits to teachers — in accordance with the sign 'No entry for pupils' on the door leading into the staff room. In most schools there is a wide enough room for decision-making between those positions to let the pupils *feel* that they also have a say in school autonomy. This, of course, should also be true for the teachers who need to experience a feeling of 'owning' their school.

The reflections initiated by such a project, which usually do not happen often enough during the routines of everyday schooling, can initiate a chain reaction; other classes are motivated to find out and present the places where *they* feel (un)happy. Teachers suddenly realize that they have not given sufficient thought to how they themselves feel about their workplace. In this sense the photos produced by the pupils are a valuable instrument of internal *self-evaluation* leading to change. It was not done by an external researcher, but the pupils were encouraged to conduct research into their own situation — with the aim of improving the social surroundings of their situation (Elliott, 1991).

Figure 15.10   One of the posters resulting from group work

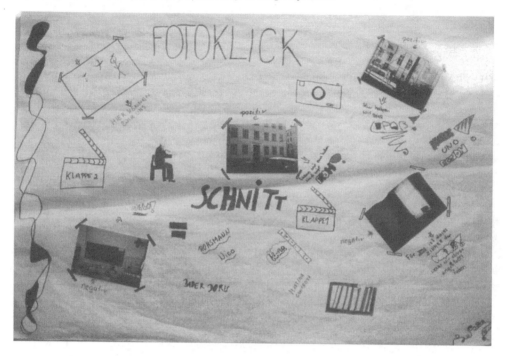

Figure 15.11   Another poster resulting from group work

Curricular Matters

Our society is highly dominated by the culture of the word. Therefore writing takes a high (if not the highest) priority in the school curriculum, which is also shown in the dominance of the subject area (see for example the role of language and orthography). With the increasing relevance of education the non-verbal culture has lost influence in learning, because in 'teaching in general and in the final exams of schools and universities, which are decisive for the social future, both the verbal culture and the intelligence manifested to the written word dominate persistently' (Rumpf, 1987, p. 32 [our translation]).

Therefore the knowledge to be learnt cannot be challenged, but remains an instrument of dominance which has to be acquired (and further reproduced) within the framework of socialization and selection. Mr Keating, the teacher in the cult movie 'Dead Poets' Society', has convincingly tried to break out of this socialization process by tearing pages out of classic books he read with his pupils. Mere *deconstruction* itself, however, does not in itself lead to an enhancing educational process. Moreover, it is necessary to *reconstruct* cultural knowledge in such a way that it becomes accessible and can be challenged and manipulated. For this purpose photography is a medium which grasps reality in its *whole complexity* as a frozen image. According to Susan Sontag (1979, p. 88) photos are not only the evidence of what an individual sees, not just documents but an evaluation of the world (view). Therefore they present a 'vision' of the relationship between subjects and objects, which manifests itself in the snapshot. The 'interconnectedness' between places, rooms, areas and feelings, emotions, associations has received little attention in pedagogics, and even less in schooling where teaching is mainly based on cognitive aspects of the curriculum.

Compared with filming and video, photography as a medium lives from the conscious separation of particular elements (such as language or movements) and asks for the intensification of the remaining possibilities, such as the focusing on the sense perception of the Gestalt, the appreciation of the strangeness in the familiar culture, through the parameters set by the angle of vision of the lens. What is distant in thoughts suddenly comes close and becomes accessible through focusing. Horst Rumpf (1986, p. 135) justly asks: 'Where else should one still learn how one can accept the irritation caused by seeing reality differently and noticing that things do not always look the way one wants them to, if not through school and university?' According to him, both institutions seem to do anything in order to repel those irritations, because then you achieve membership in the community of specialists.

Apart from the practical value to the pupils and teachers involved, using photographs has an added value for theory building. On the one hand, the experiences bring new insights into research of teaching and learning, as different aspects run together in an interdisciplinary way through photography (for example the connection of the areas of media education, educational sociology, teaching German and the arts, evaluation as part of educational studies). In this sense photographs cannot just be occupied by a single subject area, because they grasp the experience of schooling in its whole complexity by means of a snapshot.

Conclusion

The case of children taking photographs in school has shown that visual images can be very powerful. On the first level, they contribute to bringing the pupils into discussion with each other about the personal relation to the situations and locations depicted on the pictures. On the second level it is the teachers who are confronted with the motifs and their emotional responses depicted, which helps them in gaining access to the appreciation of their pupils' experience of their reality of schooling. Thus the pupils' photos can contribute to making visible the invisible (Schratz and Walker, 1995), such as the feeling of (none) well-being of the pupils in their school, the quality of communication within the school and between the school and the community, aspects of school democracy, the teaching and learning culture as well as the effect of the school site on the children. These effects can be seen not only in the pictures to be discussed i.e., after exposure but also during the process of picture taking, when the school rules do not apply. Thus, the acceptance of such a procedure is an indication of the confidence the school has in itself. Since there is a lack of tradition and of experience in self-evaluation in most schools, it is necessary not to overtax anyone and to make sure that there is sufficient communication and negotiation between everybody involved. As with any form of (self-)evaluation, taking pictures with a view to improving the social situation and physical surroundings is an intervention in an institution, and that is why a culture of curiosity and openness helps in starting a project of this kind.

After we had worked with children using cameras in this way at different places has also sparked off follow-up activities and new ideas. For example, schools can do the photo project again a year later and see what has changed. Not only the school has, but also the children and teachers have! We have also adopted this method and applied it successfully in inservice training workshops, where teachers took photographs and used them as powerful instruments for their own personal and professional development. Wherever we introduced photography as a means to widen the conceptions of institutional learning we found one common trait: Taking pictures has always been fun and it has not done any harm to the seriousness of the outcome — on the contrary!

Note

1   We thank Claudia Steindl and class 2A of Volksschule Stiftgasse, Vienna, for their commitment in sharing their experience in photo-evaluation with us and Claudia Valsky for taking pictures of pupils' self-evaluation at work and for helping interviewing children.

References

BOURDIEU, P. (1981) *Eine Llegitimine Kunst: Die sozialen Gebrauchweisen der Photographie*, Frankfurt/M.: Europäische Verlagsanstalt.

ELIAS, N. (1969) *Über den Prozeß der Zivilisation. Band 1*, Bern: Suhrkamp.

ELLIOTT, J. (1991) *Action Research for Educational Change*, Milton Keynes: Open University Press.

FOUCAULT, M. (1976) *Überwachen und Strafen: Die Geburt des Gefängnisses*. Frankfurt/M.: Suhrkamp.

RUMPF, H. (1986) *Mit fremdem Blick: Stücke gegen die Verbiederung der Welt*, Weinheim: Beltz.

RUMPF, H. (1987) *Belebungsversuche: Ausgrabungen gegen die Verödung der Lernkultur*, München: Juventa.

SCHRATZ, M. and MEHAN, H. (1993) 'Gulliver travels into a math class: In search of alternative discourse in teaching and learning', *International Journal of Educational Research*, **19**, pp. 247–64.

SCHRATZ, M. and WALKER, R. (1995) *Research as Social Change: New Possibilities for Qualitative Research*, London: Routledge.

SIMON, F.B. (1993) *Meine Psychose, mein Fahrrad und ich: Zur Selbstorganisation von Verrücktheit*, Heidelberg: Carl Auer.

SONTAG, S. (1979) *On Photography*, Harmondsworth: Penguin.

WALKER, R. (1993) 'Finding a silent voice for the researcher: Using photographs in evaluation and research', in SCHRATZ, M. (ed.) *Qualitative Voices in Educational Research*, London: Falmer Press, pp. 72–92.

Chapter 16

Cartoons and Teachers:
Mediated Visual Images as Data

Terry Warburton

Abstract

Reflecting on cartoon representations of teachers and education in the press, this chapter describes the use of a semiotic approach to develop a methodology for using cartoons to help reconstruct and reify public narratives about education.

Introduction

This chapter examines a study of cartoons used to depict narratives about education in the UK national press. It describes the use of a semiotic approach to the analysis of visual images. Rooted in the ways teachers; teaching; issues; themes; key figures and moments concerned with both education policy and practice are represented visually by the media, it addresses what such visual images count for publicly and their role as part of a range of communication systems. Visual material exists in a wide variety of forms, for example, photographs; maps; cartoons; paintings; drawings and sketches; film; video; diagrams and even forms such as graffiti. Taken singly the nature of each form as a cultural artefact is different. The differences are fixed by two cardinal factors. First, the process and method of production. In other words how the image is mediated. Second, the use for which the image was intended or perhaps more precisely the use to which it is put. These factors imbue a particular form of existence on a specific image form. Collectively, each of the examples listed are not only visual-sensory information but are also coded culturally. Mediated images communicate. They are a 'sign system' in themselves. Messages they carry are always representative.

When visual images, in this case cartoons, form a major constituent of research data, the process of integrating them into a systematic methodology becomes an imperative. Charting the organizational scheme used as the methodology develops centres around a number of key questions. These are in the first instance, what are we actually looking at? How can we describe it? What does a cartoon count for publicly? What are its characteristics? What is its place and status in respect of the communication system or systems it is a part of? For what was it intended? In the second instance, probably the most problematic questions to be addressed for a researcher are, how are we going to treat or handle it, what can we say about it and how are we going to make use of it? Answers to the first series of questions can best be explored by examining a cartoon as a cultural artefact generally and discussing its nature. As Hartley (1992) points out:

No picture is pure image; all of them, still and moving, graphic and photographic are 'talking pictures', either literally or in association with contextual speech, writing or discourse. (Hartley, 1992, p. 28)

Cartoons are public pictures. 'Public pictures are those designed to catch a wider audience' (Goffman, 1976, p.10). The second series of questions (to be addressed later) rely on a much more systematic approach which is underpinned by some sort of theory, in this case semiotics.

Describing a Cartoon

Figure 16.1 shows a Brook cartoon published in the *Daily Express* on 23 November 1994. It portrays a scene imagined by the cartoonist to be played out on the morning of the publication of the 'league tables' for schools. (*Daily Express*, 23 November, 1994, p. 17). Caricatured here are two sets of teachers from two different schools. Inside the school, in the playground looking out, are two teachers, both male. A further four teachers, one female, three males, are pressed against the school railings looking in. Using satire, applying it to the visual content, three of these teachers pull faces and perform gestures

Figure 16.1

'God, I hate it when St Winifred's do better than us in the league tables'

intended to deride and the fourth thrusts his naked backside through the railings in a further act of ridicule. These contemptuous acts are performed, as the caption indicates, by teachers from 'St Winifred's'. The reason for such behaviour is signified by the same caption which runs . . . 'God, I hate it when St Winifred's do better than us in the league tables.' Interestingly, the style of representation makes use of stereotypes, clearly depicting teachers, symbolically, in the traditional cap and gown as badges of office and identity, or tweed suits and plaid skirts, which may be considered equally recognizable. Similarly, the setting, the brickwork of the school itself, school railings and netball court marked out on the playground, all clearly indicate that the context is of schooling. The caption also signifies this if any doubt remains. Other subtleties of penmanship also develop the iconic public characteristic emblems of the teacher. Note the patches on the elbows of the teacher in the tweed suit, looking out. Likewise the pens in his breast pocket. These are 'inter-textual' and 'multi-generational' elements, images synthesized from what Weber and Mitchell (1995) call the 'cumulative cultural text of teacher'. These are a cultural resource. They become figures of speech and so lose any sense of anachronism. Actively used, they communicate meaning which assumes shared knowledge and understanding. Generated in one text, they transfer meaning from one context to another. They resonate. One example of such a concept might be the notion of 'Mr Chips'. Taken from the novel by James Hilton, written in 1934 and repeated in the films starring Robert Donat in the original and Peter O'Toole in the remake, it has been used in many contexts subsequently as a figure of speech representing the traditional 'caring' values of teachers (see Warburton and Saunders, 1996, p. 316). Such a device can become active because it becomes de-reified and decontextualized and so develops an 'after-life' as a figure of speech. Thus, the age, style and nature of the moustaches worn by the male teachers, for example, reflect more of the traditional image of the public or grammar school 'master' than the modern image of the state sector comprehensive teacher. Nontheless these depictions bear the hallmarks of public recognisability for all that.

As well as the images, symbols and text actually drawn in the cartoon, it can be argued, there can be perceived an underlying content. In terms of this implied content, the theme is one of competition and moreover competition within a public arena. The attitudes and values to this public competition, held by the teachers in the cartoon, can also be inferred. Status associations can be applied to the depiction. The teachers placed lower in the tables 'hate' to be so. We are told this in the caption. The teachers from St Winifred's, representing higher placed schools, are entirely happy to make a public show of their placing. What is also interesting to note is that the teachers inside the playground, representing the lower placed schools, take no reciprocal action but are, or have to be, content to stand and watch taking the criticism. In this sense, drawing together these implied strands, the entire depiction is a symbolic, metaphorical parody for actual events and circumstances, reifying them.

As Kress and Van Leeuwen (1996) argue 'The process of sign-making is the process of the construction of metaphor' (p. 7). Aptly, they term this process, 'social semiotics'. As part of this process the content of a sign consists of actual images and other iconic and textual devices — what is denoted. The 'other additional implied meanings' (Hall, 1973) can be described as codes of connotation.

Cartoons are part of a communication system. They represent one 'sign' made up of signifiers. Meanings are conveyed via that system. Warburton and Saunders (1996) argue that:

Cartoons, which are distinctive cultural artefacts, rely on the communication of
stereotypes. They synthesise and amplify cultural narrative. Barthes (1964), terms
this a 'system of signification'; that is, what is said takes the form of a system of
'signs' made up of representations which are intended to convey meaning —
'signifiers' and 'signifieds' which represent what is understood by a 'reader'.
(Warburton and Saunders, 1996, p. 307)

'Signifiers' conform to what is denoted. 'Signifieds' conform to what is connoted.

Publicly recognizable images; metaphors; themes; resonant texts; issues and standpoints are drawn together within cartoons. Political cartoonists represent particular strands
of political opinion. The political cartoon is a device which communicates its message
— its perspective — succinctly, attempting to universalize particular points of view. 'Narrative content is visually charged with status associations, iconographic and political meanings and satirical twists expressed in signs and symbols' (p. 310). Cartoonists use other
visual devices, in turn, to achieve this within a cartoon using caricature and other iconographic representations of literary forms such as metonymy and rebus. Fundamentally,
cartoons are metaphorical but the metaphors become reified in visual devices. Certain
of the visual devices become central to 'reading a cartoon's meaning'. These might be
termed *key signifiers*, the most imperative symbols, those which draw the attention of the
reader above other things. Their reading might be isolated or cumulative, inter-textual or
multi-generational but it is dependent on the public recognizability of stereotypes which
are amplified and resonant within and/or across contexts. Such signs have a public history
— a particular chronology, which is, at one and the same time, public in cultural terms
and private in terms of the personal text-resource of the reader. However, these need not
be the same. There is a resonance *not* a correspondence. Thus, a cartoon is a sign system
iconically representing a conjunction of strands of meaning in a pithy synthesis. These
strands of meaning, which might be termed narrative threads, depict, represent and comment upon the events, values, influences and personalities which define 'social reality'.
Narrative threads . . .

> . . . are essentially mythic in nature conforming to what Barthes (1972) describes as
> 'modern myths'. A myth is the message held within a system of communication.
> It is a system of values read as if it were a system of facts. (op. cit., p. 308)

Content and the Public Context

The cartoon above is an example of work produced to coincide with, resonate with, and
comment upon specific educational events, in this case the publication of league tables
each November. Certain educational events such as this are fixed in time each year and
represent an Educational Calendar. The publication of School Performance Tables in
November is only one such event. Other examples might be the publication of A-Level
and GCSE results in August; the publication of the Annual Report of the Chief Inspector
of Schools in February and the teacher union conferences in April. As well as these
examples, there are a whole range of fixed events which prompt educational news to be
reported and commented upon. The newsworthiness of such events is attributed by their
applicability and relevance to a large section of the population — a series of specific publics
(Herbst, 1993) The messages — the ideas, themes, issues, standpoints, perspectives and

values they communicate are also relevant in the same way. Other depictions concerning education may not relate to moments arising from key dates in the education calendar but may instead feature key figures and their actions or policy pronouncements that they make. Official reports and other 'official channels', particularly press notices are key sources of both content and inspiration for educational stories and debate. In 1996, for example, the Department for Education and Employment (DfEE) released over 350 press notices. These are sent directly to journalists by arrangement and are available over the internet. Other government agencies such as the Office for Standards in Education (Ofsted) and the Schools Curriculum Assessment Authority (SCAA) release fewer but these are still none-the-less significant. Politicians, political parties and parliament in general are other signific-ant sources of material for cartoonists and journalists when depicting narratives relevant to education. Education policy is rooted in party politics and the work of parliament in the UK as elsewhere. Individual personalities and the choices of key players — the 'shakers and movers' — personal foibles, peccadilloes and public gaffes are metaphorical 'meat and drink' to editors, leader-writers, journalists and cartoonists.

Thus, cartoons are understood to be part of a communications system. This system has a form, or more precisely a number of forms, peculiar to it, namely newspapers and the print media generally. Meaning is signified through, amongst other things, headlines; subheadings; texts; cartoons; photographs and diagrams. The preceding elements, it can be argued, might also be viewed as key signifiers. Other elements are also important in signifying meaning and include such things as 'by-lines' and other indications of author-ship; layout — the exact placing on a page; format — positioning within the structure of a newspaper; size and prominence of text or other element and, the juxtaposition of related articles and other elements designed to facilitate the continuation of a particular narrative thread throughout a single edition of a newspaper. In turn, this communication system (one edition of one newspaper) is one part of a series of other similar commun-ication systems (a range of different newspapers) that form the press. In total these form an aggregate inter-textual communication system across newspapers and similarly are part of the wider media in general. Journalists use the entire media as a resource. It can be argued that the media, of which the press is a major contributor, is *the* common ground for educational debate.

The press provides public forms of discourse. Public discourse as opposed to private is important as it forms 'part of the public dialectical process of consent and contestation which has influence on policy formation' (Warburton and Saunders, 1996, p. 322). Char-acterizing the national press as a site for the display of public narrative is that, when taken as a whole, it is dialogic in nature. Narratives from different print and media sources repeat and coalesce becoming inter-textual; some become dominant and achieve resonance; some are expressed in stereotypical terms that are multi-generational and are diachronic; others are synchronic, in other words of the moment. This then is the cultural setting in which dialogue via narrative takes place. Cartoons are an iconic pithy synthesis of public narratives which represent the key points of this dialogue.

Methodology

Deciding how to 'treat' cartoons as visual data and, in turn, finding something useful, informative and instructive to say about them is one key element essential for a meth-odology to address. A second key element relates to the use to which such a synthesis is to be put. However, these are the fundamental issues to concern all using mediated visual images for research purposes. Hopefully, the methodology outlined below will contribute to the debate.

The first stage in the methodology for handling the visual material, a cartoon, in order to make an interpretation as to what an image counts for, what it communicates, is to synthesize a description which in effect makes an inventory of the actual visual and textual devices depicted. In simple terms the first act is to describe what one sees and to make a judgment about what counts as a signifier and particularly a key signifier. Thus, 'denotive references are taken from the visual and textual material contained within the cartoon "sign"' (Warburton and Saunders, 1996, p. 307). The second stage entails attempting to 'confirm' strands of meaning carried by signifiers denoted in the cartoon by identifying where 'messages' are duplicated in supporting text of different forms. These different forms might be headlines, subheadings, the text of reports, leader-columns and the like. Besides the message being duplicated, the supporting text will also supplement and amplify the message indicating possible connotations — implied meanings. This forms a range of possible 'signifieds'. Third, a similar process is undertaken across a range of newspapers for relevant and resonant material, recognizing the characteristic public dialogue that this form of communication system produces. Finally, the preceding stages allow for the construction of a series of 'narrative threads'. 'These are essentially mythic in nature conforming to what Barthes (1972) describes as "modern myths"' (1996, p. 308). An exemplar for this methodology follows to illustrate and operationalize this sequence.

Stage 1: Initial Description

The cartoon shown in Figure 16.2 was published on the front page of the *Guardian* on Thursday 14 October 1976. It presages the Ruskin College speech made by the Prime Minister, James Callaghan on Monday 19 October (*Guardian*, 14 October, 1976, p. 1). The cartoon shows a busy street running alongside a school. Coming out of the school, in the left foreground, is a teacher leading a line of school children. Confronting the teacher, stopping him dead in his tracks, is a school crossing patrolman in the guise of Mr Callaghan. He bars the way to the zebra crossing towards which the pupils are heading. Questioning the teacher, the PM says 'And what, may I ask, is wrong with walking the same way as the traffic?' This appears as the caption of the cartoon. Travelling down the road by the school are two heavy lorries. They move swiftly towards a group of factories in the distance, over which the words 'Industrial Needs' are placed, in the centre of the cartoon between the two men, the teacher and the Prime Minister.

Stage 2: Immediate Connotation

Headlines point the way to connotive interpretations. Next to the cartoon itself a headline reads 'Eagle eye put on schools'. The accompanying article reports the fears of ministers that 'standards are dropping', referring to plans to monitor standards as a 'multi-million pound emergency programme'. Public support is being gained for such measures, generated by 'people such as Dr Rhodes Boyson (ibid.).

Terry Warburton

Figure 16.2

'And what, may I ask, is wrong with walking the same way as the traffic?'

Of the speech to be made at Ruskin College, Oxford, the article says that:

The statement will call for a major change in educational thinking, stricter standards in schools, more attention to be paid to the training of Scientists and Tech-
nologists, and the creation of a basic national 'core curriculum' for schools. (ibid.)

The *Yellow Book* (supposedly named thus because of the colour of its cover) is cited
as the template for the content of the speech. Disclosure of the existence of the memorandum, prepared by DES officials as a briefing paper for the Prime Minister, the article
relates, was highlighted the previous day in the *Guardian*. Under the front page headline
'State "must step into Schools"', David Hencke reports 'a radical departure from an
educational tradition of 100 years'. Of the memorandum he says:

Its 63 pages constitutes a severe indictment of the failure of secondary schools to
produce enough scientists and engineers and the memorandum calls for drastic
measures to change the attitude of children entering schools and for much tighter
control by inspectors of the education system. (*Guardian*, 13 October, 1976,
p. 1)

Quoting the document as warning that 'in the face of hard irreducible economic
factors', the major thrust of the argument in the *Yellow Book* is that the 'time may be ripe
for major changes in the curriculum . . .' ending the traditional 'rights' of teacher control.
Teaching methods in both primary and secondary schools come under fire, described as
becoming 'too easy going and demanding too little work'. Schools permitting pupil
choice of subjects at 13 or 14 years of age, it continues, have resulted in

'unbalanced or not particularly profitable curricula' or of pupils opting in numbers 'insufficient for the country's needs for scientific or technical subjects. (ibid.)

Indeed, it goes on:

Some schools may have over-emphasised the importance of preparing boys and girls for their roles in society compared with the need to prepare them for their economic role. (ibid.)

Teachers 'not able to cope with modern methods', it argues, contribute to falling standards. A return to more formal methods is put forward as being necessary to 'correct the balance'. Other measures designed to ameliorate the position are examination reform; reconstructed teacher training; enhanced powers for inspectors and an extension of vocational training in schools and colleges.

Stage 3: Systemic Connotation

On the same day (13 October, 1976) the *Sun* reports a story from a complementary angle of approach, illustrating the nature of the dialogue in press narratives. Under the headline 'Battle of the Third "R"' and the subheading '"Thousands of pupils cannot add, subtract or multiply"', John Hill relates that mathematics is being 'squeezed out' of the curriculum in order to make room for more novel subjects. The report states that

Instead of being boosted to meet the complex demands of the modern technical age, arithmetic — and mathematics as a whole — is being challenged for its place in classroom timetables by new subjects like community studies. (Sun, 13 October, 1976, p. 7)

Citing Professor William Bonner, head of mathematics at London University's Queen Elizabeth College, who had 'just resigned from the governing body of a comprehensive school because of conflicting views on the issue', as condemning the 'all-in concentration on non-academic and "social" subjects as "bosh"', the report goes on to argue that a lot of children would 'benefit from a traditional education'. Continuing it argues that maths, physics and chemistry 'are the very subjects necessary for any sort of technical work'. Thus, portrayed as a 'row' over the 'Third R' and set against a 'background of deep concern', support is cited as coming from the Engineering Industry Training Board who respond that 'Thousands of youngsters coming into apprenticeships simply cannot add, subtract or multiply'. Similarly, Ruth Bradbury of the National Education Association, representing parents and teachers is reported as saying

There is no doubt mathematics is being pushed aside in schools — with the result that for example girls applying to join banks are scarcely up to operating a shop till.

The reason is that pupils have been given soft options in what subjects they have taken at school. (ibid.)

Two Sundays earlier, on 3 October the *Sunday Times* carried an article under the title 'The flight from the factory floor' which highlights industry's difficulties in finding 'both junior apprentices and already-skilled workers for the manufacturing sector'. Suggesting that apprenticeship was 'unattractive' to young people leaving school, it argued that the reason was, at least in part, because careers advisers, in school or elsewhere, failed to make this type of work seem 'desirable' (*Sunday Times*, 3 October, 1976, p. 16).

This cartoon then draws the focus of attention to the confrontation between the government, represented by Mr Callaghan and the teaching profession represented by a teacher, over meeting the needs of industry, implying that teachers are failing to do so intentionally. Synthesizing and amplifying cultural narrative the cartoon relies on the symbolic juxtaposition of signifiers for the teaching profession; children; the school; the government; industry and the textual signifiers given in the caption and that emblazoned in the centre of the cartoon itself. The visual metaphor of the school crossing patrolman, which again reifies notions concerning the 'guardianship' of government within society, is also notable. This is an interesting process which has been touched upon several times throughout this paper. An actual image or event at 'reading', and/or as it acquires a 'public life', is de-reified, de-contextualized and transformed into metaphorical speech as part of the process of transferring denoted references into connoted codes. As a figure of speech it has both 'use' and 'transfer' value for communication purposes. But in some forms, for example a device such as a cartoon, it is re-reified — it gains an 'after-life' but it is also transformed into a state of resonance rather than correspondence. Then because it is both reified and public the process repeats. Yet this is also a further abstraction. Thus, a state of resonance has the characteristic of being a meta-abstraction which is essentially the nature of the 'modern myth'. Elizabeth Chaplin (1994) describes the process in this way

> 'Representation' is a complex term ... it implies that images and texts ... do not reflect their sources but refashion them according to pictorial or textual codes, so that they are quite separate from, other than, those sources. (Chaplin, 1994, p. 1)

Stage 4: Establishing Narrative Threads

In summary, the visual depiction begins as a common basis for the construction of meaning. Secondly, the headline 'Eagle eye put on schools' adds another layer of meaning. Thirdly, the headline 'State "must step into schools"', from the previous day's *Guardian* adds a further layer. The focus becomes narrowed, centring on curriculum content with the headline 'Battle for the Third "R"' appearing in the *Sun* on 13 October with its subheading '"Thousands of pupils cannot add, subtract or multiply"' indicating that pupils are not achieving the required standards. Supplementing this the *Sunday Times* on 3 October, provides the headline 'The flight from the factory floor'. Finally, the text of the respective reports themselves clearly indicate the perceived deficiencies of informal teaching methods linking this to declining standards. Narrative threads, structured in respect of the messages synthesised in this cartoon and confirmed in its supporting and complementary texts, forming a public dialogue can be described as follows.

- There is a confrontation between the government and teachers.
- It is about standards and meeting the needs of industry.
- This is because teachers are not teaching subjects that pupils, industry and the country needs.
- New 'social' subjects have replaced traditional subjects like maths.
- New subjects are associated with 'progressive' philosophy.
- These subjects are 'bosh'.
- Consequently pupil standards of achievement are low.
- This is the fault of teachers — particularly 'trendy' teachers.
- The State must take control (of the curriculum).

Narrative threads thus represent connoted content.

Conclusion

This chapter has been concerned with how political cartoons are used to depict narratives about education in the UK press. Political cartoons which portray educational matters, their nature, content and role, tell us about the ways teachers; teaching; issues; themes; key figures and moments concerned with education policy and practice are understood and valued publicly. They are extant evidence of public discourse about education in its wider social and cultural contexts. As Hartley states, such pictures are 'neither scientific data nor historical documents but they are, literally 'forensic evidence' (1992, p. 29). Harold Silver (1992), has argued that 'so far as mass schooling is concerned, there is no social history of the classroom'. However, political cartoons, as they are treated above, are evidence which can be used to reconstruct a social history of education as it is represented in public discourse. Such visual images reify the stereotypical narratives we all use to discuss education as a social phenomenon with each other. As such these artefacts are important in themselves and worthy of consideration.

In using such mediated visual images, for that is what they are, as data for research purposes, certain important points of procedure need to be agreed on and fixed. First, it can be argued that finding a consistent way to describe such an image, discussing its nature, characteristics and describing its status in respect of the context in which it appears is the key starting point. Second, a researcher must also pay attention to how such data might be treated or handled and how it is to be used as part of the research. Not only should they receive attention but the process should also be made explicit. The methodology described above attempts to do this. It allows the focus to centre on the study of press visual and textual material as extant evidence and uses cartoons as both 'topic' and 'resource' (see Ball and Smith, 1992, p. 14). In effect this produces a new synthesis which reconstructs and reifies the public narratives which represent attitudes and values about education which are culturally resonant. Thus, this methodology contributes to the process of recording social history.

References

BALL, M. and SMITH, G. (1992) *Analysing Visual Data*, London: Sage.
BARTHES, R. (1964) *Elements of Semiology*, New York: The Noonday Press.

BARTHES, R. (1972) *Mythologies*, London: Jonathan Cape.

CHAPLIN, E. (1994) *Sociology and Visual Representation*, London: Routledge.

GOFFMAN, E. (1976) *Gender Advertisements*, London: MacMillan Press Ltd.

HALL, S. (1973) 'The determination of news photographs', in COHEN, S. and YOUNG, J. (eds) *The Manufacture of News*, London: Methuen.

HARTLEY, J. (1992) *The Politics of Pictures: The Creation of the Public in the Age of Popular Media*, New York: Routledge.

HERBST, S. (1993) 'The meaning of public opinion: Citizen's construction of political reality', *Media, Culture and Society*, **15**, pp. 437–54.

KRESS, G. and VAN LEEUWEN, T. (1996) *Reading Images: The Grammar of Visual Design*, London: Routledge.

SILVER, H. (1992) 'Knowing and not knowing in the history of education', *History of Education*, **21**, 1, pp. 97–108.

WARBURTON, T. and SAUNDERS, M. (1996) 'Representing teachers' professional culture through cartoons', *British Journal of Educational Studies*, **44**, 3, pp. 307–25.

WEBER, S. and MITCHELL, C. (1995) *That's Funny, You Don't Look Like a Teacher*, London: Falmer Press.

Chapter 17

Images and Curriculum Development in Health Education

Noreen M. Wetton and Jennifer McWhirter

Abstract

The authors set out the challenge posed by curriculum development in health education for young children. They describe the principles of curriculum development and argue that 'starting where children are' is rarely applied to education in health. They describe what non-sense children can make of images in materials when this principle is overlooked. Finally the authors describe their own research with a novel strategy — 'draw and write' — which is open ended and illuminative, yet which can provide quantitative data. Through 'draw and write' children's own words and illustrations can be used to inform researchers and teachers about the way children perceive and explain health and safety related concepts.

The Challenge

What is the best way to help young children to develop an understanding of abstract concepts of health and well being? What is the best way to devise and develop classroom materials which enable children to explore these difficult concepts? For many children, particularly those in the early years of their schooling, concepts of health, of being and staying healthy and safe, are difficult to grasp. Health and safety, by the very fact that they are described through abstract nouns are seen to be the responsibility of other people, of someone 'out there'. Children see these issues as the concern of parents, teachers, doctors, police officers, crossing patrols in fact anyone except the children themselves (Williams, Wetton and Moon, 1989a, p. 32).

Some aspects of health may cause children to feel vulnerable, may seem full of inconsistencies which are insoluble. On the one hand being adult is the most desirable status, a time when the children will feel they will be able to take control. It is also a time when disease can strike, when apparently attractive adult behaviours such as smoking and drinking alcohol lead to illness and death.

Faced with these *challenges* what kinds of teaching materials are available to help children acquire the skills and knowledge to be and stay healthy? If we examine many examples of curriculum materials for the youngest children in our schools, we might be led to think that the best starting point is to conjure up a cartoon character to embody the concept or function being taught. The younger the children for whom the materials are being written, the more likely this is to happen.

Health-related concepts are recognised as difficult to communicate to children so writers of materials search for analogies, often image-based, which will amuse and educate the children. The purpose of the analogy is to help the child to internalize the abstract concept, by turning it into a character with whom the children will empathize. In this chapter we dispute this approach and suggest an alternative which is derived from the principles of developmental psychology.

If we are to help children have a more positive understanding of health and their role in being and staying healthy, to feel at ease and unthreatened by growing and growing up, we must offer them the kind of curriculum which aids this understanding, illustrated with images which are truthful and reflect the developmental stage of the children (Bruner, 1960).

The Role of Developmental Psychology

The principles of child-centred education are well known. Children are not empty vessels to be filled with knowledge and understanding by the teacher. Children come to their education with their own unique explanations for the world in which they have lived successfully for the last four or five years. As they encounter new information they constantly construct and reconstruct new meaning.

According to Piaget (1970) knowledge consists:

> neither of a simple copy of external objects, nor a mere unfolding of structures pre-formed inside the subject, but rather . . . a set of structures progressively constructed by continuous interaction between the subject and the world. (Piaget, 1970)

Piaget also demonstrated how children learn, through assimilation of new information into existing constructs, or if the dissonance between the old construct and the new information is sufficient, by accommodating the old and the new information into a new construct (Piaget and Inhelder, 1958).

Bruner (1960) emphasized the importance of truth when teaching. He proposed that 'any subject can be taught effectively in an intellectually honest form to any child at any stage of development'. As Bruner recognized this requires the teacher or curriculum developer to be 'courteous enough to translate material into [a child's] logical form' and for 'instruction to begin as intellectually honestly and as early as possible in a manner consistent with the child's forms of thought'.

Bruner also emphasized the importance of research to discover how children's ideas are constructed before building a spiral curriculum.

Although these principles of:

- starting where children are;
- offering honest, relevant and appropriate information;
- providing a spiral curriculum which revisits topics in increasingly demanding ways, with more specific language as the child matures; and
- maintaining a positive approach

are well known, those who develop curriculum materials for young children don't always apply these principles to health education. In particular authors of curriculum materials in health education fail to 'start where children are' in terms of the information, the language and the images they offer to children. Perhaps some suppose that young children's understanding of health-related concepts is non-existent or so immature that it is not a productive starting point. Others may recognize that it is important to tap into children's perceptions and knowledge, but are unaware how to go about this in a valid and rigorous way.

The major techniques which appear to be available to researchers in this field, such as observation, and one to one structured interviews are time consuming to conduct and analyze. They are also open to the criticism that the findings may not be easily applied in a class of thirty or more children. Perhaps the answer is to use a simplified form of questionnaire.

Questionnaires do not readily provide insights into children's changing perceptions. They fail to tap into the children's own images and the language the children themselves use. Rather, they provide answers to questions which *adults* have posed in *adult* language with predetermined answers in language which *adults* have chosen.

Children who:

- have not yet mastered reading and writing;
- have difficulty with comprehension;
- have difficulty retaining several responses in mind whilst selecting the most appropriate;
- have a home language which is not the language of the questionnaire (English in our case); and
- have special educational needs

are not able to participate in questionnaire type research strategies.

Yet if we don't start with the understanding which children bring to their learning, the language they use to communicate their understanding and the images they themselves draw, we shall be guilty of making some very serious mistakes. We might believe that children are interpreting our images in the way that we intended, when actually they are making a very different interpretation.

The Importance of 'Starting Where Children Are'

Figure 17.1a shows an example of classroom material produced for the dental health education of children aged 4–7, which illustrates some of the pitfalls of the cartoonists' approach to educational materials. The key messages contained within these materials were:

- the importance of children brushing their teeth to prevent decay and plaque; and
- recognizing the dangers of sugar.

The materials included images of animated toothbrushes, toothpaste tubes and teeth. The concepts of decay, plaque and the seductive nature of sugar were portrayed as cartoon characters who were the central figures in a story (Wetton, 1987).

Noreen M. Wetton and Jennifer McWhirter

Figure 17.1a

Suzy Sugar

Try to avoid her

Children have little or no difficulty in understanding inanimate objects — toothbrushes, toothpaste tubes, which have hands and faces, or with teddy bears and trains which talk. They have grown up with these images in picture story books, on television (particularly in advertising). They know that this is fantasy (and may dismiss the character's message because of this). They have everyday proof that toothbrushes do not run around or talk. When a novel, abstract concept is presented this way, they have more difficulty, since there is no every day reality to which to refer for confirmation.

Our research with 244 children who had used this dental health material in their schools revealed how they perceived these images and those of the other characters in the story. The characters appeared to the children to fall into two distinct groups — 'goodies' who had smiling faces and 'baddies' who had ugly, frightening faces. According to the children's interpretation, all goodies gave the same message 'Clean your teeth', while the baddies' message was 'Don't clean your teeth'.

Pretty, smiling Suzy Sugar, shown in Figure 17.1a, representing how sugar is attractive, but bad for teeth, was seen as a 'goodie'. Her main messages, in keeping with her image, had to be positive — 'Clean your teeth'. Secondary messages included 'eat lollipops', which is somewhat contradictory.

When asked why Suzy had one eye closed (a seductive wink) the children responded by overriding the dental health context and replied with reference to their own personal experiences. They deducted that Suzy must have something in her eye — most likely shampoo, possibly the lollipop stick! When questioned further it became apparent that the children were particularly confused by Suzy's provocative hand on the check. The children thought that this meant Suzy had toothache — in conflict with her main message of 'brush your teeth'. And experience told the children that the cross-legged pose meant Suzy needed to go to the toilet in a hurry!

In order to make sense of Suzy's image the children had attempted to assimilate the information about her into their understanding that images of smiling people suggest goodness and kindness. Conflicting information, such as the wink, was dismissed because it could not be assimilated or because it fitted another construct unrelated to dental health. There was not enough information available to help the children accommodate both the old and the new information into a new construction. Rather, they made their own liveable with sense out of the image. To the image maker this would have been nonsense. To us this is only 'non-sense'. Suzy Sugar's value is not in its contribution to dental health education, but in the way her image demonstrates the remarkable skill which children have of constructing sense out of a confusing world.

If the image maker had started where the children were, it would have been possible to discover how much the children actually understood about the seductive nature of sweet foods and the effect on their teeth. As a follow up to this research, 300 children aged 4–11 were given a verbal description of the character and motivation of Suzy Sugar — and asked to draw a picture of her. They were told that Suzy Sugar looked very pretty, but wanted children to eat a lot of sweet things which were very bad for their teeth.

Not one child drew anything even remotely resembling the provocative Suzy of the original materials. The warnings in their pictures were explicit and unambiguous. The characteristics of sweetness were conveyed through imagery soaked in childhood conventions. The dress worn by their character was prettily patterned or beribboned, with matching hair ribbons or hats (see Figures 17.1b, c, d). But every child from 4 years upwards drew Suzy with an ugly black mouth. Interestingly, the task proved more difficult for children in the older age groups who attempted to portray the contradictory

Figure 17.1b

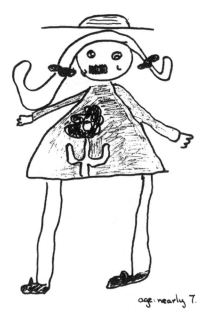

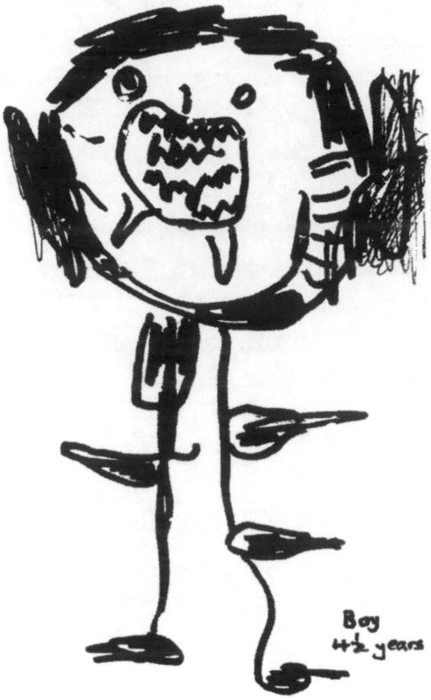
Boy
4½ years

Figure 17.1c

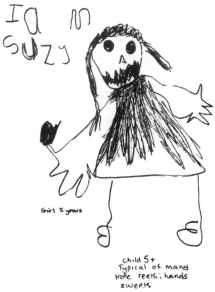

I am
Suzy
Girl 5 years
Child 5+
Typical of many
Note teeth, hands
sweets

Figure 17.1d

age: nearly 7.

nature of Suzy's character by drawing two almost identical people, one smiling and one with an ugly mouth. Whatever way the children used to represent Suzy, there was absolutely no ambiguity in their images. There were no hidden concepts as in the original material.

We question whether the original Suzy Sugar comes within Bruner's definition of intellectual honesty. We believe, like Bruner, that children are entitled to the truth, providing that the information, language and images are appropriate for the age and developmental stage of the child. How then, can we best avoid the pitfalls of presenting images to children which are at best misleading and at worst dishonest?

Using the Images Children Draw

One answer to this is to ask children to draw images which depict their ideas about a specific aspect of their world. Williams, Wetton and Moon (1989a, p. 84) published images drawn by children to illustrate a 'story' about a person who had dropped a bag of drugs. To most children of 7 years or over, such people were either easily identifiable baddies: male, bearded, with scars, eye patches and sad or angry faces, or teenage punks with multiple ear piercing. Few children over the age of 8 years perceived drugs as legal substances which might have had a legitimate use or owner (see Figure 17.2).

It is important to note that children's images consist of a mixture of stereotypes and drawing conventions. Children know that women are not triangular (Figure 17.1d) and that all houses are not detached with chimneys which smoke, but they use these images as a short hand for the concept of woman or home. Stereotypes are more persistent — and more worrying. Many children believe it is possible to recognize a bad person by their appearance. This is a cognitive trap into which both children and adults fall.

One approach to curriculum development, then, is to ask children of different ages to carry out a relevant drawing task without prior discussion or consultation. The results of this will reveal a spiral of children's changing perceptions. In the following examples, children were asked to imagine they could take their skin off and to draw or paint a picture of what was inside them. Figure 17.3 shows three examples of children's images (Williams Wetton and Moon, 1989b, p. 9). From these images it would be possible for a teacher to decide when it would be appropriate or inappropriate to teach about the circulation of blood, the digestion of food and the intricacies of the skeleton. The teacher would also be in a good position to recognize appropriate images to present to children on these topics.

This approach has many strengths, in terms of curriculum research:

- Children's-drawings can provide a personal, relevant starting point for a one to one semi-structured interview or focus groups to explore a deeper understanding. Childrens' responses can be recorded on the paper as they describe their images;
- The children can repeat the task at a later date and child and teacher can evaluate their personal progress (see Figure 17.3b);
- Children's images can be used to illustrate curriculum materials providing teachers with a realistic view of how children respond to such tasks; and
- The tasks are quick and cheap to administer and provide instant feedback for the teacher.

There are also some limitations. The more complex the concept the children are asked to draw, the more ambiguous the meaning can become. Wakefield and Underwager

Figure 17.2

<u>Who do you think lost it?</u>

10 year olds

a punk
rocker

This man is a drug Steala
he stole the drugs &
di dnt notice them fall

Figure 17.3a

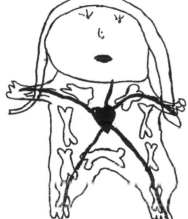

Figure 17.3b1

Figure 17.3b2

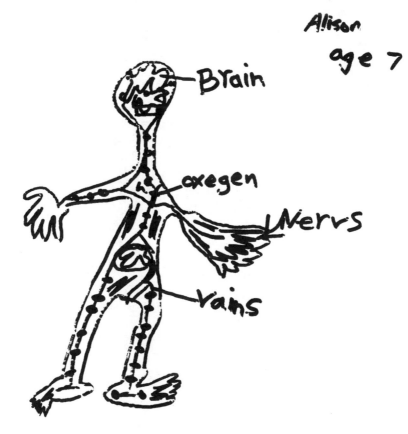

(earlier in this book) underline the dangers of over interpretation of meaning from children's images. The analysis of childrens' drawings is always subjective and has been criticized on these grounds.

It was with the knowledge that children were able to understand and illustrate quite abstract concepts, but with the recognition of the limitations of interpretation of their pictures that a new approach to curriculum development was devised.

The Draw and Write Technique

For an assignment as part of a master's degree in curriculum development at Nottingham University, Noreen Wetton (1972) described her action research approach to promote the development of the language of children's emotions. The project consisted of three phases. In the first phase student teachers presented a short dramatic story in mime to a class of 7–8-year-old children. Following this the children were asked to draw the two main characters at key moments of the story. The children were then invited to write around each picture words to describe the character's feelings. Children who felt unable or unwilling to write for themselves were able to call on a student to act as a scribe.

The words the children had used were analyzed and compared with their pictures. It was the ability of the children to capture feelings in pictures while lacking an equally expressive written, or (as shown by later interview) spoken language, which moved the project into its final stage. Some of the commonest words the children used were mad, bad, sad and silly. The pictures and words provided a starting point for one-to-one semi-structured interviews in which the children were asked to explain more fully the emotions behind the words they had used:

- mad like you want to explode;
- bad like when you know you shouldn't have done it;
- sad like when no-one believes you   and you *are* telling the truth; and
- silly when you know you have been rumbled.

It became apparent that the children experienced and empathized with a wide range of emotions including anger, frustration, despair, remorse, guilt, embarrassment and relief as well as delight, enjoyment, excitement. The children differed only from adults in that they did not have the vocabulary to express themselves.

One of the features of the 'draw and write' strategy, as it later became known, was that the emerging data could be quantified. It was the quantitative description which demonstrated the pervasive poverty of the children's language. These critical data enabled the writing of a programme of classroom activities for the teachers to use to develop the children's language of feelings. (The importance of emotional literacy has recently been brought to prominence again by the publication of Emotional Intelligence by Daniel Goleman, 1995.)

The 'draw and write' technique may have remained as an interesting but undeveloped strategy but for the launch in 1983 of a new Primary School health education curriculum project. The brief for this project was open and comprehensive. It was to research and develop flexible guidelines for primary schools which took account of current issues and concerns in health, including sexuality, child abuse and drugs.

Using 'Draw and Write' to Investigate Health-related Issues with Children

Research was to be carried out in England, Wales and Northern Ireland with 22,600 children, 9,600 of whom were 8 years old or under and 900 of whom were under 5 years old. Pupils of 9 years and above were considered to be able to respond to a questionnaire. A research strategy was sought through which the spiral of children's changing perceptions of health-related behaviours could be identified.

It was necessary that the strategy did not rule out any children through lack of reading or writing skills, nor because English was not the home language. It had to be non-threatening for teachers, governors and parents. The protocol had to seem like an everyday classroom activity but be sophisticated enough to answer meaningful research questions. The research instructions had to be practical enough for the usual classroom teacher to act as researcher while working with the whole class. The task carried out by the pupils had to meet research standards of validity and reliability. Finally, the responses had to be capable of providing both qualitative and quantitative data.

The earlier work by Wetton into the language of children's emotions provided the starting point for devising the 'draw and write' strategy which was used (Williams, Wetton and Moon, 1989b, pp. 65–9).

In the study, which led finally to the publication of a primary school health education programme: Health for Life 1 and 2 (Williams, Wetton and Moon, 1989c,d), children were asked to:

- think about and then to draw themselves doing all the things they did to make themselves healthy and keep themselves healthy; and
- write at the side of each picture what it was that they were doing.

Extra adults were available to act as scribes for those children who felt they needed them. It was emphasized to the children that 'I don't know' was a valid response.

Because only the written words were analysed there was little ambiguity in understanding the children's meaning (as long as you could read their creative spellings!) Where the meaning of the words was unclear, however, the images often provided clarification (see Figure 17.4)!

From this research (Williams, Wetton and Moon, 1989c, p. 24) were able to draw up a scope and sequence chart which described the spiral of changing perceptions of children aged 4–11 of health related behaviour (Figure 17.5).

One observation which can be drawn from the pictures alone was that, for children, health is not limited to physical aspects but includes mental and emotional health. The majority of the pictures showed smiling people (Figure 17.6). Those images where the people were not smiling carried written health warnings such as don't smoke, don't take drugs or beware out of date food.

This negative response to a positive invitation emerged to a greater and greater extent as the research was replicated with pupils aged 7 and over (see Figure 17.7).

The study revealed that primary school aged children knew much more about healthy lifestyles than the researchers expected. Although food and exercise were the largest categories of response, children stressed the social aspects of being healthy — having a home, having a family and friends, playing and working hard, as well as environmental health.

Figure 17.4

At age 8–9 years a significant change occurred in the nature of the children's responses. Children of this age seemed more able to generalize about aspects of health, as revealed by their use of more collective and more abstract nouns (see Figure 17.7). The pictures and words revealed many of the sources of their knowledge and misunderstandings. Characters and situations from current TV programmes were evident (Figure 17.8).

Indeed, the influence of TV may have helped to eliminate geographical and social differences. The results from schools from different geographical or socio-economic settings, or with different ways of organizing their teaching, were remarkably similar. The pictures also revealed a wide range of style and drawing ability. The images drawn by the children were a major contribution to the success of the teaching materials.

Figure 17.5   A spiral of children's changing perceptions of health lifestlyes

10 - 11   We have to deal with   10 - 11

- greater freedom
- greater peer support and interaction
- more rules
- more 'do's' and 'don'ts'

Our view of healthy lifestyles continues to widen. We are more aware of the value of medication but see drugs as a hazard. We are beginning to understand the need for regular exercise but some of us see it in terms of

- power
- strength
- achievement

Some of us link it with looking good. A healthy lifestyle is as much to do with 'don'ts' as 'do's'.

8 - 9   Our view of health is widening. We are beginning to understand how exercise and food affects our bodies and how we look and feel. Some of us see exercise more in terms of fitness, some of us are more aware of the importance of food. We are beginning to see why adults emphasise hygiene and sleep. Being with our friends is of growing importance. With growing independence comes a list of 'do's' and 'don'ts'. We are confused about the gap between what people say and what they do. Food and exercise for some of us is much more to do with how we look, for others, exercise means games and being fit and food is part of this.   8 - 9

6 - 7   More of us know what is meant by 'being healthy'. We think a healthy lifestyle involves   6 - 7

- exercise and food
- play
- good relationships
- work

We're starting to realise

- healthcare
- hygiene
- fresh air

are important.

4 - 5   We don't all know what being healthy means but we think being healthy is being happy, being loved, and being with family We think healthy people (including us) keep healthy with   4 - 5

- food
- exercise
- play

276

Figure 17.6

Above all the children's words and images revealed the wealth of the children's knowledge. In trying to pin down the essence of being healthy in pictures and a few words, the children revealed the sense they had woven from a multitude of sources. Sometimes the meaning was non-sense, when conflicting information had been forced to fit pre-existing constructs with which the children were comfortable. More usually it matched or went beyond narrow, adult, medical constructions of the meaning of health.

From the words and pictures together it was possible to:

- tease out a stage by stage developmental spiral of children's changing perceptions of being healthy and staying healthy;

Figure 17.8

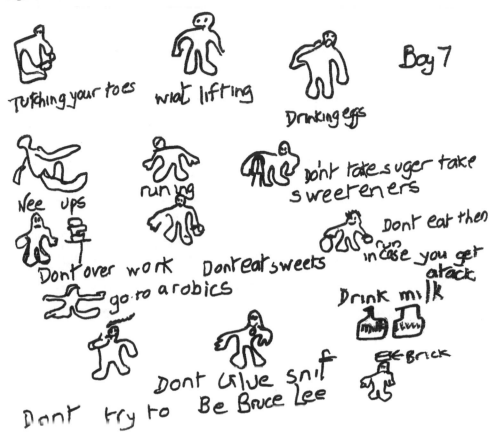

Tuthing your toes   wiat lifting

Drinking eggs

Boy 7

Nee ups

run yng

don't take suger take sweeteners

Dont over work   Dont eat sweets

Dont eat then run incase you get atack

go.to arobics

Drink milk

Dont try to   Dont give snif   Be Bruce Lee

Brick

Dont tri copying Film stars and saying I can jump off a Bus like supergran.

- determine, within the spiral, the critical ages at which important conceptual change occurred;
- detect signals which suggested readiness to make conceptual leaps; and
- recognize stages in the development of children's drawing conventions and stereotypes and the development of corresponding vocabulary.

The whole school planning programme Health for Life 1 which resulted from these data reflected the philosophy behind the research. Many of the lesson plans began by asking the children to draw and write or draw and talk about their drawings. The activities were trialed in classrooms and the materials illustrated with children's own images. Teachers recognized drawing and writing as a valuable and meaningful starting point from which to develop their health education programme.

Establishing Draw and Write as a Valid and Reliable Research Tool

Since the original research programme, the draw and write technique has been used by the authors and by other researchers to discover how children perceive and explain a wide range of health-related issues. The purpose of these studies has included curriculum development, needs analysis, market research, and educational evaluation.

The original draw and write investigation — 'what makes me healthy and keeps me healthy' has been replicated in Hungary (McWhirter, Wetton and Williams, 1995, unpublished observations), and in the former Yugoslavia (Zivcovic *et al.*, 1994). Many studies using draw and write strategies have been carried out by staff employed by local authorities and health authorities. These were conducted to determine local needs and have guided training for teachers, health professionals and informed budget holders as to priorities for spending. These studies are often published as internal reports. Others have been devised and used by Masters students as examples of action-research (Schratz and Walker, 1995; Hamilton, 1994; Ashwell, 1996).

A comparison of these data with each other or with the original published studies demonstrates the validity of particular draw and write strategies. For example, research into children's perceptions of the world of drugs (Williams, Wetton and Moon, 1989a) has been replicated many times in different parts of the UK, and in Australia with similar findings. In these studies pupils were invited to illustrate a story about a child who was walking home from school one day. On her way she found a bag of drugs. The children were first invited to draw the bag and what was in it. (Some of the youngest children drew jugs, but older children drew packets of white powder, labelled herring, so this research is fondly known as Jugs and Herrings.) Children were then asked to draw a picture and to write about the person who had dropped the bag (see earlier in this chapter). Next, children were invited to draw and write about what the person who dropped the bag was going to do with the drugs, and then what the child in the story would do. Finally children were asked to draw and write about what they themselves would do if they found the bag of drugs.

Copies of unpublished data available to the authors of this article collected since 1989 and a study by Collins and described by Schratz and Walker (1995), reveal many consistencies in the children's perceptions. The names of the current drugs have changed with time, but stereotyping of someone who dropped the bag as a recognizable baddy persists. Also reproduced in these studies are the ages at which children begin to perceive 'drugs' as illegal substances, and the ages at which this is universally understood.

Other studies (Box and Landman, 1994) have demonstrated the usefulness of a draw and write approach, when compared with other more established techniques. The data emerging from interviews with children about what they ate for breakfast, could be matched by a draw and write approach, with the advantages that the questions asked were not immediately overtly about breakfast; the data did not have to be transcribed before they could be analyzed; the task appeared to the children to be a normal classroom activity and the responses could readily have been used in curriculum materials, or for follow up work after an intervention.

A number of studies see for example (McWhirter, Collins, Bryant, Wetton and Newton Bishop, 1997; and Mortimer, 1997, both in preparation) have demonstrated the reliability of the analysis of draw and write responses if pilot studies are carried out to refine categories. In these studies a sample of the response sheets were independently re-coded by a second researcher. When the two analyses were compared the coding was found to be identical in this case.

Since Wetton described the first draw and write strategy for investigating children's perceptions of health, some thirty different protocols have been devised. Children's perceptions of puberty (McWhirter, 1993) of risk (McWhirter and Wetton) of cigarette smoking (Porcellato *et al.*, 1996) of the effects of sun on skin (Wetton and Collins, 1993; Hughes *et al.*, 1996) and numerous other health related issues have been researched using draw and write techniques.

The drafting of these different health-related draw and write protocols has led to the development of a process model, clarifying the stages through which a researcher would go in order to devise novel 'draw and write' research strategies:

- consultation regarding key questions to which answers were needed;
- development of a research strategy from the questions;
- pilot stage;
- redevelopment of strategy;
- writing specific instructions for the teacher/researcher;
- sample selection;
- analysis;
- reviewing the data;
- dissemination; and
- curriculum development.

Conclusion

Since the first studies were published in 1989, the draw and write technique has emerged as a valuable tool for investigating the perceptions of children in health-related issues. The strategy has many strengths:

- It is practical for use with a target group which has been difficult to consult — young children.
- It is valid and reliable as a research tool.

- It can generate a large amount of data, which can be analyzed both qualitatively and quantitatively.
- It can be administered by teachers acting as researchers.
- It yields information about the development of key concepts in children and can inform the development of a spiral curriculum.
- It can inform policy development.
- It can be used as for educational evaluation.
- It can guide teachers who want to develop or adapt classroom activities for a specific group of children.

Most importantly, we believe, the draw and write strategy demonstrates the language and images which are appropriate for children at different ages and stages of development, enabling teachers and curriculum developers to be truthful, while respecting and being consistent with children's own logical construction of meaning. Curriculum development strategies which start where children are value the children's knowledge and understanding, and the sense they make of the world, providing a firm foundation for constructing more sophisticated meaning in a complex world.

References

ASHWELL, V. (1996) 'I'd catch the horse', MSc thesis. University of Southampton.

BOX, V. and LANDMAN, J. (1994) 'A breakfast survey of primary schools in low income families in inner city areas of Southampton', *Health Education Journal*, **53**, pp. 249–61.

BRUNER, J.S. (1960) 'Readiness for learning', in BRUNER, J.S. and ANGLIN, J. (ed.) (1973) *Beyond the Information Given*, London: George Allen and Unwin.

GOLEMAN, D. (1995) *Emotional Intelligence*, London: Bloomsbury.

HAMILTON, A. (1994) 'The exploratory development of an injury awareness programme for 1–12 year-old children in Southampton', MSc thesis, Southampton University.

HUGHES, B., WETTON, N., COLLINS, M. and NEWTON BISHOP, J. (1996) 'Health education about sun and skin cancer: Language ideas and perceptions of young children', *British Journal of Dermatology*, **134**, pp. 412–17.

MCWHIRTER, J.M. (1993) 'A teenager's view of puberty', *Health Education*, May, pp. 9–11.

MCWHIRTER, J.M., COLLINS, M., BRYANT, I., WETTON, N. and NEWTON BISHOP, J. (1997) 'Evaluation of safe in the sun', A report to EAC: University of Southampton.

MCWHIRTER, J.M. and WETTON, N.M. (1994) 'Children's perceptions of risk', *British Journal of Health and Safety*, **10**, pp. 21–9, Birmingham: British Health and Safety Society.

MCWHIRTER, J.M., WETTON, N.M. and WILLIAMS, T. (1994) 'What makes me healthy, and keeps me healthy: Research in Hungarian elementary schools', Unpublished observations: University of Southampton.

MORTIMER, F. (1997) 'Adult perceptions of risk', MSc Dissertation, in preparation: University of Southampton.

PIAGET, J. (1970) 'Piaget's theory', in MUSSEN, P.H. (ed.) *Manual of Child Psychology*, London: Wiley.

PIAGET, J. and INHELDER, B. (1958) *The Growth of Logical thinking from Childhood to Adolescence*, London: Routledge and Kogan Paul.

PORCELLATO, L., DUGDIL, L., SPRINGETT, J. and SANDERSON, F. (1996) 'Attitudes beliefs and smoking behaviour in Liverpool primary school children: An interim research report', Liverpool Institute for Health: Liverpool John Moores University.

SCHRATZ, M. and WALKER, R. (1995) *Research as Social Change*, London: Routledge.

WETTON, N.M. (1972) Unpublished assignment, Nottingham University.

WETTON, N.M. (1987) 'Dental health perception of young children (5–7 years)', in CAMPBELL, G. *Health Education: Youth and Community*, Brighton: Falmer Press

WETTON, N.M. and COLLINS, M. (1993) 'Children's perceptions of the sun on the skin: The missing link', in *Safe in the Sun*, Dickenson and Pizzala: South East Thames Regional Health Authority.

WILLIAMS, T., WETTON, N.M. and MOON, A. (1989a) *A Way in*, London: Health Education Authority.

WILLIAMS, T., WETTON, N.M. and MOON, A. (1989b) *A Picture of Health*, London: Health Education Authority.

WILLIAMS, T., WETTON, N.M. and MOON, A. (1989c,d) *Health for Life 1 and 2*, Walton on Thames: Thomas Nelson and Sons.

ZIVKOVIC, M., MARINKOVIC, J., LEGETIC, B., PAUNOVIC, P. and VIDANOVIC, A. (1994) 'Evaluation techniques for the healthy school project in Yugoslavia', *Health Promotion International*, **9**, pp. 73–9.

Chapter 18

Making Meanings in Art Worlds:
A Sociological Account of the Career
of John Constable and his Oeuvre, with
Special Reference to 'The Cornfield'
(Homage to Howard Becker)[1]

Elizabeth Chaplin

Abstract

Following Becker, art is work that some people do; and for an art work to appear as it does requires the cooperation of a wide range of participants — which presupposes a situation of relative stability. This essay tests and confirms that set of propositions via an analysis of accounts of the life and work of John Constable. However those accounts show that Constable's reputation, and in particular the meaning and value of 'The Cornfield', have been continually subject to contestation and renegotiation. The essay suggests, therefore, that the domain of Fine Art can equally be seen as a site of cultural struggle in which meanings are never finally fixed.

Introduction

When I was a child, our local library ran a picture-lending scheme. My parents subscribed to it for a while: each month we returned a picture to the library, and took out another. Most of the pictures in the scheme were reproductions of famous paintings. One of these was Constable's 'Cornfield', and I can remember it on the dining room wall; we took it out more than once. I grew up assuming that Constable was a genius, and that 'The Cornfield' was a masterpiece. As a sociologist now, I want to revisit those widely held assumptions, and subsequently to propose a quite different way of thinking about Constable, 'The Cornfield', and the rest of the artist's oeuvre.

In a broad sense, the idea that Constable was a genius who produced a series of masterpieces is part of the Romantic ideology which emphasizes the individual rather than the collective. This ideology has given rise to what Howard Becker has called the folk theory of art.[2] This proposes that the artist is a special kind of individual — but that every now and then there emerges an artist who is extraordinarily gifted: his gifts (and it usually *has* been a 'he') impel or allow him to create works of exceptional beauty and depth which express profound human emotions and cultural values. An implication of this seems to be that the quality of the work — the artist's special gift — is exuded, given off by the work; and the sensitive viewer in front of it will be struck by this quality and recognize the masterpiece for what it is. This way of thinking was deeply ingrained into me. It has also been fostered by British art schools. According to the researches of Madge and Weinberger,[3] fine-art students in the 1960s and 1970s — and probably before and after that period — were educated into being special, one-off, self-reliant. They were encouraged to develop their own 'inner resources', to nurture a hot line to inspiration; and were discouraged from acknowledging social influences. They were educated into a virtual state of anomie. Following this line of thinking, then, the artist Constable, an individual apart, an individual with very special gifts — and many have written that he was a genius — produced a series of masterpieces, one of which is 'The Cornfield'; and by looking at the work, we can see this genius manifested. Indeed, 'The Cornfield' is widely reproduced, as we have seen, so the work *must* be a masterpiece to have been singled out for this treatment. Then, of course, the original hangs in a grand room in a very prestigious art gallery (The National Gallery, London) alongside other famous paintings.[4] All this seems to suggest that the Cornfield image has extraordinary qualities which will become evident to the sensitive, perceptive viewer standing in front of it.

As art world[5] members we may think along these lines, but when we adopt a sociological approach, we find ourselves questioning the Romantic ideology. Sociologists take very seriously the idea of the individual genius producing a masterpiece because it *is* so widespread; and they tend to be interested in how it might have arisen and taken hold. Speaking more generally, though, sociologists regard our culture (using this term in its broadest sense) as an active, ongoing process, in which social relationships are largely directed towards negotiating meanings, especially those of cultural artefacts. As the relations of power between individuals and groups shift, those meanings are subject to contestation and are renegotiated. Meanings are never finally fixed. So, instead of the idea that an artwork gives off a finite meaning or cluster of meanings, sociologists maintain that it is people in unequal but shifting power relationships who create, contest, edit, and are forever recreating those meanings. Of course, relative stability is required for a particular cluster of meanings to become at all widely shared, but within this condition of relative stability there will, nevertheless, be a running series of small changes which constantly nudge at that cluster of meanings — at 'the meaning of the work'.

Methodology

Relative stability and yet change is a theme running through Becker's *Art Worlds*. In this book he proposes that art is the work that some people do, and that all art, like other forms of work, requires the cooperation of a network of participants in order for it to appear as it does. Recently I read C.R. Leslie's *Memoirs of the Life of John Constable*,[6] a near-contemporary account of the artist's life and work, and as I did so I was continually struck by the relevance of that proposition. Now the intention of Leslie's account was, I think, to promote Constable's reputation along the lines of the Romantic ideology; and as Leslie's editor, Jonathan Mayne, remarks in his preface:

> The great authority of Leslie's memoirs arises from the fact that the story is told largely in the subject's [that is Constable's] own words.

Yet Leslie's memoirs actually indicate that in order for the Cornfield — and Constable's other works — to have been made and then preserved for us to see today, a degree of sustained, routine, efficient cooperation was required, during the course of which the meanings and aesthetic value of those works were continually contested and renegotiated. In this article I shall use evidence from Leslie's account, and occasionally from other sources, to show the various types of collective activity which were involved in the production of Constable's work, and their role in creating meanings for the work;[7] and I shall do so according to a number of overlapping themes drawn directly from Becker's *Art Worlds*. Those themes are human and material resources, conventions, patronage and distribution, aesthetic rationale, editing, art and craft, change and reputation. In short: to explore how the meanings of Constable's works get made, and are then contested and renegotiated, I superimpose the template of Becker's themes on Leslie's account (and on one or two other accounts).

Resources

Leslie made Constable's acquaintance in 1817 and became a regular correspondent. He starts by telling us something of the artist's background, and this alerts us to the *human resources* — indeed, the sheer number of named people whose cooperation or lack of it — Constable's art production involved. First of all, there was his father. Though comfortably off (potentially a plus) this Essex miller wanted his second son to go into the Church. When that didn't work out, he determined to make a miller of him, training him at home (a minus). But as a young boy, Constable formed an alliance with the local plumber and glazier who painted in his spare time. Leslie remarks that his early work was done under the plumber's roof and not under the roof of his father. Without the cooperation of this plumber, John Dunthorne, and the encouragement of a master at Dedham Grammar School, and later, the advice of the artist Sir George Beaumont, who had relatives in the vicinity — and was (through an introduction engineered by Constable's mother) impressed with John's pen and ink sketches — without this network of relationships (these human resources) Constable's life would have taken another course. This is not necessarily to say that he wouldn't have become a painter, or even a famous one; just that things would have turned out differently. Numerous people later became part of the division of labour necessary for Constable to produce his paintings as they were produced; people who were part of the support system. Here are just a few named by Leslie. First, Joseph Farington, the so-called dictator of the Royal Academy. According to Leslie, Constable first met Farington in 1798 and he continued thereafter, until the older man's death in 1821, to visit him, for advice and help. For example (says Farington):

> 25 May 1801 — Constable called, and brought a small landscape of his painting. I recommended to him to unite firmness with freedom, and avoid flimsiness.

Much later, Leslie records Constable as saying:[8]

> February 1822 — I have been with my wife to look over Mr Farington's house. I could scarcely believe that I was not to meet the elegant and dignified figure of our departed friend, where I have been so long used to see him, or hear again the wisdom that always attended his advice, which I do indeed miss greatly.

Once more or less established as an artist in London, Constable's art was not popular; that is to say, many art world personnel (i.e., human resources) criticized or merely ignored his work. Leslie tends to play down the adverse criticism according to his own editor; but despite this, we gather that few were instrumental in advancing Constable's career. For example:

> 1814 — So little was Constable's art as yet appreciated that the sale of two of his pictures, this year, must be mentioned as an extraordinary event; a small one exhibited at the British Gallery to Mr Allnutt, and a larger one of a 'Lock' to Mr James Carpenter.

We also learn that Constable did not *wish* to take advantage of some human resources; for example, he was averse to France and the French:

> 22 June 1824 — Had a letter from Paris. Mr Arrowsmith informed me of the safe arrival of my pictures, and how much they were admired; he talks of coming again the end of next month; I shall be ready for him; his letter is flattering, but I have no wish to go to Paris. I hope not to go to Paris as long as I live.

Yet Leslie makes it clear that Constable had a small circle of friends whose continual enthusiasm for his work was vital to him. For example, there was Samuel Strowger, Suffolk farm hand turned soldier in the Life Guards, turned Royal Academy (RA) model and head porter, who was always trying to influence the RA in Constable's favour. But the main patron and promoter of Constable's work and aesthetic ideas was Archdeacon Fisher:

> Fisher to Constable, 27 January 1825   I was impatient to hear how you fared at the visit of the King of France to the Louvre. Your medal could not have given you greater exultation than it did me. Indeed I always consider your fame as mine, and, as you rise in slow and permanent estimation, pride myself that I have formed as permanent a friendship with a man of such talent. . . . Later: Your letter with its uncomfortable details has just reached me. If you can get the consent of the mother, bring your poor boy down here directly; . . . and he shall have the best advice the country affords, with sea air, sea bathing, and good food . . . if he does well, we will see what can be done for him in the way of education.

And Constable writes to Fisher in 1829:

> I know not if the landscapes I now offer to your notice will add to the esteem in which you have always been so kind as to hold me as a painter: I shall dedicate them to you, relying on that affection which you have invariably extended to me under every circumstance.

Patrons help advance an artist's career, but the very notion of a patron implies that the work keeps on being produced. A whole host of people helped Constable to continue painting. For example, Leslie talks of John Dunthorne the younger (son of the glazier/plumber) who came up from Dedham to work for Constable as a studio assistant/pupil. He mentions the housekeeper, Mrs Savage, and a governess, both of whom Constable engaged when his wife died in 1828, leaving him with seven small children to raise. There was also Lucas the engraver: Leslie notes that:

> In 1832 Mr Lucas undertook to engrave 'Cornfield' at his own risk; the plate was afterwards purchased and published with its companion, the 'Lock' by Mr Moon.

And on Sept. 1829 — Constable says of Mr Lucas:

> His great urbanity and integrity are only equalled by his skill as an engraver; and the scenes now transmitted by his hand are such as I have ever preferred.

And then there was Leslie himself; friend, patron, co-creator, through his writings, of the aesthetic rationale which ran counter to the British view of artistic excellence:

> January 1826, Constable to Leslie — the 'White Horse' did me credit at Lisle. I am honourably mentioned in the final discourse of the prefect, and a gold medal was voted to me, which I received yesterday . . . All things considered, the medal should be yours . . .

Later, after the artist's death, there was Ruskin, who downplayed Leslie's champion, Constable, and promoted Turner instead. These, then, are just some of the people who helped to ensure that what happened did happen. All artistic work, like all other work, involves the joint activity of a number, often a large number, of people.

But besides human resources, the artist depends on *material resources*. Into this category come paints, canvases, brushes, varnishes — all the paraphernalia which make painting possible at all. Constable didn't invent his art form, though he may have pioneered a new way of conceptualizing it and putting it into practice. He relied on an art world and its productions that was already ongoing and relatively stable. From Leslie we gather that Constable did not grind his own paints, nor make his own stretchers (for example, those famous six footers he often mentions — he once said: I do not consider myself at work unless I am before a six-foot canvas). He routinely depended on the colours that were created, manufactured and sold by firms like Reeves, and Windsor and Newton, in order to produce the effects he did produce. (And even if he had made his own, he would have depended on the knowledge of others, the transport, and so on, to enable him to procure the right raw materials.) Of course, behind these material resources, as it were, are another set of *human* resources (the makers of paints, the stretchers of canvas, the frame makers, the carters); which shows that an art world is not a distinct entity, but is part of a wider social world and linked to other smaller more specialized ones.

Another material resource is money.

> 1826 — My dear Fisher: . . . My large picture is at a stand owing to the ruined state of my finances.

But his life was radically altered when his father-in-law died:

> 1828 Spring — My dear Fisher — Mr Bicknell has left us a fortune that may be £20,000! This I will settle on my wife and children, that I may do justice to his good opinion of me. It will make me happy, and I shall stand before a six-foot canvas with a mind at ease, thank God!

Yet even in his more impecunious days, he did not always take advantage of material resources:

> 1 July 1824 — Received a letter from the Institution offering monetary prizes for the best sketches and pictures of the Battles of the Nile and Trafalgar; it does *not* concern me.

So, resources make some things possible, some easy and others harder — for example, painting the subject matter you want to paint. There is always a division of labour. The activity of painting is traditionally seen as the core one, while engraver, printer, studio assistant and model are seen as support personnel; and others are usually hardly acknowledged.

Conventions

I have said that Constable entered an art world that was established and ongoing. That is to say, it was was already operating relatively smoothly and efficiently — according to a set of *conventions*. Now these conventions interlinked with the broader cultural conventions of the section of British society into which Constable was born. And Leslie notes that in those moderately affluent Tory circles, art as a career was not very highly regarded. Indeed, Constable's future grandfather-in-law objected to his marrying Maria Bicknell, since he was

> without a profession.

He did not want his granddaughter to marry 'below herself in point of fortune'. Seeing that he was determined to buck this Tory convention however, Maria urged him at least to become a portrait painter. She wrote to him that portrait painting was

> the path the most likely to bring you fame and wealth, by which you can alone expect to obtain the object of your fondest wishes . . . .

that is, herself. Constable ignored this method of reaching rich and influential folk. He wanted to paint landscapes. But he does seem to have taken for granted that he had to move to London, away from his beloved Essex and Suffolk countryside, in order to be taken seriously as an artist. We know from Farington's diary that he wanted to be accepted as a pupil at the Royal Academy — that is to follow the conventional career path. But the desire to combine landscape painting with a conventional training inevitably brought problems. Farington records:

> 26 February 1798 — Constable called and brot. his sketches of landscapes in neighbourhood of Dedham. Wishes to be in the Academy. I told him he must prepare a *figure*.

> 2 March. He showed me a drawing of a torso, and I gave him a letter of introduction to Wilton, Keeper of the Academy.

It was a situation in which Constable reluctantly complied with the Academy conventions, because he knew he could not advance independently of them. But at the same time he continued to pursue landscape painting; and in doing so he was, however, drawing upon another less fashionable but long-established set of conventions — as the following quotations show. The first is from Farington's diary:

13 July 1801 — Constable called on me and I on him to see a picture, a view of Mr Read's House near Dedham. It is painted on a coloured ground which he has preserved through the blue of his sky as well as the clouds. His manner of painting the trees is so like Sir George Beaumont's that they might be taken for his.

Constable himself said, in 1799:

I fancy I see Gainsborough in every hedge and hollow tree . . .

Leslie notes that he was especially influenced by Poussin's 'Landscape with a Man washing his Feet at a Fountain'; and by Sir George Beaumont's Claude of 'Landscape with Hagar and the Angel', of which he is recorded as saying:

This is the most affecting picture I almost ever stood before.

And here's an interesting diary entry by Joseph Farington, which shows that artists — guided by the convention of what counted as a paintable landscape — would come upon each other at the very same spot.

19 August 1791. At 9 o'clock we entered Dovedale, I made a sketch of the first appearance of the entrance, and while I was so employed Mr Constable came up to me, He having come a 2d time to make studies here.

Constable fought until 1822 to be accepted as an Associate of the Royal Academy, and then for another seven years to become a full Academician because this conventional career route, he knew, was the one by which he was most likely to be authenticated as a notable British artist; the one which could put the British stamp of excellence on his paintings. But Leslie remarks:

On the 10 February 1829 he was elected an Academician. That this distinction should not have been conferred on him at a much earlier period of his life is a proof that the progress of an original style of art, in the estimation even of artists, is very slow.

So, to summarize, we could say that one of the main reasons why Constable's work was noticed and discussed, and why we can now appreciate what he did, is because he made sure he was associated with the Royal Academy, thereby becoming part of the mainstream London art scene. And while he attempted to reject the favoured genres of history and portrait painting, he nevertheless absorbed, rehearsed and then, importantly, developed further the less favoured convention of landscape painting, with the crucial support of a few steady patrons. These are some of the factors which allowed him to be perceived, following his death, as an avant-garde landscape painter.

In one of his most well-known letters, Constable said:

There is room enough for a natural painture . . . The great vice of the present day is bravura, an attempt to do something beyond the truth.

Later commentators on his work have claimed that this remark is key to his distinctive approach. This may be so, but his idea of 'truth to nature' was informed by the convention of what currently counted as natural, and as paintable nature. The landscapes that Constable painted were of humanized nature: the cultivated fields, paths and buildings of Essex, for example. They did not depict swathes of virgin forest or tundra. People had worked the land in order for it to look as it did; and some of these workers are represented in his paintings — as in 'The Cornfield'. But even when we acknowledge that Constable's landscapes are of nature-filtered-through-culture, there is another perhaps more important aspect to that 'truth to nature' concept which needs to be questioned. This is that he reproduced exactly what he saw — like the idea of a scientist observing nature and acting as its midwife to the scientific community and the outside world (which doesn't hold either). Constable made a *representation* of what he saw. In fact, John Barrell has argued[9] that Constable painted a conventional Tory view of the landscape, in which idealized images of hardworking peasants, apparently rewarded by the efforts of their own labours, merge into a scene which suggests a view of social harmony that was very far from actually being the case.

However, my aim is far from trying to undermine the aesthetic worth of his paintings. I am instead suggesting that for new and exciting work to emerge, there has to be a whole raft of conventions *already* in existence which the painter absorbs — contesting some, modifying and extending others; and equally, a shared understanding of this process and a condoning of it by at least a few other art world participants. Without these conventions and a degree of shared understanding as to what counts as an exciting development or violation of them, work tends to go unremarked. Leslie writes that in 1818 Constable sent to the Academy:

> 'Landscape, Breaking Up of a Shower' and three other landscapes; and to the British Gallery he sent 'A Cottage in a Corn-field' . . . But these and other *latent* beauties passed wholly unnoticed in the Exhibitions; indeed the pictures . . . were for the most part unheeded, while more showy works, by artists whose very names are now nearly forgotten, were the favourites of the day [my emphasis].

Yet it is Leslie's defining of Constable's paintings as 'latent beauties', his contesting of current convention, his belief in their worth, that helped these works travel the precarious path to more widespread acclaim at a later date.

Distribution

One reason why artists, including Constable, were keen to be associated with the Royal Academy and other major institutions and galleries in the early nineteenth century was because this was a way of getting their work known and distributed; it attracted patrons. A crucial task performed by patrons as purchasers was that of integrating the artist into their society's economy by transforming aesthetic value into economic value, and thus making it possible for artists to live by their art work. After a public exhibition of Constable's work early in his career (1814), Leslie notes:

> These last two pictures were purchased by Mr Francis Darby, of Colebrook Dale. Constable was highly delighted that they had attracted the notice of an entire stranger to him.

And although this indicates how important it was to attract new purchasers, Leslie also seems to imply that Constable routinely relied on the support of a few consistently enthusiastic patrons. Indeed he shows that the lives of Constable and Archdeacon Fisher were closely entwined for many years — that artist and patron cooperated in such a way as to get the work produced and distributed. For example, in 1822 Constable asked Archdeacon Fisher a financial favour:

> I have had some nibbles at my large picture of the 'Hay Wain', in the British Gallery. I have an offer of £70 without the frame to form part of an exhibition in Paris. I hardly know what to do. It might promote my fame and procure me commissions, but it is property to my family; though I want money dreadfully; and, on this subject, I must beg a great favour of you, indeed I can do it of no other person. The loan of £20 or £30 would be of the greatest use to me at this time, as painting these large pictures has much impoverished me. If you can, I know you will oblige me. If not, say so.

Later, Fisher sent his congratulations on Constable's promotion to a full member of the RA, but Leslie says,

> . . . he rendered Constable a service which was, perhaps, of more importance to him at that crisis of his life [his father had just died] than it would have been at any later period: he purchased the 'White Horse'.

Fisher was a stubborn patron, secure in his judgment and sound in his practical advice. Constable did not seem to want his work to go to France, but Fisher could see that distribution there might lead to distribution at home. He says:

> 18 January 1824 — Let your 'Hay Cart' go to Paris by all means . . . I would, I think, let it go at less than its price for the sake of the eclat it may give you. The stupid English public, which has no judgment of its own, will begin to think there is something in you if the French make your works national property.

And again:

> 1824 — You have long lain under a mistake; men do not purchase pictures because they admire them, but because others covet them . . .

And Fisher encouraged his association with Lucas:

> 11 December 1825 — I am pleased to find that he is engraving your pictures, because it will tend to spread your fame . . .

Later, Leslie gives us a glimpse of the different levels on which Constable was to become bound up with patronage.

> 4 September 1832 — While Constable's mind was agitated by the near prospect of losing John Dunthorne, to whom he himself had been a useful patron, having assisted to establish and to procure him employment as a picture cleaner, he heard of the death of that friend who had been his own and only patron, when patronage was of the greatest importance to him [Fisher].

Distribution of art works is also affected by the *state*, as the *Art and Power* exhibition recently made clear.[10] Some states censor certain works, or destroy them. But the early capitalist world of Britain did not censor Constable's work, and thus implicitly encouraged its distribution as a commodity. Constable did have some fairly direct connections with the workings of the State. Leslie tells us his father-in-law was a solicitor to the King. And Farington, with whom he had a good relationship (even buying Farington's house, after his death) knew the men of state, including those at Court; some of whom believed that an ability to pick the best artists and commission the best work demonstrated a nobility of spirit and character commensurate with being powerful and wealthy. But Jonathan Mayne, Leslie's editor, notes that during Constable's lifetime the distribution of his work was very limited, and that:

> ... he had achieved no resounding worldly success ... Such public praise as he received had been grudgingly bestowed, and his posthumous sale (of one hundred and forty items) realised little more than 2,000 guineas.

Aesthetic Rationale

In *Art Worlds*, Becker quotes the philosopher Arthur C. Danto: 'To see something as art requires something the eye cannot descry — an atmosphere of artistic theory, a knowledge of the history of art: an art world' (*Art Worlds*, p. 148). In other words, Danto is saying that visual works don't become art just in the physical act of painting, and in the physical act of observing them; they have to be associated with an understanding, a rationale — an *aesthetic*. This is our next theme (though it does tend to overlap to some extent with that of convention). Aesthetics range from the informal to the fully formalized. Thus, an aesthetic may be tacit, something that art world members — people 'with their eye in' — agree about without much needing to be said. And artists may contribute to that aesthetic through their choice of materials and forms. However it becomes more prominent, gets developed and is then articulated in the course of discussion between artists, critics and knowledgeable patrons, after which there will often be evidence of it in writing. A fully formalized aesthetic will almost always find expression in writing. One of the principal functions of the Royal Academy during Constable's lifetime was to provide and sanction a fairly formalized aesthetic by which art works could be given meaning and judged as art, and which would then allow their authors to compete for resources, such as prize money. Leslie shows that Constable's work was continually judged according to the Royal Academy aesthetic, and found wanting; thus causing him much unhappiness, and a troubled relationship with this guardian and promoter of British aesthetic standards. There was constant criticism of his 'lack of finish', which prompted the remark that:

> My art flatters nobody by imitation, it courts nobody by *smoothness*, it tickles nobody by petiteness, it is without either fal-de-lal or fiddle-de-dee: how can I therefore hope to be popular?

But perhaps even more seriously, as Leslie explains:

> The Royal Academy considered high art to be inseparable from historical art

whereas Constable's paintings belonged in

> the humblest class of landscape

He was admitted as a student at the Royal Academy in 1799. His name appeared for the first time in the RA exhibition catalogue as an exhibitor in 1802. Thereafter, he was a regular exhibitor; but as we have seen, he was not elected an ARA until 1819, nor a full Academician until 1829, because his aesthetic ran counter to that of the Academy. From an entry dated 1822, we can glimpse the zig-zagging, the day-to-day ups and downs which result from the coupling of a desire to be accepted by the art establishment with a contesting of its aesthetic:

> Several cheering things have lately happened to me, professionally. I am certain that my reputation rises as a landscape painter, and that my style of art, as Farington always said it would, is fast becoming a distinct feature. But I am anxious about this picture. My neighbour, George Clint, who expects to be an Academician before me, called to see it. He has always praised me; now he said not a word; till, on leaving the room, he looked back and said, he hoped his picture would not hang near it.

But even the most established aesthetic rationales are not inviolate; and by 1824, Constable's counter-aesthetic was at least gaining ground in Paris. On 24 July of that year he gives an account of the contest within France itself where regular critics were desperately trying to retain their aesthetic hegemony over artists whom they saw were becoming influenced by Constable's work.

> The French critics have begun with me, in the usual way, by comparison with what has been done. They are angry with the artists for admiring these pictures, which they 'shall now proceed to examine' etc. They acknowledge the effect to be 'rich and powerful, and that the whole has the look of nature, and the colour, their chief excellence, to be true and harmonious; but shall we admire works so unusual for these excellencies alone; What then is to become of the great Poussin?' They then caution the younger artists to 'beware of the seduction of these English works'. All this comes of being regular critics. The execution of my pictures, I know, is singular, but I like that rule of Sterne's: 'never mind the *dogmas* of the schools, but get at the heart as you can' and it is evident something like this has been attained, by the impression these pictures have made on most people who have seen them here and abroad. [my emphases]

And dogma is what an aesthetic becomes when there is more concern for *how* a work is executed than with *what* is executed. Constable, who seems to have been convinced of the supremacy of all things British, did not take the French very seriously whatever their aesthetic opinions. What mattered to him was that the Academy should revise its aesthetic to accommodate his. But this entailed a lifelong struggle, during which his confidence was sorely tested and sometimes badly eroded. On 8 April 1826, and still not yet a full Academician, he says:

I have dispatched a large landscape to the Academy ['The Cornfield'] upright, of the size of the 'Lock', but a subject of a very different nature: inland corn fields, a close lane forming the foreground; it is not neglected in any part; the trees are more than usually studied, the extremities well defined, as well as the stems; they are shaken by a pleasant and healthful breeze at noon. I am not, however, without my anxieties, though have not neglected my work, or been sparing of my pains . . .

And Leslie, co-producer of Constable's competing aesthetic, indicates that his anxieties were not allayed even after becoming an Academician:

1829 — Constable called, according to custom, after the honour that had just been conferred on him, to pay his respects to Sir Thomas Lawrence, who did not conceal from his visitor that he considered him peculiarly fortunate in being chosen an Academician at a time when there were historical painters of great merit on the list of candidates. So kind-hearted a man as Lawrence could have no intention to give pain; but their tastes ran in directions so widely different . . .

Editing

Becker has remarked that all the choices, made by all the art world participants over a work's life, are what give meaning to the assertion that art *worlds*, rather than artists, make works of art. He suggests that the entire process of choosing, and indeed contesting the choices of others, can be thought of as *editing*. Artists get the credit for art works; but all support personnel who helped make the work what it was and not something else can be thought of as editors. For example, critics and museum personnel allow some art works to die, through ignoring them: in this way, the work of women artists was edited out until recently. And conversely, art gallery and museum staff do editing work by conserving those artefacts which are deemed to be of value. It is not difficult to find examples of the editing — including visual editing — of Constable's art works during his lifetime; and indeed, Leslie remarks in 1830:

I have often observed with surprise, how readily Constable would make alterations in his pictures by the advice of persons of very little judgment.

A would-be editor of what we now know as 'The Cornfield' was Mr Phillips of Brighton. Having seen a preparatory sketch, he wrote to Constable, suggesting some plants which would be suitable. In a letter dated March 1st, 1826, he says:

My dear Sir, I think it is July in your green lane. At this season all the tall grasses are in flower, bog-rush, bullrush, teasel. The white bindweed now hangs its flowers over the branches of the hedge; the wild carrot and hemlock flower in banks of hedges, cow parsley, water plantain, etc.; the heath hills are purple at this season; the rose-coloured persicaria in wet ditches is now very pretty; the catchfly graces the hedgerow, as also the ragged robin; bramble is now in flower, poppy, mallow, thistle, hop, etc.'

Figure 18.1   John Constable, *The Cornfield*, 1826. Oil on canvas, 142.9 × 121.9cm. London. National Gallery (reproduced by kind permission of the National Gallery)

This advice seems not to have been heeded. The finished oil painting appears to depict the countryside in autumn.[11] However, Leslie cites a Mr Allnutt who made sure his editing ideas were carried out — and lived to regret it.

> 1843 — Dear Sir, many years, ago, I purchased at the British Institution a painting by Mr Constable. But as I did not quite like the effect of the sky, I was foolish enough to have that obliterated, and a new one put in by another artist which, though extremely beautiful, did not harmonise with the other parts of the picture.

Some years after, I got a friend of Mr Constable to ask him if he would be kind enough to restore the picture to its original state, to which he readily assented.

A somewhat similar visual re-editing, and re-re-editing happened to one of Constable's works at the Academy on varnishing day, April 1929. Leslie says:

Chantrey told Constable its foreground was too cold, and taking his palette from him, he passed strong glazing of asphaltum all over that part of the picture; and while this was going on, Constable, who stood behind him in some degree of alarm, said to me 'there goes all my dew'. He put it back in afterwards.

Editing work is also accomplished by the verbal title. Constable himself sometimes referred to 'The Cornfield' as 'the Drinking Boy'. This gives a specific meaning to the work, focusing attention on one particular part of the composition. However, when it was first exhibited at the Royal Academy — whose editing rules allowed only the briefest of titles — it was re-named 'A Landscape', which gives the work a different meaning. In 1827, Constable re-edited it again (with the help of a poet who had been dead for a hundred years) in order to make it more likely to attract a buyer. He titled it 'Landscape: Noon', and attached to it lines from Thomson's 'Summer':

Which now a fresher gale, sweeping with shadowy gusts the fields of corn . . .

And the editing process goes on: In 1835 it was exhibited at Worcester, entitled 'Harvest Noon; a Lane Scene'. The current title 'The Cornfield' seems to have been first used by the group of patrons and friends who bought the painting and presented it to the National Gallery shortly after Constable's death in 1836. Then began a different kind of verbal editing. George Constable (a friend but no relation) writing in the *Art Journal* of April 1869, says of the 'The Cornfield' that though much of the landscape can be precisely identified,

. . . the little church in the distance never existed.

This verbal remark, and all subsequent pieces of writing about the Cornfield, continue the process of re-editing the work, and thus altering its meaning.

Those who decide where a painting is to be hung also do editing work. I have alluded to the august climate in room 34 of the National Gallery, which contributes to the specialness of 'The Cornfield'. On the subject of hanging, and the aura lent by certain gallery sites, Constable writes to Archdeacon Fisher:

24 December 1824 — My Paris affairs go on very well. The director, the Count Forbin, gave my pictures very respectable situations in the Louvre in the first instance, yet on being exhibited a few weeks, they advanced in reputation, and were removed from their original situations to a post of honour, two prime places in the principal room. I am much indebted to the artists for their alarum in my favour; but I must do justice to the Count, who is no artist I believe, and had thought that as the colours are rough, they should be seen at a distance.

Leslie himself did much editing work. Indeed, Jonathan Mayne, Leslie's *own* editor (and thus himself an indirect editor of Constable's oeuvre) comments upon his 'too careful editing' (Leslie, 1951, p. xi). Later Ruskin, competing with Leslie's *Handbook for Young Painters* (Leslie, 1855) to say what counted aesthetically, downplayed Leslie's champion, Constable, and promoted Turner instead (and 'unhappily Ruskin was a far more influential writer than Leslie', remarks Mayne) (Leslie, 1951, p. xii). And so on, up to the commentary on the audio-cassette, and the information on the National Gallery computer — especially that section which visitors can print out and taken home. Some very significant editing work was done by Lucas the engraver, which brings us to our next theme: the activity of distinguishing art from craft.

Art and Craft

In *Aesthetic Theory*, Theodor Adorno states that 'if any social function can be ascribed to art at all, it is the function to have no function' (1984, p. 322). By contrast, craft objects serve a practical purpose, while at the same time displaying a degree of skill and beauty. The greater their practical efficiency, skill and beauty, the more highly they are regarded as craft objects. Becker observes that art world and craft world personnel between them maintain a running distinction between what is art and what is craft, and that each world has need of the other. Leslie makes it very clear that Constable the artist had need of Lucas the master craftsman-engraver, and that between them, they continually reproduced the distinction between the two worlds. For example:

> September 1829 — Constable was now engaged in preparing the *English Landscape* for publication, having secured the valuable assistance of Mr David Lucas; and it led to the magnificent engravings that gentleman afterwards executed of 'The Cornfield', and others.

There are many references to the artist's warm and close partnership with Lucas. Constable says, in September 1829:

> His great urbanity and integrity are only equalled by his skill as an engraver; and the scenes now transmitted by his hand are such as I have ever preferred.

And in a letter to Constable in January 1831, Lucas refers movingly to the illness of the artist's son:

> Don't think of me or my concerns for a moment; your business is with yourself. I mention this only to relieve your mind from all other anxiety, as I well know your great integrity, and that you are always too ready to devote yourself to others, or at least to me.

However, it seems clear that the division of labour was such that, overall, the artist instructed the engraver. For example, Constable writes to Lucas in 1833:

> All who have seen your large print ('The Lock'?) like it exceedingly; it will be, with all its grandeur, full of detail. Avoid the soot-bag, and you are safe; Rembrandt had no soot-bag, you may rely on it. Be careful how you etch it, that you do not hurt the detail; but there is time enough. I hope you will not injure your family by so large a print.

Yet it was a complex relationship in which the artist often relied on the engraver's skill and judgment, in which respect directions were given with the greatest tact and deference:

> 1836 — Dear Lucas, I am greatly pleased to see how well you are preparing for the new bow (rainbow); the proof is about what I want; I mean that you took hence. I took from the elder bush a blossom to the left, you will possibly do the same. Go on as you think proper . . . We cannot fail with a proper bow.

While overall the artist directed the engraver, lower down the scale — as it were — the engraver directed the printer who was also indispensable. Lucas's printer fascinated Constable who was from a quite different social stratum:

> 18 March 1836 — Dear Lucas, Mr Cook, the Academician, said yesterday that the 'Salisbury' was 'a grand-looking thing'. I hope that obliging and most strange and odd ruffian, your printer, will be allowed to have just his own way in printing the plate, for I now see we must not be too full, otherwise it will, as he says, 'only be fit for a parcel of painters' . . . I hope you are better. I must now dismiss the ruffian, for he is getting too knowing for John [his son] and me.

Soon afterwards, he writes to Lucas:

> Your man [the printer] is a droll fellow. I have given him two shillings, but it was before he had told me that he 'is given to break out of a Saturday night, but it does not last long, and generally goes off on the Sunday morning' . . . This is his own gratuitous account of himself. What a creature is man, either cultivated or not, either civilised or wild!. I offered him some rum and water, and gin and water, all of which he refused almost with loathing; perhaps his hour is not yet come.

Another indication of the hierarchical but complex distinction between art and craft is that Constable was at pains not to blame the engraver for failures.

> 1831 — Years must roll on to produce the 26 prints, and all this time I shall not sell a copy. Remember dear Lucas, I mean not, nor think one reflection on you. Everything with the plan, is my own, and I want to relieve my mind of that which harasses it like a disease. Do not for a moment think I blame you, or that I do not sympathise with you in those lamentable causes of hindrance which have afflicted your home.

And Lucas's own commercial ventures (e.g., *New Series of Engravings of English Landscape after Constable*) were a failure; he ended his life miserably in the Fulham Workhouse. Constable's socio-economic status and art world connections could not, I think, have made it possible for him to share the same fate.

Change in Art Worlds

Making highly crafted representations of Constable's unique art works does not seem to have boosted Lucas's reputation during his own lifetime (and the fate of the 'ruffian' printer is not, to my knowledge, even recorded); but the engravings helped to make Constable more widely known. And thus we come to the theme of *change in art worlds*, and then finally to that of *reputation*. Even though art worlds may be relatively stable and enjoy a firm organizational basis, they nevertheless change continuously. No-one can do anything exactly the same way twice; and consequently, there is always a slow drift away from what was done before, though this will probably not be seen as change by those experiencing it. But at a later date art historians, for example, may try to establish the chronological sequence in which an artist's work was executed; and they gradually become expert at detecting the fine changes that took place over a period of time, whether these were intentional on the part of the artist or not. In rather the same way, an old Academician, looking back over his career at the Academy, might note that things are done rather differently now from how they were done in the old days. However, Becker observes that besides gradual change, there is another kind: dramatic change. This tends to be intentional — to involve concerted effort, in which a successful attack is made at a particular time on the existing aesthetic and organisation of an art world. Constable, writing in 1829, discusses the two kinds of change in terms of a contrast between the dominant British aesthetic and his own. He claims that adherence to the former — as exemplified even in the best works — produces only gradual change, whereas the latter inevitably involves dramatic change:

> In art, there are two modes by which men aim at distinction. In the one, by a careful application to what others have accomplished, the artist imitates their works, or selects and combines their various beauties; in the other he seeks excellence at its primitive source, nature. In the first, he forms a style upon the study of pictures, and produces either imitative or eclectic art; in the second, by a close observation of nature, he discovers qualities existing in her which have never been portrayed before, and thus forms a style which is original . . .

But deliberate, dramatic change is usually only valued and applauded at a much later date, if at all. For, as Becker notes, art history usually deals with winners — with innovations and innovators that won organizational victories — those who mobilized enough people round them to cooperate in regular ways that sustained and furthered their ideas. Although, posthumously, Constable did achieve this sustained organization, he did not do so during his lifetime. In a continuation of the above passage, Constable gives a sociological explanation of the situation:

> . . . The results of the one mode, where they repeat that with which the eye is already familiar, are soon recognised and estimated, while the advances of the artist in a new path must necessarily be slow, for few are able to judge of that which deviates from the usual course, or are qualified to appreciate original studies.

We might add that other reasons why 'the advances of the artist in a new path must necessarily be slow' are because people tend to experience their aesthetic beliefs as natural, proper and morally right, and feel these advances as a personal attack; and also because the old guard establishment knows that if it doesn't try to resist change, it stands to lose control of the aesthetic/moral high ground. Now, change is bound up with reputation; and quite dramatic changes in attitudes to Constable's work were to occur after his death, as the final section shows.

Reputation

We have seen enough now to know that the idea that Constable was a genius and 'The Cornfield' a masterpiece, was scarcely entertained in his lifetime; though associating 'artist' with 'genius' was not unknown (for example, Joshua Reynolds had previously referred to Michelangelo as a genius). Constable was always mindful of his reputation, and was always aware that he had few admirers. However, the activities of Archdeacon Fisher, C.R. Leslie, 'the French', Lucas and his 'ruffian' printer helped to create such reputation as he had while he was alive. Leslie says that after his death and before the property Constable left, in pictures, was dispersed:

> It was suggested by Mr Purton that one of these works should be purchased by a subscription among his admirers, and presented to the National Gallery. He proposed that the large picture of 'Salisbury from the Meadows' should be chosen . . . But it was thought by the majority of Constable's friends that the boldness of its execution rendered it less likely to address itself to the general taste than others of his works, and the picture of 'the Cornfield', painted in 1836, was selected in its stead. One contributor said: 'The great number of his works left in his possession proves too clearly how little his merits were felt by those who could afford, and ought to have possessed them; and that, unless some such a measure had been adopted as that which, to the honour of his friends, has been carried into effect, it is too probable that his works would have fallen into the hands of artists only, for a mere trifle, and remained comparatively buried, till dug up, as it were, and brought to light in another age. . . . In the picture selected for his monument in the National Gallery, we find all his truth of conception, with less of the manner that was objected to, than in most of his later works.'

The subscribers certainly acted shrewdly in choosing a painting which represented a compromise, and 'addressed the general taste'. For once the National Gallery acquired 'The Cornfield', it seems that things began to change. Richard and Samuel Redgrave in *A Century of Painters*, 1866, put it like this:

> Constable. . . . had worked hard for appreciation and fame, and it must have been with pain that he said of himself in reference to a work of his engraved by Lucas — 'The painter himself is totally unpopular, and will be so on this side of the grave.' But his conviction that his pictures would be valued by posterity soon found its fulfilment. His friends purchased his fine work, 'The Cornfield', and presented it to the National Gallery. *A better feeling for his art at once arose*, and his pictures are now treasured in all collections, and prized at their proper worth. [my emphases]

Leslie, whose own *Memoirs of the Life of John Constable* was published six years after the artist's death, also contributed to the 'arising of a better feeling for his art'. For the book, according to his editor, Jonathan Mayne was favourably received, though he added:

> . . . this cannot be said to have reflected a high contemporary estimate of Constable's genius.

Note that for Mayne, in 1951, Constable is a 'genius', a man apart. Mayne continues:

> If Leslie's biography stimulated interest and even perhaps helped to create a demand for his works, this was no more than a preparing of the ground for the full re-evaluation which was to be delayed almost another 50 years. The key date in the establishing of Constable's reputation in England is 1888; in this year Miss Isabel Constable, the artist's daughter, bequeathed to the nation over 300 of his drawings and paintings.

So — despite the efforts of Ruskin — the buying of 'The Cornfield' for the National Gallery, the publication of Leslie's book and the bequeathing (at a significant moment in the rise of his reputation) of 300 works to the nation, helped to ensure that Constable would go down in history as a winner rather than a loser.

Changes in art worlds and changes in reputations are often connected to advances in technology. In the first half of the twentieth century, increasingly cheap reproductive techniques enabled 'The Cornfield', now on public display, to become widely known in the form of book illustration and on postcards: it became part of the discourse of mainstream art history, and an object of middle-class 'art appreciation'.[12] Consequently, Constable's reputation grew even more; and this, coupled with further advances in reproductive techniques, resulted in the Cornfield image being imprinted on all manner of objects — for example, wallpaper (see Figure 18.2). Then in the 1980–90s, the Thatcherite

Figure 18.2 Mr and Mrs Jackson. 'Cornfield' wallpaper. Photograph by Anne Painter (reproduced by kind permission of Colin and Anne Painter)

ideology, which combined 'heritage' with 'enterprise', gave it a further boost. The Cornfield image now contributes to a thriving 'heritage' industry, and features on a wide range of craft and consumer goods.[13]

The extent of this range was made manifest in the recent exhibition, *At Home with Constable's Cornfield* (1996). The exhibition organizer placed an advertisement in a free South London newspaper, and in it he appealed for anyone who had the Cornfield image in their home to contact him. Forty-five people did so. A similar notice was placed beside the painting in the National Gallery. This received 509 responses; including 180 from countries other than Britain. Some of the respondents were then interviewed and subsequently invited to exhibit their Cornfield artefacts alongside the original at the National Gallery, London. The result was a selection of plates, pictures, tea towels, fire screens, thimbles, clocks, wallpaper, each showing a version of 'The Cornfield' (see, for example, Figure 18.3). It transpired that some people who answered the newspaper advertisement were unaware of the existence of the original painting and had never heard of John Constable: their Cornfield artefacts had become quite detached from the original and had acquired a separate set of meanings. So while the painting itself, and most early engravings and prints of it, have become highly valued and preserved for 'specialist' attention, the fact that the image has been reproduced on all manner of household objects takes it into another realm. Imprinted on plate and tea towel, thimble and clock, and brought back as a gift from a relative on holiday or simply purchased in order to make ordinary domestic life and its tasks more pleasurable, the Cornfield artefact has acquired a special place in the home where it takes on personal meaning.

Figure 18.3 Elizabeth Pett. 'Cornfield' fire screen. Photograph by Anne Painter (reproduced by kind permission of Colin and Anne Painter)

The exhibition included a video, in which 'Cornfield owners' were shown, alongside their artefacts, explaining what the Cornfield image meant to them. For some, it clearly brought to the fore their dissatisfactions with the harsh realities of urban industrial life today. For the world of the Cornfield is in stark contrast. It provides an antidote to modern living. It is, in part, a mythical world where work is satisfying, unwearisome and indeed rather remote; where class divisions, and other forms of inequality are suppressed; where life, as several interviewees said, seems really worth living. For others, it fuelled — and temporarily satisfied — a longing for the innocence of childhood. It evoked real memories of relatives and friends now gone; it was a reminder of a youth spent closer to the countryside, or of exceptional days out, days of leisure. And even though these visions, these interpretations, may rely in part on active work by the imagination, the *effect* produced by the image is palpable: it really does improve the quality of participants' daily lives. This, then, is the cluster of meanings that 'The Cornfield' reproduced on artefacts in people's homes has taken on. And it is the real effect in the *present* of this image of a better life in the *past* that the Jordans Cereals advertisement plays upon (see Figure 18.4). 'If your breakfast cereal has been sprayed with chemicals', it seems to say, 'how can you even hope to taste the purity, the naturalness, the simple pleasures, the authenticity, the value (spiritual, aesthetic, financial) of the countryside of yesteryear?' And then, of course, the exhibition itself has taken 'what "The Cornfield" means' a stage further. In effecting a cross-fertilization between the worlds of high art and more popular culture, the exhibition will have contested or reaffirmed — certainly modified and augmented — the meanings that the contributors previously gave to *their* Cornfield artefacts; while at the same time those meanings (e.g., as articulated in the video) will feed back into artworld perceptions of the *original* 'Cornfield' painting in the gallery, causing viewers (at any rate those who know about the exhibition, including readers of this essay) to revise their interpretations of it. And thus, the process continues . . .

Figure 18.4 'Most People Prefer the Original'. Jordan's Oat Cereal advertisement, 1987 (reproduced by kind permission of W. Jordan (Cereals) Ltd.)

As we have seen, the work of making meanings for Constable's Cornfield now involves many people and the overlapping of several different social worlds. At the micro-level, we can say that each time 'The Cornfield' — or any other art work image — is viewed or used in a different context, its meaning gets altered and extended. And at the macro-level? When an artwork starts to become widely known and admired, usually one cluster of meanings begins to dominate; a cluster which enmeshes with the dominant ideology of society. (The meaning of the 'Cornfield' image has long been informed and bolstered by conservative Romanticism; and Thatcherite ideology — a recent commercially-orientated variant — has injected it with a further feel-good factor.) And only when the dominant ideology of society changes does the hegemonic meaning, the definitive account of it, begin to falter and lose credence. So, we make meanings *for* the Cornfield; but then we make meanings *with* the Cornfield — i.e., we use the Cornfield meanings to bolster the dominant ideology, which then informs subsequent meanings we make *for* the Cornfield . . . The meanings we make for visual artworks are both an aspect of the way we represent our culture as a whole, and an aspect of the way our culture is represented to us.

Notes

1 This article is based on a lecture given on 2 March 1996 at the National Gallery, London, in association with the exhibition 'At Home with Constable's Cornfield.' This exhibition was originated, researched and curated by Professor Colin Painter, then Principal of Wimbledon School of Art.
2 In *Art Worlds*, University of California Press, 1982.
3 Published in *Art Students Observed*, Faber and Faber, London, 1973.
4 For example, Turner's 'Fighting Téméraire'.
5 A term coined by Howard Becker in his book of the same name — see Note 2.
6 Phaidon Press 1951 (originally published 1843).
7 If this evidence is available, we might ask how it is that it gets left out of the current popular account. To pose this question is to ask about the workings and the power of ideology.
8 All subsequent quotations in this article are from Leslie, unless otherwise indicated.
9 In *The Dark Side of the Landscape: The Rural Poor in English Paintings*, 1730–1840, CUP, 1980.
10 *Art and Power*, Hayward Gallery, London, 26.10.1995–21.1.1996.
11 This opinion is also voiced by the commentator on the audio cassette guide to the pictures at the National Gallery.
12 e.g. It was available to borrowers at Rugby Public Library in the 1950s (see my Introduction).
13 Obviously 'The Cornfield' was not the only one of Constable's paintings to receive this treatment; and if anything, 'The Haywain' image has become even more ubiquitous — for example, the National Gallery markets a fridge magnet of 'The Haywain', but not of 'The Cornfield'. I am focusing on the career of 'The Cornfield' because this was the image that featured in the National Gallery exhibition.

References

ADORNO, T. (1984) *Aesthetic Theory*, London and New York: Routledge and Kogan Paul.
BARREL, J. (1980) *The Dark Side of the Landscape: The Rural Poor in English Paintings, 1730–1840*, Cambridge: Cambridge University Press.

BECKER, H. (1982) *Art Worlds*, Berkeley, Los Angeles and London: University of California Press.

BISHOP, P. (1995) *An Archetypal Constable: National Identity and the Geography of Nostalgia*, London: Athlone Press.

CHAPLIN, E. (1994) *Sociology and Visual Representation*, London and New York: Routledge.

FARINGTON, J. (1922?) *The Farington Diary, Vol. 1* (July 13, 1793, to August 24, 1802), London: Hutchinson & Co.

LESLIE, C.R. (1855) *A Handbook for Young Painters*, London: John Murray.

LESLIE, C.R. (1951) *Memoirs of the Life of John Constable*, London: Phaidon Press.

MADGE, C. and WEINBERGER, B. (1973) *Art Students Observed*, London: Faber and Faber.

PAINTER, C. (1996) *At Home with Constable's Cornfield*, London: National Gallery Publications.

THOMPSON, K. (1997) 'Regulation, De-regulation and Re-regulation', in THOMPSON, K. (ed.) *Media and Cultural Regulation*, London, Thousand Oaks, New Delhi: Sage/Open University.

Notes on Contributors

Clement Adelman is Professor of Education at the University of Reading, UK. His main publications are in qualitative research methodology, evaluation, history of pedagogy and curriculum, action research and music education research. Early in his working life he almost made a living as a musician and photographer.

Michael Ball is a Senior Lecturer in Anthropology and Sociology at Staffordshire University, UK. His research interests and publications are in the area of the analysis of visual data, encompassing ethnomethodology, anthropology, post-modernism, and the ethnographic method.

Marcus Banks trained as an anthropologist at the University of Cambridge and studied documentary film at the National Film and Television School, Beaconsfield, UK. He is a lecturer in social anthropology at the University of Oxford where he teaches visual anthropology and conducts research on early ethnographic film and visual representation. His most recent book is *Rethinking Visual Anthropology* (co-edited with Howard Morphy, Yale University Press, 1997).

Howard S Becker is Professor of Sociology at the University of Washington, USA, and is also Adjunct Professor of Music at the University. In April 1996 he received the degree of Doctor Honoris Causa from the Université de Paris VIII in St Denis. He has written widely on such topics as sociology, qualitative methodology, art, music, photography, and education. He has recently finished *Tricks of the Trade: How to Think about Your Research While You're Doing It* (to be published by the University of Chicago Press at the end of 1997). Contact http://weber.u.washington.edu/~hbecker/

Richard Chalfen is Professor of Anthropology at Temple University in Philadelphia, PA, USA. He is former Department Chair and past Director of the Graduate Program in Visual Anthropology. His most recent book is the revised edition of *Through Navajo Eyes* (with Sol Worth and John Adair, 1997). Current research focuses on the visual culture and home media of modern Japan.

Elizabeth Chaplin teaches Cultural Studies at the Open University, UK, where she is a member of the Sociology Course Team which has recently produced *Culture, Media and Identity* (published by Sage, 1997, in five volumes). Her particular research interest is in sociology and visual representation. Her book, *Sociology and Visual Representation* was published in 1994.

Órla Cronin is a research psychologist with Unilever UK. Prior to moving to Unilever she worked at the Institute of Education, University of London. Her research interests are diverse ranging from the meaning and psychological significance of family photographic collections to children's understanding of the physical world.

Douglas Harper is Professor and Chair, Department of Sociology, Duquesne University in Pittsburgh, Pennsylvania, USA, where he teaches qualitative sociology. He is founding editor of the journal *Visual Sociology*. His current research is on agricultural labour and technology, as constructed through historical photographs.

Paul Henley has been the Director of the Granada Centre for Visual Anthropology, University of Manchester, UK, since its foundation in 1987. After doctoral and post-doctoral research in Amazonia whilst based at the University of Cambridge, he trained as a director-cameraman at the National Film & Television School for three years. In addition to publishing extensively on the anthropology of the native peoples of Amazonia, he has made nine documentaries, two for British television and the remainder for more academic audiences.

Ron Lewis is also a member of the Centre for Education and Change at Deakin University, Australia, and has a background in media, in music and innovative distance learning education. Contact http://www2.deakin.edu.au/E&C/DCEC/Assoc%20Researchers/Lewis.html

Jenny McWhirter is a Senior Research Fellow in the Health Education Unit at the University of Southampton. Since 1989 she has been researching children's perceptions of health issues, principally children's perception of risk. She has also conducted evaluation studies of curriculum materials developed for use in schools. Dr McWhirter is currently managing an international curriculum development project, working with Noreen Wetton to develop novel research methods for use with young people.

Claudia Mitchell is Associate Professor in the Department of Curriculum and Instruction, McGill University, Montreal, Canada. She teaches courses on children's literature, qualitative research, popular culture, and teacher education. Her research interests include: cultural studies, teacher education, children's literature, literacy, and gender studies, and she has published widely in these areas. Dr Mitchell began her career as a high school teacher, and, along with her three daughters, is an avid collector of children's cultural artefacts.

Jon Prosser is a member of the Research and Graduate School of Education at the University of Southampton, UK. He teaches qualitative methodology, management and institutional culture, and is course director of the doctorate in education programme. His research interests include institutional effectiveness and improvement, the visual representation of institutional culture, and child abuse investigation. Contact http://www.soton.ac.uk/~jpross

Michael Schratz is Associate Professor of Education at the University of Innsbruck, Austria. His main interests are in educational innovation and change with a particular focus on management and leadership. He has taught in Austria and Great Britain, did research at the University of California, San Diego, and worked at Deakin University, Australia. His latest books are *Research and Social Change* (he co-authored with Rob Walker), and *Die Lernende Schule* (The Learning School) (he co-authored with Ulrike Steiner-Löffler).

Dona Schwartz is an Associate Professor at the School of Journalism and Mass Communication at the University of Minnesota, USA. Her area of specialization is visual communication and qualitative research, and she has taught both documentary photography and photojournalism for more than a decade. Her most recent book *Contesting the Super Bowl* (will be published by Routledge and is due to appear in October 1997).

Ulrike Steiner-Löffler is a consultant for school development at the Pedagogic Institute of Vienna, Austria, and works as a grammar school teacher, in in-service training, as a researcher and as a lecturer at the University of Innsbruck, Austria. She has taught school management and educational development in many European countries. She is mainly interested in how to combine pedagogical and organizational innovation of schools; her special focus: ensuring that students' voices are heard in matters of school development. Her latest book *Die Lernende Schule* (The Learning School) (she co-authored with Michael Schratz).

Hollida Wakefield and **Ralph Underwager** are licensed psychologists at the Institute for Psychological Therapies in Northfield, Minnesota. They provide treatment to victims, families, and perpetrators of child sexual abuse and have consulted or testified in cases of alleged sexual abuse throughout the United States and in several foreign countries. They have presented workshops and seminars on the topic and are the authors of 'Accusations of Child Sexual Abuse,' 'The Real World of Child Interrogations,' and 'Return of the Furies: An Investigation into Recovered Memory Therapy.'

Rob Walker is a member of the Centre for Education and Change at Deakin University, Australia. He teaches courses in classroom research and distance education and chairs the course team for Deakin's professional doctorate in education. Contact http://www2.deakin.edu.au/E&C/DCEC/members/Walker.html

Terry Warburton is a Lecturer in Research Methods for the Education subject group in the Faculty of Arts, Science and Education at Bolton Institute, UK. His research interests are the professional cultures of teaching; images of teachers and teaching, particularly political cartoons and education and the media.

Sandra Weber was Associate Professor at the University of Alberta, Canada for eight years before joining the Department of Education at Concordia University in Montreal where she teaches courses on second language acquisition, qualitative research methodology, popular culture, and curriculum theory. Professor Weber's publications include articles on French immersion education, qualitative research, teacher education, and narrative inquiry. Her current research focuses on teacher education (with particular emphasis on the process of becoming a teacher), popular culture, gender studies, and autobiography. Dr Weber began her professional career in Montreal as an elementary school teacher and, along with her daughter, Stephanie, is an avid, albeit critical consumer of popular culture.

Noreen Wetton is a Senior Research Fellow in the Health Education Unit at the University of Southampton. She has had a long and productive career as a teacher, headteacher and teacher educator, before moving into curriculum development in the field of health education. She is perhaps best known as one of the authors of Health for Life, a major curriculum programme in health education for primary schools in the UK, for which she developed the 'draw and write' technique.

Brian Winston is Professor and Head of the School of Communication, Design and Media at University of Westminster, UK, having recently moved from the University of Wales in Cardiff where he was Director of the Centre for Journalism Studies. Prior to that he worked on Granada Television's World in Action programme, and taught documentary film production at the National Film School and New York University. In 1985 he won an Emmy for script writing. His most recent book is *Technologies of Seeing* (published in 1996 by the British Film Institute).

Index